GIANTS
in the Cornfield
The 27th Indiana Infantry

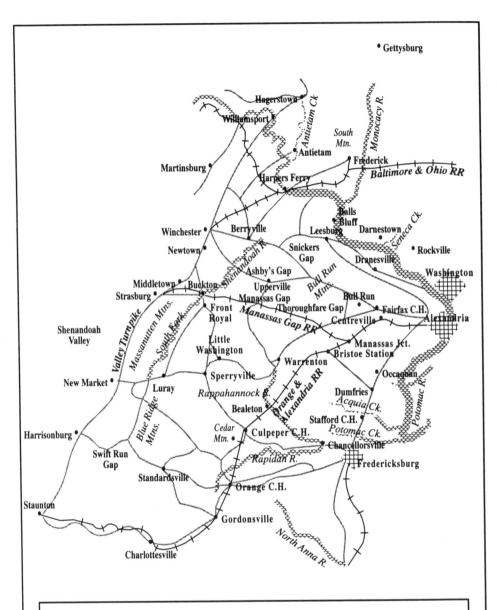

EASTERN THEATER AREA OF OPERATIONS
27th Indiana Infantry
September 1861 to August 1863

MAP SOURCES:
Principally Official Military Atlas of the Civil War.

GIANTS
in the Cornfield
The 27th Indiana Infantry

by
Wilbur D. Jones, Jr.

 White Mane Publishing Co., Inc.

This White Mane Publishing Company, Inc. publication
was printed by
Beidel Printing House, Inc.
63 West Burd Street
Shippensburg, PA 17257-0152 USA

In respect for the scholarship contained herein, the acid-free paper used in this book meets the guidelines for permanence and durability of the Committee on Production Guidelines for Book Longevity of the Council on Library Resources.

For a complete list of available publications
please write
White Mane Publishing Company, Inc.
P.O. Box 152
Shippensburg, PA 17257-0152 USA

Library of Congress Cataloging-in-Publication Data

Jones, Wilbur D.
    Giants in the cornfield : the 27th Indiana Infantry / by Wilbur D.
Jones, Jr.
        p.   cm.
    Includes bibliographical references (p.) and index.
    ISBN 1-57249-015-2
    1. United States. Army. Indiana Infantry Regiment, 27th
(1861–1864)--History. 2. Indiana--History--Civil War, 1861–1865-
-Regimental histories. 3. United States--History--Civil War,
1861–1865--Regimental histories. I. Title.
E506.5 27th.J66 1997
973.7'472--dc21   97-17172
                                                                      CIP

PRINTED IN THE UNITED STATES OF AMERICA

TABLE OF CONTENTS

ILLUSTRATIONS

MAPS

viii

PREFACE

Finding Barton Warren Mitchell

In the middle of the rural southcentral Indiana hamlet of Hartsville is a small park with a weathered blue and gold historical marker trying to catch the eye of drivers hurrying by on Route 46. I would have missed it also if I had not parked alongside to purchase a soft drink across the street on a steamy day in August 1987. With my two sons, I was headed for Bloomington to enroll the older one as a freshman at Indiana University. Because I had been a history major 32 years ago, I glanced at signs like that wherever they were out of both casual interest and eternal guilt, because my parents paid my way through college and I had never "used my degree."

Ah, this one was a Civil War marker. Drawn to it immediately, I had to write down the information and then go home and do something about it. Strange, but that sign had been waiting for me for 24 years, in Hartsville, Indiana.

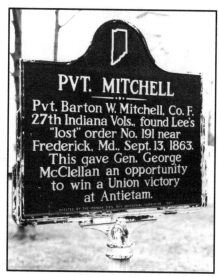

Pvt. Mitchell

Pvt. Barton W. Mitchell, Co. F, 27th Indiana Vols., found Lee's "lost" order No. 191 near Frederick, Maryland, Sept. 13, 1863 [*sic*]. This gave Gen. George McClellan an opportunity to win a Union victory at Antietam. Erected by the Indiana Civil War Centennial Commission, 1963*

Historic Marker, Private Barton Warren Mitchell, Company F

Located on Route 46, Hartsville, Indiana, where Mitchell's wife and children lived during the war.

Photo by author

---

* A replacement sign erected in 1992 changed 1863 to the correct 1862.

I thought I was knowledgeable on the Civil War, but who was Mitchell, and what was it about the "lost" order I should remember but didn't? Soon I toured Antietam and Frederick, Maryland, visited libraries, wrote to sources in Indiana, and here are my notes about what I learned.

Mitchell family lived in Hartsville during war. He is buried there. September 1862. Clover field south of Frederick. And a Sgt. John M. Bloss. McClellan knew Lee's plans, pursued, forced Lee to fight at Sharpsburg. Bloodiest day in American history. Military standoff, but strategic Union win. Lee withdrew to Virginia. Lincoln issued Emancipation Proclamation. France and England refused to recognize South. The Union was saved. All because of a "lost" order and some Indiana soldiers.

Soon the "lost order" became a commitment to write a book about the 27th Indiana, eventually a nearly six-year project. I became heavily involved, and was inspired by experiences like the following soliloquy at Gettysburg, which I wrote upon returning home and intersperse here within the preface. My son graduated from Indiana University in 1991, also with a history degree, but he paid most of his own way.

Sunday, July 3, 1988

The sun rose quicker than I had anticipated. I wanted to reach out and suppress the daylight until I was in place. I awakened at 2:00 a.m. at home in Alexandria, Virginia, planning to arrive at my destination by first light. The hour advanced toward 5:00 a.m. as I hurried my Cadillac north on Steinwehr Avenue through the sleeping town of Gettysburg. For months I anticipated this day, and even made a dry run several days before. I must be on time and experience every moment with them.

I wheeled right on to Baltimore Pike and, seeing no one, sped the remaining 1½ miles to my destination, Spangler's Spring, at the southern base of Culp's Hill. The sun was ready to break out over the trees on Rock Creek to the east as I turned on to Colgrove Avenue and parked off the single-lane paved road opposite their monument. Grabbing the camera bag, tripod, and tape recorder from the car, I walked across the road and placed them on the large, flat rock on which their monument rests. Then I sat still on the rock and waited, alone.

I had arrived in time. It was a little after 5:00, or 4:00 their time. Closing my eyes, as if commanded, I immediately drifted into a reverie, abstaining from the present world. My imagination was conditioned to flash them to the picture screen of my mind. I was ready now. Boom! Boom-boom! I heard the cannon fire begin on schedule behind me along Cemetery Ridge, and wisps of sulphur quickly reached my nose. The total sensual imaging was working. As the 125th Anniversary of the Battle of Gettysburg's Third Day began, I entered my very personal communion with the men of the 27th Indiana.

For years I walked in their footsteps, visited each battlefield, tracked marches and campaigns, viewed camp sites and tramped approximately 50 cemeteries. As well as Indiana, particularly the central and southcentral sectors ("27th Indiana country"), my research placed me in California, Georgia, Illinois, Louisiana, Maryland, North Carolina, Pennsylvania, Tennessee, Virginia, Washington, D.C., and West Virginia. I drove the Atlanta Campaign—but in reverse from Atlanta to Chattanooga (to get the Rebels' view of what was coming). In all, I logged more than 26,000 automobile miles during my odyssey to find the 27th Indiana.

For 20 minutes the Union batteries bombarded Rebel forces in the woods behind stone walls, rocks, and earthworks at the base of Culp's Hill. The massed infantry of General George Hume Steuart's Brigade which fronted me northeast across Spangler's Meadow were a primary target. Shells exploded randomly. The air was heavy with whine and smoke. Suddenly the cannons stopped. An eerie calm blanketed the meadow and surrounding woods. One by one birds began to clatter. A thin mist rose from the half-mown meadow, the other half left in its natural state with grass uniformly growing to 24 inches. I strained my ears. Yes, I heard voices coming from McAllister's Woods off to my right: quiet, stifled, but discernible voices, and the soft rattle of metal and scuffling of footsteps on leaves and broken twigs. The 27th. It was my 27th! They were about!

God be with them. They do not know, but this day will be murderous. They will suffer dreadfully, but they will help save the Union Army. How I wished I could tell them to beware. Instead, I could only observe and live to tell their story: how their blood would help hold the Union right wing and turn the course at Gettysburg.

The early morning was cool and crisp for summer. Then, about 6:00, the sun burst forth and threw shadows from the tree lines onto the meadow. The day warmed rapidly as the field became splashed with sunshine. With the exception of the roads and the woods to the west, the area looked nearly as it did then. Breaking my reverie momentarily between the shelling and the charge which would follow, I photographed the dew-shrouded meadow, the 27th's 8-foot granite monument which marks the left flank of their charge, the 3-foot granite marker at mid-meadow indicating their farthest advance, the spring, and the State of Indiana monument which lies on the edge of the meadow where her sons attacked heroically, lay, and bled.

Too early for sightseers and joggers, in the visceral solitude of this clear, fresh morning, encased in thoughts, I was there with my men. Countless hours of studying the regiment and the Third Day propelled me back in time. I was swallowed by events. I dared not hold back the tears as they came. Rarely have I shut out the world of logic with such fantasy. Then at 6:00 their time, they charged.

Down from the woods they rushed, some 331 strong, their left flank sweeping past me. Their lines touched the right flank of their comrades in glory, the 2nd Massachusetts, whose monument nearby records their own suffering in the charge that morning. My men leaped across a ditch and headed straight for the stone wall and breastworks nearly 200 yards away. They never got there. Volley after volley of flaming bullets cut them down. Within 10 minutes, more than one third of them had fallen. Six color bearers were shot. Then, withdrawal to the edge of the woods—the vicious counterattack repelled—the living twisted into holes or behind trees all day to protect against snipers firing at will—the fighting over by mid-morning—the torrid sun at high noon—the temperature near 90—the humidity unbearable—and no water, no food. Blood and sweat drenched the ground amid screams and shrieks—but no requiem for the dead, dying, or wounded, most of whom lay on the meadow without succor until dark or the next day.

The regiment's casualties were ghastly: 138, 42 percent of those engaged, and 21 killed in action.

Their sacrifice bought time for the Union forces on Culp's Hill. Because of the charge, the Confederates moved men from the Hill to the meadow, weakening their previous positions. A follow-on Union attack repulsed them from Culp's Hill, eliminating any Confederate hope of linking this fight as planned to that on the center of the line on Cemetery Ridge—the long-delayed afternoon assault by Longstreet, which was to have rolled back the Union Army. By 11 a.m., the battle was settled.

Sweating profusely, as if I, too, had charged, I walked their ground looking for signs, finding only traces of their stone fences and breastworks in dense thickets. I wondered who else has seen them. Veterans on reunion, decades ago? Descendants, yesterday?

I remained with my men until noon when I wearied of the awful moans and the smells of powder and death. The sun ripened very hot. The temperature hit the low 90s and it was miserably sticky, like 125 years before. Helplessly, I had watched the horror. Private George Bales, I will tell your wife, Nancy, in North Salem and your children, Sophonia and little George, how you died a man. Corporal Laban Williams, I promise to visit your grave in the Old Union Christian Church Cemetery in Fayetteville. Lieutenant Thomas Casey, you hurt terribly now, but I will write your granddaughter Virginia May in Indianapolis about how you return from the hospital in two months, and spend the last years of your life in Raglesville. What else could I do? Lord have mercy on them, and let their memory live forever.

The core references are overwhelmingly primary source material, much of which was previously unpublished. Interviews included a number of grandchildren who shared photographs, manuscripts, mementos, and stories. I spent hundreds of hours researching in major depositories such as the Library of Congress, National Archives, and the Indiana Commission on Public Records, and used university libraries including Depauw, Indiana, Vincennes, Wabash College, and North Carolina. I built a correspondents' network of several hundred descendants, historians, researchers, and interested parties who helped accumulate a couple thousand more documents. I also visited many Indiana state and local libraries and historical societies, and national parks resources at Kennesaw Mountain, Antietam, Gettysburg, and others. The interest, assistance, and positive response were far beyond my expectations.

I reviewed every available official and personal record on the regiment and its members, including compiled military service records, descriptive lists, carded medical records, muster rolls, morning reports, order books, records of deaths, clothing books, regimental correspondence, unpublished manuscripts, memoirs, contemporary photographs, and illustrations. Altogether I read or perused: (1) of Indiana and Civil War history, approximately 500 books, monographs, pamphlets, etc., in addition to items cited above; (2) of the 27th Indiana, approximately 1,000 official and personal letters and diaries; nearly 800 pension records; and several thousand other records and documents. I even researched many corresponding Confederate accounts to see whom the 27th was fighting.

I wanted to add a fresh dimension to Civil War literature by writing about the social environment of a homogeneous group of Union common soldiers, the young, uneducated farmers of the 27th Indiana Volunteer Infantry Regiment. I chose not to cast them in another war chronicle of campaigns, tactics, competing generals and battles, or another chronological regimental history. Historians have adequately covered these areas, but not enough has been said about the characteristics, interactions, feelings, and emotions of one particular regiment, and how its members struggled to exist. I wanted to see how men from the same state, counties, and neighborhoods assimilated into and persevered through the nation's most horrible war. Even then, this book omits some of those generic soldiering experiences about which much has been written, such as food, shelter, weapons, uniforms, and camp life.

I revisit many of their experiences to learn about army discipline, health and medicine, and being a prisoner of war—things they could not influence—and morale, internal politics and family relations, which they could.

Because they were the army's tallest regiment, called "giants," and gave and took horrific casualties in Antietam's Cornfield, the study's title "Giants in the Cornfield" came naturally.

Tied through interlocking reports, vignettes, and one-liners, I explore individual and collective actions, values and feelings in and out of combat. I see men working with and against each other, their superiors, and the enemy, in making do with what they had. I observe their maturing, endurance, resolve, and inner conflicts, and how they coped with lack of money, fear, sickness, and dying. I watch them complain, conduct personal business, face boredom, sleep on frozen ground and yearn for who and what remained behind.

Corporal Edmund Randolph Brown, Company C

Brown helped keep the reunion group together.

Provided by E. R. Brown

Antietam, where they earned everlasting respect as Union soldiers, is the lone battle highlighted and only as seen through their eyes. However, Antietam is simply the culmination of their involvement in the most intriguing military mystery of the war: the finding of Lee's Special Orders No. 191, and subsequently its fortuitous impact on redirecting the war. Antietam and the "Lost Order," the flagship stories, present new and unpublished information.*

With permission of his namesake grandson in Seattle, Washington, "ERB" helps me tell the story as a periodic commentator. ERB is Corporal Edmund Randolph Brown of Company C, who almost one hundred years ago wrote and published the popular regimental history of the 27th Indiana.

Wilbur D. Jones, Jr.
Alexandria, Virginia

---

* On the opposing side, the author has solved the mystery of who lost the Lost Order and the situation surrounding it, the personalities involved, and how the Confederate Army handled the intelligence error.

ACKNOWLEDGEMENTS

In researching and writing this comprehensive story of a Union Civil War regiment for nearly six years, while working full time on the faculty of the Department of Defense Systems Management College, I needed the periodic energy, pumping and confidence—and sleeves-rolled-up research assistance—of many people. Of special note are two friends who love and study the common soldier of the Civil War, and continually urged me onward. They are James Fletcher, Ashburn, Virginia, reenactor and living history presenter *extraordinaire* (plays both sides as movie extra), whose pickup truck plate is "HRDTACK," and Dr. Jack Dwyer, Fredericksburg, Virginia, book collector, authority on Confederate senior officers, and a man who has spent untold hours walking old graveyards making a list of where the soldiers rest.

I was extremely lucky in quickly building a super network of correspondents, some of whom were descendants of members of the regiment, particularly in Indiana. The folks accumulated information and illustrations on the Regiment's members and were helpful, courteous, opened many doors, and often escorted me. Indiana's No. 1 fan of the 27th Indiana, Harry M. Smith, of Connersville, whose license plate reads "27THIND," was a frequent inspiration and source. Key Indiana correspondents include: Mary Berry Leinenbach, Jasper; Wilma Stricklen Coats, Bicknell; Ruth Hutchison, Edinburg; Carol Ann Barrett, Indianapolis; and Eleanor Purdue, Washington—whose loyal, detailed, and lengthy assistance certainly showed they believed in my work.

Key correspondents elsewhere include: Betty Krimminger, Chapel Hill, North Carolina, who among other jewels discovered a piece buried in a 1922 *Confederate Veteran* magazine which was my basis for writing an article solving the mystery of who lost Lee's "Lost Order" (found by the 27th Indiana), to be published in the journal *Civil War Regiments*, Betty Clemmens, Atlanta, Georgia; Patricia A. Peruch, Carmichael, California; and Betty M. Majors, Tullahoma, Tennessee.

I owe a gold-star thanks to Dr. Trudy Peterson of the National Archives for bending their policy and allowing me to review as many pension records and other 27th Indiana records as I could handle at any time, an accommodation which saved me weeks of daily research time.

Other providers of essential information include, in Indiana: the late Jay Wilson, Oolitic, and Keith Houk, Jamestown, who helped get me started; Beverly Oliver, Fairland; Hon. Phil DeHaven, Union City; Robert A. McKnight, Jr., Zionsville; John and Helen Rowell, Martha G. Davis and Helen Reeve, Columbus; Janet G. Myer, Star City; Betty Burgess, Winamac; Petty Officer William J. Young, II, USN, Kerry V. Armstrong, Esther M. Ketcham, Dixie Kline Richardson, and Mary F. Long, Indianapolis; John D. Steele, Odon; Helen M. Fullerton, Loogootee; Bert Witham, Franklin; Bridget A. Young, Winslow; Mildred Cook, Brazil; L. Rex Myers, Washington; James J. Barnes, Wabash College; Mona Robinson, Bloomington; and Lillian Doane and Doris Kreilein, Jasper.

Elsewhere: William G. Willmann, Frederick, Maryland, who directed me to where he believed the Lost Order was found (I determined he is correct); Edmund R. Brown, Seattle, Washington, "ERB's" grandson; Dick Loughry, McLean, Virginia; R. C. "Dick" Datzman, New Orleans, Louisiana, who shared unpublished material on the Lost Order finding; Clay Hoffman, Bakersfield, California; Reggie Box, Traverse City, Michigan; Irene Englis, LaCygne, Kansas; John A. Sink, Memphis, Tennessee; and Fred Frechette, Charles City, Virginia.

A number of Civil War historians shared information or offered me guidance, including: Dr. Jay Luvaas, Army War College; Dr. Joseph Harsh, George Mason University; Paul Chiles and Ted Alexander, Antietam National Battlefield; Dennis Frye, Harpers Ferry National Historical Park; Kathy Georg Harrison, Gettysburg National Military Park; Robert Krick, Fredericksburg and Spotsylvania National Military Park; Connie Vogel-Brown, Chickamauga and Chattanooga National Military Park; Alan T. Nolan, Indianapolis; Guy Swanson, Museum of the Confederacy; W. E. "Bill" Erquitt, Atlanta Historical Society; Dr. David G. Vanderstel, Connor Prairie Settlement; Ted Ballard, U.S. Army Center for Military History; John Goode, Bentonville Battlefield State Historic Site; and John Michael Priest, Hagerstown, Maryland.

A few of the many librarians and archivists who went out of their way to assist me include: in Indiana, Wanda Potts, Mooresville Public Library, Mooresville; Phyllis Walker, Morgan County Public Library, Martinsville; and Marybelle Burch, Patty Matkovic, and John Selch, Indiana State Library; also, Martha Warden, Lanhom Memorial Public Library, Tullahoma, Tennessee; and Sharon Fawcett, Cindy Fox, Connie Potter, Charles Cooney, Mike Muzik, and Bill Lind, superb professionals at the National Archives; and Gerald Handford, Indiana Commission on Public Records.

I interviewed a number of grand and great-grandchildren including in Indiana, the late John Bloss Lotz, Muncie; Patsy Powell, Gosport; Virginia May, Indianapolis; Maury Melchior, Edward J. Schaaf, Ruth Buecher, Margaret Hoffman, and Urban, Lucille, Veronica, and Tony Streigel, Jasper; Judi McMillen, Bedford; also the late John M. "Jack" Bloss, Paris, Illinois.; and Colonel Rudolph F. Rose, USAF (Ret.), Manassas, Virginia.

I also wish to thank David Mannweiler of the *Indianapolis News* for his September 1990 column which plugged my work and "generated business," and Christina Shinn for indexing the manuscript.

From my extremely supportive family, I thank my wife, Carroll, for her exceptional critiques, tolerance, and patience; my sons David, Indiana University '91, and Andrew for their research assistance; and my granddaughter, Carrie, who willingly and patiently made pleasant company on many research outings.

CAMPAIGNS AND BATTLES

of the 27th Indiana Volunteer Infantry Regiment

Eastern Theater

With the Army of the Potomac (September 1861–June 1862)
    Shenandoah Valley Campaign (Virginia, March–June 1862)
        Banks' V Corps, 1st Division, 3rd Brigade
        Buckton Station (Engagement, Co. B only)—May 23, 1862
        Newtown (Engagement)—May 24, 1862
        Winchester—May 25, 1862

With the Army of Virginia (June–September 1862)
    General Pope's Virginia Campaign (July–August, 1862)
        II Corps, 1st Division, 3rd Brigade
        Cedar Mountain—August 9, 1862

With the Army of the Potomac (September 1862–September 1863)
    Maryland Campaign (September 1862)
        XII Corps, 1st Division, 3rd Brigade
        Antietam—September 17, 1862
    Chancellorsville Campaign (Virginia, April 26–May 6, 1863)
        XII Corps, 1st Division, 3rd Brigade
        Chancellorsville—May 2–3, 1863

    Gettysburg Campaign (Virginia, Maryland, Pennsylvania, June–July 1863)
        XII Corps, 1st Division, 3rd Brigade
        Gettysburg, Pennsylvania—July 2–3, 1863

Western Theater

With the Army of the Cumberland (October 1863–November 1864)
    Atlanta Campaign (Tennessee, Georgia, May 4–September 2, 1864)
        XX Corps, 1st Division, 2nd Brigade
        Resaca, Georgia—May 15, 1864
        New Hope Church, Georgia—May 25, 1864
        Kolbs Farm, Georgia—June 22, 1864
        Peachtree Creek, Georgia—July 20, 1864
        Siege of Atlanta, Georgia—July 28–September 2, 1864

CHAPTER 1

Giants in the Cornfield:
Bloodletting at Antietam

Thousands of men pressed on to conquer a peace and illustrate to all coming times, to all Christian nations, the truth of Julia Ward Howe's most beautiful sentiment that as Christ died to make men holy, the highest duty of a citizen-soldier is to die to make men free. —About the XII Corps leaving Frederick, Maryland [1]

On Sunday, September 14, 1862, at mid-morning, the 27th Indiana marched with the XII Corps from Frederick, Maryland, amid church bells calling to worship the followers of the Prince of Peace. The stars and stripes floated over prominent buildings, hung from windows, and were waved, showing that the brief Rebel occupation had not impaired the area's love for the old flag.

The regiment headed westward over the National Road (present U.S. 40), remembered by many as their migration route to Indiana. At Boonsboro they halted with loud "exuberance of spirits" to rejoice in the Union victory at nearby South Mountain and loudly cheer the presence of Major General George Brinton McClellan, Commander of the Army of the Potomac, and other generals. McClellan "with his endless retinue of staff officers, orderlies, clerks and bodyguard had passed us," his staffers riding ahead instructing the troops. "We marched gaily along through the dust cheering McClellan."[2] "But nobody appeared to be in a hurry," one private worried. "We wondered what might have happened if those generals had been nearer the front urging forward the army, pushing things along there. Is this a time for pompous displays of vanity and dilly-dallying?"[3] The day before, the common soldiers heard all the hullabaloo about their own Indiana comrades finding Confederate General Robert E. Lee's Special Orders No. 191, and that Lee had split his army by sending Jackson one way and Longstreet another. This must be the reason they were now on the march. Now the men wondered how McClellan the fox would catch the Confederates out of the coop: why not hunt, attack, kill, and crush the whole rebellion once and for always?

1

September 16, Night

> The batteries in the wood on the far right were playing vigorously, but the wind blowing toward that direction it resembled the constant flash of huge matches or jets of gas flashing out in the twilight. —*Second Lieutenant Josiah Clinton Williams* [4]

By nightfall on the sixteenth, the regiment arrived near the farm town of Sharpsburg, behind Confederate lines and 15 miles north of the Potomac River from Harpers Ferry. Shortly before midnight McClellan ordered the XII Corps to cross the Antietam Creek and support Major General Joseph Hooker's I Corps three miles north of town. They moved in murky darkness by whispers only: follow the file leaders and meditate. With their 1st Division, commanded by Brigadier General Alpheus Starkey Williams, the Hoosiers forded the creek and bivouacked near the John Poffenberger farm, about a half mile behind Hooker. They passed the night in silent thoughts annoyed by a chilly drizzle and persistent firing.

"Neither the light showers that drenched the bivouac nor the sure prospect of the morrow's fight disturbed the slumbers that exhausted nature claimed," said Private Edwin E. Bryant, a nearby 3rd Wisconsin soldier. "At daybreak the fire of skirmishers was the reveille that wakened so many thousands to their last day on earth."[5] Private Edmund Randolph Brown of the 27th wrote, "When we lay down that night there was a division of sentiment among us. Part believed that next day would witness a desperate battle. But others contended that it could not be so, as nothing had been done in the way of preparing for it."[6] A New York newspaper reporter heard Hooker say, "Tomorrow we fight the battle that will decide the fate of the Republic."[7]

Northerners ascribed the name Antietam to the battle that raged along the stream. Southerners named it for the town. At the point where the Potomac bends it is only one mile from the creek. Across that narrow neck Lee, gathering his forces, had established his lines of battle facing east, northeast, and east, from left to right. One flank rested on the creek and the other near the river on a naturally strong position with rocky ledges, stout post-and-rail fences, knolls, ridges, and patches of woodland, behind which to conceal movements. McClellan faced Lee on the left across broken and rough ground, in the center across steep acclivities and deep ravines, and on the extreme right, the 27th's battlefield, across wide, gently rolling fields, some cultivated, with small patches of woodland and broken rock outcroppings intervening.

By first light on the seventeenth the rain stopped. Mist hung like a shroud obscuring the terrain before the 27th Indiana. Looking south, the ground between two belts of timber was mostly pasture and plowed fields on the David R. Miller farm. In the middle, along the eastern edge of a turnpike linking Sharpsburg with Hagerstown to the north, was Miller's 20-acre field of ripe corn, about 250 by 400 yards wide, with stalks higher than a man's head. There were other fields of corn in the area, but later only that one would be called "The Cornfield."[8]

September 17, 5:00 a.m.

> Wounded blue uniforms came streaming back—some slightly, others limping along using their guns for crutches. They shrieked to Gordon's men how they were "driving the 'Johnnies' in front." Stretcher bearers burst forth with the severely wounded bound for field hospitals down a valley behind the line. —*About Hooker's early attack* [9]

Hooker prepared to advance at daylight. The XII Corps was held in reserve. The 27th's 3rd Brigade, commanded by Brigadier General George Henry Gordon, massed near Mr. Middlekauf's buildings, 100 yards east of the Hagerstown Pike and north of Joseph Poffenberger's house.[10] Suddenly the heavy damp air rattled with picket firing. "Muskets never seem to crack so loud and wicked as on the picket line when a great battle is expected. A few shots then sends the blood whirling to the fingertips of the whole army," Private Brown said. Cannons joined in, musketry increased, and expectations whirred. Then, at 5:30, as Hooker's I Corps was hurled through the dawn glow, Brown continued, "In a very short time the battle has assumed large proportions." Soon the brigade marched to near Middlekauf's barn to "rest at will" and stack arms. Gravely apprehensive, "We are now ready for any order that may come."[11]

Men fumbled for coffee and ate whatever they had. "Few can forget that this may be the last food they will taste in this world, or the last as well men," wrote a member of the 27th. "Some of the more excitable ones cannot eat a mouthful." Some "intend to eat all the more." Men arranged "quietly yet openly to a possible dire contingency," exchanging valuables and keepsakes or passing them to men in the rear with instructions concerning business matters at home, care of family, or messages to friends, even one's own remains. Some men threw away decks of cards or other "evil" items.[12] The wounded shuffling to the rear increased. None were demoralized, and most expressed encouragement or cheer. The only "skedaddler" the 27th saw during the battle went running by, zig-zagging through the fields as if escaping a swarm of bees. The boys laughed and heaped epithets on him, but he did not stop.

> To members and friends, the most momentous, important, dramatic day in our history was that day, one year after mustering in. —*ERB* [13]

6:30 a.m.

> Every Hoosier heart leaped as a major general, mounted an a superb white horse, wholly unattended, and looking as if victory was within his grasp, rode hither and thither, and gave the word "Forward!" —*About Major General Joseph K. F. Mansfield* [14]

The Indianians cheered the "old general," in XII Corps command three days, his "whitened locks and heavy beard flowing to the morning's breeze." He shouted, "That's right, boys; you may well cheer. We are going to whip them today."[15] They must support the faltering I Corps. Gordon assembled his 2,210 soldiers with the old regiments leading: the 27th on the left and the 3rd Wisconsin and 2nd Massachusetts on the right, and promptly moved to the front. The untested 13th New Jersey and 107th New York followed. Half of Mansfield's troops were green, and Mansfield had never led large numbers into combat. So his men would not run, he marched them in a tight formation known as "column of companies, closed in mass," showing a large convenient target. As he struggled to shift them into battle lines he was mortally wounded in the East Woods. Williams assumed corps command, conferred with Hooker, reformed the lines, and moved forward.

On the right, along the slopes of the hill which commanded the woods, the 1st Division saw stone fences and ridges of rock obstructing the march and affording easy shelters for enemy sharpshooters. The 27th Indiana had never experienced anything like that day's journey into the valley of death. At Winchester they defended, were overwhelmed, and ran. At Cedar Mountain they endured a tortuous temperature and steady uphill terrain, only to retreat. Now they marched straight ahead through patches of fog in columns, at a slow measured pace, over slightly rolling uncultivated ground, then obliquely over pasture to the top of a short ridge—all calmly, thinking they were not yet a target, and witnessed the maelstrom one mile ahead. However, passing Joseph Poffenberger's barn on the right, they heard humming sounds overhead from canister and shrapnel being slung by the ton at the troops in front but aimed too high, and felt shredded twigs and leaves sifting down. They walked closer to the cannons, and the missiles began dropping among them. The booms grew louder, soon unleashing a fury the Hoosiers compared to the devastation of an Indiana prairie cyclone, "with its snapping of trees, its creaking and grating of buildings rent asunder and toppling over, its screaming and shrieking of men and animals in mortal terror, and a thousand other ear-splitting, blood curdling sounds, darkening of clouds, dust and rumble and peal of thunder."[16]

6:45 a.m.

> There were many "narrow escapes." Nearly all the boys carry marks in their clothes or person of the thickness of the bullets. —*Commissary Sergeant Simpson Solomon Hamrick* [17]

Then Colonel Silas Colgrove commanded them to unsling knapsacks and, "Battalion, deploy into line of battle, double quick, march!" Except for the mounted Colgrove, remembered for his "unflinching courage, cool, self-poised leadership," officers took places behind the men. Colgrove turned backwards only to give commands. Corporal Robert S. Good, standing next to Second Lieutenant Josiah Clinton Williams, was killed and others were wounded, yet Colgrove rode "quietly on," without reflecting any personal danger or being "influenced by his peculiar surroundings." Sulfurous gunsmoke joined the mist hanging in gullies, limiting visibility and invoking eerie premonitions. The precise alignment was as if they were "passing the grandstand on review." Every man walked erect, head high, straight as a gun barrel, looked ahead, touched elbows, and kept perfect stillness.[18]

They climbed two fences. Private Frederick Winder fell to the ground on one, got up, and continued. The next day, ruptured on both sides, he could not walk. Company F was in the center, its columns of six-footers forming an illusionary pyramid in the line: Captain Peter Kop, 6'4^1/$_2$", First Sergeant John McKnight Bloss, Corporal James Campbell, 6'2^1/$_2$", Corporal Elijah McKnight and Private James Montgomery Foster, 6'2", Private Thomas Mitchell Gascon, 6'1^1/$_2$", and others. They were the "giants," the name people called the entire regiment, the tallest in the Union Army.

Most of the six-footers would drop that day—50 soldiers in all, nearly 80 percent of the company—on farmland much like theirs at home. The Hoosier common soldier had no real idea where he was or what was happening around him. He only did what he was told, and he was told very little. He was not party to grand strategies, numbers of muskets, or tactical maneuvering, and just kept moving toward the densest smoke and sounds. He put his trust in his officers, his friends, his God, and himself, not always in that order. A man who had been shot at had some notion of what to expect, but the terrifying artillery awakened the senses to new heights of expectations and apprehensions. The seasoned ones braced each other and buoyed the raw ones. Each man sweat profusely in the cool dampness. Bowels of the sickly could not be restrained, and every man burned in the bladder. Thoughts intermittently flashed fear, then courage, death, then survival, anything to pass those interminable minutes.

Only Ransom's Battery of four Parrott guns supported Hooker's center. Exhausted men on both sides were waiting for reinforcements to resume the offensive, for it appeared the battle would be decided within the narrow cornfield. But the battery's men and horses were "shot down in heaps" with nothing serviceable left. The Hoosiers reached the position and saw a single artilleryman trying to extricate an uninjured horse, his cap pulled down over his eyes, slowly moving around as though he had a whole day to do his work. "He appears utterly oblivious to all the surroundings. He is evidently in bad mental health."[19] "By nobly standing her ground," the 27th took credit for saving the battery until it could be remanned.[20] Years after the war Lieutenant Josiah Clinton Williams still discussed it. "The brave fellow was trying to fasten the trace chain link over the whiffle tree hook, hammering as coolly as if in a harvest field of peace and plenty, instead of war, death and devastation. I would like to know if he survived and who he was."[21]

The battlefield, little changed since Hooker's assault, now opened before them. Both sides advanced, stalled, wavered, and under extreme artillery and musket fire, retreated, after sacrificing rows of gallant soldiers. During the morning on the Union right, ground was gained and lost for no advantage or consequence. Blue and gray lines swept across the field an estimated 15 times like out-of-control arms of a giant pendulum. Brave young Mississippians, Pennsylvanians, Georgians, Ohioans, Texans, and Indianians were force fed into the cornfield grinder of bloodletting, and thousands were killed or maimed.

When the 3rd Brigade, leading the corps, with the 27th on the left, reached Miller's pasture, the enemy occupied nearly all the corn. The clashes there had been raging for over an hour and Hooker's troops, badly cut up, were slow in retiring, not recognizing the extent of their welcomed reinforcements. Gordon's men absorbed but could not return fire because the green and disorganized 128th Pennsylvania was in the way. An eternity passed before the 128th scattered and fled rearward, and Gordon continued the advance, firing rapidly. Hooker's bloodied men went "wild with joy and enthusiasm at the sight of reinforcements," and, showing "true grit," reformed and continued fighting. The hazy enemy stayed put, bobbing up and down dispatching their flashing rifles toward the Federals. Facing south, Miller's farmhouse was 150 yards on the Hoosiers' right. Colgrove commanded, "Guides post!" and galloped to his position behind his lines. "This is where we are to do our bloody work," one of his soldiers predicted, "and where the bloody work is to be done to us."[22]

Not until the Pennsylvania fugitives had passed did the 27th deliver their first volley. "The firing was heavy on both sides," Colgrove said, "without any change of position on either side. It was very evident the enemy was greatly superior in numbers. At one time during this part of the engagement the fire from the enemy was so terribly destructive it seemed our little force would be entirely annihilated."[23]

Antietam, Miller's Cornfield

The average 27th's soldier was 5'9", attempting to fight through the 7' high corn stalks ready for harvest.

Photo by author

It was difficult to see them lying in the corn. We finally opened irregular fire when we saw gray forms, taking deliberate care not to hurt any blue uniforms. Rebels were more than 400 yards away. Soon after we halted they started toward us. In the still air all flags hung down showing the same colors as stars and stripes. —*ERB* [24]

7:00 a.m.

They deserved a better fate than to have been, as they were, sacrificed for the want of proper support. —*Colonel William Tatum Wofford, CSA, about his Texas Brigade* [25]

Seventy steps ahead was a partially torn down wooden fence bordering a cornfield, creating something like a right-angled triangle. The side next to them, faced by most of the 27th, was its shortest side. The longest bordered the road to the right, or west, and the third a clover field, faced by the regiment's extreme left. Immediately to the east were thick woods. Across the fields ahead to the right was a small white structure clouded with smoke and dust, with thick woods behind it. A farmhouse on the left front was ablaze.* The 3rd Wisconsin in the center of the line followed the crest of the slight swell, and the 2nd Massachusetts on the right flank was temporarily lost from view as it passed into Miller's orchard. The 13th New Jersey and 107th New York supported. They had run into the Texas Brigade of Brigadier General John Bell Hood's Division.

Colgrove's clarion voice rang out: "Battalion, make ready!" Instantly a hush fell on the line. Locks clicked as hammers were pulled back. "Now, aim good and low, boys! Aim low boys, aim low!" Line officers repeated the orders. "Take aim, fire! Fire!" Their first volley blew down perhaps half the enemy line. Other enemy halted, confused. Officers waved swords threateningly and seized men, turned them around, and shoved them forward. "The officers were hard put to keep the line from demoralization."[26] Instead of advancing they dropped into the corn and returned fire. Then the Hoosiers fired at will.

The 1st Texas, aware they had advanced 150–200 yards farther across the cornfield than their flanking comrades, suddenly faced Gordon on the left. "Thought [they] would be attacked and annihilated," a Texas officer recalled.[27] The 1st Texas carried 226 into combat and lost 182: 80.5 percent—the largest suffered by any unit on either side on any one day of the war. The 18th Georgia helped drive the I Corps until Williams' 1st Division threatened their left flank, and fell back. The 5th Texas allowed the Federals to get within 75 yards with unbroken lines before firing, but soon retired. Three of Wofford's four regiments advancing through the cornfield halted before reaching the fence between it and the 27th, and came no closer than the 75 yards. Wofford's right reached the fence in advance of their line, crouched behind it, and "gave us the trouble."[28] Wofford had been on the field for an hour and was being mauled. When the 27th encountered them they were disorganized elements fighting valiantly and holding the field against vast odds. Hood beat back the I Corps. But the XII Corps, too late to help Hooker, arrived in time to save Hooker. Terrific fire hit Wofford's "thinned and almost annihilated ranks." After Gordon advanced, Wofford, "having suffered so greatly," exhausted and without relief, almost out of ammunition, retired to their starting position in the West Woods.[29] The Texas Brigade lost 560 of the 854 taking the field—an incredible 65.6 percent. Hood later called it "the most terrific clash of arms, by far, that has occurred during the war."[30] Hood's assault ended about 7:30, but stabilized the Confederate left wing.

The Southerners drew plenty of Indiana blood. Second Lieutenant William Van Orsdall, the only 27th officer killed in action, died instantly from a gunshot to the head. A bullet over the left eye knocked down Corporal

---

* The landmarks were The Cornfield, Hagerstown Pike, East Woods, Dunker Church, West Woods, and Mumma Farm.

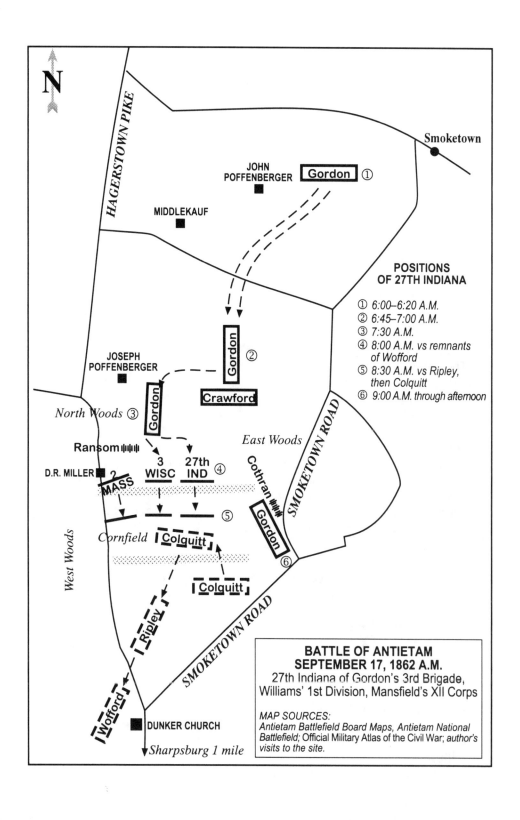

N

HAGERSTOWN PIKE

Smoketown

JOHN
POFFENBERGER
Gordon ①

MIDDLEKAUF

**POSITIONS
OF 27TH INDIANA**

① 6:00–6:20 A.M.
② 6:45–7:00 A.M.
③ 7:30 A.M.
④ 8:00 A.M. vs remnants
   of Wofford
⑤ 8:30 A.M. vs Ripley,
   then Colquitt
⑥ 9:00 A.M. through afternoon

JOSEPH
POFFENBERGER

Gordon ②

Crawford

North Woods ③

Gordon

East Woods

Ransom

D.R. MILLER

2

3
WISC

27th
IND ④

MASS

SMOKETOWN ROAD

Cothran

Gordon

⑤

Cornfield

Colquitt

⑥

West Woods

Colquitt

Ripley

SMOKETOWN ROAD

Wofford

**BATTLE OF ANTIETAM
SEPTEMBER 17, 1862 A.M.**
27th Indiana of Gordon's 3rd Brigade,
Williams' 1st Division, Mansfield's XII Corps

MAP SOURCES:
Antietam Battlefield Board Maps, Antietam National
Battlefield; Official Military Atlas of the Civil War; author's
visits to the site.

DUNKER CHURCH

Sharpsburg 1 mile

Ebenezer Quackenbush, rendering him temporarily insensible. The wound broke and ran like a boil during his remaining service. Private William M. Elliott, one of the few neither wounded nor missing muster during the war, helped the wounded Captain John Wilcoxen off the field. Of Company D's four Fiddler relatives, all Lawrence County privates, Joseph was killed three weeks after mustering in; his brother Christopher Columbus lost his right forefingers; and William lost his left arm and died of wounds October 5. As fast as the men were shot down, the ranks closed up. "They were bound to win, who could stand the hardest knocking."[31]

7:15 a.m.

> They finds me laying under a crib shed wounded. The other boys are all wounded but I think we will get well. I have not the ability to write much. I fired 30 rounds before I fell. The battle was one of the most severe, shell & shot flew thicker than hail. Our line was cut down like grain before the sickle.
> —*Private Eldridge Williams* [32]

As Wofford's remnants withdrew, fresh gray lines on the left advanced. "Their shouts of exultation could be heard distinctly," Gordon reported.[33] Firing as they came, eager and persistent, "stooping forward like a hunter stalking his prey," they dashed to the fence and dropped behind it. Those men, Brigadier General Roswell S. Ripley's Brigade of Georgians and North Carolinians, avenged the Texans and dealt the 27th their "worst punishment," remembered Brown.[34]

"Who ever tried to stand before a more withering, consuming blast than we do now?" one man thought, as everyone seemed to fall. "A soldier makes a peculiar noise in loading his gun which attracts attention, but when we turn to look at him he falls. Another makes what he considers a good shot and laughs over it." Then he falls. "Another tells a man in the rear rank not to fire so close to his face." Others glance there only to see both fall. Seemingly all that happened simultaneously. True to tactics of the day, they stood erect in perfectly open ground with only blades of grass for shields. No one kneeled or lay unless hurt. They constantly touched elbows, and as bodies fell out they closed ranks to maintain an unbroken front—"Close up! Close up!"—as the ranks dwindled. Privates John W. Hansell, Martin Layman and John H. Parr died immediately from gunshots. First Lieutenant Jacob A. Lee, Sergeant Lewis D. Payne and Corporal John Lervis, Jr., lay mortally wounded on the field for hours before being treated.[35]

Each soldier discharged 80–100 rounds, replenishing from those on the ground. Muskets fouled from overheating or jammed cartridges and were exchanged for any dropped on the field. While carrying ammunition to the lines, Private Lewis King, returning to the ammunition wagons for a fresh supply, ran into the rear guard who were preventing straggling. "Hold on, young man, you are going in the wrong direction. Go back to your regiment." King finally persuaded them that he was hauling ammunition to them. To King, detached to the ammunition wagons, the ebb and flow "was too hot to be comfortable" on the 27th's line.[36]

A gunshot fractured two ribs in Private Howard H. Hensley's chest. For two days and nights he lay covered by dead men before being hospitalized. Wounded in the right knee, Private James Henry Burk, "a fine soldier," used his gun as a staff and fought for two hours "until knee swelled so I had to quit."[37] Private Daniel Burk, shot and on his stomach, saw Corporal Phillip McManus fall with a shell wound in the left thigh and groin. While trying to crawl to safety, McManus drew a ball in the right shoulder. Men left the field unauthorized to transport wounded and for other reasons, and were later pressed to explain their absence. Daniel Burk ("I am not educated, but I am not a liar or a coward") said, "One of my comrades was badly wounded & begged me to take him away. I got orders from an officer to do so. I carried him 200 yards & then returned immediately to the front, was gone about 20 minutes."[38]

Many of Ripley's soldiers used old smoothbore muskets which fired buck and ball, three buckshot and a standard ball, which sprayed shotgun-like blasts, creating a high proportion of wounds to kills. Over the few hundred yards separating them, the 1st and 3rd North Carolina severely punished the 27th.* "Our men began to fall on every side (we were on the right wing then)," wrote Lieutenant Williams. "All companies lost severely. We kept closing ranks to the right as fast as they thinned & when they were within some 100 yards of us put in a heavy front & flank fire, which made them skedaddle."[39] A "typical" Hoosier, "tall gaunt slow-spoken every inch a hero," was desperately wounded. He calmly laid down his gun and went a short distance toward the rear, drawling, "Wall, I guess I'm hurt about as bad as I can be. I believe I'll go back and give 'em some more." So he did.[40] Mortally wounded Private Robert W. Faith, exposed to further injury, refused his brother Private Thomas' offer to move him to safety, bidding him to remain where he was needed more. Robert had been a soldier four weeks, Thomas three.

Private William Thomson, only five weeks in the army, suffered a weird bullet wound. It first passed through his haversack filled with hardtack, then through his dress coat, pants, pocket, pocketbook, and drawers. Then the battered ball passed through his left thigh above the middle going between the femur and femoral artery, cutting off in two parts the sciatica nerve, and passing out through and badly tearing the bicep. He became

---

* The 1st & 3rd North Carolina regiments also fought the 27th Indiana at Chancellorsville and Gettysburg. The 3rd was raised in and around Wilmington and New Hanover County, coincidentally as was the author.

numb, weak, easily exhausted, and partially paralyzed, with a feeling like a cramp or his leg being asleep. Placed beside a rock ledge behind the line, he lay with other wounded till late in the afternoon. Then he was taken by ambulance to the White House hospital almost a mile away and lay in the garden. Years later Thomson recalled the head doctor's name was Donnely.

All three finders of Lee's "Lost Order" fell. First Sergeant John McKnight Bloss was shot in both legs, Corporal Barton Warren Mitchell in the left calf, and Private David Bur Vance in the right hand and left knee. A soldier whose arm was injured helped Vance off the field. Moving to rear, Vance's partner was struck in the head by a cannon ball, scattering brains and blood over Vance. He took refuge in a straw stack with a badly wounded Confederate. The man knew he would not live and gave Vance a ruby stick pin to pass to his kin. Later Vance gave the pin to his own great-grandson.

> It seems a miracle that anyone should still remain unhurt. There is scarcely a man on whom blood has not been drawn in some way. —*ERB* [41]

8:00 a.m.

> I was struck in left breast with a spent ball. I thought it went plum thru me, it would not have hurt more if it had. I thought it strange that I did not fall down. I felt for the hole in my breast but found none so I kept on fighting all day. After the battle I examined my breast & found it was black & blue. I never had anything done for it. —*Private William Charles Riley* [42]

A brilliant sun now lit the scene. On the field for more than an hour, the 27th in trying to regroup was about to receive their heaviest blow. At 8:30 a.m., as Indiana losses mounted, Colonel Alfred Holt Colquitt's Alabama and Georgia brigade came up on the left to relieve Ripley. Colquitt quickly pushed to the rail fence bordering the cornfield on the north, directly opposite the Hoosiers, and eventually forced their withdrawal behind the batteries in front of the East Woods. Gordon wrote, "So strong was the enemy that an addition of any force I could command would only have caused further sacrifice without gain."[43] But morale remained high. Gordon added, "If only a few of us are left, the enemy has suffered in at least equal proportion."

Those behind the fence where Indiana fire was hottest "doubtless think it is raining lead where they are." (After the battle they found a single rail peppered with 45 balls.) Confederates in the corn kept changing positions as a steady stream passed rearward. The 27th wished themselves at the fence or able to enfilade the enemy. Either would have saved "much of the sad, sad loss" in the 3rd Wisconsin and 27th Indiana.[44]

Colonel D. K. McRae's brigade arrived on Colquitt's right—a new threat to the Union line. "But Gordon's three trusted old regiments stood firm on the Miller pasture high ground" just above the cornfield, and, as reported in a New York newspaper, "crowned the hill and stood out darkly against the sky, but lighted and shrouded over in flame and smoke. There was no more gallant, determined heroic fighting in all this desperate day."[45] Colquitt became extended without flanking support and withdrew when Federals appeared on the crest of the hill the 27th had occupied. Hooker rode up, his wounded foot dripping blood, and ordered the 3rd Brigade to pursue. Colgrove's "Fix bayonets!" pierced the din, rallying his men. Before they charged, however, Colquitt retired briskly, the Federals going "wild with joy and begin to cheer with all our might."[46] Colgrove's men followed.

8:45 a.m.

> This field was a low piece of ground, the corn very heavy, and serving, to some extent, to screen the enemy from view, yet the colors and battle flags of several regiments appearing above the corn clearly indicate the advance of the enemy in force. —*Colonel Silas Colgrove about The Cornfield* [47]

"With a whoop and a hurrah" the Badgers and Hoosiers swiftly moved down the slope to that "tragic fence" and over and between bloody corn rows, "with their cut and hackled corn stalks." Pushing through the cornfield, Hooker "leading like a captain," they continued until near the post-and-rail fence bordering the Hagerstown Pike as the enemy entered the West Woods.[48] A bullet hit Private Theodore M. Nance in the throat. First Sergeant William H. Holloway commanded all five men left in his Company I, Nance among them. All officers were disabled and in the rear. "I picked a piece of collar button out of his neck & told him if it had come a $1/2$" closer he would have been a dead man," Holloway wrote. "It cut the skin & bruised his throat, mashed the collar button. He was standing sideways loading his musket when the ball struck him."[49]

The corn was strewn with dead greycoats, but the enemy continued firing. When the Indiana color bearer was shot, Sergeant John L. Files caught the flag before it hit the ground. Then Files, his big Navy revolver blazing, fired 37 rounds before being shot. "Our men routed the rebels in our front as they got up to run. I shot 3 times at the rebel color bearer & he fell to ground."[50] Colgrove said the frenzy lasted about two hours, "without any perceptible advantage to either side."* Federal fire soon "proved too hard for them. They broke and fled, in utter confusion, into a piece of woods on the right."[51]

By 9:00, the widely scattered I Corps attack had fizzled; the XII Corps, with almost 25 percent casualties, had lost all aggressiveness. The XII Corps held parts of a line extending from Miller's house to Dunker Church, with the 1st Division a half mile from the church. Williams signaled McClellan at his headquarters: "Gen. Mansfield is dangerously wounded. Gen. Hooker

---

* Years later he said two hours, forty minutes.

wounded severely in foot. Gen. [II Corps Commander Major General Edwin] Sumner I hear is advancing. We hold the field at present. Please give us all the aid you can."[52]

The aid became Sumner's reckless uncoordinated attack, led by Major General John Sedgwick's Division, which entered the West Woods' lions den and was savagely repulsed. After 9:00 a.m., while the 3rd and 27th were engaged near the pike, lying amid the dead and dying of both sides avoiding cannon balls and shells on every side, just as their "little band was pluckily getting into shape to charge deeper into the woods," Sedgwick arrived.[53] "The work of dislodging the enemy from the woods, designed for [Gordon's] shattered brigade, had been assigned to them."[54] "This was all that prevented us from assaulting a position with about 150 men, which a few minutes later Sedgwick's Division with 4–6,000 failed to carry," a Wisconsin man remembered.[55] The two regiments backtracked through the cornfield gathering up several rebel flags as trophies, their day's fighting essentially ended. But it was not without contact: a bullet hit Private Edmund Randolph Brown left of his navel.

A Hoosier lieutenant paid homage:

> The [Confederates] fell thick & fast. We finally got a crossfire on them which made them right about & take to their heels rapidly, then we charged amid the dead & dying up through the corn after them. Gen. Gordon rode up in the corn complimented us very highly as brave soldiers having done our duty, & the 27th as being one of the best regiments in the service— received with cheers while the bullets were flying thick & fast...When we charged into the corn my Captain T[ighlman] H[oward] Nance & myself were the only officers left of the [27th's] entire right. [Private] John [Robert] Rankin was the entirety of Co. A. Four color bearers were shot down with the colors in their hands. I was surprised to see our own men and the foe lying thickly intermingled o'er the ground. It was hot both naturally and artificially. All were crying for water. We gave to each alike while our canteens lasted.[56]

Corporal William Muster survived two attempts to put him under. While loading his gun a "missile" struck the gunstock just below the lock, breaking it in two. The lower portion or the missile, or both, punched him in the pit of the stomach, bending his belt plate and knocking him senseless. A comrade thought he was killed. He lay for many hours until carried to a field hospital by the burial party, who were about to inter him. The wound at times caused derangement and bloating of the bowels and stomach, and he had to keep his pants loose at the waist, rendering him unfit for duty.

The cornfield was a ghastly final breath for hundreds who fell. Countless poor souls lay in utter agony as the inferno roared above, dumping debris and more broken bodies, and hoof and foot steps, on top of them. As firing diminished, Antietam's northern phase, centered there, had ended. In three and a half hours of hell on earth, some 8,000 men were casualties. Soon the clash would shift one mile south for possession of a sunken country lane.

9:15 a.m. through the Remainder of the Day

> I severely wounded my right arm which paralyzed it & hand so much that it did not pain very bad at the time. Dr. said [arm] was bad, said arm would have to be taken off. I then left the hospital, didn't want my arm removed. After we had gone back to rear 3 ladies came to us & dressed the arm. I was taken to hospital at Harrisburg Pa. After I had been there a few days the doctors wanted to amputate the arm. I told them I could not have it taken off. —*Private Philip A. Lane. He died in 1919 with both arms intact.* [57]

Retiring from the cornfield, the regiment stopped to support a battery, lying 100 feet in front while six 6-pounders fired overhead "playing heavily on the enemy" with "very frequent and loud reports." Sergeant George Mehringer never forgot the "loud cannonading."[58] Sergeant John L. Files' hearing was impaired from the "sharpest guns we had. Men who lay close to me had blood run out of their ears (none from mine). Continual firing made my hearing so bad that after the battle at 3:00 p.m. when roll was called I could not hear my name. All I heard was a roaring sound; a man put his hand on my shoulder & said 'here he is.'" His head roared for 3 months after— "was 2–3 weeks before I could distinguish plain conversation. In service I was never free from roaring in both ears equally." Private William Thomson said the jar and concussion was "so great as to make me nearly deaf for some time after that."[59]

By the time Captain John D. McKahin was wounded between 10–11:00 a.m. in the "very severe hit fight," one-third of his Company H were lost.[60] Private Dennis W. Ogden finished a very bad year. Run over by Confederate cavalry at Winchester, and shot in the left temple at Cedar Mountain, Ogden took a ball in his left thigh. Placed in a barn on the field, he lay there one week before going to a Frederick hospital. He lived 32

Brigadier General
Alpheus Starkey Williams

The 27th Indiana served under him for nearly three years; they loved and respected him.

National Park Service, Gettysburg

more years. Sergeant Oliver P. Shepherd was hit in the left thigh and ne-
gotiated himself off the field using his gun as a crutch. That night Private
Francis James saw Shepherd nearly dead from blood loss. Later Private
William Muster, a temporary nurse, saw Shepherd and Corporal Jonathan
Baker lying side by side for eight days in a Boonsboro hospital bleeding
profusely. Private Josiah W. Tobias, supposedly killed, "presently raised
himself to a sitting position" and asked to go to the rear. Sergeant Thomas
H. Adams and Private Thomas Hunt carried him to a tree uprooted by wind
and then returned to the line.[61] Stretcher bearer Private Harvey Deputy
saw Private Elmer Perry Booher fall from a bullet graze to the head. Booher
lay there 20 minutes, then ran to the rear.

On shifting to the East Woods, the 27th replenished stomachs and
cartridge boxes, and cleaned or exchanged guns. "All told not enough were
now present to make one fair sized company."[62] They relocated again and
were never far from the battle lines for the rest of the day. Yet their work
was not finished. Shortly the 3rd and 27th were ordered over the same
ground again to support their comrades posted near the West Woods. But
the move was called off. Having survived the day untouched, Captain
Peter Kop was then mortally wounded in the lungs by a stray bullet. For
some reason he exclaimed in great pain that both legs were wounded.
While being carried to an ambulance, he surprised everyone by walking,
but soon died on a field hospital bed of straw.

The Hoosiers grimaced at the horrors on the field where they had fought:
dismembered dead and wounded men; corn trampled to shreds; broken
guns and swords; dismounted wrecked cannons; and mutilated equipment.
Horses, with pieces of harness hanging to them and maddened with terror
and pain, "made it the hideous spectacle which none but the retreating or
the conquering soldier ever sees."[63] The pathetic wounded screamed for
mercy like nothing the living could ever experience. Brigadier General
Williams, under fire from sunrise to nearly 2:00 p.m., having missed breakfast and dinner, wondered how anyone escaped injury:

> All over the ground we had advanced on, the Rebel dead and wounded lay
> thick, much more numerous than ours, but ours were painfully mingled in.
> Those we were obliged to leave begged so piteously to be carried away.
> Hundreds appealed to me and I confess that the rage of battle had not
> hardened my heart so that I did not feel a pity for them. Our men gave them
> water and as far as I saw always treated them kindly. The wounded Rebels
> had been carried away in great numbers and yet every farmyard and hay-
> stack seemed a large hospital.[64]

"Col. Colgrove and Lt. Col. [Abisha L.] Morrison are the proudest men
living of the manner the regiment acquitted itself," bragged Commissary
Sergeant Simpson Solomon Hamrick.[65] Both escaped injury while riding

their horses throughout the battle, although Colgrove's horse was shot from under him, and were "at all times in the thickest of the fighting encouraging the men." First Lieutenant Robert B. Gilmore was mortally wounded. "If we lose him we lose the best company officer in the regiment."[66] Hamrick considered Gilmore "the pride of the company," and the dead Second Lieutenant William Van Orsdall, as "respected by all. It will be difficult to fill their places."[67] Hamrick had charge of getting the ammunition wagon to the front and was on the field from beginning to end.[68]

Gordon's brigade was under fire from before sunrise until after dark. Although the main fighting was in the forenoon, all day long they were exposed to heavy artillery shelling. That night Colgrove temporarily commanded the brigade and marched them to the front nearest the enemy again to support batteries. "Although our men had gone into the fight without breakfast and had fought all day, they performed this arduous duty without grumbling, but with cheerfulness," he reported. "I saw no man or officer who took a backward step during the whole day, unless ordered to do so."[69] Soldiers were not alone in the field. Surgeon Willis H. Twiford operated on wounded until 3:00 p.m. when ordered to another hospital. And Gordon wrote:

> Grape and canister mingled their hissing scream in this hellish carnival, within all this and through it all the patriots of the North wrestled with hearts strong and nerves unshaken—wrestled with the rebel hordes that thronged and pressed upon them as to destruction; never yielding, though sometimes halting to gather up their strength; then with one mighty bound throwing themselves upon their foes to drive them into their protecting forest beyond.[70]

Post-mortem analysis praised the 3rd Brigade. "The admirable troops of Gordon's brigade," one observer reported, succeeded in clearing the cornfield "with some aid from [Brigadier General George S.] Greene's men." The Federal pressure had caused the Confederate line which was to the left of Confederate Major General Daniel Harvey Hill to fight really at right angles to his line. "It may have been at this time and place the disparity of the numbers was the greatest."[71] "Gordon turned the tide," wrote another, and Hood's brigades were gradually forced back through the cornfield to Dunker church. "A great gap had now opened in [Stonewall] Jackson's line."[72] Hamrick's view was colored. "Our regiment is praised by all and is said to have turned the fortune at one time in our favor when other regiments wavered and run. When it comes to fighting Indiana always shows herself equal to the emergency."[73] Gordon said the Indianians "had made the noblest stand ever" and the men deserved the nation's thanks and praise.[74]

We saw nothing of Gordon. Where he was during this fiery ordeal, or why some move was not ordered by him that might easily have relieved the situation and saved many valuable lives has never been explained. After the crisis was passed he dashed up to our colonel and, with his customary effusiveness and attention to stage effects, took off his cap and said, in the hearing of all, "Colonel Colgrove, I want to congratulate you and your men. You have covered yourselves all over with glory." Yet, in his official report we find nothing of the kind. *—ERB* [75]

Federal troops now held the Miller and Mumma farms, East Woods, Hagerstown Pike, the fields along Smoketown Road and the cornfield. To Hooker the price was ghastly: "Bodies were in heaps amid the broken corn-stalks near the pike...every stalk of corn in the northern and greater part of the field was cut as closely as could have been done with a knife, and the slain lay in rows precisely as they had stood in their ranks a few moments before."[76] As Williams wrote:

In front of the position of my corps, apparently a whole [Rebel] had been cut down in line. They lay in two ranks, as straightly alligned as on a dress parade. There must have been a brigade as part of the line on the left had been buried.[77]

The exhausted 3rd Brigade then "slept upon the bloody field of our victory."[78]

September 18 and After

Eldridge was wound in the thy & rist but is getting along pretty well. John A. Henshaw was killed. Laben is wound in arm. Daniel is wound in knee. George Phillips wound in leg. Them 3 is at another hospital & I have not saw them. Joe Fiddler is killed. Chris Fiddler wound in hand. I cannot tell all that is wound. I was struck in the left side by a piece of shell but I soon got over it. I am waiting on Eldridge & will stay with him until he gets well. I think the boys will all get well. I will try to get Laben & Daniel with Eldridge where I can tend to all of them. *—Private Rufus Williams* [79]

Tough Rufus, also wounded at Winchester, Gettysburg, and New Hope Church, completed his service and lived until 1926. "I think the rebel army gets out of Maryland. I think they will leave the big part of their army here."[80] Private Eldridge Williams died from his wound on November 12. Corporal Daniel B. Williams recovered, was wounded at Gettysburg, and discharged in November 1863. Corporal Laban Williams was later killed at Gettysburg. Private George W. Phillips was discharged in 1863. Private Christopher Columbus Fiddler was discharged in November 1862. The Williams boys likely were related. (Private Adam Williams, Daniel's brother, had died of lung congestion in 1861.)

Major General George Brinton McClellan
Commander of the Army of the Potomac at Antietam.

Brady Collections

Early casualty counts were rarely correct, as typified in reports by two lieutenants. "Was an awful struggle of life & death," Josiah Clinton Williams wrote. "Fought all day. There were only 15 or 20 men left on the right wing of once 500."[81] But, noting "On the Field of Battle," George Tarvin Chapin penned home to Putnam County:

> Near as I can learn our regiment lost 18 killed & 192 wounded. Men never fought better than our Company I but as far is known 3 killed & 16 wounded. Poor Jim Hall I am afraid will die of a wound in right breast. Charles Kimball is well. Gabe Lewis was not in the fight. Company A lost a bigger portion of their number. John Rankin was not hurt & is well. We drove the enemy with great slaughter.[82]

After burying their compatriots on the eighteenth, the Hoosiers spent the night south of Miller's barn. The next morning they marched across the pike and through the cornfield, visited the burial places of Sergeant Robert S. Good and other comrades, crossed Antietam Creek at Burnside's Bridge, and left the horrible spectacle they helped create. "The Dunker Church we fought in front of was literally riddled on every side. The little town of Sharpsburg had a bullet hole in almost every building."[83] They stopped where the enemy dead lay thickest. The repulsive enemy carcasses were now swollen and blackened beyond all recognition, as Private Lewis King remembered:

> They were all as black as the blackest African and the stench was horrible...in some places two or three deep. I observed a cavalrymen who had taken from under the pile of dead men one that was not dead. He lay there faintly breathing. What had attracted their attention was the fact that his skin was still white amid a multitude of black ones. I observed a well dressed lady in the crowd of spectators sitting on a horse, looking coolly on those horrible scenes. Later I learned she was one of McClellan's spies.[84]

"It required stout nerves to be able to look at them. Probably many had lived after being shot, some until recently, some faces had freshness even peacefulness of sleep." One face, a "mere boy" not over 17, had light hair, blue eyes, a high forehead, and refined, classical features. "The purest strain of our Anglo-Saxon blood was in his veins and with it were lofty ambitions and a dauntless courage." His face was up, his uniform of fine English broadcloth, suggesting a "Southern home of wealth, culture and refinement robbed of its idol, some proud aristocratic mother had paid the extreme penalty of secession."[85]

McClellan's army trekked toward Virginia pursuing the resilient and elusive Lee, whom they knew they could defeat but wondered if they could ever destroy. Their sacrifice at Antietam had redirected the course of the

Civil War. The 27th Indiana, now skilled practitioners at bloodletting but gored in the vitals, added their own evaluation. "No other battle of the war contributed so much towards the final settlement of the question of the relative fighting qualities of Northern and Southern soldiers, and the ultimate possibility of putting down the rebellion by force."[86]

Almost as an afterthought, an Indiana newspaper reporter wrote, "I hope our people [anxious] for their sick and wounded ones will find some comfort in the assurance I give them. Every care and kindness possible under the circumstance attending so bloody a battle are being extended to their loved ones. In passing over the fields of bloody Antietam, the evidences of honor as well as success of our forces are everywhere."[87]

And history would eternally know "The Cornfield," the bloodiest phase of America's bloodiest day, glorified by honor and success. "Its effects will be seen & felt in the destinies of the Nation for centuries to come."[88]

CHAPTER 2

For Union, Flag, and Lincoln:
Cause, Morale, and External Interactions

It was the best type of the American volunteer regiments, made up of sturdy, resolute boys, animated by a sincere love of country and an earnest desire to do their whole duty...a crowd of raw, undisciplined country boys, making all sorts of blunders and fun-provoking mistakes, who through the fires and trials of military training and hard service became hammered and shaped into as fine a body of soldiers as ever stood under a flag. —*John McElroy, National Tribune Editor, about the 27th Indiana, circa 1900* [1]

By mid-Summer 1861 the wheat crop had just been harvested, and most other major crops had been planted. This made the farmers more comfortable about leaving their farms and freed them for service. The men who comprised the 27th Indiana, most of whom eked out meager livings on the fringes of the broad prairie or in the hilly, rocky soil of the state's central and southcentral regions, were intensely patriotic. They also had shown their practical side, and, substituting keen common sense in tracking the news for deficiencies in book learning, they awaited the appropriate time to respond to their country's peril.

In the spring of 1861, President Lincoln's calls for troops to crush the rebellion reached the villages and farms which would become "27th Indiana country," an expanse from north of Indianapolis south to the Ohio River. The impact was immediate, and rosters filled. Let us get on with it and come home, the volunteers chided, in time to fix the stable roof before the first snowfall.

Soon the music of fifes, drums, and bands filled every Indiana town of size, attracting crowds of prospective soldiers in sweltering heat to the town park to hear patriotic speeches and pleas for service, joined by curious veterans of the War of 1812 and the Mexican War. Preachers, politicians, and civic leaders incited the audience and set the stage for other men who were raising local companies of volunteers. Young soldiers accompanying the entourage smartly displayed their uniforms and muskets at attention. Old men clapped, and the tanned, strapping youths, straight

Indiana's Citizens Entering Cincinnati to Enlist for the Defense of the Union

Leslie's Illustrated Weekly

from the wheat shocks and hog pens, reacted anxiously to every word and note. Volunteer now with your school chums, your friends of the neighboring villages! The Union must be preserved! The words, songs, and huzzahs rang in their ears.

Thomas J. Box, Lawrence County farmer, enrolled immediately. While working his field the fifes and drums enticed him into Bedford. He left his mule and plow right where he stopped. Less than three years later, Box earned the Medal of Honor for valor at the Battle of Resaca. Other prospects wanted time to think or get parents' permission.

Most Indianians joined the army to save the Union, very few to free the slaves. Some joined from quest of adventure or expected glory; this was borne out in Indiana's record in the field. Some did mean to let the army straighten out their lives. On the whole they just went, fed in part by similar actions of others they knew. Traits of youthful masculine invincibility, wrapped by Hoosier individuality, drove them on the surface, but deep down they realized their country needed them.

Like thousands of other youngsters leading quiet and monotonous lives, far away from the madding crowds, I was destined to be swept into the maelstrom of the Civil War. I begged to go earlier but finally obtaining my parents grudging consent I enlisted in the 3-year service in July. I was gone a year before I saw anyone I had known before leaving home. We could not forget that we were starting on a long journey, with the prospect of a long absence, and that our errand was war! It was well for us that we had no real foresight as to the very large number among us who would never return. —*ERB* [2]

The 27th Indiana Volunteer Infantry Regiment was mustered into service in the Union Army on September 12, 1861, at Camp Morton in Indianapolis. Colonel Silas Colgrove formed the regiment and was its only commanding officer until wounded on June 22, 1864, in the Battle of Peachtree Creek in the Atlanta Campaign, requiring hospitalization. The original regiment numbered 38 officers, 995 enlisted combatants, and 24 band members, a total of 1,057. During its three years of service, the 27th Indiana enrolled 1,181 men, including replacement recruits. On September 1, 1864, one day before Atlanta fell, the regiment was mustered out of service, its arduous, loyal, and productive duty done.

Morale within the 27th Indiana varied between weak and strong, highly questionable and decidedly superior, not always the result of success or failure on the battlefield. Other factors impinging on morale included regimental officer and noncommissioned officer leadership, the relationships of men with each other, interactions with external parties such as the U.S. Government and general officers, obtaining furloughs, and not the least, pressures from home. Periodically the war seemed so close to being over, and they could return home. But then hopes were dashed, and fighting resumed again. In 1861–63, the men frequently discussed the elusive topics of victory or even a cease fire. Blame and resentment were easy to affix for young, uneducated farmers trying to sort out—and adjust to—the complexities of army life, combat, rebellion, and Washington and Indianapolis politics.

As the abolition of slavery became a central issue for winning the war, a potential issue certainly recognizable to Indiana farmers in 1861 but accelerated by Lincoln's Emancipation Proclamation following the Battle of Antietam, it also impacted morale in the 27th Indiana.

In 1864, the final year of service for the original members, with the war turning towards a Union victory and their days in uniform numbered, morale improved steadily and the "cause" of 1861 grew dimmer in their memories. Survival became paramount, defeating the rebellion only important.

The southern and southcentral areas of Indiana from which most members came were full of "secessionist sentiment," even to the point of outright hostility toward enlistments, the draft, Union soldiers in general—including friends and neighbors—and the war effort. Other Hoosiers from those areas were lukewarm about the war and gave it only tacit support.

Besides posing continuing political problems for Indiana Republican Governor Oliver P. Morton, these sentiments were manifested the first two years of the war upon targets in the 27th Indiana through insults, ostracism, and pressures to desert. Overall, the soldiers were little influenced by those politicians, newspapers, family or friends at home, and were quick to rebuke them. Most members responded with loyalty to their flag, but in numerous cases relationships with home folks were rankled.

Opposition in strongly Democratic and anti-war Dubois County was particularly abusive. Answering taunts to the front, Company K Captain Richmond M. Welman, on June 18, 1862, wrote home, "If you be not for us don't be against us, but let us fight it out in peace within our own breast. For the sake of our country, help us. Put no stumbling blocks in the way."[3]

Members of Company K took the offensive in letters to the Jasper paper, including one from "a Dubois Volunteer":

> Can you in clear conscience stay at home and see your comrades enlisting in this bloody struggle? Our liberties are at stake and it depends on men of true patriotic sentiments to preserve our blessed Union. If you have property to protect, take your musket in your hand and fight for it. If a man makes excuses and tries to influence others not to go he is a coward. If you are Union men lay aside politics and fight for your country. If we die, we die in a good cause, but run ain't our name.[4]

Welman continued to chastise the people of Dubois:

> Do people in their quiet homes...think of the floods of tears now flowing from the eyes of those mothers, widows, and orphans? Do they think of these things as soldiers do? Then pray tell them to hold their peace a little longer. Prate not so much over dollars and cents; make not so many speeches about abolitionists, negroes and democracy. Let not your first object be to repair old political parties or build new ones—that is after the country is safe.[5]

Opposition split parents and sons. In 1861, Second Lieutenant Josiah Clinton Williams wrote his grandfather, "I have not heard from Pa or any of our folks for some 3 months. I strongly suspect them as being actual seceshers since I have joined the army."[6] Mr. Harden Edwards railed in a December 1861 letter to Private George Edwards:

> Your letter found us doing as well as Linconn your damned abolitionist will allow us. Now you bragged about sending your flag on the oytside of the envelop. I would hate to send that flag anywhere if I believed such damed stuff as you are fighting for. That flag was a flag of liberty but they have got it over the principle of tyrony. You talk of dying in defense of your wife and children. If you thought mutch of your wife and children you would go home and take care of them and not be afighting to take other peoples propertys

away. I will not take your advice if I fight atol. I will be bound to fight for principal and not for a damed negro.[7]

Colgrove reacted strongly to harping from home: "Everything is right & if editors, croakers & politicians at home will mind their own business all will be right. I have no sympathy or even patience with demagogues at home who are too cowardly to fight & are too mischievous to suffer men who have a right to know something about the matter to control it."[8]

Pressure on men to come home or desert was greatest in the Winter of 1862-63. "Our boys constantly receive letters from friends at home chuck full of treasonable trash, just such as will excite soldiers to suspect the cause." Some men flirted but none wavered in spite of the army's malaise. "I can't see anything encouraging ahead of us. I am just as confident as when I started out. If the North was as united as the South the end would soon come. It does look gloomy."[9] The letters "sounded the same: the rebellion could never be put down in force; we were waging a war solely to free the nigger; the war had lasted longer than anybody first believed; money was getting worthless." The writers were "lonesome and melancholy, some destitute. Weak parents and other relatives obviously were being used as tools by the wide, treasonable [Indiana] conspiracy."[10] The majority was frustrated but optimistic, as Sergeant John L. Gilmore said: "I think [the war] will close this summer. The rebels are about 'played out.' I am willing to fight them until doom's day before I will give them any place unless they lay down their arms, come back into the Union, pay for government property they have stolen & destroyed & agree to let the majority rule. Until they do this I say fight, show them no quarter, offer them no terms of peace & let them know we are determined to conquer or die trying."[11]

In the early days of the war soldiers were optimistic with tongue-in-cheek reality, as Private Ferdinand Grass typified: "Tell the boys who have the fever so high to come ahead; we can cool them down in 3 nights by giving them a bed on the ground, where the mud is about 4" deep, and a few nice crackers for breakfast, and work it off with rice soup for dinner. I tell you there is no mistake about our bravery. By the time we meet the enemy we will be so hungry as to become mad. They want Hoosiers to do the fighting, and we intend to do it. I am happy to hail from Indiana."[12] Colgrove wrote the governor before being tested under fire, "I undoubtedly have the largest finest looking regiment on the Potomac. General [Nathaniel P.] Banks says it is the finest regiment of men he ever saw."[13]

Men of the 27th Indiana were unabashed about criticizing army and government leadership, and began griping immediately after entering the service. What had they expected? After one month "some of the boys are quite tired of soldiering," a sergeant remarked. "The way you can tell they complain about their rations, say they don't get enough to eat, and find fault with everything."[14]

Commissary Sergeant Simpson Solomon Hamrick wrote home in 1862 after the army was run out of Virginia, "[Our troops] are universally badly discouraged and demoralized. All confidence in our head generals is gone. I think McClellan more than any other man [is] to blame for the failure of the Union Army. Is now just where he started a year ago with a disorganized army."[15] His complaint was typical.

The early days brought little good war news, but in February 1862 "the quiet monotony of the Hoosier City was broken up today." The regiment thought they were marching. Instead, Captain Peter Kop announced the fall of Fort Donelson out West and the capture of 15,000 prisoners, and waved his cap high. "One thousand Hoosier lungs expanded to their utmost, and such a shout the good people of old Dubois never heard," Welman exclaimed. The band played and the men reacted in a "wild state of excitement, some jumping, some throwing snow and shaking hands; all shouting at once."[16]

However, complaining was endemic to soldiering. In September 1862 in Maryland, coming after the disastrous Virginia Campaign, some, like Hamrick, felt the army moved too slowly and was poorly led. But others disagreed, saying morale had soared on entering Maryland. "At once, as if by magic, a wonderful change came over our army, buoyant and full of confidence, that General McClellan was restored to command, the only general who could lead the army to victory."[17] And he did; victory at Antietam redirected the war, but weeks of sacrifice exhausted the soldiers who understood none of the strategy and politics—only their personal deprivation. Hoosiers marched to Antietam "a set of long-haired, filthy, lousey tatterdemalions." Many were entirely shoeless, while the shoes of some "scarcely hung on their feet." Pants were out at the seat and knees, frayed at the bottoms from the ankles upward. Many had no coats or ones with holes at the elbows, rips at the seams, no tails, and were soiled and discolored. Clothing reeked with vermin and men turned garments wrong side out at night to give temporary relief from the lice until dropping into sleep.[18]

> There never was so much to dishearten and demoralize at any other stage of our service. We had been exposed to all kinds of weather, day and night, opportunities to cleanse our persons or clothing had been so infrequent, we had been reduced to such extremes of destitution in many ways, that we were really objects of commiseration, if not loathsome in our own eyes. —*ERB* [19]

Earlier in 1862, the critical Hamrick told home folks, "All quiet along the Potomac is getting to be so common that it is used by the soldiers to ridicule those in command."[20] Chasing Confederate Lieutenant General Stonewall Jackson about the Shenandoah Valley without serious action was frustrating. In May 1862, they felt they "belonged to an army intended only for occupation, not aggression. It was hard for us to bear it with any cheerfulness; we wanted something to do and we could not see that our weakened constitution gave abundant promise of it."[21] Their general felt that "when properly led, Union soldiers were quite capable of meeting the best efforts of Jackson's famed 'foot cavalry.'"[22]

By late Summer 1862, the war going badly, loyalty was put to the "supreme test." First Lieutenant Williams wrote, "Disheartening reverses imposed on their love of country and their faith in its ultimate deliverance." The men seriously questioned whether "Northern soldiers were not equal to Southern soldiers." The "most fatal" and "most discreditable thing" that could happen was "distrusting one's own prowess and overestimating the foes. If this army was out-maneuvered, taken at a helpless disadvantage and pounded mercilessly yesterday; resolutely and hopefully if not smilingly it squared itself for the encounter today." He continued, "There has already been enough sacrifice of life & blood spilled. If there had been enough management skillfully employed the war would have ended by now. All we can do now is fight it out & look for the best."[23]

Welman wrote the Jasper paper:

> Now the greatest, the most glorious government and country on earth is on the very brink of ruin. [Tell] the politicians not to clog the wheels of the war chariot. The rebellion can't be quelled by legislation. The country is in a dire extremity; the principles of self-government are undergoing a fiery trial; dread war is upon us. Your neighbor's house is on fire, will you now stop to enquire the cause, or philosophies upon preventative engines, etc., or will ye help extinguish the flames and inquire into the cause later?[24]

Marching through Washington to fight at Antietam were Union soldiers, including the 27th Indiana, whose pay was in arrears four to eight months. Many died defending a weakened, embarrassed government unable to pay the "small pittance owed them for their previous service."[25] In January 1863, Colgrove was "afraid to let us out of his sight for fear we will strike out for home or else he is entirely indifferent. Thank fortune he is about as near strapped as any of us and has to beg his tobacco occasionally wherever he can find it. I haven't a spark of pity for him."[26] "If the soldiers were paid up promptly and things managed more energetically there would be less discontent," Hamrick added.[27]

In the Winter 1863, Major General Joseph Hooker reorganized the Eastern army, a move the Hoosiers received well. "By his rigid system of discipline & almost daily inspecting & reviewing has put everything in the best & most efficient fighting trim. All are confident of ultimate success with such a leader," and by April they were anxious to end their "masterly inactivity" and strike the Rebels. "We are tired of surveying a sea of un-fathomable mud & pine forests almost interminable. 'Fighting Joe' will ei-ther advance or retreat, whip somebody or get whipped, & fast too."[28]

By April 1863, the regiment was "in excellent health," wrote "40," the 27th's unofficial and prolific correspondent to Indiana newspapers on regi-mental affairs, 10 days before Chancellorsville. "Chaplain [Thomas A.] Whitted said he could whip any man who accused us of being demoralized....Our rations are better & the commissary department is more efficiently managed. Now armed with Springfield rifles & fitted out with clothing, camp & garrison equipage complete. The absence of the pay-master has rendered our financial affairs unhealthy."[29]

The man with the *nom de plume* "40," Quartermaster Sergeant John A. Crose, had a certain feel for the state of the regiment. "We are better encouraged at the present aspect of affairs and more determined to put down and wipe out this accursed rebellion than ever. The utmost good feeling and harmony prevails among the officers and men. Everything moves along quietly, smoothly and without any jar or discord."[30]

Morale was never better than in April 1863. Yet, throughout the war, the men were sensitive to the degree of respect shown them. This respect often affected group and individual morale. Governor Morton's represen-tative Mr. T. Bullard reported on visiting their camp after Antietam: "The boys greet anyone from home with pleasure. They seem to expect that whenever there is a battle you or someone to represent you will soon be there to look after their wants. This adds to their courage & willingness to fight.[31] Morton's private secretary and military agent also visited the regi-ment, but saw only Colgrove. "They [Morton's men and Colgrove] appear inclined to drink the whiskey all among themselves," the observant Hamrick opined. "If they are looking after the interests of the soldiers of Indiana they probably could find out more of the wants and wishes if they would consult them some and not take the colonel's word for it. If these are the kind of agents Morton sends he had better not send but few for it has a bad tendency. The soldiers see how indifferent such men are to their interests."[32]

Relatives, friends, and officers' wives visited, some on sad missions connected with casualties. But having Hoosier visitors cheered the troops. "It was a veritable Godsend to have a refined loyal lady in camp."[33]

The men constantly wrote home concerning regimental business or gossip, particularly about each other. "By this time we are well used and acclimated to the hardships that we are getting along tolerably well," wrote an officer. "[Commissary Sergeant Tarvin C.] Tarve and [Private] Lewis [P., his brother] Stone have both made good soldiers. Lewis is somewhat cut down being too young to stand it as well as older boys. Both the com-panies that left our [Putnam] county are greatly reduced. Such is the effect of war."[34] Not being able to go home all winter of 1862–63 peeved Second Lieutenant Williams. "I may try again. It is necessary to keep in the front those who have been absent nearly 2 years from home to protect band-box straps [officers] of the Potomac from smelling gun powder. Enough. A soldier should be but a machine without the links. I can stand it."[35] A depressed First Lieutenant Thomas W. Casey shared those feelings. "Can't get a furlough to come home. I can stick it out without one." He added, "I see but little prospect of the close of this war. I think we have not seen the worst of it yet. We have very comfortable shanties and are getting along fine. But I expect we will have rough times when we get to marching again."[36]

Money as well as shelter also influenced morale. Back in December 1862, the men had been due six months pay, and First Lieutenant Hamrick begged his family repeatedly. "Still in want. Need some funds. Don't send all in one envelope."[37] In two weeks he wrote, "My health never better in my life. Can march as far as the best of them. The boys all say I look 10 years younger." Still no pay. "The administration and Gen. [Henry] Halleck don't merit the confidence of the American people."[38] Another week passed. "We have almost lost confidence in our government officials. Of all the outrages heaped upon us this is the greatest. There is scarcely a man in camp has money to buy tobacco or even a sheet of paper to write to our friends."[39] In February 1863, now seven months: "Some of the legislators are debating the propriety of reducing our pay. Should they curtail it much the government will have to feed us or else we could not run the machine long at a time."[40] And then, "I am satisfied the government intends using us for some time to come."[41]

July 4 observances were inspirational as after Gettysburg, when both armies rested with memories of their common heritage. A year later a band awakened them in the Atlanta trenches playing "most beautifully" the "Star Spangled Banner" and other patriotic airs. "No soldier of those old days has ever heard what seems to him such impressive soul-stirring band music as he heard then," and "considerable cannonading to celebrate our independence and hurrying the Johnnies retreat."[42] On Washington's birthday in 1862, First Lieutenant John A. Cassady read Washington's Farewell Address as the Company F flag, given by Bloomington residents, was raised. Colgrove's remarks were his standard rally: "George Washington was all right, the country was all right, and the 27th was all right" except "that we had no chance for a scrap with the 'Johnnies.'"[43]

The thrill of soldiering peaked in the Winter 1862–63. Any member who missed it was "like a man without a boyhood." There were hardships, bad weather, much sickness, inconvenience, and deprivations, "but the good cheer far overbalanced the things of a different nature," and when they were off duty they were always comfortable and usually happy.[44] They were adequately fed and sheltered and duty was not burdensome.

Comforts and joys in this world are wholly relative. No man or family ever felt better satisfied or happier on moving into a mansion, or felt more gratefully its warmth and shelter, than did we happy-go-lucky soldiers in our occupancy of this soldiers' cantonment in 1863. Nothing could be truer than this: Fraternity indeed, if not in word, marked everywhere for the true soldier. —*ERB* [45]

At Chancellorsville in May, Hooker got whipped, and the men quickly lost the faith he had been nurturing. Retreating bedraggled back to Stafford Courthouse, the regiment experienced a horrible time, an abrupt change from April. "Some whole messes [eating groups] were completely wiped out; not a man was left to claim the deserted hut." In other messes only one or two remained. One company at roll call looked liked an ordinary guard detail. Those known to be dead left un-

Major General Henry Warner Slocum

He commanded the XII Corps (27th Indiana) at Chancellorsville, and the Union Right Wing at Gettysburg. This statue is on Culp's Hill in Gettysburg, which Slocum saved for Union victory.

Photo by author

buried in hands of enemy henceforth to fill "nameless graves"—"it almost broke our hearts." The Company C glee club broke up. The soprano, who helped lift spirits, a "glorious good soldier," was mortally wounded, and other singers were badly wounded. Duty called. They cleaned up "camp, equipment, clothing and arms, and were reviewed by [XII Corps commander Major] General [Henry Warner] Slocum."[46]

Later during a parade review for Slocum, morale rebounded. "Smiles, compliments and cheers greeted the 27th." Previously their army comrades had treated them coldly, but he "fairly beamed upon us," and aides and orderlies clapped hands and waved guidons as they passed corps headquarters. First Division commander, Brigadier General Alpheus Starkey Williams, "stern, gruff old 'Pap,'" said, "That's a fighting regiment for you!"[47] They had a month to pick up the pieces before heading for Gettysburg. "I want to just say that I am proud of the old 27th regiment," boasted a private. "They are as brave as men as there is in the service of the United States. I believe not because I belong to it but I feel proud that I do belong to the 27th as long as I am in the service."[48] Soon it was off to Gettysburg.

Throughout their service, the question of slavery remained topical with members of the 27th Indiana and provided for interesting discourse. One fact was that most members saw and had dealings with black people for the first time. "What I saw of the city [Washington] was very commonplace. Take out the public buildings and it will not vie with Indianapolis. Principal part of the inhabitants are negroes. The boys kept asking if that was Nigger Town," wrote 1st Lieutenant George Whitfield Reed in October 1861.[49]

In the day's lexicon, no offense was meant, but the white Hoosier farmers, most never away from home, simply had not been around negroes. They owned no slaves and knew little about slavery. Few if any negroes lived in their areas except along the Ohio. Daviess County had about 10 and Jennings County had an Underground Railroad "village." But Washington, Southern by culture and tradition, was home to many, and the soldiers were naturally inquisitive. The accepted name for black people was "negroes," the term most Hoosiers used. The army called them "colored." The term "blacks" was not used often, and the familiar nickname was "nigger."

By federal decree, after August 6, 1861, fugitive (runaway) slaves escaping into Union lines became contraband of war. The fugitives, or contrabands, were not emancipated but virtually set free. In Southern areas where the 27th Indiana campaigned they roamed freely, assembling near Union camps. An Indiana observer noted, "Most [were] profoundly ignorant" and could only do manual labor, and "some had sufficient intelligence to furnish the North with valuable information regarding the enemy. Officers complained they were "obstacles to good order and discipline."[50] The negro population increased as the regiment went south. "Negroes tell me their masters was all secesh until the Union troops came," wrote Hamrick. "Now they are all Union men. The negroes say their masters are awful good to them since the soldiers came but they would be glad if we stayed home."[51]

Following the Union Army's retreat from the rout at Winchester in May 1962, a controversy raged over whether negroes rode while soldiers walked. Hamrick blamed Private Philburd S. Wright for writing home about the negroes riding. "It is well known in the regiment that his father is as rank a traitor as those in the army against us. All he lacks is the courage."[52] "Secesh would like to make a great hobby" of that, said Captain Theodore H. Nance: neither army commander Major General Nathaniel Prentiss Banks nor regimental commander Colonel Silas Colgrove would let negroes ride rather than sick soldiers. Nance added:

> Some of the teamsters might have let a negro or two ride for all I know. I suppose they [Indiana Southern sympathizers] think we are all Abolitionists. If they don't like the way the war is conducted I would suggest they come out and help us. [They would] rather stay at home and find fault with those that are trying to do the best they can for the country in this hour of her peril. If they will not come to fight like men I say tax them so they will feel it. [53]

The U.S. Government employed some negroes as cooks and hands. In 1862, Quartermaster James M. Jameson had a mulatto servant named Henry. A Dr. Bussard came to camp claiming Henry as his property. Henry was hidden and Bussard was told where to go. Later a member took Henry to Indiana. A sergeant wrote, "Taking Henry away has done more to abolitionist the 27th than anything. The more we see of slavery the more detestable it appears. I have a dislike for slave owners though there are exceptions." He thought Henry would go to his house because "I have always told him I intended to take him with me when the war was over. He always showed a preference for me."[54] He missed Henry, who washed his shirts and drawers "in the absence of a better washerwoman."[55] Later the sergeant said Jameson's new "black boy doesn't fill the bill like Henry. I am tutoring him as fast as possible."[56] He added, "Our Negraw says the Hoosiers all have the biggest and longest whiskers that he ever saw."[57] An officer said he was "enjoying good health & revel in the luxury of having a nigger man to cook at $10 per month. Who would not have a nigger?"[58]

Some former slaves saw their first Union soldiers when visiting the 27th's camp in July 1862, and hailed them "with unconcealed cordiality and delight." They would "Pat Juber," sing, dance, or do anything for amusement, and the boys kept them busy. Colgrove formed a squad of them and went through the manual of arms. When "shoulder arms" was given, they "all showed their ivory." One old "glossy ebony" man said, "You needn't think I don't know that much," and laid the rifle on shoulder hunter fashion.[59] One officer lumped all Virginians regardless of race:

> Southern men women & children are no more like northern than if they were of different colors (almost). Old log or tumble down stone houses with white-washed picket fences surrounding, thus enclosing a few decent pigs, chickens, dirty white & ragged little nigger children & a half dozen starved dogs generally constitute the scenery surrounding a country or farmer's

home. Let them be rich or poor it is about the same only there are a few more of the above mentioned articles."[60]

The regiment first encountered negro soldiers in Tennessee in 1863, and were impressed with their exact execution of orders. The men felt "if a negro could stop a rebel bullet, or better still, if he could stop the rebel from shooting the bullet, let him come on." Someone asked a 27th Indiana private home on furlough whether he wanted "a nigger to stand aside him in battle." The soldier promptly replied, "No. I want the nigger to stand in front of me." Some white troops in the rear disliked being relieved by colored soldiers and sent to the front, but the 27th found no such fault. Hoosier enlisted men laughed when some of their officers inadvertently strayed close to the negro guard line and were marched off to the officer of the day.[61]

While the regiment was posted in Tullahoma, Tennessee, in 1863–64, Corporal Michael Henry Van Buskirk went to "a debating school." The question was: "Is it politic for the Blacks to be colonized outside the present limits of the U.S.?" Yes, it was decided.[62] The men never saw negroes in Confederate service but did see their handiwork. Near Marietta, Georgia, the Rebels used several thousand to construct defenses. This "gang of slaves increased the effective strength of the rebel army as much as if they had been mustered into it."[63]

Several men applied for commissions with colored regiments, but none was accepted. First Lieutenant George Tarvin Chapin wrote, "There is not the least doubt about the slaves being good material to work on. I believe they can be trained easier than white men and there is no end to their faithfulness or devotion to the cause of freedom...yet the Union soldiers curse them just because they are black."[64]

Passing through Strasburg on May 24, 1862, all sorts of camp followers and hangers-on were on the move. The most pathetic spectacle was the throng of colored people, often whole families, from the gray haired wrinkled parents to the little pickaninny carried in arms, loaded with bundles, pressing forward, their fear and consternation plainly showing upon their ebony features. —ERB [65]

References in 1861–62 to the abolition of slavery as the war's goal upset many members, as Welman said in June 1862. "The soldiers here have often talked of sending up to the Federal Congress their united petition to...stop their daily introduction of negro resolutions, and give their time and every effort to the suppression of the rebellion."[66] Hamrick conjectured, "The Southern and Northern states will never know harmony in one government as they used to. The prejudice and bitter feeling here against the North is too great to be easily overcome. Seems impossible to convince them that our object is anything else but to abolish slavery."[67] Private Edward G. Fugate believed the war was "to free the negro, & the ternips [farmers] will not fight much longer for that. At least i will not & ther is a grate many in our regt. have the same notion that i have."[68] Private John Parham in 1863 wrote his sister Henritty, "I am for the union. I am willing to die for it, but to have a negro constitution I am not in favor of it."[69]

The issues of slavery and black people, spirited but not divisive among the Hoosiers, never went away. "There is really more danger of northern traitors running our government than those armed at the south," wrote Chapin in January 1864. "Slavery is not undoubtedly the great curse of our country the cause of all our trouble or the cause of the war. I hope the war will wipe it from the face of the country forever. Its crimes cannot be written, eternity alone will reveal them."[70]

Brigadier General
George Henry Gordon
Commanded the 27th Indiana's 3rd Brigade, of the 1st Division, XII Corps at the Shenandoah Valley Campaign.
Leslie's Illustrated Weekly

As with the morale swings, the regiment's fortunes in battle also fluctuated, whether or not a Union victory, until the successful Atlanta Campaign of 1864. Early-war disappointments such as the loss at Winchester on May 25, 1862, were bitter pills. Colgrove, a proud and sensitive man, took criticism personally and defended his regiment against official and civilian critiques. After Winchester he commiserated to an Indiana citizen:

> I am [obliged] for the kind sentiments and assurances of confidence in my Regiment by yourself and the good people of our State. Such assurances at any time would be gratifying to a soldier and to the 27th Regt. at this time are peculiarly so. The events of May connected with the retreat from the Valley will be long remembered; the fortitude and bravery of our troops displayed in the 53 miles made in thirty hours without food or sleep fighting every inch of ground in the face of an enemy more than six times the strength of our little army—will scarcely ever be fully and duly appreciated.[71]

Newspapers were blamed for faulty reporting. A senior enlisted man added: "Some of the Yankee correspondents try to make it appear that the 27th led the retreat but it is such a malicious lie. The truth is we are connected with one of the most detestable Yankee brigades. They try to build up their fortune by trying to put us down."[72] "By now the character of the 27th is established, although our Yankee rivals would try to throw disgrace on us.

We understand Gen. [Nathaniel Prentiss] Banks telegraphed Gov. Morton that the 27th done the only good fighting. The 27th contains as good fighting material as any of the Hoosier regiments and all we want is half a chance."[73]

Colgrove's troops knew Winchester was "an awful defeat."[74] However, they were unprepared for their damaged reputation in Northern newspapers and Washington circles. Dubois County citizens thought "the 27th Indiana would fail in fight—on account of inexperience in commanders, and a slight inkling of pleasure is sticking out in the 'I told you so'—knew you'd get whipped."[75] The Dubois company captain defended his men as "cool and fearless as regulars; never thought of leaving there until orders were given to retire, which had to be repeated 5 or 6 times."

Major General
Nathaniel P. Banks

Commanded Union forces in the spring '62 Shenandoah Valley Campaign.

Leslie's Illustrated Weekly

Of one Rebel regiment that charged, "78 now lie on that hill, buried near which lie 2 of the 27th."[76] Colgrove said "the 27th fully sustained itself to deserve the name of Indiana Soldiers. It was the first regiment engaged and the last one that left the field," alone fighting two regiments. "[It] did not turn its back upon the enemy until ordered to do so, and that order was not given until surrounded on three sides."[77]

The controversy swirled around Banks and their brigade commander, Colonel George Henry Gordon, both Boston Republicans. Should the brigade have been annihilated or captured? With finger pointers abounding, Gordon "caved in to adverse criticism" and offered the 27th as the culprit.[78] Relations deteriorated quickly. The Hoosiers, "piping mad at Gordon and his people" for "feeding junk" to the correspondents, became incensed over Winchester, his subsequent public criticism of their action at the Battle of Cedar Mountain in August, and his failure to praise them in writing for Antietam heroics. Gordon was prejudiced against the lower caste Indiana farmers and Colgrove, whose feisty Western individuality and temperament were considered irreverent to the Harvard-educated Bay Staters.[79] Gordon called them "that incorrigible 27th Indiana."[80]

Nevertheless, from the disappointment of this crushing defeat in the Shenandoah Valley, the 27th gained composure.

> In our first engagement [Winchester], eagerly awaited, we had such an unequal and disadvantageous opportunity, but we began to get confidence in our troops and a feeling of comradeship. —*ERB* [81]

September 1863

The XII Corps (27th Indiana) leaves by train from Bealeton Station, Virginia for the 1,110-mile trip to Chattanooga, Tennessee.

Leslie's Illustrated Weekly

Another point of contention in their relations with other federal units and leaders began in the Fall 1863 when their XII Corps and the XI Corps were transported by rail from Virginia to Tennessee to bolster Union forces moving against Chattanooga. A jealous Army of the Cumberland was not quick to welcome their Eastern brothers into their territory, and looked askance at this means of their deliverance. The 27th Indiana relished its record and associations with the Army of the Potomac, and leaving their fields of glory for the unknown was traumatic even for combat-hardened veterans.

> We were very sorry to leave our old comrades, but we thought those Western troops would welcome us with open arms, and look up to us as bringing the prestige of Gettysburg and the Army of the Potomac with us. But, on the contrary, they rather turned up their noses, and with true western modesty appeared to think that all the skill and bravery in the Union Army was in the West.[82]

With ridicule the resident troops of the Western Army who fought along the Mississippi River made Slocum's soldiers feel unwelcome in their new Tennessee home. Perhaps it was the Potomac image of moving slowly and bad generalship, but the one handle each Western soldier could grasp was the Easterners were "soft bread soldiers," a reputation from their closeness to the bakeries of Washington. The fact Indianians were themselves "Western" made no difference, and new personality and unit conflicts emerged.

Although never completely happy in the East, the Hoosiers cheered lustily with mixed emotions on departing Virginia: "We seemed so far away from home there and so much isolated from the soldiers with whom we should affiliate." Their days had been made "more burdensome and galling than necessary." By then, however, the regiment developed a "full share of pride" in itself and the Army of the Potomac, which all survivors would cherish. "We believed in it, heart and soul, and we gloried in being identified with its history." Its failures and defeats were from incompetency and mismanagement rather than from better enemy troops or efforts. "We were going with many sincere regrets."[83]

"Men who carry the scars of Winchester, Cedar Mountain, Antietam, and Gettysburg do not like to be repeatedly asked, 'What have you ever done?'" wrote "40." "The force of rebellion is about played out, & as Jeff Davis will undoubtedly have to foot the bill, we would like a finger in the pie with the balance."[84] Slocum's historian wrote, "The frequency of company calls in the Red Star [the 27th's 1st] Division and the corps badge itself were special objects of derision, they having no such 'damned nonsense' in their [Western] army. The Potomac men were indifferent which angered and incited the rabble."[85]

The 27th was always embroiled in an "East vs. West, who is best" bragfest, and natural rivalries were predestined. "There is so little similarity between Eastern and Western troops," a lieutenant said. The 27th then petitioned the Secretary of War through Morton to change them to mounted troops, but it got nowhere.[86] Ultimately they fought alongside admirably in the Atlanta Campaign.

The Winchester post-mortem showed the common soldier was sensitive to press coverage. One member complained to the Indianapolis *Journal* about the attention given Indiana Western regiments, particularly those with little combat experience, but not enough for the 27th. It was more a stoical plea for facts than jealousy. "The old 27th. She never done nothing, & consequently nobody ever said nothing about it. Yet she never done anything. She ain't no fightin' regiment & haint't got no fightin' Colonel. He only says, 'Boys, I want you to take the yell out of them gray gentlemen coming up the hill yonder. Charge bayonets! Forward! Double-quick, march!' & the yell all comes out of them. Then old Coley [Colgrove] says, 'That will do, boys. Give them a few of your pills,' & the boys administer the all-healing dose. Yet that's nothing, & nobody ever says anything about it." The paper replied: "The distinction of this regiment is merely accidental, & that the 27th's uniform gallantry...is kept in lively & grateful remembrance. Editors cannot know what any particular regiment does except as members inform them."[87]

The close-knit 27th had limited contact with the comrade regiments of their brigade. They related to all except the 2nd Massachusetts, Gordon's elitist unit, with whom they were mostly aloof for three years. Except for natural sparring, the enlisted men, frequently side by side sharing pride in common adventures, were on good terms. Relations fluctuated, and the charge in Spangler's Spring at Culp's Hill on the third day at Gettysburg—regarding who assaulted and who supported—generated extremes. Both assaulted, but Massachusetts survivors mistakenly felt the Hoosiers created confusion by charging later and departing the field earlier. Postwar exchanges eventually reduced animosity, but one Hoosier dug in: "One glance is sufficient to designate the 'semi-barbarous' 27th & their Badger friend the 3rd Wisconsin, who are pretty much in the same category, from their polished bandbox neighbors."[88] The "smug, Boston Brahmins" and the "down-home Hoosiers" were of different cloth, one reason why the Hoosiers disassociated themselves from true "Yankees." Only as the years passed and reunion groups met did the two units lower their animosity, and old men realized it was time to recognize each other for what they had mutually accomplished and the many miles they had marched in arms together.

> Westerners believed the Army of the Potomac was a paper-collar, review-and-dress-parade army and could not fight. Because the 27th was from the 'wild and wooly west,' pronounced Indiana 'Ean —dy—an —ny', spoke of being 'raised,' made liberal use of word 'heap' as meaning quantity, sharpened our a's and slurred our 'ings," and were not too particular about blacking our shoes or dusting our clothes, this made us the subject of bandying and insults. We could take the jibes, but insinuations and assertions affecting our manhood and soldierly qualities were different. —*ERB* [89]

Relations between the 27th Indiana and their Confederate enemy, while aloof, were generally cordial and respectful. They did not hate the South or its soldiers. One reason was their own Southern heritage, and the fact some Hoosiers had relatives on the opposite side. Their cause was to preserve the Union, to force the South to return under one flag, but they always valued their own lives more. Indianians followed the cardinal rule of warfare: kill the other man before he can kill you.

Private Linzey C. Lamb, a poor, barely literate farmer, wrote his wife after Resaca in May 1864:

> I must [tell] you what I taken from a reb the other Sunday after the fight. I got in his pocket hankerchief and his pocket book and two combs. The Suthiren Confedecy have about slid out with him. He had only five cents and that was silver. Also he had three pen points. I have pulled the buttons off his new uniform & you no that disfigured he did not now the diference. He did not say a word. He ly upon his face with the blood pored out of his hed. A miney ball had pearced him threw the head and killed him instantly.[90]

Lamb was the only member known to remove items from Confederate dead, elsewhere not an uncommon practice. Most of what the Hoosiers said about their enemy came from dealings with the few prisoners they captured, surveying the battlefield dead and wounded, or exchanges along the Rappahannock and Chattahoochee River picket lines.

Surgeon Jarvis J. Johnson, after his capture at Winchester, attended to both Confederate and Federal sick and wounded at the local army hospital. Before abandoning Winchester shortly after his victory, Stonewall Jackson went through the hospital and shook hands with Johnson and regimental Sergeant Major John K. McKaskay, the only members known to be proffered such civility by the enemy. After Cedar Mountain the 27th participated in a truce when all dead were removed and buried. A Jackson aide wrote, "Soon the ground was covered with those who had lately been arrayed against each other in mortal strife, mingling unarmed. While burying parties collected their bloody charge, and excavated great pits in which to cover them, arguing politics and discussing the merits of their respective generals. The Federals were loud with their praises of Jackson; and declared that if they had such generals to lead them they could also win victories and display prowess."[91]

The Hoosiers first saw Confederate prisoners in the Shenandoah Valley in Spring 1862. "They generally are good looking fellows and look as though they used to be somebody. After our men get them they treat them very kind and soon become quite social."[92] In the West, they twice encountered masses of prisoners. The first was while garrisoned in Tennessee, when thousands of disheveled, sick, and starved Rebels came through after their Chattanooga defeat. The men pitied and comforted them within their limits. The other was at Resaca when they captured the colonel and some 30 men of the 38th Alabama.

In June 1864 in front of Lost Mountain, Georgia, their brigade band serenaded both sides with "Johnny Fill Up the Bowl," "Home Sweet Home," and other songs, bringing a "magical change" of cheerfulness and exuberance. One Hoosier believed the Rebels thought they had the "Billy Yanks" surrounded. Immediately an armistice was arranged. As if they were back on the Rappahannock in Virginia, where such quiescent periods and exchanges were commonplace, the pickets of both sides started talking. A few "Johnnies" of the 10th Tennessee were "skulking around." Both sides exchanged "friendly intercourse under proper restraints and safeguards," swapping newspapers and bartering tobacco and coffee. A Hoosier procured the Memphis *Appeal* brought from Atlanta the previous day. It contained "considerable important news on both sides but principally lies."[93] Cordiality between pickets continued for three days. Then, "Rebel pickets driven one mile," the records said. "This was characteristic of the times. This was war."[94]

Battle of Kolbs Farm, June 22, 1864

The ravine and stream where attacking Confederates of Stevenson's Division were annihilated by the 27th Indiana and Ruger's Brigade of Williams' Division. Hundreds of corpses lay here; the stream turned red with their blood. It was a ghastly Rebel defeat.

Photo by author

Battle of Kolbs Farm, Georgia

The 27th Indiana was on the right of Hooker's XX Corps line about ¼ mile northeast of the house. This is one of the few remaining battlefield structures. View of McAdoo-Oatman house at intersection of Powder Spring Road (Georgia Highway 5) and John Ward Road looking north.

Photo by author

At Kolbs Farm, Georgia in June 1864, the Confederates were decimated in the 27th's most one-sided victory. The dead were buried under truce, and filthy, tattered blue and gray forms mingled in conversation. "There was a constant curiosity to know more about the other fellows." An "air of mystery" pervaded between the sides who, "except in battle, really see [little] of each other." Many 27th men were born and raised in the South and knew almost as many soldiers in North Carolina, Virginia, and Kentucky regiments as their own. The Hoosiers "all wanted to compare notes with 'Johnny Reb.'"[95]

During a July 1864 truce the Hoosiers became acquainted with a 10th Georgia lieutenant and his men. They bathed in the Chattahoochee, exchanged courtesies, commodities, and tales. "In all except their uniforms they seemed like ourselves." Several days later in front of their positions at Peachtree Creek, the 27th found the names of the Georgia officer and several of his soldiers on grave headboards. A man recalled, "The 30 years and more which have gone over our heads since then have not entirely removed the pain which we have always felt when recalling the episode of war." That was the last time they met Southern friends.[96]

Later the enemy picket line was very close to the 27th's brigade, their shots a constant annoyance preventing any movement. A Rebel tired of crouching in his pit would call out, "I say, Yank." "Well, Johnny Reb, what is it?" "I'm go'n to put my head out, don't shoot." "Well, I won't. Let's all stretch our legs." "All right." Then for an hour there would be peace. Then, recalled by sense of duty, the cry was, "Time's up, Yanks, look out, we uns is go'n to shoot. Be keerful." "All right Johnnies, lay low."[97]

Hoosier spirits were high during the 1864 Atlanta Campaign as the men sensed victory. By New Hope Church in May, they were under the now more aggressive command of Hooker. With his "commonly appearance" he "is very much loved as a corps commander I think. The general expression he is a fighting man."[98] He was, but he stepped down two months later with Slocum replacing him. The Federals had more new hope. Leadership was improving significantly. Captain John McKnight Bloss wrote, "General [U. S.] Grant is trying to put some discipline in this army I would judge by his orders. Some Chattanooga correspondent calls his orders Potomacized."[99] Army commander Major General William Tecumseh Sherman was always with his men and might appear anytime anywhere. He was "always courteous and usually candid, though brief."[100] New Hope Church, in spite of the rain, brought "days of good cheer among the soldiers," often "great joy and delight." As difficult as it seemed, the men "bore all of their hardships cheerfully,"[101] and most textbook routine was relaxed or suspended.

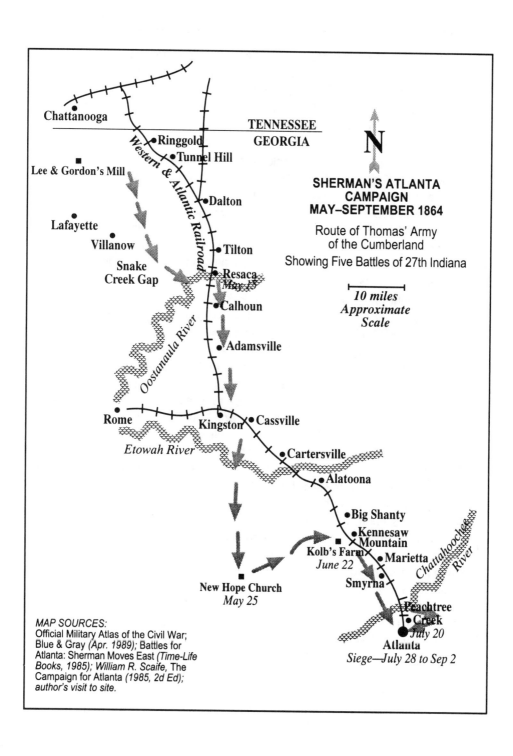

Chattanooga

TENNESSEE
GEORGIA

Ringgold

Tunnel Hill

N

Lee & Gordon's Mill

Western & Atlantic Railroad

Dalton

**SHERMAN'S ATLANTA
CAMPAIGN
MAY–SEPTEMBER 1864**

Route of Thomas' Army
of the Cumberland

Showing Five Battles of 27th Indiana

Lafayette

Villanow

Tilton

Snake
Creek Gap

Resaca
May 15

Calhoun

*10 miles
Approximate
Scale*

Oostanaula River

Adamsville

Rome

Kingston

Cassville

Etowah River

Cartersville

Alatoona

Big Shanty

Kennesaw
Mountain

Kolb's Farm
June 22

Marietta

Chattahoochee River

New Hope Church
May 25

Smyrna

Peachtree
Creek
July 20

MAP SOURCES:
Official Military Atlas of the Civil War;
Blue & Gray *(Apr. 1989)*; Battles for
Atlanta: Sherman Moves East *(Time-Life
Books, 1985)*; William R. Scaife, The
Campaign for Atlanta *(1985, 2d Ed)*;
author's visit to site.

Atlanta
Siege—July 28 to Sep 2

The Union victory at Resaca was clear cut, one to be savored. "We have possession of the field and their rifle pits and I guess they are gone," as Corporal John Michael Tomey stated.[102] It was the first such win the 27th had known. At Antietam the Federals had to wait until the Confederates left the field two days later, and at Gettysburg, the only other triumph, the impact did not hit until the Rebels headed southward.

> The night of Resaca was rainy, cold, gloomy, and cheerless. We had loss fewer than anticipated and congratulated ourselves on getting off lightly. Even small losses would cut deep as the Regiment neared mustering out, like costly pearls dropping into the sea one by one. What are pearls compared with trained courageous devoted soldiers, who have served so long and who so richly deserve to live and enjoy some of the rewards of their sacrifices? But ultimate triumph, glorious and complete, was no longer a question. Hallelujah! —ERB [103]

At Peachtree Creek in July, Brigadier General Joseph Farmer Knipe, leading an engaged comrade brigade, breathlessly requested support. He found Hooker so near the 27th he could be heard clearly. Shells and minie balls were whistling and zinging everywhere. Hooker pointed to a regiment nearby: "There, General Knipe, take that one." "Nooo, noo, I don't want that one," Knipe screamed and turned away. Hooker called, "Here, General Knipe, come here, come here!" Knipe turned back. "Hooker this time pointed to the 27th and said, 'Take that one.' 'All right, I'll take that one,' still speaking in high tones and drawing out his words." Knipe, "a mercurial, demonstrative little man" well known to the Hoosiers, approached the regiment and shrieked, "27th Indiana, I want you! This old brigade never has been whipped, and it never will be whipped."[104]

By mid-1864, as both the war and their service dragged on, conjecture and opinions about what was right or just, or reasons for continuing the fight, had diminished. The enthusiasm was gone, and grousing was less important than ending the conflict or their three-year obligation, whichever came first. Still, ERB remembered, "Our spirits were high. The enemy had again shown us his back, and under such circumstances as to encourage us greatly."[105]

> Picture the 27th soldier in June 1864: lean and weather-beaten, no surplus flesh, skin as brown as a bun, clothes soiled, hair and beard might be long and probably unkempt. The enlisted man had his only worldy goods aside from clothes, musket and its belongings, all in a small roll of stuff hanging from the left shoulder and crossing over the right hip. The roll contained a rubber poncho, woollen blanket, and piece of shelter tent. He dangled a tin pail and frying pan, sometimes light ax or hatchet. Impaled on bayonet or carried in hand chicken or other fowl or fresh meat. —ERB [106]

As the regiment's days in service dwindled, the men impatiently awaited mustering out papers and removal from the front lines. Days passed slowly:[107]

August 12, 1864. Everything is quiet along the line. Still laying in breastworks. We look to be relieved all the time. Second Lieutenant Roger Sherman Loughry reflected that 3 years ago today about 85 men of his Company C held up their hands and took the solemn obligation to defend the Constitution against all enemies, and left Edinburgh in fine health and light, except some sadness from parting with their friends.

August 20th. The 27th was expecting to be relieved today & it failed. Still no meat on rather short rations.

August 21st. We got up a petition & will send it to General [George] Thomas tomorrow to discharge us. We took it to the colonel asking him to sign it but he made us a nice little speech & we did not send it.

August 23rd. Relieved at dark, moved back to third line of works to make out mustering out papers.

August 26th. We are in line of battle guarding railroad bridge of Chattahoochee. Had no sleep last night. We did not like this much but had to grin & bear it.

August 29th. Yesterday was the first day of this campaign we [did not] hear rebel guns. Nothing to hinder us from being mustered out at any time. General Slocum rode along the lines and was cheered.

August 30th. Our time is out & we are building breastworks. Yet they have sent us an order to muster out 1st of September.

August 31st. Our brigade band are over here tonight giving us a parting salute as we leave tomorrow. The officers furnished the whiskey & they are having a high old time.

The time to muster out all except those veterans who had reenlisted and recruits who had joined during service, at last arrived on September 1, 1864, in the trenches in front of Atlanta.

Men shook hands and separated there on the bank of that far-away Southern river who through the entire three years were more than brothers. When not separated by sickness or wounds they occupied the same narrow bunk, were sheletered by the same little tent, hovered close together covered by the same blanket, divided the last cracker, and drank from the same canteen. —*ERB* [108]

On September 3, 1864, President Lincoln acknowledged the victory at Atlanta:

The national thanks are rendered by the President to Major General W. T. Sherman, and the gallant officers and soldiers of his command before Atlanta, for the distinguished ability, courage, and perseverance displayed in the campaign in Georgia, which, under Divine favor, has resulted in the capture of the city of Atlanta. The marches, battles, sieges, and other military operations that have signalled this campaign must render it famous in the annals of war, and have entitled those who have participated therein to the applause and thanks of the nation.[109]

The 27th Indiana's role in the Atlanta Campaign was really the story of the 1st Division of the XX Corps, of which it was a part, as its commander stated:

The valor, constancy, cheerfulness and general good conduct of the officers and men through all the hardships, exposures and vicissitudes of one of the most memorable campaigns in the history of wars. Weeks continuously under fire; for days and nights in succession drenched by excessive rains, and exposed on hard marches to a midday southern sun; working on breastworks and trenches by night, they have borne all with a patience and cheerfulness that creates profound admiration. Few stragglers, no skulkers."[110]

The regiment had fought its final battle and achieved its final victory. No more blood would be shed. Its non-veterans, those men who had not reenlisted, went home, and its veteran volunteer reenlistees and recruits consolidated with the 70th Indiana and later the 33rd Indiana to continue serving. With the capture of Atlanta, Lincoln achieved a political boost which helped him win re-election in November. The war was nearly won, the rebellion nearly crushed. Indiana wheat crops and hog pens awaited those who were physically able and on their way home.

CHAPTER 3

Colonel Colgrove, His Officers, and Other Enemies: Insurrection, Leadership, and Politics

We the undersigned commissioned officers of the 27th Regiment Indiana Volunteers respectfully request the immediate recall of Silas Colgrove our Colonel commanding. We have patiently submitted to insults until forbearance is beyond indurance The regiment is now on the point of demoralization for such causes as having officers called fools, liars & threatened with a knockdown while in discharge of their duties, maltreatment of the sick & ungentlemanly treatment of old & men generally. The feeling is unanimous in the regiment & unless something is done soon the 27th once the pride of the state & we believe its Governor, may become a disgrace to the state on which so far no blemish has been noted. *—The regiment's officers, November 28, 1861*[1]

This petition to Indiana Governor Oliver P. Morton, after the regiment had been together only two and a half months, drew a line in the sand. From then on, animosity and caution led the colonel to hold most of his officers at arm's length, if not at bay, and the resultant response to his leadership—and theirs—was mixed.

Four weeks earlier the same group had written Morton recommending Major John Mehringer for colonel, Captain Abisha L. Morrison for lieutenant colonel, and Captain Theodore H. Buehler for major, "believing that those gentlemanly officers at the head of the regiment will be qualified for the respective positions."[2] But Mehringer wrote Morton that his signing

Colonel Silas Colgrove

He was the only colonel commanding 27th Indiana. Shown here with Brevet Brigadier General's stars (late 1864). History of Randolph County, Indiana, *(1882, Chicago, A. L. Kingman)*

47

the petition did not relinquish his own claim to the lieutenant colonelcy should he be considered, "not that I will seek the office."[3] Such turbulence from newly formed regiments was common, and the politically sensitive Morton, under greater stress in a state split with discontent over the rebellion, was silent.

Then the company officers petitioned Colgrove to resign. "It was a heavy stroke and took the colonel completely by surprise. He disappointed all of us," wrote Commissary Sergeant Simpson Solomon Hamrick. "Instead of getting in a rage as all expected he would it humbled him right down. He called all the officers together by his appearing so severely cut." The notice hit Colgrove squarely; he preferred "losing his life to resigning and going home in disgrace," and refused. If so, the alternative was to send the petition to Morton; and they mailed it.[4] "Which will have the greatest influence on the Governor remains to be seen," Hamrick ventured. "Colgrove will be too fast for them, for he is shrewd and smarter than all the officers combined. Should he retain favor with the Governor and hold his place you may look for him to displace them. They will drop one by one, and the regiment will still be controlled by the one man power. I would censure Morton severely for sending such a man out in the first place for he certainly knew better."[5]

Were others to blame? For one, Hamrick waffled. "The great trouble is our officers. The privates are superior to almost any other regiment in the division. Colgrove decidedly is the best, but has an abuseful disposition. He is decidedly the most profane man I ever came in contact with, but with all his vices he is the [only] officer worth a notice. He would be a good officer to lead an attack but that is all. He is very tyrannical."[6] The humbled Colgrove held his ground, "but he is entirely a different man. He has become of the most familiar clever men especially with the soldiers and he is fast gaining force with them. My opinion is the colonel will out general his enemies and retain his position."[7] As Colgrove rode out the insurrection, Hamrick was right on one point. One by one his officers dropped.

Silas Colgrove, Winchester lawyer and state legislator, was the only colonel of the 27th Indiana. Morton appointed him several days before the regiment mustered into service on September 12, 1861, the customary method for filling senior positions. Colgrove, a Morton political ally, claimed he never solicited the appointment and expected to remain with the 8th Indiana, his former regiment.

A postwar opinion of Colgrove typed as the typical "old-fashioned Colonel." He was considered "at times brave and courageous to a fault; at others careful and judicious to an admirable degree....Always kind and cheerful to his men, winning not only their admiration and respect, but their love and confidence. His stanch, soldierly virtues were largely reflected in his men."[8]

Colgrove made an immediate impact on the 27th. A comrade recalled Colgrove's first night in camp when he ordered out his soldiers on dress parade. He was obviously impressed—"the number of men, their great average height, the length of the line as it stretched out to the right and left—particularly the thought of what had brought the men together and what was to be their fate," and his responsibility in their "trying, deadly days to come." These "were matters that wrought upon him with great force."[9]

Balancing his men's divergent personalities, strengths, weaknesses, and objectives with his instincts and experiences, Colgrove weathered storms of discontent until regimental management jelled. The foregoing perspective, written by a XII Corps comrade, was largely gratuitous, for Colgrove was seen internally as both pariah and savior. He kept his own counsel, often eschewing communications and relationships as leadership necessities. His internal communications were limited by the officers who would speak up for him or to him. Consequently, his son Theodore Freelinghausen Colgrove, 17, became his eyes and ears and rose through adjutant to major. The colonel's popularity vacillated more on personality and style than actions. As a soldier he was tough, organized, and demanding, and in the end extracted the best qualities in his men under fire.

The lean, 5'8" Colgrove, 45, looked every bit the soldier. His hair and beard turned white during service on the enormity of his load. He dominated and when necessary, more so in 1861–62, was also domineering. Brains and intuition substituted for a network, and his grip rarely slipped. His strong personality and will maintained a presence even when physically absent. A man of details, he knew which issues to resolve himself and which to leave to juniors. Like other militarily inexperienced commanders, he tinkered with regulations, such as with the on-and-off restrictions on gambling in camp. He established himself as a disciplinarian by reducing in rank numerous noncommissioned officers in 1861–62, but often showed unexplained leniency with returned deserters.

Colgrove never publicly criticized his men and always backed them confidently. In January 1862, he said there was "more good fighting material in the 27th than any regiment in the service." The men reciprocated. They had all "confidence in the colonel's fighting pluck although some think him too rigid and severe in his discipline. There are no doubts as to his pluck in time of danger."[10] Present at all battles, basically his combat decisions were sound, his courage and ubiquity under fire fearless and inspirational. His body and mind were rugged, and until a terrible wound at

Peachtree Creek on July 20, 1864, sent him home, he shrugged off three earlier wounds. Excluding leave and temporary brigade command (including Gettysburg), officially he was commander until promoted to general in August 1864, over three years after joining the regiment.

Colgrove did not laud his men for a good job and guarded his emotions in dealing with them. They responded likewise, with one exception. In March 1862, the officers gave him a real Damascus sword, with an elaborate, ornate hilt and scabbard. He carried it throughout the war until it, like he, was severely damaged at Peachtree Creek by a cannon shell, perhaps deflecting the impact enough to save his life. Official recognition of good deeds for either officers or enlisted men was rare. As if to compensate, survivors filed affidavits attesting to comrade "good soldiers" and deeds of heroism, mercy, kindness, and friendship. And Colgrove remembered First Lieutenant John Forlander as twice leaving his sickbed to go into action, "and behaved most gallantly," before being discharged with eye disease.[11]

Three lieutenant colonels served as second in command. The first was Archibald Irvin Harrison, the grandson of former President William Henry Harrison and brother of the future President, Benjamin, colonel of the 70th Indiana. Popular but ineffective, he resigned in two months with disability. Abisha L. Morrison, promoted from captain, who resigned with disability in January 1863, followed. John Roush Fesler, the most effective, was the last. Only Fesler, who was in the job nearly two years, temporarily commanded the 27th in battle—at Gettysburg and Peachtree Creek after Colgrove's wounding.

Colgrove had trouble keeping other officers. Whether by his design or other reasons many of his company officers departed, and within the first 15 months three staff majors (third in command), John Mehringer, William S. Johnson, and George W. Burge, had gone.

The history of the 27th Indiana bears Colgrove's impress to a very marked degree. —ERB [12]

One noncommissioned officer in particular, Commissary Sergeant Simpson Solomon Hamrick, became a self-appointed "Colgrove barometer," attempting to measure and analyze for anyone who would listen his views on who the colonel was and what he was doing. "I sincerely wish the regiment could have a colonel with a little more humanity," he wrote in June 1862. "[He] has got a hint of how things is drifting as I hear he talks of resigning and going home. His resignation would be hailed with more delight by our boys than the news of the fall of Richmond."[13] Hamrick had a unique view of Colgrove and indeed, everyone, and encountered and gave a multitude of opinions. Hamrick dealt regularly with him ("Colgrove is virtually our quartermaster") and other officers. With savvy and critical flair for gossip and speculation, through his letters he offered keen—though biased—insight into moods, quirks, heroes, and deadbeats. He studied him almost to the point of keeping a log. However, his writings were tinged by his own inferiority complex and mercurial judgments.[14]

Believing his superior, Quartermaster James Monroe Jameson, was on his way out in 1862, Hamrick said: "I think the colonel will compel him to resign."[15] "The colonel is getting more tyrannical. The officers are getting very much dissatisfied with him again. The colonel has marched the regiment several times unmerciful and then curse the officers and men because they could not go further. He is very unreasonable sometimes."[16] Later he wrote:

> There is one thing different in our regiment from others. Generally the colonel takes an interest in his subordinates welfare and promotion if they merit. He has no intimate friends. Half the officers are afraid to approach him on business matters. Morrison told me last night the colonel to his knowledge had not spoken a friendly word to one of his officers for more than a month. Why does Morton suffer a regiment of Indianians tyrannized over in this manner when he knows God never made better soldiers?[17]

Some of his former officers sought revenge against Colgrove in June 1862. "Our Major Johnson has just confidentially told me," cooed Hamrick, "that there is an effort making in the part of the State where our regiment was made up from," headed by the former major and Buehler. They had a petition signed by over 3,000 "friends of the regiment praying Morton remove Colgrove from command." He urged his father to "help the thing along." If Colgrove remained "anything our friends could do would be a great favor to us. Our regiment is already doomed."[18] "The officers of our regiment are very unpopular with the brigade. Our regiment will never amount to much while it is under the present colonel, because he has the least appreciation of merit."[19]

With Colgrove on sick leave during part of the Winter 1863, senior management was depleted. First Lieutenant George Tarvin Chapin wrote, "Our major resigned and went home last week. Colonel Colgrove got a furlough and went home in quite feeble health. It is thought he will not return. Captain [John Roush] Fesler has command of the regiment." Chapin dreaded Colgrove's son becoming major. "I wish we could get rid of the Colgroves all together for I consider that they have been an injury to us."[20] By February, Colgrove's declining health confined him to his tent, and by March "Old Coley" was unlikely to get his expected promotion. "So, we are likely to be well represented by Colgroves. We have stood it this long, and I guess we will have to endure a while longer."[21] Hamrick's commentary ended with his death at Chancellorsville, and no one replaced him to watch Colgrove. By then, the tempest had subsided.

While his popularity chart fluctuated, Colgrove slipped into an ethics morass. In April 1862, Hamrick charged, "The colonels only object seems to be selfish motives. He has managed to get one of his sons adjutant. Another one who came in the winter carries the mail at $80 per month. The colonel is partner with the sutler and extorsions off the soldiers. Also his brother-in-law is employed in the sutler dept at $125 per month. It looks like all he cares for is to advance his own pecuniary interests."[22] Even citizens reported Colgrove, as in a May 1862 letter to Morton:

> I have been shown a great many letters written by members of the 27th Regiment to their friends in Daviess, Martin & Lawrence Counties complaining most bitterly of their Colonel. The last act of said Colonel is that he is compelling them to pay the adjutant (his son I believe) 10 cents per month to procure the mail for them, that he is indirectly in partnership with the regiment sutler & using government trains to haul goods for him, that he is selling some of their rations by which they are compelled to buy the more of said sutler, & in every respect treating them very inhumane.[23]

The ethics issues boiled over in July 1862. Morrison, mad at Colgrove and feeding the discontent between Colgrove and 3rd Brigade Commander Brigadier General George Henry Gordon, officially reported the allegations to Gordon. On or about July 22, Colgrove allegedly detailed three government wagons to Warrenton, Virginia, "to get a supply of shoes & clothing for our 27th Indiana regiment"—but, as generally believed, to haul sutler goods. When the trains returned "I found them well loaded with goods for the sutler & but one small box containing 200 pairs of socks & 50 coats for the regiment." With the regiment ready to move on the twenty-fifth, the sutler had a large stack of goods to be hauled or left behind. "The Colonel could not think of leaving any of his interests behind. So he leaves his regiment, goes up into town to hire or press wagons for sutler's use. He stayed at the sutler's until everything was loaded, ordering the rear guard to assist on loading. His son is a partner without doubt."

Morrison also said the Colonel was using a government horse for his own private benefit, and "permitted his son (the partner in the sutler shop) to keep & use a stolen or captured horse."[24] Other charges included having liquor shipped in his name, supplying Rebels with clothing, cigars, and numerous articles, and "unofficer like treatment to both officers and men."[25] Official action taken on the allegations is unknown. Hamrick believed a couple of trips to Gordon's headquarters by Colgrove "set him all right" and the charges "went by the board." The Hoosiers just went through another "rush at our colonel" like the previous fall. Nearly "all hands (all officers headed by Morrison)" were again concerned, this time "very sanguine." An observer who "thought they would succeed" remarked, "They thought they had a sure thing, but old Colgrove has completely out-generalled them, and they are worse off than before."[26]

Allegedly Gordon, because of Colgrove's antics, reported the 27th "unfit for service on account of its officers," and subsequently permanently detached them from the brigade. The latter was only rumor, but the men were distraught. "We are used up so far as general service"—"ruined by one man," Hamrick said. "We will be kept as scouts and bushwhacking and will see a tough time of it. If Governor Morton lets this regiment continue to suffer the abuses it has we will hold him accountable hereafter for the manner we have been treated." Surely Morton knew there was "something wrong." Gordon apparently interviewed Morrison and insisted he "hold on" and not resign, and that he would "use his influence to get rid of Colonel Colgrove."[27]

Gordon's bias against Colgrove continued. While interviewing Adjutant Theodore Freelinghausen Colgrove, Gordon said essentially his father was to be pitied for he did not have the right kind of material for a good regiment. His men were "naturally insubordinate and cowardly." He condoled with other 27th officers that their trouble was their colonel. They could reach the top with a different commander, he said publicly at least once. Gordon was "sowing seeds of discontent and stirring up sedition in one of his own regiments," ERB noted.[28] His ear to the ground, Hamrick wrote, "The great trouble is none of our officers have the courage to denounce and expose the most shameful conduct. If us non-commissioned fellows would attempt it we would be reduced so quick it would astonish everybody. Our officers seem completely cowed and don't resent anything." He blamed Morton: "If Morton only knew the state of affairs there would be a change. Colonel Morrison is completely disgusted and says he intends resigning. Captain [John W.] Wilcoxen is the only officer on friendly terms with Colgrove. He makes a perfect ass of himself truckling to whatever he wishes. His own company make sport of him."[29]

Colgrove reported officer vacancies to Indianapolis and recommended replacements. To fill the February 1862 major vacancy he supported two: Captain William S. Johnson and First Lieutenant John A. Cassady. Regarding a third, Captain Theodore H. Buehler, he said: "I do not consider that he possesses any qualifications whatever for the place. I also consider him a dishonest intriguing man. Should the Governor find it necessary to place him there I must regard it as an indication that my services are not any longer considered useful to the service, & should act accordingly."[30] Johnson won and Buehler resigned. On replacing the Company E commander after Antietam, Colgrove wrote: "The two Lts. of Co. E are entirely unfit to command the company—the 1st Lt. is now being court-martialled for cowardice."[31]

Morrison stayed on until February 1863, Gordon as brigade commander until after Antietam, and Colgrove for two more years after that, outlasting them all. Like the earlier furor when Colgrove was subjected to the petition for removal, the records which would close this incident are missing. One wonders if Colgrove removed them from the War Department while working there after the war.

Colgrove was deeply ambitious, and he made it obvious. Citizen H. B. Hill, after a visit to the 27th Indiana in December 1863, wrote Governor Morton: "I find the men of the 27th in good condition. Colonel Colgrove is very desirous to hear from you as to his condition. He fears that some undue advantage has been taken of him or that something has been thrown in his way of which he is unadvised and it leaves him in a very unpleasant situation."[32] Colgrove's "condition" was he yearned to be a general.

Promotion never was an obsession before duties, but still he followed his political quest, as Hill's letter to Morton indicated, and an Indiana inner circle strongly supported him before Washington in spite of his controversies. That he persevered during the long quest and gained his generalship was a tribute to both man and system.

Rumors began in 1861, heating in January 1862, that Colgrove was under consideration and would leave the regiment. The Jasper, Indiana newspaper in March 1862 reported the 27th's brigade commander had been promoted to major general, and the men are "anxious that Colonel Colgrove should be promoted" to brigadier.[33] Did that imply to have him out of their way?

Colgrove eventually weeded out most of his detractors and those who remained supported him or kept silent, and avoided his ambitions. Captain Josiah Clinton Williams wrote in January 1863, "The Colonel is down to Washington on 8 days furlough. It is thought he may return with a star on his shoulders as he commenced with the war & has gone through a heavy portion of the fierce & fiery ordeal."[34] Chaplain Thomas A. Whitted in April 1863 said "he could whip any man who accused us [Regiment] of being demoralized, or said that our colonel did not deserve a 'star.'"[35] Another wrote in February 1864 that "Colonels & lieutenant colonels who 'scent the battle from afar off,' always too far, however, who thunder loudly but never strike anything, can 'see stars' as they descend upon their shoulders, while none [stars] are allowed to displace those 'two old eagles' that have perched above Colonel Colgrove's shoulders through the storms of many a battle for nearly 3 years. It would appear that faithful performance of duty is no passport to preferment."[36] Colgrove himself solicited Morton's backing directly in March 1863.

While recovering from his Atlanta Campaign wound, Colgrove's ambition was realized. In an August 7, 1864, War Department letter to Morton, the Secretary of War appointed him a brevet (temporary) brigadier general of U.S. Volunteers.[37] After serving as the president of the Indianapolis Treason Trials commission in 1864, he left the service on December 30, 1864.

Colgrove's capers diminished after the ethics charges, and the military frustrations of the Summer and Fall 1862 put matters in perspective. Still, some members sought a transfer. Second Lieutenant Joseph Balsley wrote about Company D in the fall of 1862: "When I was wounded at Antietam the company got into bad hands. The men became dissatisfied with the officer in charge [Captain George Lake Fesler] & when the offer was made them to be transferred to the regular service they readily accepted. When I got back to the regiment I found many men had transferred to the U.S. [regular] Army."[38] Lieutenant Williams wrote home, "There is a cavalry regiment to be raised. Do you know of an opportunity of a first lieutenant's position I could get in a battery or cavalry company? If you do tell me as I can be transferred from here into it."[39] He added, "I thought of my long cherished idea of changing the infantry for artillery. Hated to leave my company and regiment on account of my friends yet I resolved I would resign."[40]

The War Department allowed the regular army to recruit from the volunteer regiments, much to the chagrin of volunteer commanders including Colgrove. The recruitment drive came in October and November when spirit was dormant, and men without shoes or adequate clothing, mindful of the blood they had sacrificed, were easily attracted to less arduous artillery, cavalry, engineer, or navy duty. The temptation lured 42 privates, nearly 10 percent of the regiment's effective strength, 10 from the already weakened Company D. The high numbers were attributed to personal dissatisfaction rather than skilled recruiters, but many were marginal soldiers whose problems would not be missed.

With Colgrove on furlough in February 1862, Morrison commanded the regiment and gave "universal satisfaction." The insider Hamrick said: "Phil Wright [1st Sergeant Philburd S.] lost his position as orderly and is now in ranks as private. Phil is effectually used up by his own forwardness. All the sensible men got disgusted with him, but there is one thing inevitable in an army, everyone finds his level and if he has a position without ability he will loose it sooner or later."[41] Having lost two officers at Antietam, Company A was left in "a bad fix for Wilcoxen is not only incompetent to fill his position but he rules with an iron rod of tyranny. Many are the threats that are laid in store for him should we ever get the yoke thrown off."[42]

Petitions were used against others. Company F asked Colgrove to reassign Second Lieutenant John D. McKahin from the company "because of his domineering tyrannical conduct."[43] Sergeant William Parmemas Ellis wrote in 1864, "Our officers played shenanigan on us. They would not grant us an election. So [Second Lieutenant Bethuel M.] Clark (with assistance) pushed himself in where he is not greeted with that welcome as an officer should be. I know of no man in company (in the ranks) that wanted him as Lt."[44]

The leadership issue prompted many officers to resign. "The best officer we had Lieutenant Colonel Harrison resigned & went home," wrote Sergeant Chapin in November 1861. "Captain Morrison will take his place. He is a very fine man. [First] Lieutenant [George Whitfield] Reed & [Second Lieutenant] Williams are well but do not like the boys (judging from their actions) nor the boys them."[45] Harrison was "decidedly a military man," the "universal favorite of the whole regiment." Some wished he were colonel.[46] When speculation persisted Colgrove would be promoted, Harrison's stock rose. That would "give entire satisfaction." But the inconsistent Hamrick said, "I hope not, for I have confidence in Colgrove's ability."[47] Harrison resigned October 29, 1861, because of "domestic troubles & cases claim my presence & attention at home." In reality he clashed with Colgrove. Of Morrison being promoted: "We shall all feel very proud if he does get it."[48] He did, but he became untenable after Winchester.

Problems had surfaced in the fall of 1861. "I became more and more convinced every day because the regiment has no one to represent it or look after its interests," Hamrick said. "The truth is we are hardly noticed by the higher officers. We get no favors in proportion to other regiments who deserve less."[49] By June 1862, "nearly every officer that started out with us have resigned or what few remain intend doing so if there is not a change speedily. The privates are beginning to talk of deserting. Some have already gone home and have affected their escape. Others will seek the same relief rather than submit much longer."[50]

After the Winchester defeat, Colgrove and Morrison avoided each other for weeks as each tried to save his reputation. The 27th withdrew from the front apparently under orders from Gordon to Morrison, who at the moment believed himself commanding the regiment in Colgrove's temporary presence in another part of the line. Morrison quickly gave the order to fall back without seeking Colgrove, and Colgrove immediately tried unsuccessfully to rescind the order when he realized what was happening. Some observers said that precipitated the Union rout, and Gordon and the Eastern newspapers embarrassed the 27th. Gordon appeared to commit "palpable, intentional fraud, taking shrewd advantage" of the relationship between the two Hoosiers, and played "double dealing." He and his staff denied ordering Morrison. The affair stung Colgrove then, but the peeved Morrison still wrote about it in 1890.[51]

Dubois County, Indiana

Home of Company K, the German ("Dutch Koompany") Company of 27th Indiana.

George R. Wilson, History of Dubois County from its Primitive Days to 1910 *(Jasper, 1910)*

Brigadier General
John Mehringer

He was major of 27th Indiana early in war. Of Jasper, Indiana, Dubois County.

George R. Wilson, History of Dubois County from its Primitive Days to 1910 *(Jasper, 1910)*

When Morrison resigned, the 27th's officers recommended Captain John Roush Fesler for Morrison's position and Adjutant Colgrove for major. The latter "was a pact concern and did not express the sentiment of the officers," Chapin wrote. Captain Tighlman Howard Nance ("he stands very high") might have been a unanimous choice for major, but chronic diarrhea forced him to resign.[52]

Unhappiness with army life was hardly confined to the 27th, but its officer resignations, including Colgrove's purge, indicated unusual discomfort. His original officers had been appointed by Morton or elected by their companies. He influenced filling subsequent company vacancies but had limited influence on the field and staff ones. Officers desiring to terminate their service through disability, family, or other personal reasons were mostly free to do so, and Colgrove undoubtedly encouraged a number of them. Twenty-seven resigned, most within the first year. Surgeon Jarvis J. Johnson wrote, "And Pete resigned. Likewise Lt. Furlander [John Forlander], Lt. [Francis No. 1] Atwell, Capt. Buehler, Capt. [John T.] Boyle. The colonel did it to put in [Lieutenant Squire O. W.] Garrett as Garrett would be more easily remolded to suit his purposes."[53] Buehler's request originally was approved and he was discharged May 9, 1862. The next day Washington rescinded it, and he was ordered back to duty. Eventually he was released effective May 9.

To green Indiana soldiers, the management was in turmoil. In November 1861, one wrote, "Morrison is decidedly the only captain worthy to even hold a commission. Nance is a good easy

clever fellow but he don't know nothing, nor never will. Sigh [Second Lieu-
tenant] Williams and [First Lieutenant George Whitfield] Reed are morti-
fied at Nance's promotion over them," and "Our staff deserved better officers. I have a great deal of confidence in the privates."[54] Colgrove, "determined not to grant privileges," rejected officer leave requests in December
1862.[55]

In January 1862, Major John Mehringer, citing "serious indisposition of
my wife, threatened mental aberration, I must be at home," was the first
significant resignation.[56] Changes were "almost every week." Wilcoxen
feared he would lose his position and hurried back before finishing his
furlough. "[First Lieutenant Robert B.] Gilmore now stands the fairest of
any company officer. The colonel has promised him a promotion."[57] Johnson
wanted to resign "due to domestic affairs at home demand personal &
immediate presence—wife's health rapidly & surely declining, her constitution being naturally delicate & subject to those diseases peculiar to her
sex, I consider it my duty to be with her as soon as possible."[58] Resignations were denied Nance, Williams, Second Lieutenant Thomas W. Casey
and Captain Peter Fesler. Morrison offered to resign before officially charging Colgrove, but Gordon would not approve it. Morrison, scorned by
Colgrove, was motivated "by the same cause that has nearly ruined our
regiment—the tyrannical rule of Colonel Colgrove."[59] To his end, the out-
spoken Hamrick would have the last word.

Ultimately, reasons for resigning commissions included wounds, disability, disease or sickness, family pressures, or personal reasons, primarily disdain for army life, some attributable to Colgrove. McKahin was forced
out following a homosexual affair. Boyle resigned under charges of cowardice at Antietam. Burge confessed he simply lacked the education to
handle the job. Colgrove's officers at best were a mixed bag.

CHAPTER 4

Likely I May Then Fall:
Bravery and Bravado

We expect to fight again soon, and likely I may then fall, but I am willing to die in the cause. Death on the battlefield is not as frightful as it used to seem. A soldier becomes so hardened that he don't look at it as he did at home. —*Corporal James C. Thomas, May 10, 1863* [1]

"Hardening" may have facilitated bravery, or perhaps it was the reverse. Always after a battle, a soldier reviewed his conduct, wondered why he had been spared and evaluated future odds for survival. Bravery and bravado had little to do with such an evaluation.

The Medal of Honor awarded to Captain Thomas J. Box for valor at the Battle of Resaca was the lone official commendation presented to the 27th Indiana for performance or bravery. During the Civil War, the Medal of Honor was the only such decoration awarded, quite different from today's multiple decorations for bravery or achievement in varying degrees.

Instead, genuine acclaim or recognition from outside parties, usually superior officers, was limited to citations, or mentioning, in official reports. These were customarily politic or remarks made on the field. However, the 27th's reputation for bravery as a "Fighting Regiment" was built gradually and nurtured by those who served with them in the lines, from the rifleman to the commander, and those who wrote the war's histories.*

Second Lieutenant Thomas W. Casey, typical of many men, sent home a lock of hair just in case. Men marveled at having lived through one more clash. After Antietam Casey wrote, "I did not get hurt [but] consider myself very lucky to escape so well for it was a very hard battle."[2] I lis and other letters home divulged scant fear in retrospect.

---

* In his 1898 work *Regimental Losses in the American Civil War*, the renowned historian William F. Fox named the 27th as one of the Union Army's "Fighting Regiments" for its total engagements and casualties.

Private George Edwards wrote after Chancellorsville:

Now Ill try to tell you a little bit about how I felt during time of battle. I felt calm. I was not excited in the least when I seen our men falling all around me. It appeared to me to be a very serious thing to be a thining out of their ranks and we did thin their ranks. I never thought once of getting hurt in that action. I got tutched on the right forefinger just enough to make it bleed but I dont call that anything.[3] I dont believe that I will be killed in this war but I dont know what might be yet I have good hopes of getting through safe. So dont be uneasy about me God being my helper. I have to feel very serious when I see and think what I have went through seeing the dead laying so thick that I could hardly walk without stepping on them.[4]

In the winter of 1861–62, as the men adapted to soldiering, they itched for action. The Rebels were never far, separated only by the Potomac River. "We could get a glimpse of the enemy's pickets and the boys fired a shot occasionally," said Second Lieutenant Josiah Clinton Williams. "I climbed a tree on the river bank and saw the secession camp of artillery plainly." "If so, then they know where we are, too," Williams mused. "Our boys are nearly dead for a fight."[5] A sergeant conjectured: the colonel says bring them on. "He swears he is good for any 3 rebel regiments they can bring against him. He really is anxious for to get a chance at them."[6] So it went until innocent bravado evaporated as did any prospects for a quick, clean war.

Soon orders came to march forthwith that night. Officers shouted with heavy feeling. The effect was electrical. Blood whirled. Men went wild and cheered, screamed, shook hands and hugged. We were off to the action. When it was over, the [October 1861] expedition to Balls Bluff brought the shocking realities of war home in a way that had not been done before, but the effect seemed to be of a nature of an additional stimulant, making the men more eager than ever to go forward. —ERB[7]

On reaching Virginia's Shenandoah Valley in March 1862, they were confident but frustrated by the skill of Confederate General Stonewall Jackson at eluding them, and the ambivalence of their Major General Nathaniel P. Banks at seriously chasing him. A private said, "I have not got sight of a secesh yet nor I don't believe now that I will," and furthermore "I don't believe our regiment will get to fight any."[8] This impatience was reflected in reporting home negatively or unenthusiastically. Another man believed "we belonged to an army intended only for occupation, not aggression. We wanted something to do and we could not see that our weakened condition gave abundant promise of it."[9]

Manassas Gap Railroad

Company B guarded Manassas Gap Railroad at Buckton Station between Front Royal and Strasburg, Virginia and were overwhelmed by Turner Ashby's Cavalry.

Photo by author

Not long after, the 27th Indiana ran into Jackson's whipsaw, and the whining tempered.

Engagements at Buckton Station and Newtown, Virginia—May 23 and 24, 1862

> When Rebel yells grew threatening and defiant, Colgrove shouted: "Damn them, let them come on! They will find us here!" Coolly and calmly, obedient to commands, the Regiment marched steadily onward doing its duty but wishing it was they who were advancing. *—About Colonel Silas Colgrove at Newtown* [10]

The regiment's first combat came on May 23, involving only Company B. The company had been detached along with one of the 3rd Wisconsin to guard the railroad at Buckton Station between Front Royal and Strasburg. The small detachment, no match against the numbers of Confederate Colonel Turner Ashby's cavalry, was routed and withdrew.

But the 27th had its first hero, Corporal Henry L. Pitman, credited with a "cool and desperate act" against Ashby's riders. On picket when the first charge was made, he escaped capture by taking a circuitous route to the depot. A mounted Rebel officer sighted him and, thinking Pitman's gun was empty, charged and demanded his surrender. Pitman shot him dead, then rode the officer's horse into camp. Teamster Hiram Kinneman volunteered to take a dispatch to headquarters at Strasburg. He swam the Shenandoah River with a mule and was on his way, but help arrived long after the successful Ashby had departed.*

> This was the first time we faced enemy muskets. We could scarcely have had better men to represent us than these bright young farmers' sons from Daviess County [Company B]. Though at a disadvantage, they possessed two prime requisites of a soldier—pluck and discipline. —ERB [11]

With Banks' 5,000 troops, the 27th continued its retrograde slowly north along the Valley Turnpike to Newtown, skirmishing along the way. Artillery pounded them with "wicked terrifying noises." Sent alone to save supply wagons behind them at Newtown, the 27th hopelessly faced Jackson's onrushing forces. They climbed hills and slopes, negotiated fences, and jumped ditches and water courses, "jolting and stumbling over rough ground, scarcely a step for two miles that shells were not hissing around us."[12] They rescued the wagons and continued retreating.

> No other service of the 27th reflects more credit upon the patriotism and soldierly devotion to duty and courage than Newtown. When we were ordered to retrace our steps alone miles from the others we clearly understood we were taking great risks. Yet no one ever saw an order obeyed with more hearty cheerfulness, not to say eagerness, than the 27th obeyed the order to rescue the wagon train. ERB [13]

The Battle of Winchester, Virginia—May 25, 1862

> We were sure to whip them but they outnumbered us too. Their force being 45,000 and ours only 5,000. —Private Michael Henry Van Buskirk, May 25, 1862 [14]

Written after being captured that day, Van Buskirk's pessimism was symptomatic. The retreating, exhausted 27th rejoined Banks at Winchester at midnight on May 24. Picket duty was a task assigned to an unlucky few who would pass the night without sleep. Sleep for the others refused to come. Minds locked on home and deeds undone. No doubt tomorrow would bring their first battle and surely some men alive now would not be tomorrow night. Tonight no man heard fifes and drums, speeches, or cheers from the town folk. They heard only their own silence.

Company sergeants quietly bounced between groups and sentinels with encouraging whispers or a touch of the shoulder, performing the ritual

---

* Jackson had begun the final push of his Valley Campaign to oust Banks from Virginia.

by instinct, not by experience. For the first time since soldiering began each man now reckoned with himself and made his personal peace. What little remained of the night passed swiftly. They were unable to write letters or enter diaries. Uncomfortably crouched, lying, or sitting, their contest tonight was with themselves, and their thoughts would remain for years: Whether to stay and fight, or run.

The dawn broke before most of the cold, damp, restless men turned over. Angry stomachs would have no breakfast. A few men hurriedly prepared a semblance of coffee, and gulped one last cracker, but it was no substitute for volume. (The men would have no food for nearly 24 more hours until they reached the Potomac River.) Rumors of the Rebels' numbers grew. Before daylight, their drums rattled and wheels creaked, and the Hoosiers were posted to await their coming.

The 27th was soon initiated. Ordered to the right flank toward Bowers Hill at the town's southern edge, they ran into a heavy volley from two Virginia regiments 150 yards away. Colgrove precisely formed a line of battle and marched "with promptness and coolness as if it had been on parade," and the men their own first volley in earnest anger with a "telling effect."[15]

> The initial Virginia fire killed Corporal Jacob Michael, the first death with the entire Regiment engaged. He bravely fell with his face to the foe, a musket ball striking him squarely on the forehead and opening a one-inch hole in his skull. We broke ranks to avoid stepping on him as he writhed in his convulsions of death. —ERB [16]

Soon the Louisiana Tigers Brigade reached the base of the hill and leaped forward, their crescent and pelican flags limp in the damp stillness. "We saw a thrilling spectacle. As far as we could see was a mass of men in gray. It is doubtful we ever saw at any time afterwards as many as were in sight at that time. It was folly, but new troops do not know when they are whipped. Not a man flinched or hesitated."[17]

Having withstood the Virginians' advance, the defenders were shaken by the Louisianians' follow-on attack. The eerie, blood-curdling cheer, like nothing ever experienced, would always ring in Hoosier memories. At first the Federal line held, extracting a fearsome price, until bravery was replaced by common sense. Every Union ear tuned for the order to withdraw. "The range was so good, and the enemy so massed," a private said, "that, with any aim at all, it was simply impossible to miss. If open, face-to-face killing in war is ever murder, then murders were committed then. While loading, men picked out some conspicuous enemy and when ready, took deliberate aim and shot him."[18] But there were too many crescent flags. They "had us nearly surrounded and we had to give way."[19]

Banks' battered force fled north through Winchester's streets to Maryland, and the Valley belonged to Jackson again. But for how long? "[The boys] wants to go back and try them again," Teamster Clemens Johnson said. "I guess we will go back in a few days and help to run the rebels out of Virginia."[20]

Men absorbed in battle, noise, confusion made it difficult to bring men to attention and hear commands—conditions we would soon become used to, were new to us. When withdrawal was finally understood it was generally disapproved. Many protested we could hold our position and repulse the enemy, and retired with lagging steps. —ERB [21]

The Battle of Cedar Mountain, Virginia—August 9, 1862

With wild enthusiasm and mad resolution they overcame a thousand obstacles. —About the charge to the wheatfield [22]

The Battle of Cedar Mountain was another Union disaster of poor generalship and too few muskets. Banks' corps marched rapidly in torrid heat and humidity to get there. They barely had time for water and catching their breath before being hurled against the 3 to 1 advantage of an enemy who hid behind a wheatfield northwest of the Orange-Culpeper road.

The 27th's brigade advanced westward up a slope toward the wheatfield, a half mile away. Maintaining proper ranks was impossible. Readjusting his formation, Colgrove had to resume double quick marching. Men dropped from heatstroke in the 98 degrees. Because of the abrupt and steep woods, the left wing got 100 yards in front of the right. "The 27th passed down the slope, crossed the run, forged their way

BY TELEGRAPH.

THE DAILY JOURNAL,

NOON DISPATCHES.

WAR NEWS.

BLOODY BATTLE AT CULPEPPER.

BANKS AND STONEWALL JACKSON FIGHTING.

Our Troops hold their Position.

POPE REINFORCES BANKS.

REBELS REINFORCED

Loss Between 2,500 and 3,000 on each side.

Twenty-Seventh Indiana Badly Cut Up.

SEVERAL GENERALS ON BOTH SIDES WOUNDED

No Fighting the Day Following.

Rebel General Winder Killed.

TWO REBEL GUNS TAKEN.

Burnside to Take Part.

Fighting at Gordonsville Probable.

FROM McCLELLAN'S ARMY.

August 12, 1862, Article

Reporting the 27th Indiana at Battle of Cedar Mountain, Virginia, August 9, 1862
Daily Journal, *Indianapolis, Indiana*

to the edge of the wheatfield beyond the crest, all at double-quick, with anyone able to stand on his feet at the end, is more incredible—it was miraculous."[23] The terrain was the worst they ever encountered under arms, and the physical strain and burden more severe than at any other time.

> The line moved promptly into the jungle and parted bushes, pushed aside limbs, crawled under or broke through vines and briars, steadied or pulled ourselves up by seizing hold of roots and twigs, dodged around trees, leaped the washouts and stumbled over stones. —ERB [24]

The banks of Cedar Run were 6 to 8 feet, nearly perpendicular, with a 45-degree angle where they forded. The soldiers jumped, slid, or tumbled down to the water, rushed across and clambered and pulled each other up to the bank without realigning. Ascending the final hill, they encountered the enemy for the first time face-to-face in combat. Some Confederates ran or gave up. Others fought hand-to-hand. "One, with more valor than discretion," seized a Hoosier with "murderous ferocity and intent." A comrade of the 27th "instantly shot the aggressor dead, the ball scattering his brains over the one assailed."[25] Private Joseph B. Stimson was wounded by a bayonet jab, a rare occurrence to the 27th Indiana.

The regiment arrived at the wheatfield haphazardly. "Red in the face, panting for breath, almost ready to drop with heat and fatigue, the advance struck the fence bordering the wheatfield without knowing it was there. Not more than a dozen or 20 men of the regiment could be seen by any one person."[26] Colgrove ordered a halt at the fence but some proceeded into the field to be chased by sheets of leaden balls. Enemy on the left and more screened behind wheat stacks on the 27th's right at nearly a right angle to the line poured in a crossfire. "Trust Colonel Colgrove always to do the right thing in a battle, if left to himself," a veteran said.[27] But Colgrove knew it was going badly. "I soon saw symptoms of disorder in my ranks, and in spite of all I could do the regiment fell back and was not rallied until it reached the open ground on the [north] side of the woods." He reformed the regiment and again advanced up the hill—another "yelling attack," but again was repulsed. We "were afraid to advance for fear of their having a reserve."[28] Virginians flanked them on the right and unleashed a galling fire, forcing them back to their starting point where they collapsed.

"We will whip them yet," promised Lieutenant Williams. "I have once more been providentially spared. If I am spared longer I will write more at the earliest opportunity."[29] Private Edmund Randolph Brown recalled: "That night I suddenly remembered. Today was my 17th birthday."[30]

> This battle was a wild, frenzied, freakish affair, fought under leaders of no more military ability and experience than those in control here. It was foolishly precipitated, through a stupid misconception of orders, if not willful disregard of the same. Under such hapless, hopeless and mismanaged

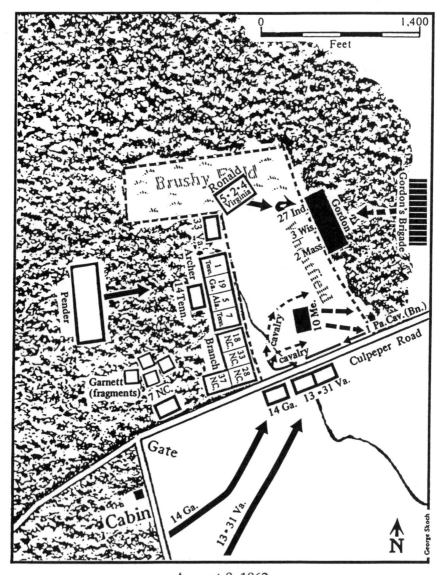

August 9, 1862

27th Indiana (Gordon's Brigade) routed at Cedar Mountain, Virginia.

Robert Krick, Stonewall Jackson at Cedar Mountain

conditions must we try to do something for our deeply imperiled country. All too many had made the extreme sacrifice of the patriot. —*ERB* [31]

Battle of Chancellorsville, Virginia—May 1–3, 1863

The battles of [May 3rd] was the hardest they had ever passed through. The 27th gained the highest credit for it gallant conduct. Gen. [Daniel] Sickles said it was the best regiment he ever saw although it was not in his corps. This is high praise, but the losses prove that it was well earned. – *Indianapolis, Indiana,* Journal, *May 11, 1863* [32]

"We was in action without a rest three hours and 20 minutes all the time under heavy fire from the enemy," wrote Private Edwards. "I fired 70 shots at them and I dont know that I killed any of them but I took good aim. I feel thankful that I came out safe."[33] Corporal James C. Thomas said, "There is a great difference between this Sabbath and last Sabbath."[34] "A week ago two armies were lying close together, watching each other as tigers watching their prey," a leader wrote. "Many a poor soldier arose that morning and soon launched into eternity, and many from the effects of that day's work are now suffering with wounds."[35] Smoke and cannon roar were horrifying, "but our boys took it coolly. I never saw such bravery as was exhibited by the 12th Corps."[36]

May 1

That night, as both sides prepared for tomorrow's certain battle, 1st Division commander Brigadier General Alpheus Starkey Williams noted:

The whippoorwills...were whistling out their 'whip-poor-wills' as if there was nothing but peace on earth. There was a solemn stillness which was almost oppressive. How easily and carelessly the heart beats on the very eve of scenes of battle and carnage. Jokes were played; the laugh and jest were as common as if we had been a part of picnickers instead of armed men awaiting the onslaught of thousands in combat.[37]

May 2

The regiment feverishly built breastworks all day. Late in the afternoon, Jackson's tumultuous surprise attack on the right crushed the disorganized Union lines and pressed eastward, threatening the entire Federal army. The 27th's brigade hunkered down to avoid the panicked, terror-stricken soldiers fleeing into their line, and then to stop the graycoats. At Hazel Grove Colgrove corralled two artillery pieces, some artillerymen, stragglers, and his men, and made a stand. "These arrangements were scarcely completed before the rebels charged our works with terrific yells," he reported. "I immediately caused both pieces of artillery to open fire first with shell & afterward with grape and canister. I am very confident the fire from these pieces did much to check their advance."[38]

That was "a supreme moment for the 27th. Would it be overwhelmed and carried away by the awful tide? How could a few of us stand alone?" Colgrove, "a man for an emergency like this, with tremendous resolution and firmness, forbade any of the fugitives from passing through our ranks; and at the same time called for the guides upon which to dress our line," which preserved their ranks. Private John Bresnahan said Colgrove "stood in his saddle-stirrups and shouted in a voice as loud as a steam whistle,

Chancellorsville: 27th Indiana Marker
on South Edge of Fairview

Marks the 27th's position late night May 2 and early a.m. May 3, 1863. Here they withstood the assault by Jackson's Corps.

Photo by author

'Steady John! [his horse] Whoa, boys. Steady, boys! Whoa, John.' He and the 'boys' understood the commands and acted accordingly."[39] Other officers were courageous, and no 27th soldier wavered. Both the Union fugitives and Jackson were halted as daylight ended. Corporal Michael Henry Van Buskirk wrote:

The rebels [were] in full pursuit yelling like so many devils. Colonel said, "Now 27th, form into line & stand firm." We formed into line as calm apparently as we ever did on dress parade. The rest of our brigade rallying with us, our line deceived the rebels. They thinking they had run into our main line & it being nearly dark they halted for the night. By morning we will be in better shape to meet them.[40]

May 3

The worst came today. Shortly after sunrise the Rebels began a steady advance, "delivering their fire with telling effect." Colgrove reported:

In a very short time [our] whole line was engaged. No part yielded an inch or wavered. The enemy poured in regiment after regiment of fresh troops, determined to break the line; but they found our fire so deadly that they were forced to halt and seek shelter behind the timber and rises in the ground. I immediately ordered the whole line to fix bayonets and charge, which was done in gallant style. The rebels fled before us like sheep...gave way and were soon thrown into utmost confusion. I have never witnessed so perfect a slaughter. Many of them...threw down their arms and came into our lines.[41]

At Fairview, Colgrove engineered the Hoosiers' defense in one of his best efforts of the war. The first Rebel attack, by Archer's Brigade, "swept on exultantly" but soon struck the 27th's 3rd Brigade, supplemented by stragglers. "That gallant regiment did not quail," an observer noted. "It gave Archer's men such a reception that they reeled back in confusion" against Colgrove's breastworks. "Archer had had enough of the brave Indianians. Colgrove was a splendid man for such an emergency. He was fearless, and filled his men with his own courage and fiery energy in battle."[42] Next the Hoosiers repelled McGowan's South Carolina Brigade. "The impetuous Colgrove, pushing forward on the left, had enfiladed the works and drove the enemy beyond them, huddling them up like sheep in 'a perfect jam.'"[43] Sergeant John L. Files wrote, "We charged the rebel works & they ran away. I called out to a rebel to halt but he went on & the 2nd shot I made at him he fell & I never seen him move again."[44] A Hoosier had to be restrained from putting a bullet in one who squinted. Many Palmettos lay dead or wounded, some "playing possum." "Humanity seemed to dictate [they] should all have the benefit of reasonable doubt." When the Hoosiers turned their backs some of the miscreants shot into their ranks, killing two who had begged to have them spared. "We have never ceased to mourn [them] in a peculiarly distressing way," a survivor said.[45]

The 27th was the last XII Corps unit to leave the field. Colgrove paid "a just tribute to the brave soldiers and officers of this brigade....The 2nd Massachusetts, 3rd Wisconsin and 27th Indiana fully sustained the reputation they won at Cedar Mountain and Antietam, is the very highest compliment that can be paid them."[46] Even in defeat, observers heaped accolades on the 27th and its courageous corps, who bore the brunt of the May 3 Confederate assault.* Their brigade commander recognized the valor:

---

* The 27th was cited postwar for their conspicuous coolness and the careful, deliberate aim with which they discharged their pieces. [*Slocum and His Men; A History of the Twelfth and Twentieth Corps* (AKA *In Memorium: Henry Warner Slocum*)(Albany, N.Y.: 1904), 165–66]

"Colonel Colgrove was, as on former occasions, conspicuous for courage and determination, and, although severely wounded, remained in command of his regiment until it recrossed the river."[47] A general fighting near the 27th wrote of the "valiant conduct" of Colgrove and his men during the "hottest of the fight. Instead of retiring with the rest of his brigade he remained with us until his ammunition was entirely exhausted. His coolness under fire, and the admirable discipline and steadiness of his men, cannot receive too much praise."[48]

The Federals retreated once more. Private Joseph Dunn Laughlin said the day the defeated 27th recrossed the Rappahannock "was the saddest day of our service."[49] The father of Captain Josiah Clinton Williams, visiting his hospitalized son, wrote: "Josiah had a very narrow escape. He was pointing out to his men with sword in what direction to shoot the rebels. In the meantime a rebel took his measure, the bullet hitting the guard of his sword, fluttered & glanced downward. We are indebted our relative is yet in the land of the living. He says this engagement does in ferocity & slaughter all others in his estimation."[50] Private Alfred Keck, retrieving wounded, "did not fear bullets. He worked hard all day fearing no danger & frequently would carry a big man by himself, never did man do his duty better."[51]

More post-mortems flowed. "I regret to say we have lost some of our best boys," wrote Sergeant Major James R. Sharp about neighborhood friends. "The boys thought Antietam was a hard fight, but they say it will not compare with this one. We fought 4½ hours and held our position until nearly surrounded. If all the troops had fought like the 27th victory would have been ours, but as it is we got licked."[52] Other comparisons differed.

> We were proud of the good reports, but we were no more willing to do our duty here than other times. The crucial test of courage was not equal here to that to which we were subjected at Antietam. —*ERB* [53]

Battle of Gettysburg, Pennsylvania—July 3, 1863

> Dismayed but cool, Colgrove pulled his nose, which he did when pondering a difficult problem, and repeated, "It cannot be done; it cannot be done." Pausing and looking upward, he said, "If it can be done, the 2nd Massachusetts and the 27th Indiana can do it." —*About Colgrove at Gettysburg* [54]

Yet the regiment's ultimate test of courage came at Gettysburg on July 3, 1863, at Spangler's Meadow adjacent to Culp's Hill on the Federal right wing. At 6:00 a.m., Colgrove, temporarily commanding the 3rd Brigade, and ordered by his superior, directed the 2nd Massachusetts and the 27th Indiana to charge frontally across the meadow into rugged enemy positions near Rock Creek.

Both regiments suffered extremely heavy casualties and were repulsed, never accomplishing their objectives. Although they dealt the Rebel counterattack a deadly blow, the two beaten regiments were forced to spend the day under a boiling sun amidst piles of dead and the ghastly moans of wounded. Later, a mile away, other Federal forces repelled Confederate Lieutenant General James Longstreet's similar senseless assault, and Gettysburg was over. In this reversal of fortune, the Hoosiers added their voices acclaiming Union victory, and the day ended with hope. However, the rationale for and conduct of the forlorn charge was indelibly framed as a major subject among the survivors.

Little tactically was accomplished by the charge. No one prevailed; no fronts changed; only hundreds more men were killed and maimed. Strategically, however, it was fortuitous for the Union right wing. It forced Confederate Major General Edward Johnson's shifts to counter the

The Swale, Spangler's Meadow

Charge by the 27th Indiana and 2nd Massachusetts on July 3, 1863, forced realignment of defending Confederate forces leading to Union victory on right wing of Culp's Hill.

Photo by author

Foot of Culp's Hill

McAllister's woods where 27th formed for charge across meadow. Monument placed by State of Indiana to 27th Indiana and other Hoosier units fighting at Gettysburg.

Photo by author

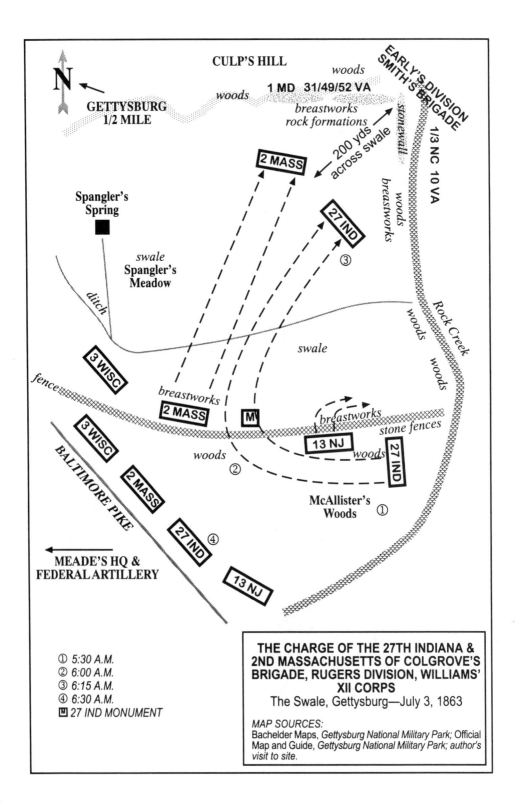

CULP'S HILL

N

woods

1 MD **31/49/52 VA**

GETTYSBURG
1/2 MILE

woods

EARLY'S DIVISION
SMITH'S BRIGADE

breastworks
rock formations

stonewall

200 yds
across swale

1/3 NC 10 VA

2 MASS

woods
breastworks

Spangler's
Spring

27 IND

③

swale
Spangler's
Meadow

ditch

Rock Creek

woods

swale

woods

3 WISC

fence

breastworks

2 MASS

M

breastworks

stone fences

3 WISC

②

woods

13 NJ

woods

27 IND

2 MASS

BALTIMORE PIKE

27 IND

④

McAllister's
Woods

①

**MEADE'S HQ &
FEDERAL ARTILLERY**

13 NJ

① 5:30 A.M.
② 6:00 A.M.
③ 6:15 A.M.
④ 6:30 A.M.
Ⓜ 27 IND MONUMENT

**THE CHARGE OF THE 27TH INDIANA &
2ND MASSACHUSETTS OF COLGROVE'S
BRIGADE, RUGERS DIVISION, WILLIAMS'
XII CORPS**
The Swale, Gettysburg—July 3, 1863

MAP SOURCES:
Bachelder Maps, *Gettysburg National Military Park;* Official
Map and Guide, *Gettysburg National Military Park; author's
visit to site.*

From Spangler's Spring, Showing the Position and Monuments

Woods in center right was ultimate position of 27th Indiana and 2nd Massachusetts after charging and repelling Confederate counterattack. Charge went from center to left. McAllister's woods on left and up the incline. 27th regimental monument in center.

Gettysburg National Military Park

perceived threat (the sudden charge), gambling how strong (were more blue lines to follow?), and unbalancing his line. His original task was to turn the Federal right flank; suddenly he notioned an attempt to turn his left—his army's left. If initially interested in the Baltimore turnpike, the Federals' supply and escape route weakly guarded only by the 27th's brigade, with the Army of the Potomac commander's headquarters only a couple hundred yards further, he reoriented and never reconsidered. Consequently, Johnson was thrown off Culp's Hill at mid-morning. As Johnson hemorrhaged, General Robert E. Lee's oft-delayed assault disunited his planned concurrent left-center offensive, and for all intent and purpose the Battle of Gettysburg ended by 11:00 a.m., a Confederate failure long before the immortal Pickett's charge.

The charge by the 2nd and 27th of course was a blunder, as their generals concluded, in a war replete with errors and a battle directed verbally. Each principal was responsible: the Union right wing commander for ignoring the XII Corps commander in the chain of command; the 1st Division commander for failing to write the specific order; his officer courier for miscommunicating what he *intended*; and Colgrove, temporarily commanding the brigade, for failing to query the order or direct a simultaneous assault. Simply, brigade command broke down. An elementary multi-unit evolution, lacking basic intelligence data, uncoordinated and unsupported, never achieved efficient use of numbers, tactics or firepower, and failed its mission. The meadow, later called The Swale, along with Antietam's Cornfield and Chancellorsville's Fairview, became synonymous with the 27th Indiana's bravery, suffering and pride.

> Our case was foredoomed; persistence meant annihilation. Indomitably, a little more energy and unity would give us success. We were invincible. However, the assault was not entirely unfavorable, but whatever happened was largely the result of chance. Regardless, the men recalled one genuinely glorious Fourth of July. —*ERB* [55]

Battle of Resaca, Georgia—May 15, 1864

> I have the honour to inform you that on the 15th instant before Resaca, the 27th Regt. in a fair and open fight defeated the 32nd [*sic*] and 38th Alabama Regiments killing and wounding a large No. and taking about 100 prisoners among whom was Colonel [A. R.] Lankford, 38th Alabama, also the battle flag of the 38th; enscribed on it—Chickamauga, Lookout Mountain, Missionary Ridge & Tunnel Hill. —*Colgrove, May 22, 1864* [56]

At Resaca, on the Atlanta Campaign, the 27th did something they had never done or seen, or would ever do again. They raced into their foe's midst after startling them with vicious rifle fire, locked grips in mortal vengeance, seized their colors, and captured many prisoners of war. Usually it was difficult to identify enemy unit names because of smoke, noise, and confusion, but at Resaca they knew instantly, as Colgrove proudly reported to his Governor.

Following winter garrison duty in Tullahoma, Tennessee, and 10 months since Gettysburg, by the time the Hoosiers reached Resaca with Major General William Tecumseh Sherman's advancing army, they realized they were back at war. The familiar smells and sights of powder and blood were shocking only to the handful of recruits who joined them over the winter, and each man anxiously anticipated driving the Rebels into the nearby rivers. The night of May 14 passed before they saw action again. In line of battle they dug in and lay on their arms in a steady, chilling rain. Their brigade again occupied the army's flank position, this time the left.

The next day, while the enemy formed for a 4 p.m. assault, Colgrove dispatched skirmishers to drive their pickets. The Confederates opened

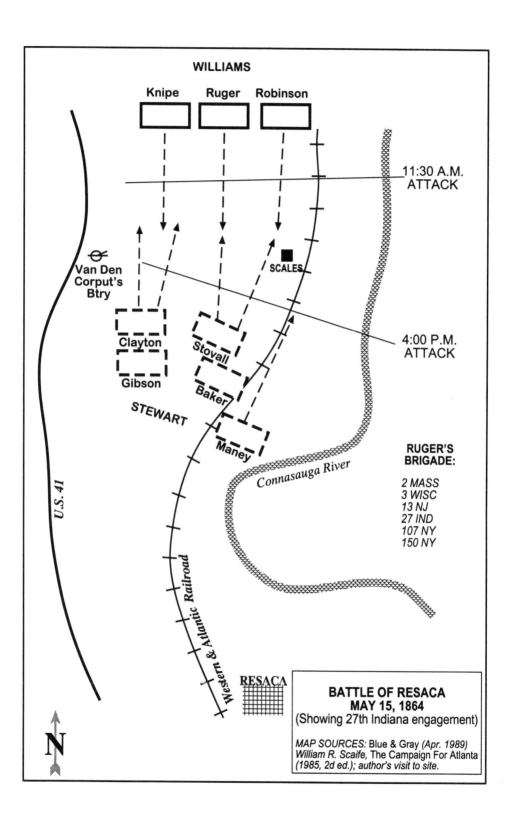

WILLIAMS

Knipe   Ruger   Robinson

11:30 A.M.
ATTACK

Van Den
Corput's
Btry

SCALES

4:00 P.M.
ATTACK

Clayton

Stovall

Gibson

Baker

STEWART

Maney

Connasauga River

**RUGER'S
BRIGADE:**

*2 MASS
3 WISC
13 NJ
27 IND
107 NY
150 NY*

U.S. 41

Western & Atlantic Railroad

RESACA

N

**BATTLE OF RESACA
MAY 15, 1864**
(Showing 27th Indiana engagement)

MAP SOURCES: Blue & Gray *(Apr. 1989)*
William R. Scaife, The Campaign For Atlanta
(1985, 2d ed.); author's visit to site.

with heavy artillery and musket fire on the 27th's positions, but the Hoosier skirmishers were ordered to fire only "under very strong provocation." Colgrove galloped out to see Captain Peter Fesler, commanding the forward line, and saw the enemy infantry pouring out of the woods in force with their bayonets bobbing over their heads. Expecting an imminent assault, Colgrove told Fesler to hold as long as possible and then quietly fall back into place.[57]

Colgrove then set a trap. He moved the regiment nearly halfway to the enemy works and had his men lie in a thicket on the back slope of a knoll where they could not be seen, to remain there until ordered. On his command they were to rise up and fire a careful, deliberate volley into their ranks, then charge them with the bayonet. As the yelping columns swept toward them "no soldier will ever forget the surging emotions started by the announcement, 'They're coming, boys!' or what is still more thrilling, the actual sight of the advancing column! A moment under such circumstances seems an age."[58] Down the hill into more level ground they came. Every Indiana head pounded. The enemy were "unconscious of danger at this point, their steps were firm and their ranks in order. Will Colonel Colgrove never break the silence?" They got within 35 yards. Colgrove, speaking over the swirling sounds in slow, distinct tones, finally said, "Now, boys. Ready, aim, fire!" Standing, he shrieked at the top of his lungs: "Charge!"[59] Officers repeated. "Poor men of the misguided South! It was all over in one terrible minute."[60]

Thirty-three members of the 38th Alabama lay dead at Hoosier feet and as many were so badly hurt they could not move. The 27th quickly surrounded 35 more, including the colonel, and all surrendered. The rest turned and fled so fast the Indianians did not think quickly enough to pursue. "They yelled, then broke and ran."[61]

The 27th also seized their battle flag, which Lankford was waving defiantly with one hand with his sword brandished in the other. Private Elijah White wrested the flag from Lankford and gave it to his company commander, Captain Thomas J. Box. When White reached Lankford, Private Thomas J. Acton was at his side. Either man could have taken the flag. Lankford knew what was happening and would surrender only to an officer, but by then Box had not come up. The two privates "did not think of the point of honor involved in a person surrendering to one of his own class; Lankford was quite strenuous about it. Before he could make himself understood, more than one soldier would have shot him if others had not prevented. They thought he was too slow in giving up his sword."[62]

Box arrived and settled the issue. Lankford brought his sword down on the hilt of Box's sword and instead demanded Box surrender. Box ordered a Hoosier to "blow out the colonel's brains."[63] Lankford, a "short, stout-built man and when taken was sweaty, red in the face, and puffing like a wood chopper," was persuaded.[64] What happened after the capture is unknown.*

Box was awarded the Medal of Honor. White and Acton received nothing. The "gaudy" flag was the only flag captured that day.

During the battle Second Lieutenant Roger Sherman Loughry recorded it was a "Terrible fight of an hours duration. Thank God I escaped unhurt. We have lost some good officers and men."[65] Captain Williams wrote: "The noble old 27th not only retained her former dearly bought honors of a half dozen battlefields but covered herself with glory & added new laurels to her war-worn veterans," creating "a general state of rejoicing for it was a glorious victory."[66] Private Lewis King recalled:

> The men got nervous and could hardly be restrained from firing. Finally the colonel gave the command to fire! We fired two or three rounds. Then we charged. Up to this time I had not seen a single rebel. Many of our boys had been laid low by their bullets. Among them was the nearest and dearest comrade I have ever known. He was a brave, honest soldier, a big-hearted man and true friend. He was shot through an arm and the opposite leg by the same bullet. He started to the rear in an ambulance. Then a stray ball struck him in the unwounded arm. In his dry, joking way he said he did not think it fair to shoot him again after he had left the field.[67]

Battle of New Hope Church, Georgia—May 25, 1864

> They drew us into a masked battery supported by a heavy line of infantry. We retreated under a very galling fire. In this retreat I was struck on the right shoulder by a piece of shell which knocked me down. For a moment I was confident I was shot thru & thru, but I soon found that I was mistaken & made up my mind I wasn't a dead man yet. —*Corporal Michael Henry Van Buskirk, May 25, 1864* [68]

For the 1st Division, just getting to New Hope Church had been hazardous enough. The terrain was almost wholly covered with brush and timber and loblolly pines as thick as canebrake, a forest reminiscent of the Chancellorsville wilderness. The oppressively hot day itself was nearly like Cedar Mountain—minus the wretched briars. The Confederate defenders had enough time to "plant and protect the batteries which wrought our repulse." With no time to rest, the fatigued, parched division was hurled into the melee. Without flinching, each man obediently followed the guidon and entrusted his fate to God.[69]

---

* Colgrove and Lankford met after the war. Lankford was "very friendly" and jokingly accused Colgrove of playing a "Yankee trick." Colgrove did not deny it: "Anything is fair in love and war."—*ERB* [475]

The jogging troops could see only a few yards in front of them as the defenders poured "into us canister and shrapnel from all directions except the rear." The division drove back skirmishers right before the enemy unloaded "shot, shell, and canister in murderous volleys."[70] During no attack anywhere did the 27th face such ferocious artillery fire. After nearly three years, the onrushing infantryman's gravest fear—looking down the cannon's mouth—exploded into their lives, ending some. It was each man's Armageddon. Grapeshot severely punctured Private Mark Hoover's right hand and right hip, destroying his thumb and two fingers. Screaming in pain, he dropped his rifle and hobbled toward the rear, dragging himself along using a broken tree branch for support, dropping all accoutrements to lighten the load. He was in five hospitals. Private Reuben Lucas was lying in front of the enemy works. Obeying orders and rising to fire, he was struck by a ball in the front upper part of the right shoulder, which fractured the bone and passed out the rear. Battlefield pain was old; Cedar Mountain and Gettysburg had already taken pieces of his body.

As the Indianians passed another brigade while going to the front they thought, "While there were so many good soldiers there could not be a battle" without including the "Old 27th." The command "Forward!" rang automatically in their ears. The Hoosiers bore stubbornly onward "beating their way through the jungle together," believing "we had been decoyed to our death." Shot and shell shivered off limbs, blazing and splitting trunks, "like tremendous bolts of lightning." Colgrove "finally decided" the enemy could not be dislodged and to continue was a "needless sacrifice," and withdrew the regiment a short distance until eventually relieved.[71]

Corporal John Michael Tomey saw it another way: We "shamefully broke and run off the field."[72] Second Lieutenant Roger Sherman Loughry said, "The regiment broke in confusion, our whole brigade driven back in confusion with heavy loss. I have so far escaped unhurt."[73] The 27th's brigade maintained positions "with obstinacy" for about an hour. Then, through diminished smoke they saw that some portions of their lines reached nearer the enemy's works than any other troops. One of the dead was Private Manfort Kutch, whose body was found near the cemetery closest to the works than any attacker. "Brave Kutch," a comrade lamented.[74]

> It is impossible to conceive of a more appalling, terrifying if not fatal rain of lead than this one. The canister and grape hissed, swished and sung around and among us, barking the trees, glancing and bounding from one to the other, ripping up the ground, throwing the dirt in our faces and rolling at our feet, until those not hit were ready to conclude that they surely would be hit.
> —ERB [75]

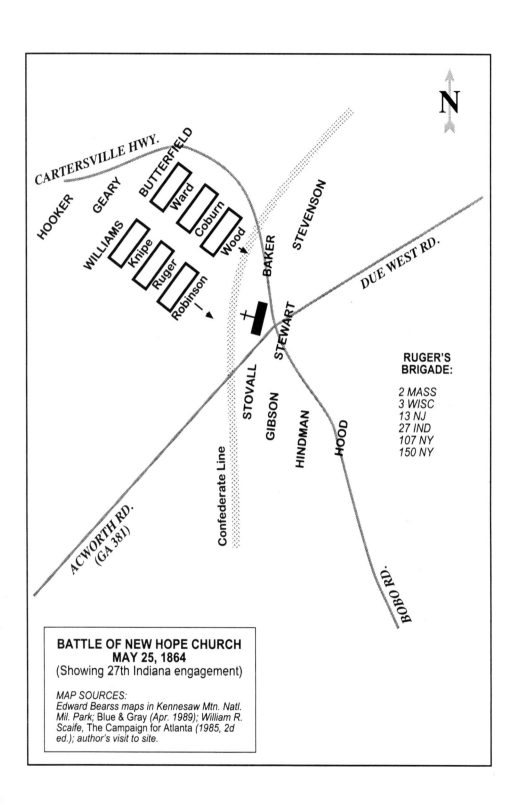

N

CARTERSVILLE HWY.

HOOKER

GEARY

BUTTERFIELD

Ward

Coburn

Wood

WILLIAMS

Knipe

Ruger

Robinson

BAKER

STEVENSON

DUE WEST RD.

STEWART

STOVALL

GIBSON

HINDMAN

HOOD

Confederate Line

ACWORTH RD.
(GA 381)

BOBO RD.

**RUGER'S
BRIGADE:**

*2 MASS
3 WISC
13 NJ
27 IND
107 NY
150 NY*

**BATTLE OF NEW HOPE CHURCH
MAY 25, 1864**
(Showing 27th Indiana engagement)

MAP SOURCES:
Edward Bearss maps in Kennesaw Mtn. Natl.
Mil. Park; Blue & Gray (Apr. 1989); William R.
Scaife, The Campaign for Atlanta (1985, 2d
ed.); author's visit to site.

For some time dark clouds had been gathering with the sense and smell of a brewing storm. All of a sudden, about 7 p.m., the sky became extremely black, and the heavens opened its mission of mercy on each soldier in the field. A tremendous electric storm broke, with deafening thunder claps drowning out the belching cannons, and fierce lightning bolts flashing nearby across the sky. All eyes and ears were turned to the violence overhead, as torrents of rain dumped on the exhausted human beings clutching the earth or trees for safety. The woods became "weird and spectral." In this "battle in the dark" men aimed at flashes and reports of enemy guns, and the smoke from their guns, which normally would have risen and dissipated, clung to them at ground level.[76] It was so black Private Bricen Carter, suffering from moonblindness, could not see his way out of the woods. He wanted to continue fighting, but Box ordered him to the rear immediately. Then all shooting stopped. Amidst the awesome storm and darkness, the likes of which many Hoosiers never saw again in their lifetime, the battle was over.

For the 27th, it would be their final assault, the last time they would be asked to do the impossible in crushing the rebellion. As brave as they were in that "very warm fight," what had it gained? "There was no living through it," an officer groaned.[77] It was nothing else but running blindfolded into a "hornet's nest." Union New Hope veterans never forgot the term, and invoked it together with the name each of Sherman's survivors gave the entire several days of death along the Dallas-New Hope-Picketts Mill line: "the hell hole."

The Battle of Peachtree Creek—July 20, 1864, and the Siege of Atlanta, Georgia—July 21–September 2, 1864

> We have good works now & are willing for the rebels to try us. But we aint willing to charge them. —*Corporal John Michael Tomey, August 6, 1864* [78]

Bravado in the earthworks, or trenches, before Atlanta with its rain, mud and filth was out of place, as Tomey alluded. The men marked time until Atlanta fell, or they were mustered out, whichever came earlier. But at Peachtree Creek which preceded the siege, the Confederates had turned and attacked the advancing Federals. The 27th was rushed into action as the assault began to shore up Brigadier General Joseph F. Knipe's flank. A sergeant of Knipe's 123rd New York witnessed a scene involving an unknown Hoosier:

> One of the skirmishers came running...toward our line. As he ran he was loading his gun, and when he reached us he turned to give the enemy a parting shot. He was a straight young fellow at least 6' tall and looked every inch a soldier; on his cap was "27," noting the 27th Indiana. As he was

bringing his gun down after firing I heard a dull thud and saw him fall. A bullet had hit him squarely in the forehead. He was dead, and as his body was in the way of the gunners it was carried back of the line. I have often wondered if his fate was known to his people back in Indiana. He was separated from his regiment and none who saw him killed knew him. He died when men's lives were cheap; I doubt if any effort was made to notify his regiment.[79]

Captain Richmond M. Welman, formerly of the 27th and now the 9th Indiana Cavalry surgeon, visited his old unit. "The boys are all in good spirits, anxious to charge into the city. Those in the hospital are improving," including Corporal James C. Thomas, recovering from Atlanta wounds. "To him honor is due—having fought and bled for his country."[80] Fifteen months after opening this Chapter, Thomas had fallen, but the "hardened soldier" lived until 1911.

Why should we start and fear to die

With timorous worms we mortals are

Death is the gate of endless joy

And yet we dread to enter there.

Oh if my Lord would come and meet

My soul would stretch our wings in haste

Fly fearless through deaths iron gate

And feel the terrorists as they passed.

—*Private George Edwards, October 6, 1863* [81]

Edwards, ready for finality, did not cheat death as did Thomas. Wounded in the head and hand at Resaca, he died the next day. On September 2, after non-veterans had mustered out, those of the Old 27th who remained marched into Atlanta. *The city is ours. Long live Sherman. Long live the Union.* *

---

* Men of the 27th Indiana rarely touted or reacted to killing, wounding, or otherwise harming the enemy. They boasted, "we'll give it to them Secesh!" but those epithets hardly curdled blood or revealed fratricidal tendencies. They gave few descriptions of actually inflicting casualties except capturing prisoners of war and some remarks about dead bodies. The Hoosiers took their jobs seriously, and to them it was only a job. They signed up for the cause: to save the Union. To do so, killing was necessary, if unrelished.

CHAPTER 5

Boredom in Polecat Den:
Picket Duty

On picket, raining. The pole cats have a regular den here. They play around
while we are on picket. No lack of perfumery. —*Corporal Michael Henry
Van Buskirk, February 11, 1863* [1]

Stafford Courthouse, Virginia, in the Winter 1863 was a "lonesome,
weird, ghostly locality." [2] No one knew why the army established its winter
quarters there. The area was difficult to access and required great care to
traverse, but it had to be secured. Hardly anything lived near the camp
except polecats.

Several nights the creatures almost stampeded the 3rd Brigade picket
line, including one night in heavy wet snow, when the 27th Indiana's men
could not return to camp from their isolated post, and the relief had difficulty getting there.* A Hoosier private wrote, "Snows caused branches to
strip, continuous snapping and roaring in the forests, crash of falling timber
as if at battle. A picket fired at an old horse thinking it to be a mounted
rebel; everyone knew he was tired of being out there alone. Nights were so
inky dark could see nothing. Dangerous footing over footlogs over creeks.
Reliefs fell into raging freezing torrents." [3]

Indeed, the weeks at Stafford became etched forever. "We had many
heavy snows here," said Private Lewis King. "One of 16 inches deep I
remember when I was on picket. What a dreary, never to be forgotten
night. There was little fire, no sleep, plenty of pine bushes covered with
snow making huge caverns, to my boyish imagination, hiding panthers,
bears and bushwhackers." [4] Private George Phillips caught a cold, fever
and consumption during a 12" snowstorm February 25, causing his death
in 1866. Sergeant Joseph B. Sellers said, "The hardest duty the 27th done
was winter of 63 doing picket duty." [5] Diarrhea, the infantryman's curse,

---

* That picket post was known as "polecat den," remembered Private Joseph Dunn
Laughlin. "I was one of the relief next morning." [Family Records of Joseph
Dunn Laughlin. Provided by Kerry Armstrong.]

Union Army Winter Quarters, 1862

Typical of what 27th Indiana quarters looked like at Camp Halleck ("Hoosier City"), Frederick, Maryland.

Brady Collection

was doubly so on guard duty, and the logical excuse for trying to avoid it. Private Michael Leikauff had diarrhea so bad he could not stand guard or leave his post, and had to run nearly all the time. "Thick heavy set, fleshy," Leikauff "was too fat to keep up on the march, spent much of the time in field and other hospitals."[6] King vividly remembered the Stafford post:

> The night I got scared was a rainy night and dark as Egypt, too. Contrary to orders I went on duty with an unloaded gun. I had heard various stories of pickets having their throats cut by bushwhackers who had slipped up on them. I did not believe the stories. I did not enjoy drawing the load from my gun and washing it out every two or three days so I risked it that night with an unloaded gun. It was raining when I went on post at 10:00 p.m. I wore my rubber blanket. By and by it stopped raining and I hung my rubber blanket on the lower limbs of a tree and stood about three feet away. When I moved a distance down the beat I heard a rustling of leaves in my rear. I suddenly faced about and there within three feet of me stood a man. Immediately all the stories of the pickets who had been murdered flashed through my mind. In obedience to an early, unused and almost forgotten drill, my gun went over my right shoulder at the command, "Butts to the

front, strike!" Just as I was putting all the force at my command into the "strike," I realized my rubber blanket was about to get the benefit of the "strike." So I didn't.[7]

Each regiment and each picket detail, including those working together, had an officer of the day (OOD) in charge for a certain period, reporting to the commander. The OOD looped his sash over his shoulder, passing it across his breast and wrapping it around his waist. Everybody understood his position and saluted when he passed. Officers took the duty seriously. "I have heard so much grumbling in the army I take everything as it comes & am getting to be a model boy," Captain Josiah Clinton Williams wrote home in 1862. "Being officer of the day today I have seen to strapping 30 lbs. of rocks each to 2 prisoners & others policing."[8]

One night a 27th sentinel challenged an OOD on his rounds. "Who comes there?" "The officer of the day." Quickly the sentry responded: "To hell with your officer of the day! It's high time the officer of the *night* was getting around."[9] In July 1863, the 27th guarded the Rappahannock River at Kellys Ford. One dark, rainy night the 13th New Jersey OOD felt the pickets, which included Hoosiers, would be "gobbled up," and ordered all to stay awake. The 27th's corporal of the guard allowed two of his men to be alert and others to sleep on their guns, ready in a flash. As the OOD made his stealthy rounds the Hoosiers immediately sensed him, waked each other, challenged him loudly and properly, and drew praise for their vigilance.[10]

Guard duty was a military necessity but an unwelcome chore. "I have just come off guard & delivered my report concerning the general management etc. of 77 guards, forming 3 reliefs of 23 each, & the arts & care of 4 prisoners," wrote Williams. "Report of considerable writing, having to sit up till 3 o'clock in morning out in open air by the bright campfire with 50 odd men of my command (after I got them awake) with a beautiful moonlight night & almost everything to attend to. I call our present location Camp Necessity, where we had the pleasure of destroying a fine secesh straw stack to lie on."[11]

Reuben Hendrickson
Company F, from Monroe County, Indiana.
Provided by William Young

Williams described coming off 24 hours of picket at Strasburg, Virginia, where posts were a mile into the pines and the reserve in an old log house. "After night are the very personification of gloominess especially when by oneself and looking sharp for the secesh game."[12]

Senior officers also performed guard duty. While commanding the combined picket post at Collins and Pipers Fords, Maryland, on the Potomac, in November 1862, as was his daily custom, Lieutenant Colonel Abisha L. Morrison started out to visit the pickets up and down the river to communicate the countersign. His horse stopped suddenly, passing over some rocks where the fence was down before passing on to the picket camp, threw him and injured his spine severely, precipitating his disability discharge two months later.

Often opposing pickets were posted near enough to discern voices, but the only boundary separating them was fear or deceptive, transparent boundaries such as Virginia's Rapidan and Georgia's Chattahoochee Rivers. In October 1861, before the Hoosiers learned signs and countersigns and where their own were posted, tragedy struck. Patrolling the Potomac in Maryland after the Battle of Balls Bluff, Private Henry McCaslin was mistakenly shot dead by a 27th comrade when he appeared on Harrison's Island, and became their first combat zone casualty. A year later they were still watching the Potomac, as Williams wrote:

> We are constantly watching one another's actions. There are 3 sitting under an apple tree within good shooting distance. Yesterday we tried the nerves of one brave fellow by drawing up 6 men & aiming at him. I ordered them not to fire but knew it was a dangerous experiment as I expected a bullet would come whizzing at any moment. The fellow stood bravely. Grim winter stares us in the face once more. This picketing is a freezing business.[13]

Amusing incidents happened on duty. An officer apprehended a regular army soldier "who was very irregular in getting a jug of whiskey," and wanted him to take it so he could leave. Leaving under escort, the regular "took a parting horn," stepped behind the sentry, and smashed the jug on a stone wall.[14] Private Jacob Varner, who served in the most army units, four, saw three secesh and a dog together. He halted them and two whirled to run. He fired his gun at the other man and picked up one of his sleeping comrade's guns and shot it off with the plug in it, bursting the barrel. "No one was hurt but the gun," and no blood was spilled. Williams, taking it all in, mused, "Who wouldn't be a soldier?"[15]

During the summer of 1864 Siege of Atlanta, guard duty was absorbed in consummate trench warfare: artillery duels, constant skirmishing, random picket firing, unnecessary deaths, and with minimal territorial gains. First Division commander Brigadier General Alpheus Starkey Williams in

August described the trench warfare new to the Western Front and new to the 27th Indiana:

> While pickets on both sides of my front are popping away at one another, those of my division have not fired a shot for days, but are on quiet and joking terms with the Johnnies. I am always glad when picket firing stops. It has no effect on the results of the war and is a miserable and useless kind of murder. Pickets are mainly intended to give notice of an advance or movement of the enemy. This constant popping obviates and destroys this valuable purpose.[16]

Private King portrayed what picket life was like in the trenches:

> Eventually our pickets were instructed to watch but not to shoot. However, the rebels continued to watch and also shoot. They were getting some of our fellows every little bit. I stood this for some days, but then came the last straw. I volunteered to take a number of canteens to the rear for water. My way led to the right along the works for about 100 yards to the railroad cut, which was piled with cordwood at least one rick and 6' high, so that after a man reached the railroad he could walk upright. In passing over the 75 yards of open ground he had to crawl along the works, or else be a target for sharpshooters. A number of shots were fired at me, all coming close. On the return trip after getting water I again drew their fire. When I got back I was "mad as a wet hen" at our commanders for prohibiting our shooting, mad at the rebels for shooting, and madder still at the cowards who had called me to get down.

> The sergeant warned me not to shoot. I cocked my gun, took deliberate aim and fired. The sergeant yelled, "Get down, King, they will get you for sure." He took my blouse and jerked me down. A bullet tore up the dirt under where I had been. That afternoon a shell from a battery in our rear, which fired a shell into Atlanta every five minutes, day and night, exploded before it reached us. A piece of it as big as my fist stopped within reach of my hand.[17]

Life on the picket line was extremely dangerous. Exposure above the earthworks could mean instant death. "[Private] Thomas Pratt killed on picket," recorded Corporal Michael Henry Van Buskirk in his diary on August 1. "Not having any men for detail I volunteered to help bring him in. We had to carry him about a quarter of a mile exposed to their fire all the time. I would rather go through a battle than try that over. Worked half the night making a box and burying him."[18]

Thomas' brother Private Arthur Pratt and Private Dawson Denney assisted Van Buskirk in digging the grave. Denney had to quit and was taken out of the grave alleging heart trouble. "He seemed to suffer greatly" and complained of smothering spells, but revived when water was poured on him. At one time his Captain John McKnight Bloss had only three men present but "scarcely able for duty; two had nightblindness, and I remember that Denney and these two men had to be frequently excused from duty." Denney also complained of "shortness of breath and nervous prostration" but was not hospitalized. Bloss carried their guns and led them about six miles at night back to the Chattahoochee.[19]

Bunkmates Privates Washington Akester and Joseph R. Jones were skirmishers one night until 4:00 a.m. and captured a number of pickets. "When they found out their pickets were gone they opened fire on us from a fort," Akester said. The Federals built a shelter. Jones and a New Yorker were carrying a log toward the line, and he strained himself badly. "The log was heavy, and in the excitement Jones hurt his back. We stayed there about an hour and then went back to our original picket line." The two were relieved at 8 a.m. Jones could not travel or do arduous duty, his "gait not so lively (good marcher before that)."[20]

Picket life in 1862–63 along Virginia's Rappahannock River fords had been different times of bartering, story swapping, epithet hurling, questions about relatives and occasional nastiness. Zealots might break cordiality, but usually after gentlemanly warnings. Still, neither vigilance suffered nor killing ceased. Anything could erupt. "There is firing left & right. Being Sunday it seems as though the higher powers are content to respect the Sabbath for once by not fighting, at least up to 4 o'clock. Did my first picket duty yesterday at an old reb's (Mr. Whearly's), where his son had been on as a reb picket but an hour before, & I presume is still close by."[21]

The strangest guard duty the 27th Indiana encountered, however, was in New York City helping to quell the aftermath of the draft riots of August–September 1863, where they protected Northerners

Germanna Ford, Virginia

The 27th Indiana was the first Union regiment to cross Rapidan River on the way to Chancellorsville.

Photo by author

Germanna Ford, Virginia

Pilings of Civil War era bridge at Rapidan River, Virginia, destroyed during the war.

Photo by author

from each other. Rested after the Gettysburg Campaign, the regiment was one of the units sent by ship to New York. A confused private wrote, "I took my gun, for I did not know but that the same gun that had shot at rebels at Gettysburg and other places, would have rebels to shoot in New York City. However we watched those New York rebels for 10 days and never got to shoot a single one of them."[22] It was mostly uneventful, and the Hoosiers got to see a bit of the country's largest city.

Garrison duty a distance from the front, no matter how less stressful, could become drudgery fast. Compounding garrison and railroad guard duty was enough to make time stand still, and among men of the 27th Indiana at Tullahoma, Tennessee, during the fall of 1863 to the spring of 1864, boredom reigned. Except for the occasional interference by guerrillas, or Confederate cavalry from Generals Nathan Bedford Forrest and Joe Wheeler, the usual sentry report was, as Corporal John Michael Tomey wrote, "Nothing strange going on."[23] When winter came, attention to security dropped in spite of the threat. Men of the 27th were unaccustomed to such extended guard duty.

Tullahoma, Tennessee

House used as hospital (by both sides). In 1863–64, the 27th Indiana garrisoned there 7 months guarding railroad.

Photo by author

The situation in the Middle Tennessee hills was much different from Virginia, where partisan activity was nil and guerrilla activity, with which the Hoosiers had little contact, was limited to organized Confederate army units. Now Tullahoma presented the Federals with a special problem and point of confrontation: guerrillas. Some Middle Tennessee pro-Confederacy people became irregulars, or "bushwhackers"—citizens by day, marauders by night. The Hoosiers felt unconstrained around town and its environs but venturing too far without protection in numbers was an invitation to trouble. The wooded region south of town with steep rocky hills was guerrilla vantage ground. They would attack the railroad in late afternoon and be gone before pursuers lost them in the dark, and by morning would be "harmless and inoffensive citizens" again. Twice railroad trains were thrown from tracks supervised by the 27th. No lives were lost and the property damage was never large, and the guards responded quickly to the "villain" before he could do harm to any extent.[24]

Private Joshua Deputy went on guard daily from 10 a.m. one day to 12 p.m. the next, "so we are on about half the time."[25] It kept them occupied, but a bored First Lieutenant George Tarvin Chapin, detailed as Tullahoma post adjutant, wrote his brother, "[This] is a position of very little responsibility and only serves to keep me from more severe duty as going on picket post twice a week. I still retain the position and will probably while we air here. I have a good time to read and improve myself."[26] He might as well, for the grueling march to Atlanta was still weeks ahead.

Tullahoma was frigid that winter, the coldest the Hoosiers had experienced, with unusually high snowfall. After the tedious routine settled in, they would long remember the coldest day of that most frigid winter, a day they called "That Cold New Years," when 1863 became 1864. The feet of Sergeant Bricen Carter were severely frozen and frost bitten while on picket duty that night. "His feet were not properly protected against intense cold," a comrade wrote about Carter. "When his boots were pulled off next morning a part of his skin came off with them."[27]

For Carter, he had to remain in his tent for three months and was unable to walk at all. Corporal Ebenezer Quackenbush, his messmate, was with him and waited on him. Carter suffered continually and often fell out of ranks while marching and came up with the wagons or the best he could.

On January 2, the temperature dipped to minus four degrees in Bridgeport, Alabama, the railroad terminus about 50 miles southeast. "To go on picket every other night under the open sky through an entire winter is an irksome, slavish, health-destroying life," a weary soldier wrote.[28]

For three days in late December 1863, Second Lieutenant Roger Sherman Loughry was sent 20 miles on a foraging expedition. He arrived January 2 with a severe chest and lungs cold and cough, making him unfit for duty. "He never seemed as strong after that or able to stand the campaign as before."[29] Tennessee got cold long before then. Corporal Van Buskirk noted for November 29: "The ground is frozen right smartly this morning. It snowed a little last night, first we have had yet." For December 18: "Still cold as Boston." For January 1, he underscored everyone else: "The coldest New Years Day I ever saw. The citizens say it is the coldest day they have had here for 12 years. Wind is blowing like all Boston."[30] For January 1, Corporal John Michael Tomey recorded: "Cold and frosty and some snow. As cold as Greenland. Spent all day in bunk" staying warm, not volunteering for guard duty. The next day Tomey lay around the picket campfire. "One side burnt while the other side froze." Snow fell January 5, 7, 8, 15, and 18.[31]

Second Lieutenant
Roger Sherman
Loughry, Company C
of Columbus, Indiana
Provided by Richard Loughry

In mid-February corporal of the guard Tomey made his rounds, starting out at 1 a.m. and covering six miles. The ground was "froze hard," and he pitifully wrote, "God bless all of us." Tomey checked on friend Private William Fugate, detailed with corps headquarters in charge of the U.S. mail. Fugate had "the worst feet I ever saw." On February 23, Tomey headed the third relief. He started at 5 p.m., made six miles, returned at 9 p.m., then got ready to go again at 5 a.m. and return at 8—walking most of the way, brutalizing his own feet. Tomey's squad drew picket duty often in Braggs Graveyard. One February night, the weather radically looking like spring, "Old General [Alpheus Starkey] Williams" visited the graveyard post with the 13th New Jersey's Colonel Ezra Carman. The OOD, from the 13th, approached Tomey. "Corporal, what is your instructions?" Tomey said the usual. The OOD asked him what he would do if attacked by cavalry. He replied, "I would have the boys to do like one of the 13th New Jersey told his men—skirmish around in the woods and not come back where I am." The officer rode off and asked no more questions.[32]

The brief flirtation with spring ended with snowfall on March 14, 15, 16, and 25, and feet again became soaked and frozen. On March 3, seven cars jumped the track but were soon put back by railroad crews, and no one was hurt. Tomey's squad was at the McMinnville tracks three days later when the order came to let no one in or out without a pass from the provost marshal or the colonel, and to keep pickets on post all the time and walking. On March 17 guerrillas raided Company F four miles south of Tullahoma, captured seven men, burned two cars, "and din a heep of devilment." As Easter dawned, Tomey sat on a railroad car door on picket. "This is Easter Sunday & I think that I will go out and have myself an egg." He would fondly record March 30 as the very first day he had been off duty in six weeks. Finally spring broke through and April 25, as the regiment packed for their final campaign, was beautiful. "I can almost see the grass growing."[33]

We understood that a soldier, whatever his rank or station, is simply one wheel or one cog in a great piece of machinery, and for the whole to be perfect, means every one must do his whole duty. Then we first became imbued with that invisible something, called the military spirit, which once in a man never leaves him until he is ready for his coffin. November 1861 dates the development of the 27th into a regiment of volunteer soldiers. Before that we were not really ready for active service; after that we were. —ERB [34]

CHAPTER 6

Letters, Loved Ones, and Likenesses: Families and Friends

If you know of any other pretty girls you think I take an interest in just send the little face and smiles along and I will pay the bill. I assure you I am getting quite mannish (I fear dotage). If I am in the same state of mind when the rebellion is crushed I will be content to settle down and lead a different life. —*Captain Josiah Clinton Williams, December 1, 1862* [1]

Williams wrote again to thank his sister. "I was the happy recipient of a neat letter from Mollie Buckingham and happier to discover her photograph in it. She has improved wonderfully and is quite pretty and lady-like from the representation." [2]

The photograph was a likeness, or portrait, a favorite memento exchanged with families and friends. They carried them in folding cases, as miniatures, or loose in knapsacks, hats, pockets, and haversacks. Many survived the war. Likenesses were taken in camp by roving photographers but usually in a city studio. One man wrote he paid $4 to the "best dagnarrean in Indianapolis" for his "military likeness," and later noted he preferred photographs or on copper plates as easier to carry than those in cases. [3] Private Wesley Slider, writing home about "solgering," asked his mother to send pictures. [4] An officer receiving his brother's likeness said, "The boy has so changed I hardly knew him. I presume he has grown taller." [5]

Private Enoch Anderson told his father, "I would of liked to of had my likeness taken before I got sick but I had no

A Likeness

Private Nelson Purcell, Company E, of Washington, Daviess County, Indiana.

Daviess County Museum

92

chance to go to town. I will send [it] home as soon as I can get it taken." He asked for one from each of the family—"get 2 or 3 taken together."[6] Commissary Sergeant Simpson Solomon Hamrick said yes to a request for a likeness, "but I can't get it here [Fairfax Station, Virginia] and doubtful if I can get to Washington or Alexandria for it."[7] Sergeant William Parmemas Ellis wrote from Nashville, Tennessee: "PS for Indiann [sic]—I ordered some photographs while in Indianapolis but did not get them. I left your address. Send one to [other sisters] Becca, one to Sally, one to Caroline, one for yourself, and one for mother—and send me two. The other two someone else may have."[8]

Ways other than photographs wooed the girls back home. A friend of Second Lieutenant Roger Sherman Loughry, visiting in Virginia in 1863, wrote about the boys' "passtime lottery." Names of the hometown "ladies" were written on slips of paper, placed in a hat, and shaken up. Each soldier drew one and to that lady he promised to send his card and ask her to write the lucky man so they "might get up on interesting correspondence and have some fun. We had a big laugh after the drawing was over to see how well matched some of the parties were. If some of the girls could see some of the ducks that drew their names they would be sure to fall in love with them, and others it would be the reverse. You must give the list to some of the girls that go to school and tell them not to get mad at the boys for using their names."[9]

Affection also went out to others' kin. First Lieutenant Robert B. Gilmore, wounded at Antietam, died at home in Greencastle. On furlough, Williams called on his widow, "on two accounts: one was to see and speak to a Hoosier lady and also for Ma and the girls. I confess I feel quite flattered at her most favorable report, especially as she is a pretty widow left a lonely representative of her country's honor. Poor lady, I am sorry for her situation."[10]

Young men away from home for the first time also shared warmth with parents, as Teamster Clemens Johnson did in 1862: "I well remember your kindness to me and long to see the time come when again can share the joys of home and a kind father and mother, and exchange the confusion and bustle of camp life for the comforts of home, and the associations of loved friends." Johnson, both married and divorced in 1860, had a reason for parental affection.[11] Sergeant Stephen Rayburn's "great desire" was to go home to care for his old parents. Home on furlough shortly before his death at Gettysburg, he anxiously told his mother as soon as he got back to draw his pay he would send it to her.[12] Captain John A. Cassady was granted emergency leave in April 1863 to attend to his father's estate which had been badly handled by an agent. The day after he returned from leave he was shot in the abdomen and left on the field to die at Chancellorsville. At least they got home. Corporal Bricen Carter wanted 20 days in 1864.

His mother was very sick with no one to attend to her, and his father and three brothers had died since he left home for the service. But the request was disapproved.

Some men received the equivalents of "Dear John" letters. "Sarah never intimated a word in her note that Maggie had married," lamented one. "I see a notice in the [Putnam County *Republican*] *Banner*. Surely she ought to have appraised me of the fact knowing I was interested. Doubtless she thought I couldn't bore it all at once." Confidently he added, "She should have no fear. I am prepared for almost anything."[13] His ego regained, later he told his brother of his favorable opinion of the young ladies of Belleville, including "Miss Fletcher and Miss Papes and several others."[14] Another soldier wailed after being away from home only three months. "I used to have an occasional 'special correspondent' whom I wrote in Camp Morton, but she also has forgotten me."[15] The men gave heartbreaks, too. "i rote letter to the morgain girl & i got the answer she had herd that i was maried," Private Linzey C. Lamb wrote his new wife. "She give me fits but she did not now wher to beleave what had herd or not. She can do as she likes."[16] Other soldiers wanted to forget. First Lieutenant George Whitfield Reed hesitated suggesting Private Amos W. Nicholson send money to his wife. "I am under the impression he volunteered for the purpose of leaving her. If he sends any more [money] by me I will talk to him and try to induce him to send any spare money to his wife." Nicholson later deserted the army as well as his wife.[17]

Other love affairs lasted, such as Sergeant John McKnight Bloss' affection for Emma McPheeters, of Livonia, where Bloss was school principal. "You have been so constantly with me mentally and I am glad it was so," he wrote her in August 1861. "I am constantly reminded of your lovely image to keep out difficulties. You know we both love as we love no other nor can we ever love others as well. You can't imagine how badly I hated to part from you. I will do whatever it might cost if you would prefer our union before I leave for the seat of war it shall be so. For Emma you know we both love as we love no other nor can we ever loves others as well. Please remember me in your prayers."[18] They were married after the war. A number of men were married within a few months after discharge, indicating an ongoing relationship which postponed marriage until service was completed. They included Captain William H. Holloway to Caroline Lancet in Owen County and Lieutenant Loughry to Martha J. Mitchell. Others married sweethearts in Indiana on veterans' reenlistment furloughs in March 1864. These couples decided not to prolong their engagement until his new commitment was served. They included Lamb to Mary Catharine Heaton at North Salem. Winter 1864 also was when First Lieutenant George H. Stephenson married Sarah.

Homesickness could be "downright depressing." The men sat around talking about home and the good things they would have to eat and kindred subjects, "until apparently they lost every spark of energy. It could be 'demoralizing' to participate and to listen."[19] It came quickly for men not well travelled. Private George Edwards wrote from Washington, D.C., nine days after mustering in he was "homesick fighting for liberty and children."[20] In 1862 he whined, "It is nearly eight months since I left home and it seems to be three times that long."[21] An officer told his parents, "I was never much of Boo Hoo homesick kind of soldier, but I assure you I should like to see you all (and the new piano) awful swell. If you felt like visiting the seat of war or making a trip East I would be quite happy if you would pay me a visit."[22] Children were missed. Teamster Johnson asked to be remembered "to Daniel's children Michel, Sarey and Leuisa. I have not forgot you and want you to be good children and obey your mother and try to help her all you can and prepare to go to heaven."[23] Private William Thomson wrote his wife, "I would be mighty glad to be at home now & stay or even to be there & see you & the children. I want to see them very bad. Kiss them for me."[24]

With veracity, negligence, and nonchalance, the men handwrote their official and personal legacy. Writing letters was a significant pastime for soldiers of the Civil War, and their principal means of communicating with friends and loved ones. The low literacy level and writing ability of men of

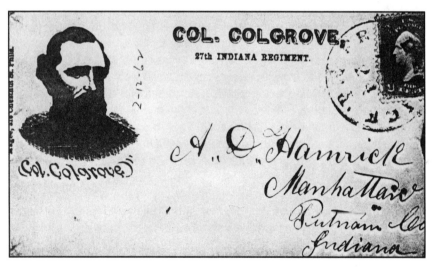

Letter Sent by Simpson Solomon Hamrick to Father

Hamrick was a frequent letter writer and critic of the regiment's administration.

Indiana Historical Society

the 27th Indiana was bound to cause some problems in communicating. "I cannot give you anything about your case in the letter you wrote," Captain Albert Dodd, army commander at Columbus, Ohio, wrote to Private Edwards in November 1862. "You do not give your company or regiment nor tell anything of the circumstances under which you are at home whether on furlough or discharge. State more particular the circumstances and then I can tell you better what you ought to do."[25]

Dodd was confused that Edwards, a paroled Winchester prisoner, had been at nearby Camp Chase since July before going home in November. How or why was uncertain. Dodd wanted to help, but his response showed official frustration with the manner in which this soldier selected his words.

All official headquarters and regimental orders, notices, and general news were handwritten and copied as often as necessary for distribution. Clerks with good handwriting were assigned those duties, and generally those documents were clearer and more proper than personal ones. Telegraphic messages were not used. Through personal letters the men opened their world and bestowed their feelings, opinions, and accounts to history. Letter writing was a pastime to some and a chore to others, and a frame of mind depending partly on the man's family or social bonds. Soldiers were concerned when previous letters, especially with valuables, were not acknowledged by the recipient's own return letter.

The writer used a pencil, similar to today's, or pen with ink bottle. Lined tablets or bond-like paper were normally available but protected and utilized so sparingly that virtually no margins remained on a sheet. He wrote small, again conserving space, in styles very difficult for us to read, especially if the ink showed through flimsy paper to the other side, which he would write on anyway. Envelopes were normally the size of today's cordial notes. Paper and envelopes were purchased from sutlers, sent from home, or were scraps. Desks, tables, and chairs were for headquarters' use and normally unavailable to the common soldier. He wrote on a hardtack box held on the knees, or "on a tin plate on my knee," or (if "wondering about my penmanship") "on top of a tent 3–4' high that two boys are sitting under," which the writer sits beside—or, while on the ground, or his bunk, or against a tree.[26]

The men used glued postage stamps early in the war, but they became a mess when soaked with rain or perspiration and had to be separated and dried out. Rates were three cents for a letter not exceeding 1–2 ounces, if not going over 3,000 miles in the U.S. Postage stamps were hard to obtain. During their six-month drought without pay in late 1862, men requested stamps from home. "I hate to make more requests but would you please send me some postage stamps?" wrote one broke soldier.[27] Corporal George Donica sent his father "$32 of Uncle sam's greenbacks and you will send me $1 worth of postage stamps, and the rest is yours to do what you want."[28] Sergeant Ellis found it was impossible to get stamps during the Winter 1863 camp. "The preacher nor no one else will not bring any here to sell. I have a great many letters to write," to home and men in other regiments. "Just as soon as this comes to hand if not sooner," send me some more stamps.[29] Eventually the postmaster general allowed soldiers to send letters without prepayment. On the envelope they had to write "Soldier's Letter."

Chaplain Thomas A. Whitted was responsible for regimental mail and was criticized more than praised. Who took over when he resigned in June 1863 is unknown. Mail service was erratic, but occasionally faster than one would expect considering delivery means and difficulties in locating units in the field. The mail in Virginia in 1863 "came regularly."[30] Letters were delivered on New Year's Day, 1862, "some of them nearly eat up with mice."[31]

Single members wrote more than married men. Therefore, more letters to parents survive than those going elsewhere. Men wrote more letters early in their service than toward the end [ergo there was less correspondence during the 1864 Atlanta Campaign]. Some wrote girl friends more than other men did. Recruit Private Vinson Williams told his parents to "Tell Nancy that she needn't be uneasy about him [Hiram, who had been busy] if she don't get any letters from him. Consider when you get a letter from me that you all have got one from me and Hiram both." And he signed it, "Your affectionate son until death."[32] Four months later Williams died of Gettysburg wounds.

For men in the field there were never enough letters or "quality news." Pathetically, Private Lamb, who aptly earned his nickname "Granny Lamb," wrote his wife of one month:

> I have looked for a letter for the last 5 or 6 days but my looking has bin in vain. The mail comes in every night at 8 o'clock. I never go to bed until it is divided. I always wait to get a letter from Mary. You do not know how much good it would do me to get a letter from you. Mary I will wait impatantly until I get a letter from you. I have rote 8 or 9 letters since I got back and have not received one air yet. Rite soon and do not fail.[33]

Three weeks without mail prompted First Lieutenant Hamrick to say, "If you only knew the satisfaction and gratification it was to us [soldiers] you certainly would do better."[34] In what was probably his final letter before dying at Chancellorsville, Hamrick complained to brother Charlie: "Long time since I had any news from home. Lonesome this evening as I sit around the tent tinkering over things. I almost get out of patience. When the mail comes nearly every boy in the company gets a letter but me," giving the impression he had few friends. Surely his six family members were intelligent and capable of writing. "I almost came to the conclusion to be as negligent as you all appear." How shameful they must have felt after he was felled by a cannon ball.[35] Second Lieutenant Thomas W. Casey's sister said, "I wouldn't mind writing long letters if I could make them interesting"—they always seem more lengthy than important. Her Emma said to tell uncle "Tom'ma" she wanted to see him, to answer her letters, and say if he was a Freemason. "She thinks because you are in the army that you belong to everything in the world."[36]

Soldiers could not always match inspiration with the act of writing. "I do not have no chance to rite for when we stop we air so tired we file down in the shaid and go to sleep," Lamb wrote Mary during the Atlanta Campaign, perhaps getting even.[37] Ironically, five days later a gunshot smashed his right hand at New Hope Church, and he lost his index, or writing, finger.

Men of the 27th Indiana felt obligated to help their families, many of whom quickly grew to depend upon receiving a few dollars of their sons' pay each month to supplement their meager income. "I knew Henry Allbright 16 years before he entered the army," wrote Private Leonard Davis about his comrade. "His mother was a widow. He worked for her and supported her and his sister. I messed with Henry and was taken prisoner with him at Winchester. I stayed with him until he died in the Winchester hospital. Just before he died he told me he wanted me to bring his money home to his mother, and I did—about $40."[38]

Civil War Monument,
Daviess County Court House

Daviess County, Washington, Indiana sent Companies B and E to the 27th Indiana.

Photo by author

Allbright died in Winchester, Virginia, June 7, 1862, from a leg wound. The reaction of Davis, soon paroled and discharged for disability, who delivered the money when he returned home, was commonplace. Men going home did that for one another. But Allbright's actions were even more commonplace, because many unmarried men partially or fully supported their parents.

Life expectancy in the mid-nineteenth century was much less than today. Rural Indianians seemed to grow old fast. They labored arduously without adequate health care for debilitating ailments. Consequently, many fathers of the 27th's soldiers were limited or unable to work by what to us is middle age, and therefore depended on others, primarily their children, for livelihood. Daughters did little work outside the home. Sons, even teenagers, had large family responsibilities planting, harvesting, and marketing crops; maintaining acreage, animals, and structures; and frequently toiling for others to add income. With these sons at war, the families often struggled to survive and a soldier's pay became vital sustenance. Having only $13 a month the private soldier had serious decisions to make: how much to send and keep. He had his expenses for sundries and was docked for replacement uniforms and accoutrements, and transportation home if he obtained a furlough. Some owed gambling and loan debts, and nearly everyone owed the regimental sutler.

The year Sergeant Elijah McKnight was killed during the charge at Gettysburg, his parents had no employees on their 100-acre Washington County farm and generated only $250 income. His father had been in "feeble health" for almost 10 years, could not do manual labor, only light farm work. Their land was poor soil and the "outlay for its cultivation nearly exhausted all revenues therefrom." Elijah had managed the farm. Subsequently most income came from Elijah and the other two army sons, Robert M. and James R., of the 16th Indiana Infantry. Elijah had sent money home and also left some personal property with his parents which later was sold to pay family expenses after his death.[39] Before the war Sergeant John Parker Fletcher supported his farm family. Before dying at Gettysburg he sent his money home to a Morgantown man who distributed money for various soldiers as directed. Fletcher's invalid father died in 1862, leaving his mother. Private Samuel Lemming, killed at Antietam, supported his widow mother with her boarding, clothing, and all necessities of life. She was "too old and feeble to labor for herself."[40]

Private George W. Herrendon was the sole support not only of his parents but, after they died of typhoid fever in October 1862, also his younger brothers and sisters, one of whom was only three. Herrendon, wounded before Atlanta, mustered out and headed for home in an ambulance train on September 12, 1864. Five days later he succumbed to the wounds and diarrhea at Marietta, Georgia.

Three of the four Fiddlers of Company D, Lawrence County—Christopher Columbus, John W., and Joseph, Jr.—were brothers. Their father, who lived alone in a log cabin, was opposed to their enlistments because they supported him, particularly Joseph, Jr., "the only help the father had."[41] Antietam killed Joseph three weeks after he mustered in, and wounded Christopher, bringing his discharge. John was later discharged with disability. Another Fiddler, William, who may have been related, lost his arm at Antietam and died three weeks later. Hamrick reminded his father about Uncle Bill Roberts, then suffering for food and clothing, who begged for money or something to eat. "You really ought [not] allow anyone to suffer in that land of plenty, especially an old Hero of 1812, and now the father of three sons in the Union Army. See to this, won't you? Married men often tell me of getting letters from their wives saying they was neglected by their neighbors. Such things ought not to be."[42]

McKnight's situation was typical of a son-parent support relationship. Mrs. Nancy R. McClanahan's was typical of a husband-wife relationship. The widow of Private Robert McClanahan, mortally wounded at Chancellorsville, she wasted little time expressing her need to the Indiana Military Agent at Washington, DC: "I see in the paper you are directed by the Governor to collect and remit money due wives and children of deceased soldiers. I have a case to put in your hands." The mother of two, she felt he had about three months "wages" due, and asked whether she was allowed a pension.[43]

Besides financial aid, the men felt obligated to provide their presence and moral support in crises. Captain John W. Wilcoxen's 20-day leave request in February 1862 stated: "My children have all had measles, three in November and are still sick. My wife who for years has been suffering with a disease not uncommon to her sex, has from constant nursing attention and exertion and extreme anxiety become prostrated on an invalid's couch. My last letter states that she is declining and unless a change takes place soon she cannot recover. My attention as a husband and father is called for." He went.[44] Private Joseph B. Stimson, wounded three times, had not been home. His father and a brother had died meanwhile, and "sister is lying very low. I should have come home immediately if I would see her alive." His request was granted.[45]

In the rush to help soldiers, the plight of wives was often treated lightly. Money and supplies "poured without stint" into the U.S. Sanitary Commission. "The people were delighted to lavish their bounty directly on the soldiers," but an immense amount of heroism among the soldiers' wives "passed unnoticed or was taken as a matter of course."[46] The soldier had his comrades, "excitement" and praise if he did well, or "pitying tears." However, "alas for his wife—what hours of dreadful suspense SHE passed, even under favorable circumstances." She had no friend to say, "well done" in raising her children or tending the farm, or to comfort her while she "stood bravely at her post keeping want and starvation at bay; whose imagination was busy among the heaps of dead and wounded, or traversing the wretched prison pens; who kept down her sobs as her little daughter offered up nightly prayers for 'dear pap to come home!'; or her son traced slowly with his forefinger the long list of killed and wounded 'to see if father's name was there.' This silent army of heroines was too often forgotten. The shouts of far off victories drowned their feeble wailings, and the horrors of hospitals overshadowed deeply their unobtruded miseries."[47]

Sending home money and personal effects became routine business. Private Sylvester Layton wrote his mother in January 1862, "This time we sent $37 to you by Mr. Hunt. I sent 2 little gold dollars to you mother, you must not suffer for anything while you have that money. If you need anything you must not lend all the money. We sent this money to keep you from suffering."[48]

Soldiers used four methods to send home money, gold, or other valuables. Some men stuffed dollar bills into envelopes and mailed them, but this obviously was the least reliable. Private Ferdinand Oestrich sent money with each letter home, which were written in German. Many turned it over to a comrade or civilian going home, which Layton did for his parents, who had to hunt down the recipient on his own time. Officers did this for their men, as Second Lieutenant David Van Buskirk did in December 1861. Some shipped it by express, perhaps the most reliable way. Or, they delivered it in person.

Their earnestness in keeping moral or financial commitments waned, in part because of the manner in which the government failed to pay them. First Lieutenant George Tarvin Chapin, keeping a commitment, when paid in November 1863 mailed $150 home. He wanted his mother to have "at least $50 as the amount to get things that are needful for herself [and] the family." He said to use it all rather than "you should work yourself too hard and that the family should do without."[49]

On what to do with cash, Lieutenant Williams unwittingly spoke for the regiment: "If a man don't send his money home he keeps it safer on his person, for put it in your trunk and if the [wagon] train is cut off everything is destroyed. So nothing is safe in a country where war is waged."[50] Later, distraught over his uncle Lieutenant Reed's death at Cedar Mountain, Williams told his parents to have "Grand Ma write an order authorizing me to draw Uncle Whit's pay. I may need it to procure the money for her."[51] But Williams hesitated to get involved in his men's financial affairs. "I don't think I will trouble myself in sending money home for the boys. I merely have done it to be sure their friends would get it. It has been a source of trouble to me each time."[52]

Early on one member chose against sending money home. "I find it is the best friends one can have with him."[53] Changing his mind, he wrote his father in June 1862 inquiring whether the $75 he sent in April was received. "I feel anxious about it. I am uneasy. You are rather careless about writing."[54] One soldier suggested his father take $40 in gold and $5 in paper and pay his taxes. Jasper citizens rejoiced in December 1861 when their Company K men sent home $800, and by February 1862 the regiment had sent home over $30,000.

Governor Oliver P. Morton's military agents also assisted. Agent B. F. Tuttle received a $2,444.50 package of money from the 27th at Winchester for express forwarding home. In April 1863, Morton established a state allotments commissioner to develop and oversee a process of rolls and checks. The commissioner later reported it was working "highly satisfactorily to all parties, except the sutlers, who complain that it leaves the soldiers with too little funds for a healthy financial operation in the field. Every [participating] soldier transmits his money from his tent to his family for 25 cents, and runs no risk of loss by capture of robbery." In January 1864 he said, "It took me several months to get the soldiers—and especially the paymasters—to get the hang of the system."[55] The government sent an allotment check to someone designated by the soldier to receive it; at payday he would get cash for the balance only. The innovative administrative measure, used within the 27th, was quite ahead of its time. However, money was not sent to a bank by either soldier or government as an allotment would be today.

The money flow often was reversed. Officers paid for their own rations (meals), uniforms, and other accoutrements. A field promotion from enlisted, as many were, caught Lieutenant Hamrick in December 1862 when the government had not paid them for five months. He borrowed from any comrade with funds, then requested his father express $50 to him in Maryland. He could probably get along, but "nearly every officer is short and it is hard to borrow here." Three weeks later he wrote, "The government is treating us shamefully in not paying us. Exceedingly embarrassing on us newly commissioned ones [regarding] substenance. Send money in a letter: even $10 would keep me off starvation for a while." His father delayed and Hamrick requests became desperate until he got $10 in January—when they were finally paid.[56]

When a man died his personal effects, or belongings, were collected, if possible, and sent to the family. Sometimes he was buried near the battlefield with his personal effects when permitted only a quick interment. Private Ira Hunt, mortally wounded at Gettysburg, died in York, Pennsylvania. His effects, 14 postage stamps, one pocket book, one ring and one knife, were delivered to his guardian, Caleb Hunt. Like many other men of the 27th, Ira claimed he was 18 when most likely he was younger. Private Thomas Hall, also mortally wounded at Gettysburg, was buried on the field with his effects still on his body. Fifteen months after Private James R. Gillaspy's death from Antietam wounds, widow Charlotte wrote for his belongings and $2 he never sent her, plus the surgeon's name. The effects, a blouse, pair of socks, ring, breast pin, and sundries (and the $2) were sent to her by Adams Express in March 1864. Sometimes the value of personal effects was questionable. Captain John W. Wilcoxen notified the widow of Private Earl Moore's death: "He left a money purse and a pocketbook but no money in them. They are considerably worn, not hardly worth expressing to you, but if you desire them I will do so."[57] That may help account for the sparse existing 27th Indiana memorabilia.

Thinking the war would be over soon, throughout 1861 and into 1862 the soldiers found it difficult to relinquish their business connections at home. Typical of attempts to manage details was a letter from Private Vinson Williams. "You can now do what you please with my wheat and corn and pay for all of the work that you have to hire and pay for the thrashing of it. Father, I want you to do the best you can until I get back and then I will try and help you some more."[58] Williams sustained interest in activities at home. A month later he asked his parents how they were working his horse "Bill," said to "take good care of him," and to sow him about five acres of wheat.[59]

Attention to personal affairs, business or otherwise, declined after the first six months. Realization the war was dragging on, difficulty in getting furloughs, and the new planting season, diminished their enthusiasm, if not their concern. After arriving in Maryland in 1861, farmers in the 27th continued farming. "Have you got the barn on my place planked in yet?" wrote Lieutenant Williams in October. "It ought to be for stock this winter and things off the meadow if not already. Have Dave got the corner finished? Tell him he must finish it while the brush can be grubbed and burned. If the boys don't seem inclined to work out that note tell them I will take it out in lumber or anything to be traded."[60]

Lieutenant Williams was a more persevering businessman than most. Later he wrote, "Speaking of swapping horses with Denny. Reminds me—did you receive pay of his $75 note for Frank's horse due last Christmas?

Please inform me how my affairs stand at present."[61] Regarding his parents' investments, he wrote, "I see no advantage in investing in 5/20 bonds. U.S. bonds are perfectly safe of course." He said to postpone deciding until he got there.[62]

Private John S. Hackler was concerned over his animals before leaving Indiana, asking his parents to care for his mare's new colt and "put fly to the horse this fall and next spring."[63] Before he died of measles in December 1861, he told them to sell his hogs when they finished fattening them. "Use the money to pay off your debts and everything that I had left there you can sell to help you. Only my horses—don't want you to let go unless you get well paid for them." If William Henry takes care of the colt "he may ride it a sparking. I still think that I will live to get home to see you all one time more. I think I will be there in time to help the boys put in a crop."[64]

The word "boxes" was the name given presents sent from home through the mail or express service and contained anything the sender wished, usually clothing and food. Receiving boxes was either the next best thing to going home or wasted expectations, depending on contents or condition. They were more popular in the beginning until handlers figured out ways to usurp them.

Sergeant Ellis received lots of letters and a box of socks. He asked for no more socks, "for to send them by mail you would have to pay the price of the socks almost to send by express. I might not be able to get over to the express office. I have two pairs I have never wore and if I knead any more I can buy them."[65] Ellis' family thought he needed socks but failed to please. However, most recipients reacted like this: "Received box yesterday containing shirts, socks, gloves, butter, apple butter, for which I am very grateful."[66]

Christmas was special. "I want to pay you a visit this winter," an officer wrote in 1862, "but furloughs are few and far between. So if you have any Christmas box or any idea of sending articles this way I could get it by directing to me via Hagerstown, Maryland. I am not suffering for one but would be nice to have. The little delicacies are quite palatable," and dried and canned fruits and maple molasses "are ahead of pies and cakes alone, which are perishable." He wanted his fur gloves "if Pa don't use them," wool socks, and white shirts.[67] Lieutenant Casey's mother wrote, "Let me know if your box of provisions kept good until you eat it. If [the pickles] kept I will send you more in the next box."[68] Lieutenant Williams was pleased with the "nice Hoosier supper we had of the good things that are in those friendly boxes from the goodly land of Hoosier."[69]

The same address was used for boxes as mail. For example:

Pvt. James Coats

Co. B, 27th Indiana Vol. Inf. Regt.

3rd Brigade, 1st Division, 12th Corps

Army of the Potomac

Fairfax, Virginia (Care Capt. John W. Thornburgh)

A box likely would arrive as fast with "Washington, DC" as Fairfax, Virginia, or any other Eastern address. Boxes arrived in company wagons. None were sent to the company when on the move or a campaign was imminent. Every space inside was filled with apples and dried apples, peanuts, potatoes, other edibles, bandages, lint, and "notes of good wishes." The Adams Express Company monopolized the shipping business, sometimes providing timely, efficient service. It took a long time for boxes to reach the men, as much as five months, spoiling goods because of storage time. Boxes were stolen or looted. Often all the recipient got on opening was broken jars and near-petrified goodies crawling with intruders. Corporal Michael Henry Van Buskirk said his arrived "after being on the roads for upwards for a month. Apples rotten, pies, cakes and boots moldy. Threw away the pies and cakes and put the boots on."[70] Boxes arrived as late as December 1863. "Everything that you sent in the box came through safe," Private Edwards wrote. "Only the can held the blackberry jam the lid came off of it and some of it spilt out. If you sent any tobacco it did not come. I got one pair of socks and them gloves they are so small I cant were them, they are nice ones."[71]

Lieutenant Reed asked his hometown newspaper in December 1861 to thank the people of Putnamville for the box of "shirts, shorts, socks, mittens, gloves, blankets, and other little notions of good things such as none but Hoosiers know how to get up. P.S. Colonel Colgrove adds his compliments to Mrs. W. B. Williams for a batch of Siberian crab apple jelly."[72] That winter men exchanged more mail and received more boxes than at any other time. The patriotism of friends and families, at least as expressed toward their men, inspired them to act out of pride, later out of obligation or loyalty, and ultimately out of guilt. A few men sent home items. One sent his mother a Bible as a birthday gift, his father a linen coat, his brother a jacket, and the children a tent. An earlier box arrived damaged without mention of the contents except the "secesh pistol." "So I don't know if you received my revolver."[73]

Families and friends continued commitment and care for their men throughout the war, somewhat easier when they were in the Eastern Theater than the Western, particularly regarding visits. Families also continued to seek help from and on behalf of their men. "I suppose you have been in a severe battle which makes me more than anxious to hear from you," wrote the sister of Lieutenant Casey in June 1862. "Thomas, it makes me shudder to think of the dangers you have been [in] and still are exposed to. I pray God who is mighty and able to do all things, to shield you from death, wounds and sickness, and to protect you from dangers of all kinds and grant you a safe return to your friends."[74]

Casey's Raglesville family was so committed to his welfare they freely invoked the Lord's help in guiding his footsteps.* His parents wrote, "My son I commend you to the care of our heavenly father praying Him to preserve you

Co. B. 27
:Captain:
Jackson L. Moore
:Lieutenants:
William F. Davis
John W. Thornburg
:Sergeants:
Thomas W. Casey
Jacob Ragle
William Hubbard
John G. Little
Ira Broshears
:Corporals:
Peter Ragle
Elisha Guthrie
Silas Wagoner
Michael Wallick
William J. Wilson
Lewis Ketcham
John Russell
:Privates:
Duncan Achor
Joseph Achor
Milton L. Allen
Thomas Anderson
Daniel Arford
William Arford
Anthony Berger
Stever Boardman
Thomas Bowers
Willis Hubbard
Hiram Hulan
Andrew J. Keller
Michael Keller
Charles W. Correll
Hiram Kinnaman
Andrew J. Williams
Vinson Williams
Abner Wilson
Joseph B. Wilson
Charley Combs
Harvey N. Correll
William Cox
George M. Critchlow
George E. Davis
Charles Lutz
William B. Matthews
James P. Denton
William McMullen

Civil War Monument, Raglesville
Lions Clubhouse

Wall commemorating 27th Indiana's Company B members from Daviess County.

Photo by author

and keep you safe from all harm and return you sound and well to your home and your friends."[75] His mother, Dicey, continued worrying, writing in January 1864, "You have the earnest prayers of your old mother and father at home,"[76] and in May 1864, "I want you to write the first chance after a battle for I always feel anxious until I hear from you."[77]

Occasionally wives or families visited the regiment in camp, guaranteed to uplift the men. In October 1862, Colonel Colgrove's wife was in

---

* Quaint Raglesville remains a farm hamlet reachable only by dusty, marginal, narrow roads. The general store closed years ago and the lone public telephone is used by the Amish townfolk, facing their horse-drawn buggies to a pole while they talk. The tiny village park where Company B formed under spreading elms and marched away in August 1861 still serves, and the same elms spread their shade. An interior wall of the park's Lions clubhouse displays the names of every member. Six of those who returned lie in the cemetery, including Casey, a significant number for the size of the place.

Lions Park, Raglesville

In August 1861, Company B of the 27th Indiana formed here and marched off to Indianapolis.

Photo by author

camp a few days, and Captain John Roush Fesler's wife had just arrived. "It looks like home, makes things cheerful and one almost wish he had a wife," bemused one lieutenant.[78] Three women related to Company E members remained with the company for several months. The colonel's son, Lafayette, visited the Regiment our leader in him."[79] Mr. A. M. Kern visited his sons, Second Lieutenant James M. Kern and Corporal Samuel F. Kern, in January 1862, unaware they would be discharged in one month for ill health. Andrew Mehringer, brother of Major John and First Sergeant Joseph, took Joseph home from camp after his discharge in November 1861 of pulmonary consumption. He died within 11 months.

Indicative of family ties, Mr. William Dinsian wrote a relative regarding Private Benjamin Franklin Landes after Antietam. "We have not heard from Frank for several weeks, but an old lady from Greencastle got a letter from her son yesterday. He saw Frank come out safe. There is nearly all of my acquaintances are wounded save that regiment. Poor Frank has fought through two of the bloodiest battles of this war and has never got hurt any, but oh how I dread to think he must get into it again. All we can do is trust that will come out safe in the end."[80] Landes did just that. He was one of a few present at every muster and apparently was not seriously injured or sick.

People were not shy to seek help for their loved ones. Mr. G. H. Voss of Greencastle wrote Morton about Private George W. Allen, hospitalized in Georgetown, D.C., for four months. He "will soon die if not discharged. I fear he will not last long. His parents are much distressed about him. He is a good boy and having lived long with me I feel a deep interest in him."[81] Perhaps this helped. He was discharged in December 1862 because of phthisis.

Morton, called "The Soldiers' Friend," assisted citizens seeking relief for their men. Political ties helped. Mr. J. S. Smith Hunter of Bloomington asked Morton for a furlough for Private Henry Clay Gabbert, son of Michael Gabbert, Esq. (the Union candidate for sheriff in the late election). Henry was wounded at Winchester, where he narrowly escaped capture, and Antietam, after spending the first winter hospitalized with measles. But, he refused a discharge. Hunter insisted, the colonel "will not suffer him and others" to go to the hospital. "He will not survive until spring."[82] Whom shall Morton please?

Indiana Governor Oliver P. Morton

Monument at Morton's burial site, Crown Hill Cemetery, Indianapolis. He supported Lincoln and the war effort.

Photo by author

Voss' and Hunter's letters were typical of those seeking help through sympathy, exaggeration or implications. And they were men. Mothers and wives rarely wrote—"a woman's place" was being inconspicuous. Based on postwar documents signed with their "X," women appeared less literate than their men. Often third parties wrote for the immediate family. Once an army surgeon wrote to the Secretary of War requesting a furlough for Corporal Christopher C. Showalter, convalescing at Harrisburg, Pennsylvania, under his care after an Antietam wound. He cited ill health of Showalter's mother, whom he supported at $5 per month. Divorced in 1861, and with only $100 worth of property, she was poor. The furlough was granted.

When Showalter was mortally wounded at Gettysburg he left $410 to his mother, brother, and sister.

Relatives and friends often asked that wounded men be sent to hospitals nearer home. Edinburg citizens petitioned Morton to have local wounded Private Allen Oaks sent to near Indianapolis "to be with friends and home until able to return to regiment." He was willing to transfer at his own expense. Later the citizens also requested a similar transfer for Corporal William J. Wells.[83] Wells, at York, Pennsylvania, was working on his own behalf. "I have been absent from home for 23 months. I have a wife and one child and would like to see them. There is no furloughs granted here but some is getting transferred to their regiment's states," he wrote the Indiana Military Agent.[84] For these efforts, Oaks was sent to Alexandria and then into the Veterans Reserve Corps, and Wells was transferred to a convalescent hospital in Baltimore, Maryland, before returning.

Private George East, also in York, shared Wells' predicament. He wrote the agent about discrimination against Indiana soldiers, with "no right to enjoy the privileges that have been granted soldiers from other states. I can't tell you whose fault it is; it may be because we Hoosiers have never done anything to entitle us to any favors, or because we have no one to see after us." He struggled to get transferred or a furlough home. "I am willing to do all I can for my country but I think it is poor encouragement to us Indiana boys in the eastern army. (P.S.—I can furnish a good recommendation from my company commander if required.)"[85] East followed Wells to Baltimore but ended up closer home at Covington, Kentucky. New York City's Fort Schuyler hospital was different. Private James O. Laughlin's June 15, 1863, letter, typical of a borderline literate (if indeed he wrote it), hit a responsive eye. "I have been a pacient in this hospittle to nex too months. My friends are ancious for me to come home as they have ben nerly all sick with the meezels & dipthery & I would be verry glad to have the liberty of seeing them." He got 20 days.[86]

Men died in battle or in sickness, and families had to be informed. The task was never pleasant, but by 1863, having been through so much horror, survivors found the words came easier. In April 1863, Company D commander Captain Cassady wrote, "With feelings of sorrow the sad intelligence of the death of your son, Wesley Slider, who died April 3, 1863. We are all sympathizing with you and your family in losing one who was only known to be loved by all his companions. His place cannot be filled in our memory. Accept the heartfelt sorrow of all his associates and the assurance he was a true soldier and supporter of his country and her cause. The God of Battles has called him from the scene of trouble to that happy abode where we one day expect to meet him and enjoy that eternal crown prepared for us all."[87]

Still then, Cassady's awkward, almost platitudinous letter showed the difficulties in conveying the bad news. Information normally came from a company officer who wrote as soon as possible. If the regiment was on the move, word might reach home first through newspaper accounts of a battle, from hospital visitors, or from other soldiers. Mail was normally used instead of telegrams. Some parents went to the front or hospitals to return their son's body to his native soil, as Private John N. Jones' father did after he died of Cedar Mountain wounds. A number of bodies eventually were reinterred in Indiana.

Private Hackler's death from typhoid, one of the earliest in Maryland in 1861, was tough for Captain Jackson L. Moore to tell the family. Moore admitted, "It is hard news to send home while it is a hard task for me to convey such intelligence. John's death has cast a gloom over the company. A nurse at the hospital said he prayed one of the ablest of prayers before he died."[88] Moore asked John's parents be told for he would not write them. Captain Richmond M. Welman explained to Mrs. Margaret Cooper the administrative and medical details of her son Private James' 1862 death from measles. "I never saw you that I remember of but let me offer you my sympathies and give you a few words of great consolation," he began, and rolled from there.[89] The death of Sergeant Benjamin F. Crose en route home after his discharge was announced in the Indianapolis *Journal:*

An Unknown Deceased Soldier

Mr. Editor:—I received this morning the remains of Benjamin F. Crose, a soldier. According to the best information he belongs at Cloverdale, Putnam County. I placed him in charge of Weaver and Williams. There was about $100 in his possession.

/s/ *Frank Wilcox, Provost Marshal* [90]

Quartermaster Sergeant John A. Crose then learned of his brother's death in a letter from home. The circumstances led him to ask the Indiana Military Agent to investigate, including the state of his heart when he died.

Captain Wilcoxen, informing Mrs. Moore of her husband Earl's death, sounded apologetic: "It is with deep regret that I have to announce to you the death of your husband who died January 14, 1863. He had been complaining for a few days previous to his being taken down bad sick, and I thought it nothing dangerous until he was so seriously ill that I had him taken to the hospital immediately. He lived until the next night at 3 o'clock when he died [of heart disease]. I had him decently buried and with honors of war."[91]

Battlefield news was often jumbled. Friend Abraham Landes of Manhattan wrote Washington one month after Chancellorsville seeking clarification about Corporal William Orlando Kenyon. Originally thought killed, Kenyon was subsequently reported severely wounded. "The members of his company from this neighborhood know nothing of him as they were separated from him at the time of battle, and they left him on the field supposing him dead." His father and friends were "very anxious to learn something...where he is, nature of wounds, and probable results, whether or not he will recover." Kenyon had been killed in action, but official notification had not reached the family.[92]

The family of Lieutenant Hamrick heard of his death at Chancellorsville in a convoluted manner. Captain Williams' father wrote from Georgetown, D.C.:

> Having received a telegraphic dispatch that my son was wounded in the late engagement on the Rappahannock I lost no time in striking a bee line for his bedside. The dispatch also stated Lieutenant Hamrick was killed. This turned out to be a blunder among the telegraphic operators somewhere—Lieutenant Hamrick being the gentleman referred to, my son faking this early and quick way of announcing to the lieutenant's relatives, whom he highly respects, the sad fate of one very near and dear to them.[93]

Mr. Williams was in the military agent's office when the Governor telegraphed for Hamrick's remains to be sent home, and presumed Hamrick "was cut in two by a shell and was probably in possession of the rebels," and speculated that Lieutenant Reed, killed at Cedar Mountain, was "robbed and his resting place unknown. He could not have suffered long. While thousands of his comrades remain on their humble cots or bedsteads in all shapes of mutilation to suffer, and many to die after long sieges of pain and misery, he has escaped and been saved much suffering. The tears of affection will bedew his memory."[94]

Messrs. Landes and Williams were not alone inquiring or sharing information. Mr. Philip Jones wrote Monfort three weeks after Gettysburg about son Private Andrew: "It would be quite a relief to a kind father and mother if you could give us that information [location] and under what conditions he is, whether dangerous or not. Please forward the enclosed letter to him."[95] He was in four hospitals before returning to duty in November.

Bad news went both ways and frequently had nothing to do with the war. Family members died, farmhouses burned down, neighbors voted for "traitors," business endeavors foundered. Colonel Silas Colgrove tried to maintain control of his pre-war business from afar and returned to Indiana more often than most anyone else in the regiment, not always to rest. In January 1862, he was required in a court suit regarding the title to valuable real estate. His absence would place him in danger of a heavy financial loss. Quartermaster James M. Jameson needed 20 days in 1863 to clean up business matters resulting from his partner's death. Captain William H. Holloway needed leave for family business matters in December 1863 when his father died, leaving his mother and sister alone. He had not been absent from his company 12 hours before that.

Lieutenant Casey's sister circumspectly reacted to another sister's passing: "Thomas, I can't describe my feelings when I read of sister Sarah's death. Now I know it pains the heart to hear of a sister's death. I had never heard it until I got your letter. I know that father will take her death hard, but death is what we must expect sooner or later and the great object is in being prepared." She gladly corrected Casey: "I am happy to inform you that my husband is still alive. It was his brother's death you heard of. There has been a great deal of sickness through the past winter and more deaths than I ever knew in my life."[96] Surgeon Jarvis J. Johnson's wife casually reported, "Baby died of membraneous croup, Sallie improving from pneumonia, Marietta and Goldsmith well."[97]

Private John Parham wrote a friend, "Read yours of February 1st [1863], I found you & the children all sick, so it gave me much uneasiness. My mind has been pestered ever since so that I can't enjoy myself as I should."[98] He later consoled his sister Henrity, but also waxed patriotic, which may have been more than she wanted at the time:

> I was sorry to hear that you had lost one of your children. It is better for child to die at home than it is for a man to die at war, so you can see your child is clear of all the danger. It would have been better for me and many others if we had a died when we was young than we would have been saved sure. I must stand before the mighty army and face the big guns and probably die before I get there.[99]

Private Henry Bacon Thomas learned "the sad news that another one of our family was gone to the spirit land. It was not an unexpected event to me but it does give me much sorrow to hear of his death."[100] Corporal Van Buskirk noted the day after Peachtree Creek, "This evening I received a letter from home announcing the sad news of the death of my father."[101] Sergeant Ellis simply told his father, "I received your letter stating the death of brother John." That was the extent of it.[102] Private Daniel B. Williams said of brother Private Adam's death, "It seems so hard to lose a brother that has always treated us so kindly but it cannot be helped. Death is a debt we all have to pay."[103]

Bad news sometimes came from a soldier's comrade. "We have a heap of men sick in our regiment," said Private Thomas W. David in explaining Private George Cain's death. "He had the measles and ketch cold. He was sick about 3 weeks. He died in Frederick City. He was well taken care of while he was with us. We were sorrowed when we had to give him up." More sad news followed. "John Peterson [Patterson] and John Leister is very low. Don't think they will ever get well but while there is life there is hope."[104] Patterson was discharged but Leister died January 4, 1862, from typhoid. Sickness was a condition people of the Civil War era anticipated and coped with, and without the type of medicine and medical care we expect today, early death or disability was commonly accepted as an ordeal of life.

Notification of death could be compelling:

May 21, 1864, Cassville, Georga. To Sarah Edwards. My dear friend. I have soroful news to right to you. We was in a batle on the fiftinst and Gorg was killed. He was hit under the left eye and come out of the back of his head. He lived about two hours. Tho he noed nothing nor he could not speak of it. Gorg was a good boy and died a solder and a christian. And may the Lorde help you to live so you may meat him in heaven. Tell Margret if you sea hur that I am well. I remain your friend as ever, Benjamin Arthur.[105]

Private George Edwards died the sixteenth of wounds at Resaca after nearly three years in uniform. Margret [Margaret] was Private Arthur's wife. Edwards's final letter read, "Now my dear, I enlisted against your wishes before and I will not [reenlist] this time. Oh if this war was over so that i could come home and be with you and the children. When this you see remember me. Your true friend and husband. So farewell for this time but hope no [sic] forever."[106]

CHAPTER 7

God and Good Boys:
Religion and Morals

Notwithstanding the prevalent opinion that the soldiers are decidedly irreligious under the influences at work in the armies in the field, no class of men show more genuine piety than our American soldiers. The din and bustle of camps are not the most favorable for religious meditation. Nor are the one thousand temptations which beset the soldier in the camp likely to elevate his standards of morality. The sentinel on his lonely beat has ample time for meditation. *—Indiana version of army religion, 1864* [1]

Religious beliefs of members of the 27th Indiana were very personal and never institutionalized. Individuals found great strength in their religious upbringing and in the mores of Indiana society, and the large majority tried to live accordingly. Small groups met in fellowship in their camps, and men attended organized services whenever possible. However, while their commander, Colonel Silas Colgrove, made no serious effort to promote or encourage religious practices, he did not dissuade those who would. Colgrove kept his personal life to himself and allowed others to do likewise.

Early in the war religion became a Union political and military creed. "Ours is a Christian Nation," said the Union Army commander, "and this is a Christian war, and we must fight it out on Christian principles."[2] President Abraham Lincoln directed the army not to perform special activities on Sunday when they could be postponed. "Our side observed this," said a Hoosier, but with the enemy, "if he was inactive all week not so on Sunday."[3] Both the Federals and Confederates claimed God was on their side and would wing them to victory, either on the field or at the war's finality. Confederate General Stonewall Jackson, firmly believing his side was morally correct, was the classic example of a leader who beseeched the union of God and victory. The Federals had no such religious icon, but no doubt their military leaders communed with God for guidance. Colgrove and his senior officers left no such imprint, and Colgrove attended church at least once.

Protestants, particularly Methodist Episcopalians, predominated among the 27th's members. Most early Hoosiers had been Methodists, Presbyterians, and Baptists, and after 1840 the Christians (Disciples of Christ) competed with the larger denominations. Catholics were strong in certain areas of Indiana such as Dubois County, reflected in the composition of Company K. No members are known to have been Quaker or Amish, two visible Indiana faiths, Jews or atheists.

God found His way into official business in ceremonies and other events, often tied to patriotism. After a review by Major General John Pope in early August 1862 the men listened to "a couple of chaplains who made prayers and remarks concerning the country."[4] No special blessings were given before entering battle, but the men freely recited poems of this nature:

I am no saint,

But, boys, say a prayer. There's one that begins

"Our father," and then says, "Forgive us our sins,"

Don't forget that part; say that strongly, and then

I'll try and repeat it, and you'll say Amen!

Ah, I'm no saint[5]

Religion was accorded an obvious role in military funerals:

Away from the battlefield: A suitable escort (for a private, eight rank and file, properly commanded) is formed in two ranks opposite to the tent of the deceased with shouldered arms. The procession then forms on each side of the coffin being three bearers, without arms, immediately preceding are the eight soldiers with arms reversed. In front is the dirge music, no sadder sounds ever fell upon my ear, as they proceed to the place of burial. With slow and measured step and muffled drum they move. At the grave the coffin is placed on one side, the soldiers resting on their arms, the muzzle on the foot. The chaplain who has walked to the rear of the coffin, conducts the service: earth to earth, ashes to ashes, dust to dust. Three volleys are fired over grave and the last kindness to the comrade is over.[6]

And on the battlefield:

The grave was six feet long and 40' wide. We laid in it, side by side, with blankets for winding sheets, the forms of those who had just died for their country. We tenderly dropped evergreen branches on the sleeping patriots to break the fall of the clods, and in token that their sacrifice should ever be green in our memories. We stood with heads uncovered while the Captains of the regiments cast the first earth, and while the chaplain prayed that the sad tidings mightt not break the hearts of the widows and the orphans. The sinking sun closed the mournful day.[7]

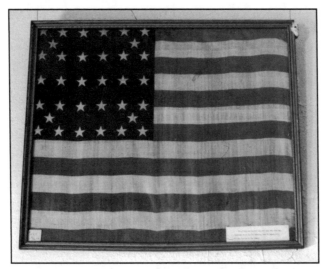

Flag Carried by Company E, 27th Indiana
Daviess County Museum, Washington, Indiana

The 27th's only chaplain was Reverend Thomas A. Whitted, a Morgan County Methodist Episcopal pastor. A frequent complainer, Whitted, 45, was best remembered for running the regimental post office and his chewing problems. His service with the mail was as roundly criticized as his ministering, and he had limited influence on the regiment's moral and religious activities. Of medium stature with a square, stout build, like all army chaplains he held a commission and wore both a uniform and civilian attire. He had no or very few teeth, was unable to masticate, and primarily ate soft food. During battle he remained in the rear near the medical facilities. He resigned on June 4, 1863, because of chronic hepatitis and died in 1871.

Whitted's comrades formed early opinions of him. In the Winter 1861: "Our old chaplain is our mail carrier. It's about all we use him for as Colonel Colgrove thinks the regiment doesn't need any preaching to at present. The chaplain hasn't addressed us but twice."[8] Eleven months later the observer called Whitted "a cleer old fellow, a Methodist."[9] In November 1861 Sergeant George Tarvin Chapin wrote, "I do not wish to complain much of our chaplain but I do wish we had a better one. He is regarded by some of the boys as a nuisance. He does very little except bring the mail to camp."[10] Private Michael Henry Van Buskirk noted the "old chaplain" preached sermons after Sunday inspection in the spring 1863. Once the chaplain left, the men attended meetings of the 107th New York.[11]

The regiment had at least three other ministers; two are named. They were Sergeant Ira Brashears, who after being discharged with an amputated right arm from a wound at Chancellorsville, tried unsuccessfully to re-enter the service as a chaplain; and Second Lieutenant Daniel R. Conrad, who died February 13, 1862, of typhoid pneumonia. The other was an unknown company captain, who once preached in Maryland while accompanied by Quartermaster Sergeant John A. Crose.

A number of men attended services, meetings or "singings" when possible. Private Thomas Deputy felt the need for spiritual uplifting in Tullahoma, Tennessee, where the 27th was stationed on garrison duty guarding the railroad for seven months in 1863–64. "I am at singing school tonight. There is a Christian Commission established here for the soldiers. They have meetings here about three times a week, all the religious books and papers that we can read and Sabbath school. We have one of the best meetings I was ever at, singing twice a week, a room and writing table. I do not think a young man that is this poor can ever start in Indiana."[12]

Collectively the men showed more interest in religion during their duty in Tullahoma than at any other time. In January 1864, Corporal Michael Henry Van Buskirk wrote of back-to-back nights of prayer meetings, singing, and "a crowded house," and "everything passed out pleasantly." Days later "one man confessed his sins." On other Sunday nights Van Buskirk and friends gathered in their lieutenant's tent to sing, and attended a "Negro meeting at Mr. Armstrong's, or rather a negro preacher congregation considerably mixed."[13] Except for the Company K Germans, members sang little on their own, but during religious services everyone always sang.

Chaplain Whitted delivered the regiment's first sermon on a Sunday after arrival in Washington, D.C., in September 1861, one of the few times the entire regiment attended divine services willingly. After morning inspection they were marched to a "pleasant spot" where he preached from the text, "Behold an Israelite indeed in whom there is no guile—John 1:47." A regular Sunday pattern was established, and when in camp they were marched without arms to services after inspection, or just dismissed.[14] Sundays were not always considered days off. The regiment held morning inspections when possible in camp. As the men matured, Sundays became less official work days, and more leisure time was granted. Three of their major battles were fought on Sundays: Winchester, Chancellorsville, and Resaca, each initiated by the enemy.

One Sunday in the summer of 1862 in Culpeper Court House, Virginia, several men attended the Episcopal church. A sergeant wrote, "The imposing ceremonies made us feel solemn until the minister, Rev. Mr. Cole, offered up a petition for the establishment of the Southern Confederacy, which effectively disturbed our devotions." Colgrove, serving as the military governor of Culpeper County, attended. To that point he had largely ignored the prayers. After that service he could think of little else, becoming "sort of an ecclesiastic," and believed he could improve the litany of that church. Cole later was taken into custody "and put a stop to his treasonable teachings by closing the doors of St. Stephens."[15]

The regular Thanksgiving Day in 1862 "went off quite agreeably" with prayers, a discourse by the chaplain, and a turkey dinner.[16] The government tried to organize at least one religious event, a fast. National Thanksgiving Day, August 6, 1863, a day President Abraham Lincoln proclaimed for "thanksgiving of praise and prayers for recent victories at Vicksburg and Gettysburg," was a kind of free-for-all along the Rappahannock River. The 27th's division commander saw a regiment having a service toward evening. "I heard a man holding forth in regular Methodistical roar, and psalm singing and hallooing prayers. There was a considerable confusion of tongues, for the adjoining regiments were singing patriotic songs with uproarious choruses, and the drums of other regiments were beating the adjutant's call for dress parade."[17] A Hoosier private added a postscript to that day of fasting: "We are doing the fasting part as we are out of rations."[18]

Deaths brought the living closer together in God, a bonding noted in a January 1862 letter from Captain Richmond M. Welman to Mrs. Margaret Cooper regarding the death of her son, Private John A. Cooper.

> Your son was a good boy, a good soldier and out of about 60 that have died in our regiment he was the second one that ever manifested any wishes or desires to get to the better world. His death was a clear Christian triumph. The hospital doctor is a very wicked or swearing man (but kind hearted). He acknowledges that he never saw a more lively hope manifested or stronger evidence of true Christianity. I think it must be a great consolation especially to a mother to know or believe that her son died in the triumph of a living faith. I did not get his last words as I could not be there all the time.[19]

The regiment's first winter in Maryland in 1861–62 presented many such occasions when almost 40 died of disease and sickness. Letters home such as Welman's reflected a genuine concern the soldiers had for each other.

Civil War morals, even to the level of the common soldier, were strongly influenced by the Victorian Age code of prudishness, respectability and bigotry. The tendency of an Indiana soldier, raised rough around the edges but knowing right from wrong, was to acquiesce innocently to the Victorian influence. As a guiding light he knew little else. In reality his compliance could be convenient, for, away from home, when tempted to break the code, he did it. Some felt guilt, others not. But he might go to lengths to disguise or hide his transgressions, particularly from the folks back home. The code was severely tested when alcohol was available, games of chance were at hand, or the company of women beckoned.

The Hoosiers cursed regularly. Colgrove was notorious for his foul language, whether prodding mules or swearing at another regiment's mistakes under fire. Their vulgarity included a number of today's expressions and four letter words, such as shit and fuck, sometimes used in slang or epithets whose translations are archaic. Because of the soldiers' prudish veneer their manuscripts contained little outright spicy language. When it did it was lightly veiled: "D..n you!" or, "F... that general." During the Winchester retreat, Colgrove halted the regiment outside of town. Major General Nathaniel Prentiss Banks was rallying his force for a stand. Banks ordered Colgrove to continue. For the first time that day Colgrove was allowed to mount his horse. "As the colonel vaulted into the saddle he used some very strong words, not learned in Sunday school, and asserted that if any man ever got him off his horse again at such a time, he would have to shoot him off."[20]

The men made few references to the Bible by chapter and verse or as tools in services. No one is known to have carried a Bible. Private Lewis King, a postwar minister, carried an 1849 pocket booklet called *Rules for Holy Living; with Questions for Self Examination*.[21] Religious tracts circulated among the soldiers, many from the U.S. Christian Commission which visited camps. Men read them but they were no substitute for hard news. Corporal Daniel B. Williams praised those who sent tracts:

> You have no idea how much the Christian soldiers of this regiment are elated and pleased. After the members of the company have read it to others they come to me every few days. We get but very few religious papers and books to read, it affords us great pleasure. I should like to have a copy every week. We need such reading in camp. It shows you have an interest in our welfare and destination.[22]

One of the most religious members, Second Lieutenant Meredith W. Leach, was suddenly taken ill on the way to church a few days before Christmas, 1861, near Frederick, Maryland, and died shortly thereafter. "He was a very brave and patriotic man and greatly loved by the soldier boys, lived a pious and devoted life, very punctual in religious duties, devoted Christian."[23] The men mourned Leach. When he was buried in Bedford with honors, "the tears shed over his grave were among the first of the many that watered the earth during that terrible struggle for the suppression of the rebellion."[24] No one stepped forward as a spiritual lay leader after that.

In those stressful times, men of the 27th Indiana sought from their deity solace and protection. Some implored the Holy Spirit in letters and diaries, indicating at least temporary expedience with faith and trust, if not permanent. Private George Edwards was more religious and meaningful than most.

> This it seems to me to almost a world of chance. But yet I am certain that there is a God that rules all things as he sees fit and if I know anything of myself I feel thankful he has been as good and merciful to me as he has. Oh he is so good to us in sparing our lives and permitting us to live that we ought to praise his holy name and obey his great and mighty commands. I want you to prepare to live for Christ and pray for me that I may live faithful. [25]

Like Edwards, many made references before and after battles, as if the writer needed the reader as a conduit to God. Private John Parham wrote to friends the day before New Hope Church, "I can only look to God for my safety. I believed when I went into the other fight [Resaca] He would be with me."[26] Parham's faith worked; he lived until 1894, but Edwards' did not.

A joyous Private Clemens Johnson began a letter to his parents in March 1862, before the Hoosiers had smelled gunpowder, with the greeting, "I am well and hearty & do truly hope that you enjoy the same great blessing of God." Later he added, after projecting the "rebels are about whipped out," the men would be home in a few months "if we live. I trust to the good Lord that it may be the case. I long to see the time when we can all lie at home together again and be surrounded with peace and harmony instead of being separated as we are and our land filled with the sound of war." One concludes Johnson was moral and religious. Badly wounded in the breast and lung at Cedar Mountain five months later, he died at home, hopefully surrounded by loved ones and his own peace and harmony.[27]

Private Vinson Williams' March 7, 1863, letter to his parents thanked "the kind mercy of God" for his ability to write them. His letters showed a deep religious fiber which no doubt was severely tested as he lay dying four months later from a wound at Gettysburg, without his parents to console him.[28] Faith helped men steel themselves to the death and misery around them and prepare them for fate, as Corporal Williams wrote in January 1863 about the dead of Fredericksburg, Virginia: "We have been oft told no matter where the body lies, where the here is cold, our souls shall not be shut out from the Kingdom of God if we serve Him acceptable no matter where we are lain for death."[29]

After the regiment's pounding at Cedar Mountain, First Sergeant John McKnight Bloss wrote, "It was while we were being shelled but I did not know but it would be the last that I should get. But God protected me. I think we will move forward soon. Desperate fighting is the watchword. I have faith that through the help of God we will live through them." He did make it through.[30]

The Sunday after New Hope Church in 1864, the 107th New York chaplain held the (27th's) brigade service in the rear. Muskets were "cracking vigorously" on the picket line, one noted, and the ping and zip of balls "united their music with that of the hymns and doxology." Another wrote, "It was rather novel sight to see men of different states all gathered together under the roaring musketry and the deep mouthed cannon to return thanks unto one common God for His watchful care. Not knowing what moment one or any one of us may be hurled into eternity." The service was finished and the men returned to the lines.[31]

Some men did not invoke the name or will of the Holy Spirit but yet implied their good and moral side by imploring the war and suffering to cease, and praying that they and their comrades come through the next conflict alive. Others showed genuine concern for fellow man, even when criticizing personalities or performances, and little rancor and hatred toward their enemy other than one would expect of brazen, confident young soldiers on a mission.

Back home, the Indianapolis *Sentinel* newspaper was concerned about public morals, but more in "carping and sneering." In 1862 the newspaper stated, "The Holy Sabbath—there is no Sabbath now. This is a time of war. It pains us to see such open desecration of the holy day, although we suppose it is absolutely necessary now." Regiments were marching and countermarching continually, drums and fifes were everywhere, glittering bayonets and flaunting flags "paraded under the Good God's glorious sun. President Lincoln's administration must be sustained, if we do smash the sacred day."[32] Later the *Sentinel* turned against Lincoln and became the principal Democratic opposition paper in Indiana. Mere carping about public morals quickly became vicious attacks on Governor Oliver P. Morton, the Republicans, and the conduct of the war, as the paper established its own credo.

> The one day of fasting and prayer in 1863 was religiously observed by a few, but not by the majority. People in the army were too much like they are at home for that. —*ERB* [33]

Rest in Peace, Jerome

> Who is there that will ever forget his cheerful face, beaming with noble, youthful vigor, always gay as a lark, even amidst the din of battle? But his smiling face will never again be seen. He has fallen, but he will never be forgotten by his comrades of the 27th. While we deplore his loss, we will try & emulate his noble example for bravery, cheerfulness, manliness & patriotism. —*Read at the funeral of Corporal Jerome Sims* [34]

The men found refuge and strength even in a comrade's death. Killed at Chancellorsville, Sims was buried on the field and re-interred at Fredericksburg National Cemetery where the author visited him. His officers paid tribute: "In after years, if any should be so fortunate to return to our homes, we will look back to the spot where fell the noble Jerome, and, quoting his favorite words, we say, 'Rest in peace, Rest in peace.'"[35]

CHAPTER 8

Scalawags, Courts, and Guardhouses:
Order and Discipline

The case of Sergeant John Meek of the 27th Indiana presents shameful evidence of familiarizing between a commissioned officer and a private. By his own confession, Captain McKahin has rendered himself a subject of trial before a court martial, charge of conduct unbecoming an officer. It is difficult to see why McKahin sent Meek to the guard house. Meek came into his tent, sat down, would not leave when ordered to. The social relation of messing together cannot fail to break down all barriers of discipline and consequent efficiency. But the offense of Captain McKahin cannot urge palliation by Private Meek. Each is an offense against military law and military decorum. A more vigorous punishment of officers would often save the time and expense of courts martial to punish privates. —*Endorsement of General Court Martial, February 26, 1863* [1]

Captain John D. McKahin, wounded in the leg at Antietam, could not cook. After assuming command of Company H on October 31, 1862, he invited then Sergeant John Meek of his company to board with him and prepare his meals. Meek, a recruit who entered service in March 1862, rapidly rose to sergeant. The two became intimates. Soon their relationship evoked an argument, and consequently exposed their homosexual liaisons.

On the night of November 24, 1862, after McKahin and Meek had supper together, they had a disagreement, and the volatile McKahin told Meek to leave. He refused and they struggled loudly. Meek struck McKahin in the face. Captain John W. Wilcoxen rushed up and, seeing the two grappling, ordered Meek to stop. Meek swung at Wilcoxen and missed, but was grabbed by two guards and arrested.[2] Convicted by court-martial, Meek was reduced to private, forfeited all pay and allowances from November 1 to February 25, 1863, and was fined $10 per month (of a salary of $13) for six months, a stiff penalty for the married man. He pulled himself together and fought honorably, but at Resaca 15 months later fell mortally wounded.

123

The married McKahin was a hulking 6'1½", 200-pound railroad conductor from Michigan City, near the northern terminus of the Monon Railroad route which had lured many men into the regiment. A good fighting soldier, nevertheless he was mostly ignored or disliked. "We petitioned the colonel not to assign him to Company F because of his domineering tyrannical conduct," a sergeant said.[3] After the Meek affair McKahin chose immediate resignation over court-martial, "in consequence of a wound received in the right leg at the battle of Antietam which has rendered me unfit for the service."[4] McKahin departed March 14, 1863. Later reinstated, he served with the 138th and as a lieutenant colonel in the 155th Indiana Infantry.

Fraternization between officers and enlisted and noncommissioned officers (NCOs) and privates persisted but never again was that kind of a problem, as long as juniors obeyed seniors. Men of the same company had grown up together, known each other well and used first names. As original officers departed, the regiment promoted from the enlisted ranks, and friendships naturally continued.

The 27th Indiana neither strove to be nor achieved status as a model Union regiment. Far from it, call it Hoosier independence perhaps, but the regiment raised eyebrows with superiors and other outside officials until settling down for their final campaign. The overall impression created was that of an undisciplined but tough fighting unit.

First Lieutenant Simpson Solomon Hamrick wrote home in March 1863 concerning an inspection by officers from another regiment: "They reported us last summer as unfit for service 2 or 3 times on account of discipline, but when it came to the test of facing the rebels we made them ashamed of themselves. Even our old Yankey general [Gordon] said we was the best fighting material he ever saw."[5] The opinionated Hamrick was on target. "What a detestable brigade we are in. We had an inspection of all the regiments owing to the prejudice Eastern officers have for us Western soldiers. They reported us in a bad condition and poor discipline. We and some other of the best regiments in the army was condemned."

Major General Joseph Hooker, commander of the Army of the Potomac, cracking down as his army neared its spring campaign, denied furloughs for those regiments, but the 27th was reprieved. "Yesterday we were again inspected" and "pronounced in excellent condition in every respect including cleanliness of camp, good arms, well clothed and well versed in drill and other matters."[6] Some vindication, but the true test would come later before the cannon's mouth.

The Hoosiers mainly came from fairly strict lifestyles guided by family, church or community norms, and therefore were susceptible to military discipline. However, the independent men were also apt to test the flexibility of regulations. Their frequent complaints are seen more as expressions

View across Potomac River

Location where the 27th Indiana crossed from Williamsport, Maryland into Virginia, May and June 1862.

Photo by author

of unfamiliarity, masculinity and boredom than inabilities to adjust. On the whole, general disciplinary problems and desertions were frequent nuisances but did not adversely affect mission or objective readiness.

Soon after the regiment was formed, the men realized discipline excused no one. By present military standards, discipline in Camp Morton was lax. The men wanted furloughs home or to get into Indianapolis, which most men saw for the first time. Camp life was interrupted by citizens' excursions to see them, but visiting of this magnitude would not reoccur. If a pass was denied, they would "run the guard." There were few enforcement patrols in the city, but one newly minted 27th officer reported, "I had the pleasure of going with two lieutenants and 30 men divided into three patrols, brought in soldiers throughout the town."[7] Aside from sleeping conditions, the harsh realities of army life played only a cameo role, and no one could forecast the hardships the East soon would bring.

Settling into winter quarters in Maryland in 1861, Colonel Silas Colgrove bore down on the regiment. His job was to harden the men for battle: soldiering was not meant to be easy. He never sought popularity, but eventually was respected as a fair, courageous officer who cared for his troops.

The most common breaches of discipline were absence without leave (AWOL), drunkenness, disrespect to superior officers, turbulence after taps, inattention on guard and gambling. Disrespect included "talking back" (strong unmilitary language) and refusal to salute or recognize an officer while on duty. Disciplinary action started with arrest and took three forms. Minor infractions such as drunkenness or failure to perform a routine assignment would usually banish the offender one or several days to the camp guardhouse: a cabin, tent, stockade, or shack. Sometimes "house arrest" relegated the man to his quarters. A serious offense by an NCO, heard before the colonel, brought reduction to private. The most serious offenses for all ranks meant trial by one of two levels of court-martial, the general court-martial hearing the most flagrant violations and officers' cases. Few recruits deserted or were court-martialed.

Provost marshals and their guards enforced discipline outside the regiment, like today's military police. They performed garrison duty, traveled with the line units, and were empowered to arrest and hold men for any offense. During marches they rounded up stragglers and in battle stood behind the front lines to maintain order and keep men from fleeing. Members of the 27th were occasionally detailed to provost marshal duty, and Captain Josiah Clinton Williams served as the brigade provost during the Atlanta Campaign.

By February 1862, "Almost every day some of the NCOs are reduced to the ranks for little offense such as being AWOL or getting drunk," and few original NCOs were left. Five resigned together to become privates, perhaps in protest. After Colgrove raided the card-playing of men in the guardhouse, a captain told him most of his best men were in there. Soon all were released.[8] Colgrove reduced nearly 40 NCOs to private. More NCOs voluntarily entered the ranks indicating pending facing disciplinary action, dissatisfaction with management, or their own inabilities to lead. Reasons included failure to perform duties, straggling on the march, or passing bogus money. Drummers, fifers, and teamsters were reduced to private with impunity early in the war.

Hiram Reynolds, reduced to private, transferred in early 1862 to the Navy gunboat service on the Mississippi River, was discharged there, and was hung for murder in Tennessee in 1864. Several hearty, raucous, hard-drinking NCOs from the German Company K felt Colgrove's justice: First Sergeant John Baptist Melchoir, reduced to private in January 1862; Corporal John David Berger, drunkenness and fighting, January 1862; George P. Mehringer, drunkenness and fighting, March 1862; and Sergeant Andrew Streigel, reduced in December 1863. Some members rebounded from discipline with promotions. John K. McKaskay began as a private, was promoted to sergeant major, was reduced to the ranks for incapacity to discharge duties, and later made 2nd lieutenant.

Company E forged a distinct disciplinary record: only one desertion and four men court-martialed, one twice, and two reductions in rank. Voluntary resignations may have been the preferred "punishment" for three sergeants and one corporal in the Winter 1861–62. Company D similarly attrited NCOs during that period when four sergeants and corporals were reduced and two others voluntarily became privates.

Arguing and fighting was commonplace, usually over gambling, a game or possessions, often while drinking alcohol. Sergeant Noah N. Sims violently assaulted Private Reuben Hendrickson over rights to an axe, was court-martialed and fined $6. Private Alexander Andrews knifed Private Richard Downing. Downing grabbed an ax and they both stood in threatening positions until officers separated them. Even officers fought. Before Atlanta, trench routine was broken up by "a right nice little fight" between Captain George Lake Fesler and Major Theodore Freelinghausen Colgrove. "Lieutenant Colonel Fesler parted them or it would have been nicer," wrote an onlooker.[9] Hospitalization, whose treatment, length and prognosis frustrated recuperating soldiers, bred violations or desertion. Private Samuel T. Osman, recovering from a Gettysburg shattered arm, struck the hospital wardmaster at a Philadelphia hospital, forfeiting a month's pay and his 60-day pass.

When the regiment arrived in New York City in August 1863 on draft riot duty, Colgrove stemmed insubordination with his sword. When three drunks (the "best of soldiers") defied their company officers and Colgrove, he vigorously whacked them "slapping, hacking and prodding, indiscriminately." Luckily it was his dress sword, "otherwise the evening might have been tragical." He decreed "the minimum of excess should meet the maximum of punishment." He sped to the saloon across from Battery Park to ask the owner not to sell his men liquor, but he would not agree.[10] Sometimes the exigencies of operations tabled action. As Major General John Pope's Virginia Campaign foundered, so did the case against Private George W. Morgan. During the Cedar Mountain withdrawal, Morgan, "giving out and excused from marching," took and rode a cavalry horse. Colgrove charged him with stealing it but became preoccupied, and he entered the hospital and never returned.[11]

By their third year, seriousness toward discipline—what really was important—should have matured. But the court-martial of Private William D. Steele, a man present at every battle without a blot on his record, in Tullahoma, Tennessee, in October 1863, for failure to salute the lieutenant colonel while on guard duty, showed it had not completely.

Sometimes we made our own discipline. Once marching in Virginia, cavalrymen constantly interfered and drove one of our wagons into a ditch breaking a part. Our commander wheeled a guard across the road to prevent trouble. A young mounted lieutenant drew his pistol on our guard; but with a dozen Indiana bayonets pointing instantly at his breast, he quickly postponed his funeral. When someone tried to make more trouble, musket butts were used with great success, the only mistake was not using the steel, for we were clearly right. —*ERB* [12]

The regiment's first court-martial was on February 2, 1862, when two men were sent to Frederick, Maryland, to a division tribunal for using abusive language on superior officers. One had struck the adjutant. Comrades knew his punishment would be severe. In June 1862, the regiment began conducting their own courts-martial using their own officers as members. They were ignorant of the military justice system, crammed to prepare, and trusted their best judgment. First Lieutenant George Whitfield Reed wrote in June 1862 about one of the earlier courts-martial:

> Drummer Boy John Messler, 16, Company A, who failed to beat roll calls and recalls, was arrested and tried by court-martial. He was guilty to charges and specifications and sentenced to three days extra beating of the calls, a slight punishment in consideration of his youthfulness and the confinement he already had undergone. [13]

Colgrove contemplated confining Messler for two or three days without subjecting him to the rigors of a trial. But then, who would beat the calls for that company? In view of their ill-preparedness and inexperience, officers who sat on the courts-martial performed honestly, fairly, and admirably in dealing with the accused, an administrative miracle in the midst of war.

The first court convened at Newtown, Virginia, for Messler and others, most charged with violations at the Battle of Winchester. Captain John A. Cassady was president and Second Lieutenant Josiah Clinton Williams was judge-advocate. Williams called the assignment an "honor—rather misfortune." The sentences were read on June 20 at dress parade and "opened the eyes and acquainted the boys regarding army regulations." [14] Williams reported the first court-martial period: [15]

> June 15, 1862. Gave report on [Private Paul] Smith of Co. K. Reported him lying down on post & letting 2 or 3 pass without challenging them. Appointed a court-martial detail. Went into council at 10 o'clock trying the cases of [Private] Thomas Morgan & [Private] William Delahunt of Company I for absence from camp without leave.

> 16th. Court-martial met at 9:30 o'clock trying cases of Sgt. Camel [James Campbell] & [Private] Barney Cullen before dinner, & Private Powell [Paul] Smith & two others in the afternoon.

> 17th. Court met at 9 o'clock. We tried 3 cases before dinner & adjourned in the evening on the third case. It was a cowardice case. We had 2 of them, quite complicated cases.

18th. Court decided on previous day's cases. One acquitted (proven he was sick) & the other sentence to have $7 of his month's pay forfeited, to be reduced to ranks & have his sentence read 6 times on dress parade.

25th. Received order to convene court-martial to meet 10 a.m. on 26th. Members Lt. R. B. Gilmore, President, & Lts. Fesler, Jerger, Stephens & Lee jurors, myself judge advocate.

Sixty-one members were court-martialed for a total of 66 courts. Thirteen men of Company H were tried and nine in F. Company A had the fewest, two. Three men were tried twice and one, Private Joseph Dingman, three times: June 20, 1862—disobedience of orders and AWOL, sentence: forfeit $1 per month for two months, carry 30-pound knapsack and march before the guard tents four hours per day, two hours at a time, for four days; confinement in the guard house the remainder of the time; September 1862—sentence: forfeit all pay thereafter; and February 4, 1863—cowardice; dismissed from the army. Privates William B. McGrew and William Dodson were both lightly punished for being AWOL from Tullahoma in November 1863. A guard that night, Private William McMullen, was convicted for lying down. His sentence was to stand at attention three hours a day for four days carrying a 20-pound knapsack with gun at support arms, and a four-month, $3 per month fine, worse than McGrew and Dodson. The harshest punishment was for a personal offense. Private Richard Morts, "incorrigible and heartless," was drummed out of the service, his bare shaved head tattooed with "T" for "thief," for stealing $20 from Private Morgan Pitcher and messmates.[16]

Sometimes there were mitigating circumstances. At Chancellorsville Private Anderson Dichert was injured when a tree, hit by artillery fire, fell on him. Unable to get to the regiment, he made it to the Acquia Creek field hospital for treatment. He obtained no proof and thus was considered AWOL. Convicted by trial, Dichert appealed to the division commander:

> Court sentence was all my pay and allowances then due me & $10 per month during remainder of my enlistment. I ask & pray to you that this punishment be stopped for 2 reasons. I am married man & have wife & 3 small children that will suffer for food & raiment. Winter is coming & it is the only source [if] my family is to be kept from want & suffering. The small allowance left me falls short of my clothing bill so I have nothing left. It is hard for me to know those near & dear are suffering with cold & hunger. I have done my duty & will continue to do so during the remainder of my term of service. If you see fit in your wisdom to mitigate the sentence of the court it will remove a mountain of sorrow & affliction. May God assist you.[17]

27th Indiana captured the flag of the 38th Alabama at Resaca, May 15, 1864 (Replica)

Flag Source: Battles for Atlanta: Sherman Moves East (*Time-Life Books, 1985*)

Dichert's sentence was mitigated to forfeit $3 per month from May 28 to August 31, 1863. The Daviess County blacksmith was killed at Resaca.

All members of the courts were governed by motives of justice and humanity, and had a praiseworthy ambition to proceed strictly in accordance with the laws. —ERB [18]

Three members of the 27th Indiana easily were "Kings of the Scalawags." They were Privates Shelly Martin, Smith Turner, and John W. Weaver.

Martin was known as a "Worthless Drunkard." Court-martialed on June 26, 1862, he deserted in Maryland in December 1862, and was arrested in Illinois in February 1865. Eventually he found Captain Peter Fesler, then with the 70th Indiana, in North Carolina and served out his term. He was well remembered:[19]

[What had Martin done] during period he deserted. He replied with oaths that he was here and there and everyplace. Spent whole time avoiding arrest. He was as likely to lie as to tell the truth. He has reputation of running with lewd women. —Corporal Andrew R. Vansickle

The Colonel was to blame for his being in guardhouse so much of the time. When we got to Harpers Ferry he got whiskey, got full and straggled, was taken by provost marshal and sent to Alexandria. Later denied he had ever joined another regiment. —1st Lieutenant Fletcher D. Rundell

He was a worthless drunkard from youth to time of death. Was driven out of Morgan County by the sheriff until he turned up in the regiment. Bad reputation prior to army. —Neighbor

Turner was known as a bounty hunter.[20] He set two unenviable and unmatched regimental records: six regiments, six desertions. He was arrested first on June 30, 1862, with more to follow. His first attempt to leave the service was rejected by a medical board at Alexandria on December 31, 1862. While recovering from a Cedar Mountain wound, he deserted the hospital on January 16, 1863. He then contracted smallpox and varioloid and was hospitalized in Washington, D.C., in February. He was returned to duty but not to the regiment, staying in Washington nursing the smallpox, eventually engineering his discharge May 6. His smallpox cured, the bounty hunter enlisted in the 117th Indiana July 16, 1863, but deserted December 3. On February 28, 1864, he was arrested in Indiana and delivered to the military in Indianapolis. On June 3 the authorities decided to return him to his command, but he deserted on June 8 while awaiting transportation. Meanwhile, in January Turner had enlisted in the 120th Indiana while a deserter from the 117th, a violation of the 22nd Article of War, and had left the 120th for good on February 1. Turner, being paid each time he enrolled, proceeded to join the 67th, 136th, and 145th Indiana Infantry regiments—deserting from each.

Weaver was known as a recidivist.[21] He never adjusted to the army. In the guardhouse 13 days for disobedience, he immediately followed with another for disobeying Captain Peter Kop, and then was arrested while escaping from confinement resulting in a court-martial conviction for attempting to stab another soldier.

No member of the 27th Indiana was executed as punishment, but the men knew of some such instances. In one, the execution of Marylander Albert Jones, of another regiment, on the Rappahannock River, Virginia, deeply impressed the approving Hoosiers. Of that September 1863 death by firing squad, Brigadier General Alpheus Starkey Williams, their division commander, wrote: "I had the unpleasant task of calling out my division to shoot a deserter. The gloom of the weather was in concert with the melancholy duty. The poor fellow sat on his coffin and fell back stone dead at the discharge, like one going to sleep. It was his second desertion. I have over 20 conscripts who probably will die the same way."[22]

After the execution, a Hoosier remarked, "The only regret was that we could not have some of our own deserters there to serve them [executioners] in a like manner."[23] Private Lewis King just missed being on the firing squad. "The orderly sergeant detailed me to be one of the firing squad. I became anxious and asked him, 'Where is [Private] Philip Cox?' He replied, 'He is ahead of you on the list, but I can't find him.' I said, 'I'll hunt for him.' I found him. He did the shooting instead of me."[24]

Incredulously, desertions in non-combat situations went unpunished once the man returned. Probably only guardhouse time was administered. Reasons for leaving ranged from the humane desire to be with loved ones to the scalawag character of the man himself, and dissatisfaction with undesirable army conditions: weather, pay, duties, food, and fear of combat, disciplinary action, or retribution. Those men who contemplated it, but stayed, were homesick or dissatisfied. The scalawags remained away. The first deserters, including Privates Needham Worrell and William Abercrombie, were gone before the regiment left Indianapolis. Colgrove offered a $30 reward for their apprehension and delivery, but it failed.

Private Henry K. Hendricks was the only one who tried to join the Confederates. He deserted August 22, 1862, was captured September third, and went to a Richmond, Virginia, prison. His captors said he was "willing to take the oath of allegiance to the Confederacy and go to work. Commissioner Baxter recommends that on his taking oath he be paroled to work for Confederacy." Ultimately they rejected him and he was discharged in 1863: "is unwilling to take the oath of allegiance & go to work."[25]

Forty-nine members in all deserted. Thirteen returned to the regiment for a net loss of 36 men, three percent of the total enrolled. Private Peter Seibel left three times: August 15, 1862, from Culpeper Court House, Virginia (returned April 13, 1863); September 17, 1863, from Satterlee Hospital, Philadelphia, Pennsylvania (returned October 1863); and December 20, 1863, from the provost marshals in Tullahoma (arrested in Decatur City, Indiana, February 3, 1865). Also court-martialed for being AWOL in June 1862, he enlisted in two other units, the 52nd Kentucky Infantry and the 17th Kentucky Cavalry, from which he deserted in April 1865. His brother, Private Daniel, also deserted and was arrested at least twice more, but finished his service in the 27th. Private Thomas J. Swan deserted twice, finally staying out.

Many desertions occurred during hospitalization or other situations away from the regiment's influence. That reflected well on the caliber of the men and the officer and NCO leadership: with the 27th's arduous itinerary and bloody battles, more desertions would have been expected. Private Christopher Sneder, recuperating from a Chancellorsville wound, deserted from Alexandria, later enlisting in the 32nd Indiana Infantry as Simon Schneider. Private Andrew Jackson Keller left a hospital recovering from sickness by paying someone there $50 for a furlough. With a $30 reward on his head, he was arrested in Indiana by citizen Henry C. Hardy on November 8, 1864, and delivered to the provost marshal. Keller eventually caught up with his comrade veterans and completed his service.

No officers and only one NCO deserted, Corporal Christopher C. Showalter, who returned to the regiment $3^{1}/_{2}$ months after leaving a hospital. Relatives sometimes went together. Privates Jonathan and Joseph L. Jones exited from Indianapolis on September 14, 1861. Both later joined another regiment and completed their service. Privates Coleman F. and James Burton were AWOL on June 20, 1862, and court-martialed. Private Barney Cullen stayed away with the Burtons and was also tried for intoxication. Like Coleman, he was fined, carried a 30-pound knapsack, and served guardhouse time. Privates William Dellahunt and Thomas J. Morgan of Company I were out with the Dubois men and similarly paid. Cullen continued on thin ice. He deserted nearly five months in 1862–63 and was returned by provost guards. June 20 continued bad for Company K. Their duty guard, Private Paul Smith, for not demanding the countersign and lying down on his beat, was court-martialed and fined $2.50 per month for two months, and made to stand more guard duty.

Few desertions came during or en route into battle, but there certainly were cowards. At Chancellorsville, Colgrove placed Private Henry Daniel behind Company F to shoot any man that would attempt to run. Private

Morgan deserted on July 2 at Gettysburg. Corporal Joshua L. Foster was convicted of cowardly and shamefully abandoning Company H in the face of the enemy at Winchester and for being AWOL 24 hours. Recruit Private Jeptha Engle ran away at Antietam, but returned after his arrest. Discipline had improved by the Atlanta Campaign, but two more men avoided combat. Sergeant James E. Smith was reduced to private for cowardice at Kennesaw Mountain, and Private Reuben Holbrook, the last member tried by court-martial, was convicted and fined $60.

Three members, Privates Joseph Dingman, Richard Muster, and George W. Wright, were convicted of cowardice at Antietam. Wright "did without permission leave from his company commander or other proper authority cowardly and shamefully and clandestinely leave his company and regiment in front of the enemy and did not go into battle but remained away for 8 days near Sharpsburg Maryland." Drummed out of the army, they were placed at the head of the regiment with a file of men behind them at the position of "charge bayonet." As fifers and drummers played the "Rogue's March," they passed between the two ranks which were facing inward, down to the left, then over the camp guard line, and out of camp. Each prisoner's head was shaved bare and the letter "C" tattooed on their heads indicating "coward." That was all. Sometimes imprisonment was added but not in their case. "Goodbye, boys," a comrade noted, "I never want to get out of the service that way."[26] Muster was killed in a railroad accident on the way home at Pittsburgh, Pennsylvania.

Officers got into trouble, too. Captain John T. Boyle, like McKahin, was a significant case in point. His letter of resignation in September 1862 read:

> I most respectfully tender you my immediate and unconditional resignation as Captain of Company C, 27th Indiana Volunteers. I am induced to make the above request from the following facts!!
>
> 1st that I was placed under arrest on the 29th day of May last.
>
> 2nd that I was tried by a general court martial on the 1st day of July last.
>
> 3rd that I have remained under an arrest all of the above time (4 months) and still remaining under an arrest, doing no good either for the government or myself, consequently it is a fact that there is a great injustice being done either to the government or myself—therefore I respectfully ask that the decision of that court may be put into execution—otherwise that my resignation may be accepted.[27]

In one respect Boyle's resignation request to General Williams was correct: the slow handling of his case was a disgrace and unlike usually swift army justice. Boyle was convicted of cowardice at Winchester. His court-martial proceedings had been approved by Williams some time before, forwarded to the corps commander and then sent to the army commander, who returned them to Williams. Williams did not concur with Boyle's "informality referred to" in the above letter and again sent the case up for review. Ultimately it went to the Judge Advocate General and Boyle's resignation was accepted.[28] The humiliated Boyle, a Mexican War veteran, lies abandoned beneath a weathered, barely legible, half-submerged stone in the City Cemetery in Columbus, Indiana.

The 27th got into trouble quickly after arriving at Washington in September 1861. Major John Mehringer and Surgeon Jarvis J. Johnson, who had gone into town on regimental business, were arrested by a Lieutenant Byrne and charged with leaving camp and visiting the city without proper papers. Their passes were taken. Colonel Colgrove retrieved them, but was put on report by provost guards who overreacted to his methods, and was charged with taking into Washington two officers without passes. Byrne told Colgrove he would report this to authorities, and the colonel replied in an "excited and unbecoming manner" that he did not care—he would do as he chose. The charges eventually were withdrawn following a letter to Washington from Major General Nathaniel Prentiss Banks, who said: "Any error [Colgrove] may have committed was wholly unintentional, and not designed to weaken the discipline, or manifest disrespect for the officers of your command. Not being thoroughly conversant with forms and perhaps not appreciating their importance, some irregularity in his proceedings is very likely to have occurred."[29]

Colgrove earned the reputation as a hard but precautionary driver. During the Atlanta Campaign, approaching Cassville, Georgia, on May 19, 1864, the 27th Indiana leading the Union advance, and not knowing the enemy strength or nature of the ground ahead, "our old Colonel" halted the entire line. "For this breach of discipline," his sword was taken and he arrested for several days. "I don't know who was to blame for this," wrote Sergeant Michael Henry Van Buskirk. "It is a burning shame to put as brave a commander as Colgrove, [who] has always proven himself, to be under arrest for halting the line while conducting a night advance, and having received word from a reliable source that if he continued in that direction any further he would be fired into by our own men. I know this to be the case."[30]

The first company officer disciplined was Lieutenant Williams, ordered confined to camp for disobeying a regimental order. Second Lieutenant Nehemiah Walton presented the most serious case. Absent at Cedar Mountain, he continued to be away and was court-martialed. Besides, Walton had imposed himself over his company both as first sergeant and officer.

He tendered his resignation August 15, 1862. Colgrove's endorsement read:

> The within named Lieut. Nehemiah Walton at the battle of Ceder Mountain left his Company and did not go into battle and was absent for 48 hours without leave, and on Saturday August 22, 1862 on the Rappahannock River about 4 miles above the Rappahannock Station while the enemy was shelling our camp, he cowardly left the regiment and was absent without leave for 6 days. His whole conduct has proven to me beyond doubt that he is a coward, and did most certainly act in a cowardly manner in the two instances referred to. I therefore recommend that he be dishonorably discharged from the service.[31]

Subsequent commands forwarded the request, but instead Walton was convicted by court-martial on October 20, 1862, and cashiered, losing all pay and allowances since August 23, and ordered discharged October 28, 1862.[32]

Mexican War veteran 2nd Lieutenant Arthur Berry resigned in December 1861 rather than be dismissed following a general court-martial conviction for drunkenness on duty, but later reentered with the 2nd Indiana Cavalry. Not all attempted resignations resulted in discharge. First Lieutenant Peter Fesler was under arrest from August 11 to October 12, 1862. He was "released without a trial and to do justice to myself and to my regiment I feel this bound to act": he submitted his resignation. Colgrove and all his superiors, including McClellan, disapproved it.[33]

The colonel's son, Major Theodore Freelinghausen Colgrove, had significant problems after mustering out of the 27th. He reentered with the 147th Indiana and rose to command as a lieutenant colonel. He was convicted of conduct prejudicial to good order and military discipline and sentenced in 1865 to be reprimanded and suspended from command, with pay losses. While undergoing the sentence he was arrested and tried again for conduct unbecoming an officer and a gentleman, and was dishonorably dismissed. He never participated in the 27th's reunion group and moved to Florida with his father, Colonel Colgrove, where he died and is buried.

> It is strange, but nevertheless true, that officers who exhibit a failure degree of ability and competency in the field will resort to ill-advised and even mischievous measures the moment they go into camp, like eight roll calls a day (like Eastern officers). It requires a share of common horse sense as well as military training and experience to cultivate and enforce discipline without breeding discontent and insubordination. —ERB [34]

CHAPTER 9

Skeletons and Scurvy:
Prisoners of War

Many of them are living skeletons, with just the breath of life left in them. The hands and feet of others are dropping off from dry rot. All are completely swarming with vermin, many are insane, and others have been made idiots from the treatment they have received in the South. My blood curdles with indignation, and I can hardly endure it. —*Nurse Mary A. Livermore* [1]

Livermore's description of freed Union prisoners of war arriving at Camp Parole in Annapolis, Maryland, in late 1862 could have included men of the 27th Indiana. Most of the regiment's 172 prisoners (121) were captured in the spring of 1862 in the Shenandoah Valley Campaign. The majority were wounded, injured or exhausted stragglers corralled by Confederate cavalry while retreating north from Winchester. A Hoosier recalled, "No organized body (company or squad) of men were captured. The enemy kept clear of all such; [it was] really only stragglers that fell into their hands." [2]

Many of these Hoosiers were processed through Annapolis on release. The 172 included men who were also mortally wounded, other wounded or injured, plus a handful who were captured (and counted) twice. It represented 15 percent of the regiment. In the fall of 1862 at Maryland Heights, Maryland, over 100 exchanged prisoners returned, "greatly pleased" to get home once more. "They underwent their full share of privations and hardships in Dixie, and bring anything but a favorable account of what they saw South." [3] All were taken while separated from the regiment as stragglers or wounded. Of the 28 captured at Chancellorsville, most were wounded and abandoned on the field during the retreat. Valley captives returned to the regiment in October 1862 or later, the ones from Chancellorsville within two weeks.

When the beaten Union forces relinquished the field at Winchester, Cedar Mountain, and Chancellorsville, they left behind soldiers with few options other than surrender, typified at Chancellorsville. In their three greatest battles, Antietam, Chancellorsville, and Gettysburg, a combined 30 members surrendered. And the member captured after New Hope Church

137

died in the miserable stockade at Andersonville, Georgia. Discounting those left on the battlefield, almost every man was taken by cavalry, not infantry.

The first prisoner of war was Private William M. Devett, captured while a picket at Smithfield, Virginia, March 13, 1862. He was paroled May 11 and discharged soon thereafter. The last was recruit Private Jeptha Engle, captured during the Siege of Atlanta, August 26, 1864. He was paroled and sent to Camp Chase, Ohio, and disappeared. Of the six officer POWs, two were surgeons whose hospitals were overrun. Captain James E. Davis was taken while away from the regiment at Front Royal, Virginia, and Second Lieutenant David Campbell Van Buskirk while trying to reorient his men in the outskirts of Winchester. First Lieutenant Thomas J. Box and Second Lieutenant Isaac (No. 1) Van Buskirk were severely wounded and left on the fields at Cedar Mountain and Chancellorsville.* Isaac died the day he was paroled, May 15, 1863, but Box and the others returned to duty.

Corporal James C. Thomas offered a compelling reason for being captured at Winchester. Having "caught cold" in his feet at Balls Bluff, marching had made them worse. So during the retreat he rode in an ambulance. At Bunker Hill he was surrounded, because his "feet could not get out of the way." After being exchanged Thomas was assigned to artillery duty where he could ride, until the Atlanta Campaign where, back with the regiment, he was wounded during New Hope Church and the Siege of Atlanta.[4]

The 27th captured Confederates several times. The most significant capture was at Resaca when, after ambushing the 38th Alabama Infantry Regiment, some 30 Alabamians and their colonel surrendered with their colors. At Gettysburg, following the regiment's charge at The Swale, Colonel Silas Colgrove coaxed two Rebels trying to surrender into the breastworks. At Chancellorsville the 27th spearheaded a brigade countercharge which bagged from 150–200 enemy. During the Atlanta Campaign, Private George Gore brought in five enemy, and others were rooted from trenches and picket posts as the regiment advanced.

Men of the 27th Indiana were incarcerated in four prisons, most of them on Belle Isle, a James River island at Richmond, Virginia. Some were detained in Libby, a converted Richmond tobacco warehouse, or in Salisbury, North Carolina. Many went to Richmond via Lynchburg, Virginia, and Salisbury.

Prisoner Corporal John Russell, taken at Buckton Station, Virginia, and imprisoned at Lynchburg and Belle Isle, wrote, "Was dragged around from place to place through the mud & rain until we reached Belle Isle, State of Virginia, & there treated for said disease by a Rebble Sergeon.

---

* The 27th Indiana had two Isaac Van Buskirks, both related. They are identified herein as No. 1 and No. 2.

Had pass to march at will, unable to march in ranks, bad case of catarrh & bronchitis."[5]

Not all prisoners were incarcerated. Some were detained indefinitely as their captors moved and then released on parole to make their own way. That happened to several captured in the Valley before the two armies agreed to a formal parole and exchange system. Others captured at Winchester were left there by the departing Confederates and met the regiment on its return in mid-June. "They all say they was treated moderately well and not so much abused as we had first heard," wrote Sergeant Simpson Solomon Hamrick.[6] Some were turned loose or rescued. Other Federals soon freed Private John Sparks, taken at Buckton Station. Private Sashwell Turner, wounded and captured at Cedar Mountain, was carried to Gordonsville where a Confederate doctor dressed his wound. Treated there for several days, he found Union forces after being released as an encumbrance.

Several men were captured twice, including Privates Robert W. Coffee and James W. Steers, at Winchester and Chancellorsville, and Private Aaron Fleener at Newtown and Chancellorsville. Men captured in the Valley and paroled in September 1862, whose places of incarceration are unknown,

Hospital at Belle Isle, Richmond, Virginia

Many of the 27th Indiana prisoners of war visited here in 1862.

Leslie Collection

likely were on Belle Isle. Half the Chancellorsville men were paroled within two weeks as encumbrances following appalling medical attention. Private Alfred Wilson, shot in the back at Chancellorsville, was neglected for 11 days, lying in mud and filth with only crackers and bread to eat, before being paroled. He died July 7. The other half, including Privates Robert R. Marshall, Berry Street, Coffee, and Fleener were held in Richmond.

Prisons on both sides were "hell holes." Little was done, nor in some instances could be done, to make the lot of prisoners habitable, much less comfortable. The fate of prisoners of the 27th was not unlike that of other Union soldiers in the same or similar prisons. The regiment's goal was to get to Richmond, but not that way.

No captured member turned his coat, but Private Henry K. Hendricks tried. Captured at Winchester, he returned to duty, deserted on August 22, 1862, was captured at Rappahannock, Virginia, on September 3, and was imprisoned in Richmond as a deserter. He became a "galvanized prisoner," one who would fight for the other side. Eventually he was unwilling to take the oath of allegiance to the Confederacy, and they discharged him as undesirable on January 10, 1863.[7] He died a year later.

Scurvy and diarrhea were nature's revenge on the pitiful masses at Belle Isle and Libby, caused by bad food, bad water, exposure, starvation, and general neglect. No one escaped diarrhea; only the luckiest avoided scurvy, to which prisoners were particularly susceptible. Those diseases drained the human system and produced an undernourished, weak, and susceptible man whose comrades would always remember as "a mere skeleton of his former self."

One such "mere skeleton" remembered was Private Andrew J. Vest.

We were messmates and prisoners of war at Belle Isle, July–August, 1862. Vest contracted scurvy, unable to get vegetables. Our food consisted of a very scanty supply of dirty blue beans & occasionally a morsel of salt pork. Sores broke out over his face hands & body, inside of mouth was raw & very sore. Unable to eat for several days, running off at bowels & complained of severe pains in abdomen & burning rectum.[8]

Despite enduring those ailments for years, Vest survived until 1927.

Scurvy decayed the teeth of Private Andrew Jones and made his mouth so sore it was difficult to eat the trifling food. Private John McConnell, "a stout heart boy" before the service, released shortly before Jones, lost several teeth and had constant toothaches. With sores on legs and mouth he dropped to 97 pounds from chronic diarrhea, "considerably reduced in flesh and frame," and was "in a bad fix generally." A comrade recalled McConnell as "one of the gritty ones that would not give up." He rejoined the regiment as "almost a skeleton," a term also given to returning scurvy-stricken Private James R. Sharp. To reach transports on the James River after his release, Sergeant Robert L. S. Foster, with badly swollen legs, required assistance from other prisoners.[9]

Exactly how many men of the 27th Indiana died in Southern prisons of sickness and disease is unknown, but probably at least 13. Private Willis Hubbard, captured by Confederate raider Mosby's guerrillas at Winchester, survived Lynchburg but died at Belle Isle on August 26, 1862. Privates Charles Robinson and James M. Wright died of disease at Belle Isle on July 13 and September 9. Privates C. William Boyd and Peter Isaac died at Lynchburg of typhoid on August 6 and September 10. Others including Privates Benjamin T. Gregory and Patrick Curley died after parole in Washington, D.C., hospitals, Curley from phthisis and prison hardships, and Gregory from exposure and diarrhea.*

Ailments were not limited to scurvy and diarrhea. Private Michael Corcoran "was very near dead with piles."[10] Corporal Michael Wallick, sliced in the shoulder by a sabre at Buckton, was never treated. He had "a sponge and much cold water applications and kept down the pus and it healed all right." Wallick, one of the few Hoosiers imprisoned at Lynchburg, Libby and Belle Isle, also contracted rheumatism, sore eyes and a cataract which went untreated. Private Jonas Davis remembered Wallick: "We were badly exposed then and had insufficient food, great deal of sickness among prisoners."[11]

Prisoner of war veterans, cursed through life, fought hard for pension benefits. Private Andrew J. Arnold wrote brothers Sergeant Samuel S. and Corporal Charles H. Weever as late as 1891: "You two comrades were captured with me on [General Nathaniel P.] Banks' [Winchester] retreat. I had organ and liver troubles while in service. Rheumatism while on Belle Isle and kidney and liver disease, contracted same while lying in cold sand without any cover at Belle Isle. Need you to sign affidavit."[12]

Hunger took its toll. Many could not walk, and when they attempted, "giddiness and blindness came on" and they fell. At Belle Isle, "lice eaten" bodies encrusted with dirt and vermin, sore from forced lying on the ground, hardly had a patch of healthy skin visible. The floorless hospital tent was always full, and some died waiting for admittance while others were discharged "still in the pangs of mortal illness." Straw beds and their coverings were dirty old quilts "shockingly offensive" from body secretions. "That any of them lived through such treatment is almost past belief," a veteran recalled.[13]

---

* Having all but given up locating the burial sites of the prison dead, believing them lost, the author by chance came upon the small, remote Poplar Grove National Cemetery south of Petersburg. Aided by the efficient directory he found the decaying, grass-covered, barely legible markers of Privates Robinson, Isaac, John Younger, Patrick Murphy, John W. Walton, and many more "Unknowns."

The impact of imprisonment on mental health is incalculable but undoubtedly was extremely traumatic. Private James H. Richards lost nearly all teeth from scurvy at Belle Isle and Libby but remained in the service. Ultimately he died in the Washington, D.C., Government Hospital for the Insane. Private James N. McCowen's "temporary fits of insanity and a general state of physical disability caused by imprisonment in Richmond" led to his discharge in April 1863.[14]

Several men succumbed in prison to wounds, including Murphy, who died at Lynchburg June 16, 1862; Private Henry Allbright, who died in the Confederate hospital in Winchester's Union Hotel two weeks later; and Sergeant John P. Beard, mortally wounded in the knee and left at Chancellorsville, who died May 11, 1863, in a ramshackle enemy field hospital near the battleground.

Two medical officers of the 27th Indiana were captured. Surgeon Jarvis J. Johnson, caught at Winchester, although disabled remained there serving the sick and wounded of both sides with relative freedom. But his regiment did not know his condition or whereabouts. Wrote Second Lieutenant George Lake Fesler to Johnson's wife, Katy, on May 30:

> We have not hered anything...reliable. We did understand to day that Dock had crossed at Harpers Ferry and was in Frederick sick but we don't put much reliance in the report. We all hope it may be the case of him making his escape from the hands of the enemy. The last that we seen of Dock was in the streets of Winchester almost in the rear of our forces. I still hope he will come up.[15]

On trying to avoid capture, Johnson had been severely ruptured when his horse threw him while leaping a fence. Fesler, his Morgan County friend, told his wife of Johnson's fate, a kind of unofficial means more customary than official notification. A week later the doctor wrote his wife:

> I have become a prisoner of war but been unconditionally [paroled] but cant get through the Confederate lines. I am at the hospital. Here I have been considerably worked attending the wounded. I was taken prisoner before I knew there [was] any retreat. I had tied my horse to late for us to get out of range of sharpshooters. I started over where I thought a fight was and when I got out on the edge of town the troops were in full retreat. I ran for my horse but he had been taken. I was surrounded and hence was taken. Surgical aid was very much needed. So far I have been well treated but to day there is a guard placed around the hospital to prevent us from going out of doors today.[16]

On June 6, Johnson followed up with his last letter as a prisoner. "I have had no chance to send you a letter since my captivity until the present. I was taken prisoner May 25th. I am in charge of an academy hospital with

58 rebel patients and 30 federals. I will write again."[17] He returned to the 27th but resigned in July 1862 from ill health. He became an influential "Union man" in Copperhead-leaning Morgan County, served in the legislature, and was an early leader in the regimental reunion group.

Assistant Surgeon Greenly Vinton Woollen, captured at Culpeper, Virginia, on August 18, 1862, was held in Libby until Union Major General John Pope rescinded his highly objectionable foraging order which dictated that civilians must help feed his army in Virginia. Woollen was paroled September 21 and returned to the regiment shortly thereafter. He wrote an incredible memoir of his ordeal with Libby director Captain Henry Wirtz, later of Andersonville infamy.

> The sick and wounded died at a fearful rate. We were comparatively unable to render them assistance, even bury them. In about three weeks rebel authorities decided to send a batch of the remaining sick, wounded, and nurses to Richmond. Not being well or especially needed at Culpeper, and hoping to be sent north, I sought to go to Richmond. With us was the wife of a wounded man who had heard of husband's misfortune and had come to his assistance. He subsequently had died and she broken hearted and alone, also joined our number hoping to escape north.

Assistant Surgeon Greenly Vinton Woollen's Headstone
Crown Hill Cemetery, Indianapolis.

Photo by author

When we arrived at Richmond we were carted across city to Libby. To my surprise I was separated from the sick and wounded and landed with 2–3 other officers in the prison room where [General] Pope's officers were being held. Captain Thomas J. Box of my regiment who had been captured at Cedar Mountain heard my voice in my inquiries as to where I was and told me where. They were being held as hostages to be treated as felons and not POWs until Pope's order was rescinded. After lunch provided by Captain Wirtz, which was only fit for dogs, I laid down on a bench near the wall to answer innumerable questions about safety of Banks and his troops in correction of false stories told them by rebels, spent sleepless night, next morning found myself alive with vermin. After breakfast Wirtz came in and called for me. Thinking I was going to be sent home or to the hospital with the sick and wounded I complied with his request to follow. We went into the end room of this famous building, nearest to the city. We then went into his private office and what was evidently his own bedroom.

Here I saw what beggars description and doubtless was never seen or known of except by three persons: Wirtz, the poor wretched woman previously spoken of, from whom we had been separated, and myself. The woman was apparently near death. Here the officer ordered me to see what the woman needed and prescribe for her and left. The room seemed to have been luxuriously furnished, was in utmost disorder, evidence someone had been fighting for life. The woman looked as if collapsed in cholera was lying on a sofa or cot almost naked and had been vomiting and purging. She cried piteously that I give her something to end her misery and shame. She told me her terrible story of night-long resistance of the horrible fiend who finally raped her. She was so exhausted from heat and fatigue together with stomach and bowel trouble as to be unable to further resist his hellish desires. Further interview was cut off with Wirtz returning with a peremptory order for me to do what I was sent for. I appealed for her removal to hospital but was checked with a curse to do what ordered to do. The prescription was ruthlessly taken from me and I was returned to prison.

I saw and heard no more from him or her till the next morning when he came in and I inquired about her, but was ordered vilely to mind my own affairs and cause him no trouble. I already had learned that "prudence was the better part of valor" and desisted. Doubtless hours before the body of the helpless woman had been dumped into the James [River] to find its last resting place with no one to know of her ill fate. I didn't even know her name. She undoubtedly was mourned by her friends and reported as were many brave soldiers: "missing."[18]

Private Michael Henry Van Buskirk was captured at Winchester with cousins Second Lieutenant David Campbell, Teamster Isaac (No. 1) and Corporal Isaac (No. 2), "Long Ike." Henry was at Lynchburg and Belle Isle, was paroled at Aikens Landing, Virginia, on September 13, 1862, sent to Camp Parole and then Washington, D.C., on September 23. Exchanged, he returned to the regiment October 9. "It was the worst thing that I had yet with diarrhea," he recalled. "Was carried by comrade to prison hospital too weak to stand on my feet. I remained in hospital 2–3 weeks in July 1862. I continued to be troubled with diarrhea the rest of my service, resulted in hemorrhoids & piles, indigestion, & heart disease."[19]

Henry's diary of his imprisonment is the only such known chronicle by a member of the 27th Indiana and reports in depth, content, and feeling, providing a memorable account of captivity. Excerpts follow from his experiences in captivity, and of "slop and slap jacks on 'scary island.'"[20]

May 25. [1862]. We held them in check for a while but then began a general skedaddle. I was taken prisoner along with Lieutenant Van Buskirk & Long Ike. We are now in the guard house of the rebels.

May 27. Still a prisoner. Have been engaged in burying our dead. They had been laying for 3 days & it was awful disagreeable work.

May 28. "Give the devil his dues," thus far they have treated us better than I expected. They have no supplies here & we would have suffered had it not been for the ladies of the place. God bless them.

May 31. We have now started for Lynchburg or some other place.

June 1. Marched to Woodstock. Pike muddy. No rations.

June 2. We are now waiting to cook some bread. The first we have drawed since we left Winchester and we ain't drew it yet. We have been started forward without rations. I think I could eat a greasy board.

June 3. This morning for first time since leaving Winchester we drew something to eat, small piece of wheat bread to the man made with cold water & no salt, & a smaller piece of meat with it.

June 4. This evening for the first time we drew full rations.

June 5. This morning while they were giving us rations they seemed scared. They began to throw the bread over the fence at us by the wagon loads, just like feeding hogs. Soon they rushed us out & all began to skedaddle. We traveled about 20 miles over very bad roads. We have 4 rows of sentinels around us tonight.

June 7. Raining again. They are taking our names. We started again on foot. We had expected to take the cars.

June 10. This morning a man escaped. Rained all day. Our camp is 6" deep in mud. We drew flour for rations but have to bake it ourselves.

June 11. We were marched through the [Lynchburg] streets to the tune of Dixie played by an old brass band. The rebs are firing off cannon.

June 12. There has been plenty of peddlers. Got plenty of rations.

June 13. Today there were 450 more prisoners came in. They say they had Jackson fairly trapped if they had only burnt the bridge at Port Republic instead of trying to hold it.

June 15. Rained a bully shower. We are all wet & no fire to dry us. Wood can't be found at all.

June 17. We moved inside the fairgrounds where a North Carolina regiment takes charge of us. We are now very scarce of water & no wood.

June 21. The boys are just now getting reduced to fighting weight. They will fight over wood, bread, anything.

June 23. Today we are getting tents. Drew an A tent, a poor thing.

June 25. It has now been 1 month since we were taken prisoner. This is my birthday. I wonder where I will be in 12 months.

June 29. I baked some nice biscuits.

June 30. All are sick.

July 1. Few more prisoners came in. We have all got diarrhea. I bought blueberry pie for 50 cts., now making some beef soup.

July 2. We are all sick, one is not able to give the other a drink of water. About a quarter mile to water. When I think of my lonely condition & see all the evils & desolations of war I reflect that those I love best are safe from its power it is a source of pleasure to me. I now find that there is a joy in grief.

July 4. This day has been one of the dullest fourths I ever saw. The rebs do not celebrate today. I was taken to the hospital with the flux.

July 5. It is $25 fine to see a paper in camp.

July 11. Still in hospital. There was 3 more prisoners came in yesterday but were not permitted to come in with us.

July 12. Out of hospital today.

July 13. Sunday spending it the same old way, laying around & cracking jokes.

July 15. Few more prisoners in yesterday from Valley. They say there is some talk of making a general exchange of prisoners of war. God grant it may be so. This horrible suspense is getting intolerable.

July 16. The guards went through the camp & made us straighten our tents in rows. This is the most military move I have seen them make yet.

July 17. Today the 1st Maryland boys were called out & their names taken. This caused the parole fever to run high.

July 19. When I think of my lonely condition shut out from the outside world, deprived of communication with my friends at home, & while confined on all sides by a strong guard line, under all these afflictions it is a source of joy to me to know that I have one friend who is ever with me & in whom is all my trust. Through his goodness & tender mercy I still hope to enjoy the company of my friends & relatives once more.

July 21. The paroles are now like the payday was at Camp Jo Holt [Maryland, 1861]: always tomorrow.

July 22. Last night one of the guards shot a prisoner. He fell against our tent & soon expired. His blood is on our tent. That will wash out but the blood that rests upon the murderers hands will not.

July 24. They are dying off very fast at the hospital now.

July 26. Still we are lying in prison, a lazy set of fellows.

July 28. It appears we are all going to be exchanged in a short time. O joy in camp.

July 30. We have the news that 1000 of us are to leave on next Thursday & the rest on the 31st.

August 1. This was the day set apart for 1000 of us to start but they have put it off until Monday.

August 3. Today we baked 5 pies. We sold 2 for 25 cts. apiece & had 3 pies to eat.

August 4. The parole fever has died down considerable.

August 5. I now think we will be out in the course of a week.

August 8. This morning we left our crowded prison at Lynchburg & took cars for Richmond, which place we reached about 9 o'clock at night.

August 9. Much contrary to our expectations we are now quartered on Belle Island near Richmond. We expect to be exchanged in a few days.

August 10. Still on "soup" island. We have fine times bathing in James River. First time we have been allowed that privilege this summer.

August 11. This is the hottest day I have ever felt in my life.

August 14. There was some more prisoners brought in from the 27th. They were taken in the fight near Culpeper. This is the first time we have heard from the regiment since we were taken prisoner.

August 15. I am getting tired of "Scary Island."

August 17. There is now about 5000 [prisoners] on the island.

August 20. There is strong talk of going tomorrow.

August 22. There was a large mail came for the prisoners. None for Henry.

August 23. Today General Row rules the island instead of General Starvation who is our general ruler. The boys have raised a crowd & are cleaning out all the Slap-Jacks bakers who have been skinning us. They allowed none to remain who do not agree to sell 4 for a quarter from this time on. The Slap-Jacks bakers are a class of men who were more fortunate than the rest of us. They happen to have a little money by them when they were captured. They now take advantage of their fellow prisoners by buying flour & baking a pancake known among the soldiers by the appellation of Slap-Jacks, & which they sell for the enormous price of 2 for a quarter. I do not much approve of mobs, but I don't blame the boys for mobbing them for such acts up to the cruel barbarities of the rebs.

August 24. They are selling bread at the commissary while last Sunday they did not have rations.

August 27. Today the sergeants of the different squads are taking the names of their men, their company, regiment, and date and place of capture. This looks something like paroling now sometime.

August 28. We have a healthy breakfast. That is, bread and water. Our slop (soup) for some cause having failed to come around. I guess it was too cool to get flies sufficient to thicken it.

August 31. We drew 4 little crackers and a little soup. We can now take up doleful lamentation "The Harvest is past and the summer is ended and lo we are not saved (released) yet."

September 1. The Richmond papers state that we are going off this week.

September 3. Were called to see who could walk 15 miles. A good sign.

September 4. It is reported that we are going away tomorrow certain.

September 5. And not gone yet.

September 7. It is now 13 months since we left Bloomington, Indiana. This morning I experienced the keenest of disappointments. Before we got done eating our soup, our squad was called out. About 40 of their names, along with three other squads, Cousin Ike's along with others, were called off and started for our lines. While the rest of us were turned back into camp to await our turn with drooping spirits. The best of it was we were in such a hurry we through our soup out, so we missed our rations.

September 12. Last night the officers were busy taking our descriptive lists prepatory to paroling us this morning. I was out peddling a little. The price of some articles selling on Belle Island. Peaches—6 for a quarter; flour—25 cents per quart; Slap-Jacks 4 for a quarter; bread—25 cents per loaf (common 5 cent loaves); pies—40–50 cents a piece; tobacco—75 cents per plug. But I am now called out to sign parole.

September 13. This is the day we have long sought and mourned because we found it not. This morning we actually left Belle Isle for our own lines. We reached the landing (Aikens) about sundown after a long and fatiguing march. Not withstanding our worn out and wearied limbs, when we saw the Stars and Stripes, that Blessed old Banner of American Liberty, shout after shout rose upon the air, as we marched to the boats, until the long column (for there was 3,800 of us altogether) had got on board. After which we all partook of a hearty meal of Uncle Sam's own. Somewhat different from Jeff's [Jefferson Davis] meals on Belle Isle. More than that we were here under our own dear flag.

September 14. I partook rather freely of Uncle Sam's hospitality, and not being used to eating much of late I do not feel well as I might. We set out early from Aikens Landing [on] the Vanderbilt.

September 15. We soon passed our line of picket gunboats when the flag of truce was hauled down and we knew we were inside our own lines. We gave three rousing cheers for the Union.

September 16. This morning we arrived in Annapolis, Maryland. We landed and went into Camp Parole where we find plenty to eat.

September 17. I started a letter home, first for about three months.

September 25. All the Indiana boys along with several others left Annapolis for Washington. We went aboard the Hero.

September 26. We run past Mount Vernon and Alexandria. We landed at Washington City where we were met by the usual amount of sutlers who were anxious to furnish us something nice to eat, provided we had the cash. We were rather poor customers without money. We went over to the soldiers home and got our dinner and then got aboard of the Swan and went back to Alexandria. We were told to get off the boat; so we went into town without any officers in charge of us. We started off and scattered around town. I went out to Fort Ellsworth and lay around a fire.

September 27. We was all in a bustle so as to draw rations. We drew some grub and cooking utensils and got dinner right out in the sun. They tried to make us stand guard but the boys refused to stand. We go just where we please.

October 5. We drew new clothes. Bully for us.

October 6. I paroled all my Belle Island lice and put on my new suit.

October 8. Still in Washington awaiting transportation.

October 9. Today we got to our regiment at last. We found them in Maryland Heights. I got a letter from home, the first in 5 months.

Camp Parole at Annapolis also was a rehabilitation camp of sorts for men released from prison in the East, including most of the 27th's. Its commander, Lieutenant Colonel George Sangster, in responding to the Indiana governor's inquiring agent, felt life there was fine.

There are about 50 Indianians in this camp now. Their every want is attended to—their clothing—rations—and quarters are everything troops could desire. Immediately upon their arrival here I furnish them with a complete new outfit, and give them all the conveniences within my power. They don't have much duty to perform and not enough to occupy their time, are prone to complain without reason.[21]

Paroled men were not allowed to bear arms until exchanged for a like Confederate parolee. Once exchanged a man could pursue normal duties. Open from August 1862 to April 1863, Camp Parole held parolees under military discipline until they either were reassigned or allowed to go home. Located at Elk Ridge near the rail head serving the Washington and Baltimore line, it was both barracks and hospital. "White flag boats" bringing prisoners from the James came up the Chesapeake Bay and landed at today's Naval Academy marina. The men went to a hospital located on the St. Johns College campus, a five-building complex, or to the "naval school." The camp processed 70,000 men although no more than 8,000 at once. One observer called the post "beautiful and well regulated."[22] Private Sylvester Layton, wounded and captured at Winchester, never left Annapolis. He died in the camp hospital December 27, 1862, from diarrhea, debility, and typhoid pneumonia, three months and 10 days after his brother Private John was killed at Antietam. The Western equivalent was Camp Chase, Columbus, Ohio, which also processed 27th parolees.

The Fort Delaware center was another story. On small Pea Patch island in the Delaware River below Philadelphia, Pennsylvania, and Wilmington, Delaware, Fort Delaware held both Confederate prisoners and Union parolees. Some of the 27th's men went through there and others through both Delaware and Annapolis. An Indiana citizen visitor, Mr. W. Wilson, was so indignant about the treatment of parolees there he wrote the Indianapolis *Journal* in September 1862:

> I visited Ft. Delaware today & saw a large No. of Union prisoners of war including 49 Indianians, 20 from 27th Regiment. They truly are in a destitute condition. Some are sick. [Sergeant] John M. Brower of Company H is very sick. I have sent to Washington, DC, to Mr. Dennis to send some things for their immediate relief. They truly had a hard time in the old tobacco house at Richmond [Libby]. Here where we can do for them it is harder to suffer the privations they have to undergo. They have no blankets. It will be chilly for them to sleep on bare boards. Many told me they get so cold at night they have to get up & walk around to keep warm. Those in the hospital are better cared for, but it is a sad picture for a government hospital. Our men speak well of those immediately in charge of them. There is a deplorable fault somewhere. Where is the relief, Sanitary Committees? Do any of their members pass in the 50 vessels that sail by the fort every day?[23]

In their freedom parolees unwittingly added a new dimension to the war's suffering made known in the North. Of them nurse Livermore wrote, "The appearance of many of these poor creatures is very peculiar. Their skin looks dead, sunburned, and faded. Their skins, from long exposure and contact with the pitch-pine smoke of their campfires, and a long dearth of soap and water, are like those of the American Indian. Their emaciated form, with the bones protruding through the skin in many instances, and the idiotic express of their protruding eyes, tell of unparalleled cruelty and savage barbarity."[24]

Former prisoners were entitled to back pay, commutation, and rations. All sought longer furloughs home or other favors while awaiting exchange. Many turned for help to the efficient office of the Indiana Military Agent in Washington, D.C. Private George Edwards, paroled home in Solsberry, wanted a pass for Indianapolis or Columbus, Ohio. Privates George W. Kent and David Brown wanted ration money and allowances.[25] While the process moved slowly, eventually it tried to reach everyone concerned. To notify current and former soldiers of his services, Agent Isaac W. Monfort ran this 1863 notice in the Indianapolis *Journal*:[26]

Exchanged prisoners of the 27th Indiana are interested in the following:

Editor Journal.—Will you please to state in your paper that the certificates for the soldiers of the 27th Indiana who were prisoners, and who were mustered some 6 weeks since for commutation and rations, are now ready, and the money can be had at any time, upon presenting the certificates. Those members who have been discharged and are now at home, can make their application directly to this office, and their money will be sent to them by express.

The 27th Indiana had a man in the Andersonville, Georgia, prisoner of war camp. At New Hope Church in May 1864, Private William Treadway was wounded and became separated from the regiment after the charge against the enemy breastworks. Disoriented, he walked into enemy lines, a mistake which removed him to Andersonville, the war's most notorious prison. There he died sometime after September 20 from chronic diarrhea. An acquaintance lived to bring the word. Treadway, 23, was remembered as "one of the truest, most unselfish, devoted friends the writer has ever known. He never returned. His white-winged soul went up to God from that Lazar-spot at Andersonville in the summer, through slow, heartless process of exposure and starvation."[27]

We were fortunate in our unusual exemption from rebel prison experiences. Except for those captured at Winchester, only small numbers fell into enemy hands. Earlier in the war, the captivity period was short compared to what befell prisoners in 1864. —*ERB* [28]

CHAPTER 10

Typhoid, Catarrh, and Soldier's Rheumatism: Health and Fitness

You wanted to know [how] the soldiers was used when they get sick. If the doctor does not excuse them from duty they are put in the guard house and sometimes with handcuffs on, and the doctor will not excuse them if they are able to walk about the camp. So you may guess how soldiers fare when sick. —*Private George Edwards, May 17, 1862* [1]

Following enlistment, soldiers of the 27th Indiana received no physical examinations unless ill and reporting to a surgeon. Even then examinations and diagnoses were cursory, and usually verbal. Sanitation was never good but did improve after 1861. It became only minimal and reduced epidemics, but affected personal hygiene little. Soldiers were not inclined to preventiveness, only to reaction once struck.

Army officials stressed neither personal hygiene nor organized fitness programs of basic exercises such as calisthenics. Countless hours of drill, shelter and fortification construction, wood chopping and 1,919 miles of marching—the distance the regiment covered on foot—were exercises of necessity. Baseball was among the few sports played, and only occasionally in the East. While much is known about the effect of diet on the common soldier's health, little is known about exercise aiding general wellness. However, normal exercise had some benefit, as Commissary Sergeant Simpson Solomon Hamrick wrote in March 1862: "We never move over 10 or 15 miles a day. That is just healthy exercise. We usually have a good deal better health on march than lying in camp."[2] Good physical shape and a strong constitution were not always enough. Without missing a muster, Private George Geisler had endured an Antietam wound and three years of arduous service. After mustering out he became ill on the way home and died at Marietta, Georgia, 11 days later.

Health problems began immediately after the regiment was formed, but erupted in Maryland in the Fall 1861, mowing through the ranks. The first ill soldier after arrival in the East was Private Samuel Waln, a "stout hearty man" at enlistment, but a few weeks later a victim of fever, measles, and bad lungs. He could not speak above a whisper, refused to accept a discharge, recovered and served his time.[3] Private Michael Henry Van Buskirk was "unwell. In the night I was taken sick. This morning I took an emetic but it did not vomit me much."[4]

Typhoid and measles epidemics nearly paralyzed the Darnestown camp in October. Private Linzey C. Lamb's legs swelled up, causing him to miss duty for a long time, and he could "do nothing except to peddle candy among the boys." Throughout the war Lamb, "broken down," was not considered a "sound man." On forced marches "of great physical strain he would invariably succumb. As a result he could only participate in those fights where there was no preliminary hard marching."[5] Private Elijah Wilkinson contracted measles, cold, and cough which always hounded him. Musician James T. McHolland, ill with measles and diarrhea, was in a Baltimore, Maryland, hospital for two years, a long time for a non-wound.

One might expect hearty country boys of the 27th to repel or endure disease and sickness. But that was not necessarily so. The Hoosiers, when exposed to "city diseases," frequently joined "the puny list," never fully developing antibodies. Isolated mostly in villages or farms, they were innocently victimized by communicable viruses and bacteria in large Eastern bivouacs. Even when maintaining robustness, a man's exposure to rain, snow, wind, frozen ground, chilling temperatures after sweating, and meager shelter caused respiratory and upper body infections.

The men were apathetic toward disease and sickness; they were "conditioned since infancy, helpless, stolid, quiet acquiescence, indifference." Indiana communities had much sickness, and the origins and unpredictability of disease were not understood. The men were accustomed to misery and death.[6] And they complained more about being cold than hot.

Health was a major topic and constantly reported to home. By late November 1861, Hamrick wrote the "health of the regiment improving since measles began to run out. Most of the soldiers weigh more than they ever did at home. I am as hearty now as I could wish."[7] Doctors were hardly immune to illness. Assistant Surgeon John H. Alexander missed nearly all of the Atlanta Campaign. Physician Captain Jackson L. Moore endured chronic rheumatism from exposure from sleeping in cold, wet clothes.

Sergeant Ira Broshears, a medical student, accompanied Moore's visits to his sick men. He wrote in February 1862, "Since leaving Indiana, 38 have died mostly of measles and typhoid fever. This is the eighth camp we have occupied. We have lost by death, discharges, etc., 62 men."[8] Private Charles Lutz contracted a cold, rheumatism, and diarrhea. Moore said, "The boy would die if he was not sent home." Lutz was hospitalized in Alexandria, Virginia, and returned to duty in January 1862, but was "still sick, bent emaciated form, hollow cough, slow stiffened gait, for he was a mere shadow of his former self." He was discharged with a "spinal affection."[9] Private George Edwards liked Maryland and hoped "they will let us stay here this winter. It will be a great help to the health of the boys."[10]

Non-combatants endured equal exposure as combatants. Band members contracted rheumatism, diarrhea, and piles during the Shenandoah Valley Campaign and performed no duty. Musician John A. Conklin contracted fever after sleeping on cold, damp ground. A gale made one night very cold, causing "pains in his back, aching joints and bones." He went to a hospital and was never well thereafter.[11]

> The period the regiment was in Maryland [Fall 1861–Winter 62] was a sifting period. I believe those who got sick or died at this stage of their service had frail constitutions or too much impaired to endure ordeals of army life. Let us drop a tear to their memory. That they did not accomplish more towards suppressing the rebellion was not because it was not in their hearts to do more. —ERB [12]

A medical discharge released a man from service but did not guarantee improved health. At home he faced treatment by his family doctor, not the government, whose skills and training were as questionable as those of army surgeons. A number of 27th men died from wounds or diseases after discharge at home and one before he left the army hospital. An Indiana NCO stated, "It is almost impossible for them [chronically sick] to get discharged. Some ought never to have come [into army]. They are a cumbrance on the regiment without any prospect of ever being of service to [the] government."[13]

The 27th Indiana lost almost one quarter of its enrollment, 275 men (23.3 percent), because of disease, sickness, and disability. Ninety-nine (8.3 percent) died. One hundred sixty-three (13.8 percent) were discharged, and 13 (1.1 percent) were transferred. Like all Civil War soldiers, they were wracked by ill health, poor preventive measures, and insufficient treatment.

However, the ratio of 99 such deaths to 158 casualty deaths, 1 to 1.6, is a marked reversal of Union Army statistics where non-casualty deaths exceeded battle deaths by some 3 to 2. Disease was cited as the cause of death 127 times, and sickness and disability five. Multiple diseases or a combination of disease and disability were cited in many deaths. Typhoid, the regiment's killer disease early in the war, particularly in the winter of 1861–62, claimed 35 lives, usually by itself and sometimes with measles. Chronic diarrhea, pneumonia, and measles each were cited in 12 cases. General "disease," "lungs," general "fever," phthisis (pulmonalis), consumption, smallpox, dysentery, and erysipelas each caused three or more deaths.

Of the war's 10 most infectious diseases of military importance in the Union Army, only five were significant to the health of the 27th. They were diarrhea and dysentery, catarrh and bronchitis, typhoid and related (presumably measles), eye disease, and inflammation of the lungs (pneumonia and consumption). Of the sicknesses, exposure to prison conditions killed three former prisoners of war. Nostalgia caused another. General "debility" and rheumatism were the disabling causes.

Disease, sickness, and disability not only killed, they generated 163 discharges which also sliced the regiment's manpower. A discharge released a member during his service, whereas mustering-out was at its expiration. Disease caused 85 discharges. Preponderant were phthisis (pulmonalis), chronic diarrhea, heart, consumption, and "lungs" and typhoid. Other interesting causes were syphilis/gonorrhea, spinal meningitis, scurvy, and eye (blindness). Sicknesses caused 27 discharges, led by bronchitis, dyspepsia, laryngitis, cough, general "sick," and a host of "itis" sicknesses, many of which have disappeared as diagnoses. Disability caused 95 discharges. Rheumatism, general "debility," injury, anchylosis/paralysis, general "disability," hernias, and epilepsy were most numerous. Others included fatigue/exposure and varicose veins/leg ulcers, deafness, and idiocy/imbecility. Drummer boy William Shaller Ottwell, 14, "a slender, very small delicate boy with rather poor and delicate health," but "prompt and faithful in his duties," was discharged because of "youth and effeminacy."[14] Thirteen transferred to the Veterans Reserve Corps (VRC) from sickness, disease, and disability. One returned. The VRC performed primarily garrison and home duty and was composed of soldiers whose disabilities prohibited them from combat duty but not from service.

The 275 losses partially address the impact of ill health. Uncounted are hundreds of men, many repeat cases, hospitalized for days or more than a year, missing the regiment's commitments and further sapping its strength. Calculating accurately all hospitalizations is impossible, but likely almost everyone was hospitalized at least once. Any who escaped were very lucky or very strongly constituted.

Diarrhea was the common denominator and equalizer. Its omnipresent pernicious impact was incalculable, but it wreaked a terrible toll in deteriorated health, reduced individual strength, wasted man-hours and productivity, and combat inefficiency. Of the service-connected infirmities, diarrhea affected most seriously the health of the survivors. Besides diarrhea, and its companion dysentery, scores of men went to the hospital for treatment of measles, typhoid, and rheumatism; many missed battles because of hospitalization. Those numbers contributed to the regiment's continual attritions, weakening its fighting capability. At least 16 original members who served their full three years made every muster. They probably visited a hospital for wound dressings, or checked in for a few days' hospitalization, but were not away long enough to miss muster.

Eventually, like most aspects of soldiering, the Indiana common soldiers came to respect the virtues of proper camp sanitation. An expression was said of the Union soldier and cleanliness, "Necessity is a capital teacher."[15] By necessity they learned to dispose of trash and other waste properly and answer their urinary and bowel calls without inconveniencing others. However tough necessity was, it was impossible to practice adequate hygiene, even in the norm of the day, and keep bodies and clothing clean while on the move. The young men generally were indifferent to how they looked or smelled while in the field.

Uncertain at first of their duties and responsibilities and unfamiliar with group hygiene, officers did not wish to offend the men who elected them and would be behind them in battle. Consequently, sanitation rules, like many others, were haphazardly established and loosely enforced. Maintaining the communal habitat required the impossible, everyone's cooperation. Regimental commander Colonel Silas Colgrove tried, but little worked as sickness and disease conquered the Union camps in the Winter 1861–62. His early directive required four men from each company for "police duty detail" to police the whole camp. "Each tent will be cleaned & swept out & all rubbish carried at least 20 feet beyond the company fires. Soldiers are required to shake their blankets out clean & hang them out for airing."[16]

In December 1861, the U.S. Sanitary Commission found Union officers were not attending to the soldiers' cleanliness, and rarely insisted on feet washing and most often face, neck, and head washing. In 20 percent of the units men did not wash shirts at least weekly. "The volunteer army is more unsoldierlike in respect to matters of this kind."[17] The 27th Indiana's company commanders "had to pay particular attention to the personal cleanliness both in the person & clothing of their men," had to inspect each mess daily before 10:00 a.m., and required tents be kept clean, dry and well ditched. An officer inspected "each & every meal," and no food was "suffered to be eaten that is not well cooked, especially the articles of meat, beans & rice."[18] In the Spring 1862, as trash piled around the camp, Colgrove directed removal of all dirt and rubbish. "No bones, meat or other refuse will be thrown inside of quarters. Company commandants will see that sinks are dug outside the color line & all slop & refuse in thrown in it." Meals were permitted only at the designated hour "& not before the hour sounded by the calls." Thirty minutes before meal time company officers inspected cooking utensil cleanliness and whether victuals were well cooked.[19]

By the Winter 1863, the general commanding their Army of the Potomac began "the best sanitary practice of the Union Army." Corporal Van Buskirk said, "We had orders to clean up 20' outside the guard line all around the camp. This is a big job & the boys are grumbling. It had almost become a case of necessity, for the litter & filth of all winter had been constantly swept over the guard line & accumulating."[20] Surgeons were awakening to the importance of their "preventive duties."[21] Medical authorities also suggested raising bunks four inches off the ground to allow air circulation, and removing all quarters sunk into the ground and placing them on the surface. To keep drinking water pure: "Hereafter all washing must be done below the spring. No working of any kind will be allowed above or around the spring."[22]

The 27th never lived in barracks or other structures with indoor water closets unless in a modern hospital. Their residences were either log huts, tents or the open air. Consequently, calls of nature were always answered outdoors. In permanent camps they built outdoor latrines called sinks, simply uncovered holes dug in the ground often upstream from camp, where soldiers were supposed to urinate and defecate. Boards or logs could be positioned as seats. Sanitary conditions always became unbearable. A camp inspector reported, "the only sink is merely a straight trench some 30 feet long unprovided with pole or rail; the edges are filthy and the stench exceedingly offensive. From the ammoniacal odor frequently perceptible in camp, men are obviously allowed to urinate during the night at least wherever convenient." Many of the boys who at home "followed nature's call to the closest and most convenient spot" ignored the sinks and went anywhere.[23] While on the move there was no time to dig sinks and the men wandered off, hopefully at some distance so as not to foul the campsite. They waived privacy and ignored modesty.

Diarrhea compounded the filth problems and destroyed well-intentioned camp sanitation planning. The human waste problem was more acute when darkness, snow, ice, or bad weather degraded access to sinks or the closest woods, or while huddled for hours behind breastworks under fire, such as after the charge at Gettysburg, or in Atlanta's muddy trenches. The men held it or went where they could. If that meant in their holes while under fire, they later dug it out and disposed of it if they had to remain there. Ingenuity substituted for toilet paper, a rare luxury. As well as the smell, the toilets attracted multitudes of flies and other insects which permeated campsites and spread everything imaginable. Soldiers had to throw dirt into the sinks daily to reduce pollutants, but camps were saturated with germs. Because medicine had not realized the causes of diseases and infection, once an epidemic broke out nothing could stop it except running out of victims.

Health was a constant topic with homefolks and often tied to sanitation. "Health of regiment continues good but not as good as it has been due to camp being more condensed, and the water is not as good," wrote one soldier.[24] Second Lieutenant Josiah Clinton Williams wrote in July 1862, "I just returned from a morning wash & had my hair cut $1/4$", sitting in shirtsleeves trying to keep as cool as possible."[25] His "wash" was not much. Camp bathing depended on the temperature and water availability. The colder the less frequently one bathed. Sponging one's face and hands with cloth or hands from a pail or canteen was sometimes all a man could do for days, if that. Enlisted men used towels only while in camp long, and then rarely. Bar soap was a scarce commodity, but pieces of soap were sometimes available from the sutler or a comrade.

Naked bathing was limited to warm days alongside rivers or creeks— if someone stood guard. Some men stripped to the flannels, or just removed shoes, socks and vests; others removed nothing. Body odor (modern deodorants were unheard of) year around was terribly offensive, but everyone had it, and was only partially eliminated when bodies, including private parts, were sponged and clothes scrubbed in streams or boiled in kettles. Skin grease and dirt was a bacteria storehouse and accelerated infections from wounds or abrasions. Many men shaved themselves when possible and some served as part-time barbers, but worn razors and scissors could be "barbarous." Some men let their hair and beard grow, never allowing dirt and discomfort to drive them otherwise. Regulations were inconsistently enforced except for certain inspections.

Dental hygiene was lax and outside the purview of surgeons. Some men used dry toothbrushes but care was worse than at home. Tooth cleansers were scarce. Halitosis, toothaches, and broken and rotting teeth were accepted adversities, particularly on those suffering with scurvy. Army dentists were few and far between.

Men washed clothes when they could be hung to dry, and since many men in the field had only those on their backs, it meant a long wait. Dirt was removed by pounding or rubbing clothing on rocks or sand, because obtaining laundry soap or lye was a problem. Uniforms wore out easily enough anyway. Sometimes officers or an enlisted mess employed a negro to do laundry in camp. Eating utensils usually were cleaned in streams or by rubbing in dirt. At one point in the Atlanta Campaign the Hoosiers took advantage of their first bonafide camp in 46 days to clean:

> July 6, 1864. We are 6 miles from Atlanta. The day was fiercely hot, and the mosquitoes of the Chattahoochee were as bad as the rebels in their thirst for Yankee gore. Time here to clean up. Boiled clothes as we had done at Sandy Hook, Maryland, after Antietam. Men stood picket while rest

boiled in suds and hung clothes on limbs to dry. A sudden call to march would have found battalions, if not brigades, in a stark condition of nativity.[26]

The common cold was a year-round curse. Most men caught colds, and shaking the symptoms was difficult. Phthisis, not diagnosed today, was the name given a severe respiratory cold, consumption-like in form but not as serious as pneumonia. Catarrh, frequently mentioned in health records but also rarely diagnosed now, was an inflammation of mucous membrane in the nose and throat. "His catarrh problems were sniffling of nose, hacking cough, spitting, complaining of head, and a stench odor when near his face," a comrade said of Private Thomas H. "Old Hound" Chiles. "He had a hacking cough with a kind of sound which some of the boys said reminded them of a choked hound. I could tell where he was day or night by the noise he made coughing, hawking, and spitting."[27]

Colds, phthisis and catarrh often preceded lengthy coughing spells, chronic bronchitis and related head and throat discomforts—each endured without effective decongestants and antihistamines. Men developed colds and other problems sleeping on frozen ground during the Balls Bluff expedition to Conrad's Ferry, Maryland, in October 1861. Veterans never forgot the anguish of awakening in the grip of ice, the product of a night's rain and sleet, their uniforms or single wool or rubber blankets bonded to the earth. Attempts to rise were stymied until pulling, chipping, or pounding loosened the hold, tearing clothes. Limbs momentarily were immobile. Only the exposed skin was spared a thin coating of glaze, and it was numb. Balls Bluff was one of two cold bivouacs rightfully blamed for life-long illnesses. Bull Run, Virginia, followed five months later.

Lieutenant Colonel Archibald Irvin Harrison caught a severe cold and cough which along with "domestic troubles and cases" expedited his immediate discharge on October 29, 1861.[28] Private Eli Edgar Barnes contracted a heavy cold, treated it with medicine, and later endured a "hard chill." Diagnosed with catarrh, Barnes had difficulty breathing the remainder of his three years' service, especially when exerting.[29] Confederate firing along the Potomac caused Private Greensbury W. Hancock to catch cold after jumping from a boat to swim back to Maryland. Captain Theodore T. Buehler's cold converted into bronchitis, sore throat and constant cough, keeping him off duty for the first winter. Surgeon Jarvis J. Johnson urged him "to resign and return home or he would not survive much longer exposed to hardships incident to camp life," which he did on May 9, 1862.[30]

Corporal Van Buskirk wrote in April 1863, "Seems as if the whole regiment was taking cold at once. I never heard the beat of barking and heaving around."[31] Corporal Ebenezer Quackenbush marked his 1863 bronchitis with a piece of red flannel around his throat. Private Enoch M. Bruner's runny nose was annoying. "He became stupid and appeared to be worn out, looked sallow and jaundiced."[32] Private Elijah S. Crawford caught a cold while hospitalized with measles, "producing almost total deafness in the left ear and partial deafness in the right."[33] In snowy March 1862 at Bull Run, they slept in the creek bottom and woke up, as Drummer William Shaller Ottwell said, with "water running in my ears. Clothes didn't dry for two days."[34]

On a bitter cold 1862 evening, Private William D. Burch "took cold, went to lungs." After four months in hospitals with "medicine [of] cod liver oil with porter and wines," he asked for duty. "The doctor said 'Young man, you had better go home than to your regiment.' I told him, 'never, I can't go home, as I never was in battle.' I would get better after a bit." He returned to the 27th in July. "They yelled to see me," but his dubious captain said, "You won't be able for the campaign. You ought to went home." "I told him and everybody that sees—take me into one battle then I will go home."[35]

Typhoid and measles always were potential scourges, and little could be done medically to prevent them. The plight of one young soldier is typical of those who died that first fall and winter of 1861 in Maryland. "Harris, Marion; Private, Company I, Died Darnestown, Maryland, December 1, 1861, of typhoid fever."

Typhoid and measles, often diagnosed together, raced through the regiment and were cited in 47 deaths. Harris and others, including Privates Green Bias, Stephen Boardman, and Erasmus Davenport, never got the chance to soldier, and because they died so soon, were not mentioned individually in memoriam by the regimental survivors group, only lumped together as comrades briefly joined—then gone—long ago. Most lie in graves known only to inquisitive descendants, if at all.

Of the early contagious diseases, measles was most numerous with "serious complications and easy communicability." Measles and other camp diseases "greatly reduced military efficiency by their high morbidity, considerable mortality, and protracted course," and could occur in epidemics. "The sick burdened the military machine."[36] Exposure was one of its origins. One private said when measles broke out, "Seemed like most all the doctor waited on either died or had a close shave." He "took with measles. Instead of answering to sick call I sent to Frederick to get some whiskey and made hot drinks. That was better and safer than the doctor."[37] Corporal John L. Files and Private John Parham nearly died at Darnestown. Private Philip A. Lane became sick with measles and almost choked to death on picket in the rain. The next night he lay on the ground without shelter in more rain. Cold settled in his lungs and they were raw and sore. He coughed up blood, his nose bled, and he had a dull headache.

Presbyterian Church Cemetery, Darnestown, Maryland

Unknown number of 27th Indiana soldiers are buried in unmarked graves in foreground to the right.

Photo by author

Living with irritating, dirty, strength-sapping diarrhea became routine even to the healthiest. Corporal Joshua L. Foster described his case: "My diarrhea caused 4–12 stools per day. The discharges are white and foamy like soap suds until it begins to check, then becomes bloody, and I suffer from gripping in the bowels. I have bleeding, painful piles, and the surface of my rectum is very sensitive."[38]

Soldiers were most likely to contract it from camp sanitation and hygiene deficiencies, but also from rancid, infested food, foul water, or a non-nutritious diet. In the "number of victims, mortality, chronicity, sequels, relapses and repeated attacks," diarrhea and dysentery were "the most important military diseases."[39]

Diarrhea caused Private John W. Cunningham to become the first hospitalization case in Indianapolis. As the men hardened into soldiers on arriving in Maryland in October 1861, diarrhea was the enemy. Private Joseph Schrader blamed "poor water and diet living off sow belly and beans, now and then a little beef. Water was greasy and brackish, started me running off at the bowels."[40] Most straggling on the march was not from cowardice but weak bowels where painful steps mandated interruptions for relief. Often men could not march. Captain John Roush Fesler contracted chronic diarrhea and piles in 1862 and suffered "occasional attacks of camp diarrhea during most of my service. I always tried to keep out of the hospital," and sometimes was carried into combat in an ambulance. After being promoted he "got to riding a horse," aggravating his rectal area.[41] In the May 1862 Winchester retreat, Sergeant William Parmemas Ellis was disabled with diarrhea and was transported on a pontoon wagon. Private Michael Leikauff stood no guard duty because he could not leave his post and "had to run nearly all the time." Thick, heavy set, fleshy, and too fat to keep up on the march, he spent much time in hospitals.[42] Musician Mathias Smith was weak and required assistance to the latrines, "spitting matter mixed with blood."[43]

Piles, a bowel and rectum ailment, struck Private Peter Jacobs. Straining himself building log huts, the bowel came out and down about one inch and was "red and angry looking. I thought it would rot off if something was not done," a comrade said, adding "diarrhea was tolerably bad on him at times." Jacobs bathed it in cold water whenever it came down, sometimes twice a day, received medicine from the hospital steward, and was excused from duty.[44] Corporal Jonathan Baker's rectum "came down," and his "lower bowel inflamed and got very sore and irritated." He used salve on the soreness and burning sensation.[45] A comrade said about Sergeant John Hayes: "I have seen his ass just stick out at different times so bad that he would almost died," and "rendered him assistance in getting it back."[46]

Rheumatism was another major ailment which afflicted nearly all in one form or another. "The day of the Battle of Resaca after sleeping on arms in the rain without tents, he [Captain Peter Fesler] had severe rheumatism. He stayed through the excitement with his company and throughout the Atlanta Campaign."[47] Called "soldier's rheumatism" in the camps, it was a pain or ailment of the joints, muscles, tendons and ligaments, usually resulting from exposure, overexertion, injury or just aging. If a part of the body hurt when moved, it was diagnosed as rheumatism.

Rheumatism was most prevalent early in the war until the men hardened, but continued to strike throughout. Often the sufferer could not pinpoint its origin. It could incapacitate an otherwise able man, causing him to straggle or be unavailable for picket duty and drill. Generically it covered arthritis, bursitis, or any inflammation, swelling or stiffness, and included sprains and torn ligaments or cartilage. Therapy was not used. Treatment included binding the area, ointments, crutches, rest, and being transported around.

Men contracted maladies on the march. Second Lieutenant John D. McKahin was "much exposed, waded streams and rivers, and for three weeks had not had time nor opportunity to change clothing." Diarrhea and rheumatism aggravated his subsequent Antietam wound. He was "scarcely able to be on duty, reduced to a mere skeleton, worn out and half starved and greatly exposed," keeping up only by riding a horse.[48] Painful rheumatism caused Captain William E. Davis to be hauled to Balls Bluff in an ambulance, and rheumatism and a Gettysburg wound sent Private Harlan Anderson on a round-about eight-month trip to rejoin the regiment.

Eye problems were numerous and annoying. When combined with other maladies they precipitated hospitalization or discharge. Little indication exists that spectacles may have been worn by only but a few soldiers. But the strangest of all health conditions faced by the 27th Indiana was susceptibility to "moonblindness" during the Atlanta Campaign, a phenomenon preventing a man from seeing after dark. Consider the plight of Private Samuel A. Duzan:

> Eye problems began in May 1864 from laying on our backs with moon and stars shining in our face. A man was detailed to lead him on marches. Suspecting Duzan was shirking, Private Rufus Williams, "who didn't think he was so blind, undertook to lead him one night. Later Williams said he knew the fellow was blind because he had led him off a [pontoon] bridge and gave him a terrible jolt." No doubts then.[49]

Moonblindness ("nightblindness" or "moon-eyed") was vividly recorded. Stricken men, complaining of sore, inflamed, weak eyes and painful eyeballs, were excused from night duty and led carefully around campfires and hazards. Eyes looked dimmer than before being moonblinded. Called a disease without accurate diagnosis or foundation, moonblindness was attributed to what we would call stress—origins and rationale were diverse and unexplained. Normally the only treatment was cold water.

The eye problems of Private Thomas H. Chiles, worn out and despondent, were attributed to debility and malaria. He "could not see a bit from the time the sun went down till skylight. Pitch dark was all the same to him."[50] At first officers and surgeons believed the condition was contrived to avoid duty. But as solid, obedient soldiers came down, they were puzzled and unable to justify it. Chiles was one of the solid soldiers, as was Private James Burke "one of the neatest men in the regiment." Burke's case came from "sleeping out in the moonshine." Lieutenant Joseph Balsley stated, "When men complained of such things as moonblindness we looked upon them as shamming, but when Jim Burke complained of being affected we knew he was ailing, for he was no shirk or coward."[51] No officers were afflicted.

The first case during Atlanta was Private John Parham who suffered "blindness" crossing the Cumberland Mountains and was often led around by Private George Washington Welsh.[52] "I am tired of this war," wrote

Parham. "I can't see to march after night unless I am led, have been that way for 20 days. There is a great many in the army the same fix. My eyes don't hurt any at all."[53] When Private Daniel Monahan developed sore eyes some comrades urged him to go on furlough. Monahan replied, "No, by golly. I think the war is about over and I want to stay and see it out."[54] As well as at night, First Sergeant Franklin Zachary Sermershein could not always see to call the roll during the day. Moonblind Private Bernard Knust squinted with one eye.

The phenomenon peaked in May–June, 1864. Sergeant Joel Kemp, Private Sanford Shively, and Private Josiah W. Tobias suffered scurvy and moonblindness during Atlanta, and along with other scurvy cases caused speculation it was associated with moonblindness. Eye problems, stress, and venereal disease had a deleterious psychological effect and reduced combat readiness. And moonblindness remained unexplained during the war.

In 1867, a physician concluded in a Virginia journal that nightblindness in the Confederate Army resembled "an epidemic." The "curious and obscure disease" was nyctalopia (night blindness), or hemeralopia. His examinations in the field tied nightblindness to scurvy, debility, weakened pulse, anemia, and coolness of skin, and showed "the affection consisted in want of tone in the nervous apparatus of the eye—a condition of enfeebled local innervation, reaching no farther than the retina, and a branch of the ophthalmic nerves. Cases frequently recovered spontaneously, after all treatment had been abandoned." Baffled medical officers just furloughed the afflicted: "a grand remedy." Therefore, the disease resulted from the meager diet and lack of vegetables and vegetable acids, including iron.[55] Home, with its improved diet, cleanliness, and relief from mental anxiety and physical exhaustion, was the best cure.*

Soldiers suffered from ancient times through the Crimean War. So, Civil War medicine and the medical and surgical history ignored it because eye problems were hard to solve. Color blindness tests were sometimes given but visual acuity was not measured, and impaired vision obviously affected routines. The practice of opthalmology was barely beginning, as Sergeant Major James R. Sharp's case showed:

> I was taken sick with fever, probably unconscious for several days. When I
> began to get better and looked around everything was dark to me. I could
> not distinguish objects unless it was right close to me. As I gradually grew
> better my eyes seemed to get stronger & could distinguish things more

---

* The moonblindness linkage to vitamin A deficiency (diet) was verified in the author's interview with Michael Piorunski, Friedenwald Library, Wilmer Ophthalmic Institute, The Johns Hopkins University Hospital, Baltimore, Md., October 23, 1990.

clearly. As soon as I began using my eyes at writing I couldn't do it at all. When I would look at the paper it would seem like there was a weight pressing on my eyes and everything looked black. I can't remember when they reached focus, but were never the same. I got spectacles but vision still became defective.[56]

Venereal diseases (VD) struck both officers and enlisted soldiers of the 27th Indiana. Second Lieutenant John K. McKaskay was diagnosed with "glans penis sloughing from phynosis caused by chancre" in February 1864, at the Carnac's Woods Hospital, Philadelphia, Pennsylvania, while recovering from Gettysburg wounds.[57] McKaskay, discharged May 20, 1864, was the only known officer treated for VD.

Venereal diseases appeared periodically but were most serious during the winter of 1863–64 and the early weeks of the Atlanta Campaign. Cases can only be estimated as records indicate only those treated, not stricken. Untold numbers neglected or refused treatment fearing social or disciplinary reprisals. The Union Army rate of VD cases *treated officially* was one in 12 enlisted men. That would be about 95 men in the 27th Indiana. Others likely were treated "unofficially" by medical personnel or private doctors.

Isolated cases were reported in 1862 and early 1863. Prostitutes called at Eastern army campsites or nearby communities. By 1862 Washington had 450 bordellos and, by one report, at least 7,500 full-time hookers. Young men were living in the height of the Victorian Age which guided manners, habits, and social relations. Therefore they masked their words in jargon and tempted the reader to "read between the lines" regarding women. Victorian or not, the Hoosiers engaged in sex whenever they had the chance and money.

Private Jesse Younger was admitted to a Pennsylvania hospital in December 1862 with a "simple chancre of the franium which was nearly healed, had fully matured bubo in left groin and some tenderness in the right." The surgeon "opened the left one [testicle] at once and applied poultices. Applied iodine and ice to right one. This treatment possibly retarded its course, but it was necessary to open it on December 22. The patient recovered without any other symptoms," and was discharged with secondary syphilis in 1863.[58] In October 1863, Private Flavius J. Potter was transferred to the Veterans Reserve Corps after a year in hospitals fighting gonorrhea and syphilis. Private John E. Hart was treated for syphilis for three months in Tennessee.

Not all liaisons were with prostitutes. Local women were available and men left camp even without permission to pursue them. From all indications the men maintained active sex lives in Middle Tennessee during the seven months of 1863–64. Such pleasures were more than casual distractions. As the regiment joined the Western Army of the Cumberland in 1863,

Nashville, with a large Union Army population about 65 miles north of Tullahoma, had ended a major effort to expel prostitutes and "suppress or limit the spread of VD. The results were highly satisfactory." Nashville was accessible to men on passes or official travel, such as the 27th's detail sent there on April 24, 1864, for 10 days.[59] Nashville began licensing prostitutes with inspections, taxation, and "certificates of soundness."[60] At first those requiring medical attention were few. "But in November, shortly after the passage of the 11th and [27th Indiana's] 12th Corps through the city, 28 new cases were received." A year later, "many of the better class of prostitute had been drawn to Nashville from Northern cities by the comparative protection from VD which its license system afforded."[61]

Gonorrhea and syphilis became acute problems as the drive on Atlanta began in April 1864. Many men had become infected and possibly continued sexual activities, naive about its causes, symptoms, and consequences. After resuming the arduous marching and field regimen the scourges extracted a toll, and the diseased ones sought treatment. Some knew what they had but preferred to treat themselves or ignored it rather than be subjected to shame, resentment, or retribution by sex partners or authorities. The men received no sex education and because sex was not discussed publicly, they were ignorant, armed only with camp talk or their own sordid experiences.

In the field gonorrhea became attached to destinies. Being dispatched to the rear with VD saved a number of men from a potentially worse fate before the cannons at New Hope Church or the filth of Atlanta's trenches. The impact on readiness was immeasurable but costly. For that the diseased men had themselves to blame, or thank.

Ruptures (hernias) were commonplace. In the face of heavy marching, running under a load, jumping on and off wagons, vaulting over obstacles, falling, or riding horses, it is no wonder that many men were injured by ruptures. Cartridge boxes improperly secured around the waist and shoulder could cause ruptures on the march. Private Asbury Allen suffered from a "hypertrophied testicle and spermatic cord of left side [from] a fall while crossing a fence. He was not treated until the organ came down to normal size, or perhaps slightly atrophied and has remained very tender."[62]

Men wore trusses to tighten and hold firmly loose testicles but they were no cure. Surgery was not prescribed. The sufferer thus became more vulnerable to sickness or further injury and lost his fighting edge.

Most ruptures occurred during combat. During the charge at Cedar Mountain, Private William Dodson fell over a stone fence, crushing his testicles. One testicle was reinjured and "painted with tincture of iodine and supported in an ensfensary bandage."[63] Private Nelson Purcell fell during a retreat marching at double-quick and then rode an ambulance. At

Peachtree Creek, Captain William H. Holloway was "hurt in the right side running over some pine tree that had been cut down and fixed to hinder us." He "tried every truss available" to fix the rupture, which distracted from his purpose of going to war "to put down the rebellion."[64] Private Samuel A. Duzan suffered a double rupture. He fell in while fetching water from a nearby spring. Within five minutes, "I had a hurting in each groin like a body with the cramp colic. The first time I knew I was ruptured was on the march to [Virginia] a month later, when it began to come down on the right side and hurt awfully." The surgeon told him only to take his time marching. Later he injured both sides. "It still hurt but I was stout in those days and didn't wish to give up and made do with my duty until the day before we took Atlanta."[65]

Marching near Harpers Ferry, Virginia, Private Isaac Adams fell on a wet road but never reported the rupture. His "relations were unfriendly" with Assistant Surgeon Willis H. Twiford and he "would rather bear his rupture and go without treatment than to go to Twiford."[66] Marching in a snowstorm, Private William H. O'Neal's testicles were "enormously swollen and were put in suspensary bandages." He ordered antithogist medicine and a supporter from New York which he wore for the rest of the war.[67]

Sunstroke claimed many victims and during hot weather impeded battle readiness. Jokingly called "*coup de soleil*" (literally, stroke of the sun) sunstroke, actually heatstroke, heat prostration or dehydration, was caused by excessive physical activity in hot, humid temperatures, failure to replenish lost fluids, and continued exposure to the sun. Today we guard against each, but Civil War personnel knew little of prevention or treatment and fluids replenishment. No member died from the heat, but residual effects complicated other ailments and degraded morale.

Corporal Arthur B. Douglas had sunstroke during the fight at Cedar Mountain. "Unconscious. Had relapse in November 1862. Was helpless, unable to move hand or foot for some four weeks, then had partial use of arms. He did not walk on his own accord until March 1863, then only with crutches."[68] Douglas, one of many Hoosiers experiencing heatstroke, never recovered and was discharged with chronic cystitis and a spinal injury.

The sun could be unrelenting, as a lieutenant wrote in July 1862: "We left Front Royal Monday & whew! it was hot! Many gave out. Must have been 95 or 100 degrees in the shade. We went into camp with only about 100 men which is about average of the whole brigade, each regiment leaving some 4–500 lying by the roadside. Many were sunstricken. We marched altogether too hard."[69]

Camps were located near adequate water, but marches, especially when forced, had no such assurances. Contents of canteens filled prior to leaving were soon depleted. Frequently the route passed no potable water,

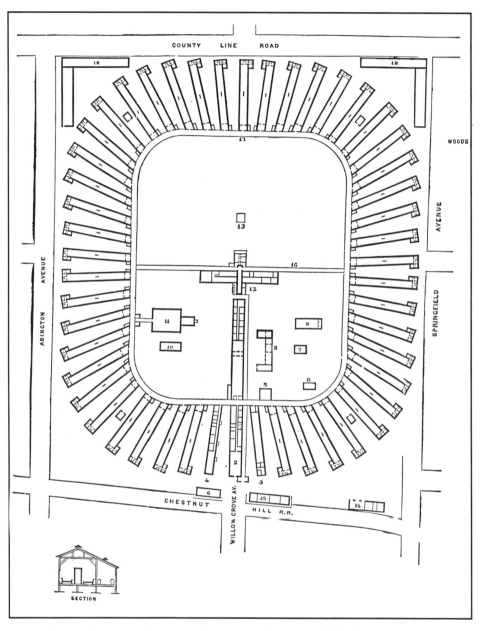

Plan of Mower General Hospital, Chestnut Hill, Pennsylvania

Medical & Surgical History of the War of the Rebellion

and famished men tried to slake their thirsts with fetid rainwater from wagon ruts, ditches, and horse hoof holes. Consuming the filthy liquid exacerbated thirst and brought stomach and bowel troubles. Dust was a protagonist with heat and thirst. Woollen, long-sleeved uniforms worn year-round choked off ventilation. But not all cases occurred while marching. Corporal Elijah Baker collapsed building breastworks at Kennesaw Mountain, Georgia. Private Seth White fell unconscious at Resaca and always complained of his eyesight.

Sunstroke was most critical in the Eastern Theater. For example, the mean temperature in Washington, D.C., during August 1862 at the time of Cedar Mountain, about 50 miles west, was 84.01 degrees. In July 1863—when the temperature at Gettysburg hit 90 degrees—it was 80.97. For June 1863, the Army of the Potomac had 58 percent of the Union Army's sunstroke cases, although constituting only 18.2 percent of the strength of all commands reporting.[70]

At Cedar Mountain the thermometer reached 98 degrees late in the day when the 27th charged. "About 10 a.m. the sweat dried on me and my skin appeared to cleave to the bone," said Fifer Potter. "Cold chills ran up my back. A glimmer came before me, got dizzy. Everything appeared to go around. I staggered and fell. Knew nothing until between 2–3 p.m. same day. I was then put in ambulance and taken to my regiment, set out and the surgeon gave me a written excuse from all duty that day. Headache did not clear up for 6 months."[71]

On August 6, 1862, the regiment marched from Washington, Virginia, to Culpeper, normally a day's march, but in the suffocating heat three days. "The dust rose up into our faces in blinding, suffocating sheets, and it appeared that wherever we went or tried to go, or whatever time of day or night we started, an endless train of wagons was in our way." At night, unable to find water, the dust was just as bad but because it couldn't be seen was breathed in more freely. "Our throats soon became as parched as the Sahara Desert."[72] On the ninth, the order came to leave immediately with their 1st Division on a forced march. No one anticipated the sun's misery over the next eight miles and during the conflict at Cedar Mountain. They moved at quick (double) time with long intervals between rests under a merciless sun. "The air was as hot as a bake oven. Our small cloth caps with narrow visors were protection for our heads and eyes, while with our heavy, regulation dress coats tightly buttoned, our bodies seemed to be a furnace of fire."[73] Canteens drained immediately. Soaking wet from sweat, the men looked for streams or springs without luck. August was dry, hot, and humid. Unused to the pace despite their training, no level of fitness prepared them for that ordeal.

The temperature possibly hit 100 as the infantry battle began, the hottest day of any battle in the East. At 8 p.m. it was 90 degrees. A 27th private said the temperature was 109. Men collapsed, some lying where they fell "frothing at the mouth, rolling their eyeballs and writhing in painful contortions."[74] Others stumbled and crawled, seeking shelter and begging for water. Officers, lacking training and understanding, and being hurried, shouted "leave them be!" Yet men sometimes stopped to pour water into a friend's quivering lips.

Private Edward A. Hoskins collapsed, suffering spasms, convulsions, and unconsciousness. He was discharged in December for epilepsy aggravated by army life and sunstroke. Sergeant James Campbell was left by the roadside. After treatment he could not walk the next day. Sergeant James M. Seibert staggered and stopped, and somehow caught up, but during the battle went down again, and was assisted from the field by Second Lieutenant Thomas M. N. Nugent. Second Lieutenant Thomas W. Casey, the lone officer overcome by heat, caught up later. Two hours and eight miles after starting out, the 27th's division halted at Cedar Run before forming their battle lines. Thousands of soldiers broke for the creek to drink, bathe their temples and fill their canteens. More were sunstruck during the battle, including Corporal John G. Wallace, Fifer Edward Kelley, and Private John C. Haddon. The negative impact on combat capability of the Union force is impossible to measure.

The 27th Indiana experienced two outbreaks of scurvy, the first among prisoners of war in Virginia in the Summer 1862 (see Chapter 9) and the second during the Atlanta Campaign. Poor diet and sanitation caused scurvy. Symptoms included pains when moving legs, discolored inner sides of legs, tender gums, teeth loss, improper bowel activity, dry skin, stiff knees, lost appetite, and ulcers. Let Private William Charles Riley describe its effects: "It poisoned my blood; I lost all my teeth. I had to be left in a field hospital before we got to Atlanta. My legs were all black and swolled up and I could not walk."[75]

The earliest case of scurvy was Private William Doyle, affected thereafter by spongy gums, loose teeth, and scars and sores on his legs. Private James Edwards' sergeant said Edwards was "so bad off his breath smelled so bad none of us boys liked to sleep with him. His offensive smell remained with him as long as we were in service.[76] Private Thomas Maginnes could not bite or chew, even tobacco. Private Robert W. Coffee caught it at Belle Isle prison and was in a "very feeble condition, almost a 'scilition' in appearance." The doctor said he could be patched up and might last a long time "but he could never expect to be much account any more physically. It had so affected his eyes that I let him have a pair of spectacles to ware."[77]

In 1864, Private John Muster had symptoms of loose teeth, swollen and discolored legs, and several ulcers on each foot near the ankle and the knee. Sergeant Henry Lange contracted "black scurvy" from eating salt bacon and crackers without vegetables, requiring two months hospitalization. Cases improved within a week on a vegetable diet, porter, and lemon and lime juice.

Personnel injuries impacting combat efficiency are infrequently mentioned by historians, and notations of injuries are missing from primary sources such as military service records. However, partial construction of records of injuries is possible. Injuries came from accidents, battle-related mishaps, nature, and animals.

During the retreat from Winchester, Private Zachariah J. Rood was barefoot and suffered cut, bruised feet on the rough, stony, graveled turnpike. He walked 35 miles from Winchester to Williamsport, Maryland. So mangled were his feet (the tendons and ligaments contracted causing his toes to turn upward), he was "disqualified from duty for 10 days and was unable to perform heavy duty such as marching."[78]

The earliest discharge was to Private Harvey Hill, who badly bruised his back during the same railroad accident that killed Private William Allen on the 27th's trip from Indianapolis to the East in September 1861. Hill was thrown about 25 feet from the car. Private Woodson Bryant missed Resaca 2^1/$_2$ years later because of a recurring side injury sustained in November 1861.

The infantryman had no machinery, and often wagons and animals were unavailable for heavy lifting and moving, such as logs for breastworks. Human power was healthy but dangerous exercise. Muscles pulled, joints sprained, lower backs tore. Private Seth White's case was common. He carried a fire log 50 paces from the woods. While tossing the log his shoulder popped out, and he was off duty for three weeks.

Safety was not emphasized. Crossing bridges, fording streams or negotiating narrow paths required great care and agility. Private Elijah Crawford partly fell through a bridge, dislocating his right ankle. A surgeon put it back in place, but he was permanently disabled. Handling animals severely jolted unwary soldiers. Musician George W. Earhart was thrown about while shoeing "unworked, wild and vicious refractory mules," necessitating hospitalization.[79] In charge of a mule team, Private Christopher Crosby was kicked in the breast and knocked senseless momentarily, then taken off for dead. Horses trampled Privates Isaac Haddon and William P. Fugate, Haddon while removing a comrade from the Cedar Mountain field.

Anything could happen to a man while on duty. Private George Pate, filling the officers' sinks, fell on to the sharp end of a tree limb, penetrating his right ear about two inches, causing hearing loss. Guard Private James

Brown, ordered by an officer, attempted to bring a drunken, resisting sergeant into camp. The sergeant bit his thumb nearly off. It became inflamed and swollen and gangrene set in, causing extensive sloughing and destroying the tendons. The thumb was removed and Brown was discharged.

Drugs, alcohol, and tobacco addicted numerous soldiers in some form. During the war Federal officials dispensed almost 10 million opium pills along with numerous drugs such as calomel, blue mass (max), and tarter enemic. Opium, the war's most commonly used drug, was easily available in pure or derivative concoctions (opiates), including laudanum, paregoric, morphine, and several patent medicines, and treated various ailments from toothaches to wounds.

Non-narcotic painkillers such as aspirin were not available yet. There was little stigma to opium's use and the Hoosiers received it in some form, such as Private John W. Hutchison. His chart read, "December 5, 1863. Much emaciated. Appetite tolerable, some diarrhea and night sweats. Course of treatment to discharge some opiate pills at night. Patient never confined to bed but for a few days. At discharge was much stronger with few paroxysms of coughing."[80]

The mood influencing and pain killing opium allowed an amputee or bed-ridden man "to distance himself from the residual pain that could hasten his recovery," and was effective in and after surgery.[81] The new hypodermic syringe injected morphine. However effective opium's application, the relief drove some soldiers into addiction which continued after the war. The drug provided escape to "maimed and shattered survivors from a hundred battlefields, diseased and disabled soldiers released from hostile prisons, anguished and hopeless wives and mothers."[82]

Alcohol, including brandy, wines, and whiskey, treated a multitude of maladies from shock to fever. If all else failed, the patient was given whiskey as either stimulant or sedative, depending on the circumstance. Contrarily, excessive alcohol use provoked maladies. No accurate measure is known of alcohol's impact on health, but since army alcohol abuse was universal, the drinkers undoubtedly harmed rather than helped their systems.

Sergeant Peter D. Jacobs "drank in the army as opportunity offered, never shirked duty when he was able to be about. He used to be on a 'burn' whenever he could get it."[83] Jacobs, "a good soldier," was trouble prone. Private Emery Howell said: "I helped Sergeant [Charles A.] Kelso arrest him one night at Hagerstown in a house of ill fame. When he refused to submit he struck at the sergeant, and Kelso struck him on the nose with the butt of his gun and smashed his nose in."[84] Private George W. Frazier was "rather slender, known to take a drink," and was "drunk from time to time."[85]

Corporal Michael Henry Van Buskirk was ordered to take Private Riley to the guardhouse. "He was drunk & we had to take him by force."[86]

The army tried intermittently to keep the soldiers from drinking and gambling, citing moral and disciplinary reasons, but usually failed. In spite of crackdowns, drinking in camp was commonplace and frequently impaired duty and sensibilities. Two of the 27th's officers and some enlisted men were disciplined for drunkenness on duty. The officers left the service after being court-martialed. Outside of camp jurisdiction, many soldiers could not hold liquor and injuries, arrests, punishment, and second thoughts followed. For instance:

> Today I had a merry time. We got hold of some whiskey & for the first time in my life I got pretty tight. I was ashamed of my condition & slipped into my bunk. I got into a deep sleep when one of my messmates came in & sat on my feet. This roused me up. I went right out & climbed into the swing but the motion so unstrung my nerves entirely. I could not hold on to the swing but down I came in a lump. It pretty near busted me & this sobered me up in a hurry. From this time on I aim to stay sober.[87]

In Maryland camps, lager beer was available at the sutler's "for five cents per every small glass, while commissioned officers get something stronger if required."[88] Company K had two brewers, Sergeant Franklin Zachary Sermershein and Private Orbagast R. Volmer, and a saloon keeper, Private Paul Geppner. In 1862, the army ordered that no sutler could keep on hand or sell within the lines any wines, liquors, or intoxicating drinks. Only officers could have it and only if approved by the brigade commander. Soldiers and suppliers tried ingenious ways to sneak whiskey into camp where bottles were disguised or hidden or smuggled in official shipments. Some got through but many were confiscated. When the regiment divided in July 1862, the sutler remained with the group at Hazel River, Virginia. His merchandise included "long black bottles" intended for the officers "for medicinal purposes only." The men caused all kinds of mischief for the detachment commander.[89]

In Tennessee, compared to earlier consumption, the men drank a lot because whiskey was more accessible and army routine hardly textbook. The men frequently referred to sprees, drinking, and other partying.* On January 10, 1864, Second Lieutenant Roger Sherman Loughry "found the old doctor quite agreeable drunk." Then Loughry "resolved this day not to drink any more whiskey while I remain in the service."[90] In Tullahoma a man saw a "whiskey seller standing on the head of a barrel with a guard to

---

* Tullahoma is about 12 miles from Lynchburg, home of the Jack Daniels distillery, whose product was likely available for a price.

keep him there as punishment for selling to the soldiers."[91] Garrison tedium spawned alcohol problems, and undoubtedly the 27th did their part in that aspect of history. A soldier noted, "Today is Christmas. There is a few drunk men in camp. Otherwise everything is quiet as common."[92]

Sergeant James S. Wood was court-martialed in January 1864 for allowing Private Alonzo Olmstead to be posted on guard while intoxicated. During Atlanta the men received whiskey officially at least twice. On June 18, 1864, "We have drawn a ration of whiskey and some of the boys are rather merry," and the night before the non-veterans departed for home, "The officers furnished the whiskey & they are having a high old time."[93]

Tobacco was more important than alcohol. The extent of tobacco use is unknown, but most users chewed it. (The constant spitting added to sanitation woes.) It was bartered for coffee from the Rebels, who had more. Otherwise they bought it from the sutler, each other or teamsters coming from supply depots. The price was expensive and depended on supply. "Got one plug of very wilt tobacco, 150 cts.," a corporal noted in a time of low supply.[94] Some men smoked pipes or dipped snuff, both practices noticed in Southern women. The men did not smoke cigarettes and usually only officers smoked cigars. Ironically, whether anyone smoked the three cigars found with the "Lost Order" prior to Antietam is also unknown, but suspected. They would make good trade bait. (See Appendix A)

Linking tobacco use to ailments was unheard of, but smoking conceivably caused coughing and bronchitis. Private Robert Kutzich was a "large consumer of tobacco and alcohol." Drunk almost constantly, his "sprees" sometimes lasted Saturday night to Monday morning. He suffered "delirium tremens," saw snakes in his boots, and became so nervous and feeble he could not "perform locomotion." Allegedly wounded after Cedar Mountain by a shell, causing fits and spasms, it was another excuse for obtaining a January 1863 discharge for "epilepsy and fainting spells."[95]

When medical officers were unable to cure diseases, fevers and assorted ailments, soldiers of the 27th—like their counterparts universally—used patent medicines for attempted cures. Sutlers and quacks sold them, and rural mothers supplied sons with home concoctions. Patent medicine firms and products boomed. "I only got medicine once or twice from regimental doctors," recalled Captain William H. Holloway. "I had home send me some Roback's Pills by mail, and about every other night I took a dose and thus was able to keep my stomach and bowels moving through the Atlanta Campaign. If I hadn't done this I couldn't have been on duty but half the time, because of piles and sick headaches caused by a bad stomach.[96] Private Amos Kersey remembered Holloway took pills nearly all the time while on the march.

At first men used patent remedies "on the sly," but later they were widespread and advertised in newspapers such as this one in the Indianapolis *Journal:*

> Advertisement: Soldiers, Attention! Pain, disease & exposure, with a hot climate, muddy water & bad diet will be unavoidable, but armed with Holloway's Purifying & Strengthening Pills you can endure all these & retain good health. Only 25 cents per box.[97]

(These were not *Captain* Holloway's pills.) Janes Expectorant was popular in fighting cold and cough symptoms. Private Henry Daniel "took three bottles which brought him out of a bad spell."[98] Various field sicknesses were treated with quinine and Dover's powders. Private Peter Jacobs caught cold from lying in wet, muddy rifle pits during several days and nights of rain before Kennesaw Mountain, without shelter or chance to dry his clothes. Jacobs' cold settled in his lungs and throat causing hoarseness and a "terrible, dry hacking cough." Jacobs got quinine and Dover's, but he never got over the cough.[99] Second Lieutenant Josiah Clinton Williams, feeling "quite unwell," took "the biggest dose of quinine I ever saw" to quiet a severe headache and fever "that almost took what strength I had."[100]

Other diseases and ailments took a toll on unit health and military preparedness.

Pneumonia, often developed from colds or catarrh, was a serious disease in the regiment's early Eastern service but tapered off considerably. Second Lieutenant Meredith W. Leach was pneumonia's most prominent victim and the only officer to succumb to disease, sickness, or disability.

Consumption, or tuberculosis, led to the December 1861 discharges of Lieutenant John F. and Private Jasper N. Parsons from hereditary causes and aggravation of camp life. Private Jehu Davis was discharged with tuberculosis "caused by severe exposure when the regiment lay in bottom land near Bull Run in mud and water. Was attacked immediately with pain in side and chest and severe cough."[101]

Jaundice struck Commissary Sergeant Simpson Solomon Hamrick. But he "attended to business all the time," and wrote that cousin Private Frank Landis was also recovering from jaundice.[102]

Varicose veins tormented both young and old legs on the march. The malady was near-rheumatic swelling and aching of shins and calves, sometimes with large, bulging vessels due to improper footwear and constant pounding. The condition drove Private Michael Corcoran, who could not march, to transfer to the artillery. After Chancellorsville, Private Joseph Rice had rheumatism and his "legs were swollen and stiff, veins were puffed and knots formed on the calves and hollows of my legs. Veins were red and full of blood, looked like they were ready to burst." A sergeant saw him pull up his drawers and breeches to show his legs. Private Anthony Berger rubbed liniment on them. Rice was a "good soldier," but "kind of a weakly man."[103]

Little was known medically about *epilepsy*. Recruit James Edwards, two weeks after joining the regiment, was "overcome with fright" and "excitement" in September 1862 at South Mountain, Maryland. He had a disabling fit and hit the ground in "kind of a nervous jerking fit, didn't know anything." In December, "nervous and not in his right mind," he was discharged for "idiocy caused by epilepsy in early life, want of sense, and improper enlistment."[104] Edwards and other epileptics were improperly treated. Private Edward A. Hoskins' discharge read: "Has fits, has been subject to them for over five months, becoming more frequent, has four or five some days. Not able to perform duties of soldier. Epilepsy. Afflicted with disease before coming into service past five months greatly aggravated."[105]

Aside from the ravages of scurvy on teeth and gums, and conditions of prisoners, records make scant reference to *dental hygiene*. Several men reported toothaches and one man was sent to a general hospital for a tooth removal because the regimental surgeons had no instruments for the task. Union soldiers were not required to carry toothbrushes, although some did, and there was a "prevalence of toothaches and swollen faces in our camps."[106]

Hearing trouble was common, mostly caused by artillery firing. No one wore ear plugs, but at least the artilleryman could cover his ears when anticipating a blast. At Antietam, Company H was supporting a battery which was firing over their head checking the advancing enemy. Color guard Corporal Files was affected by the concussion. During the Atlanta Campaign 20 months later he still failed to understand conversation unless spoken loudly. Private Patrick Ryan became deaf in his left ear from rheumatic fever.

The nebulous diagnosis *heart disease* was as elusive in post-war examinations as then. Many survivors attributed infirmities of age to it. Victims told of shortness of breath, palpitations, strain, sweating, being smothered, and chest pains. Treatment was rest. As arduous as their service was, no death was attributed to "heart disease." In helping comrade Private Arthur Pratt dig his brother Private Thomas Pratt's grave before Atlanta, Private Dawson Denney had to quit work and be removed from the grave with heart trouble. Water was poured on him, but he suffered greatly with "smothering spells."[107] Private George Washington Welsh said heart disease caused his weight to drop from 165 to 130.

Smallpox never threatened because nearly all men were vaccinated soon after enrollment. A private wrote on November 7, 1861, "The smallpox was among a regiment that was quartered close by us. I was vaccinated and have been puny from that two or three days, but I am getting better."[108] Isolated cases broke out such as Private Abel Deats in 1864, late in the war for this controlled disease. Private Jacob B. Gilmore, wounded at Chancellorsville, contracted smallpox while hospitalized. In May 1864 he was diagnosed: "On each arm are large scrofulous ulcers constantly emitting pus and blood. Ears have to be lanced frequently to prevent too great collection of pus. On hips posteriors and legs, at least a dozen running scrofulous sores, emissions seem to come from bone. Much emaciated." He became "too offensive for treatment."[109]

Urinary problems occurred more often than *kidney problems*. Suspect drinking water quality caused gastrointestinal and bladder ailments. The quality of the staple coffee varied, but its method of cooking did not. It was boiled black and strong, often with extraneous matter, and coupled with a high fat, high sodium diet irritated the urinary tract. Private Enoch M. Bruner had "trouble with his water works."[110] Captain Tighlman Howard Nance complained of kidney problems during marches. He would stop to urinate and noticed "it would take a long while to do so with expression of pain on his face."[111]

Mumps hampered Sergeant Robert L. S. Foster, "quite critical for a while," which reduced the size of his left testicle.[112]

Older age accelerated debility. Private William H. O'Neal had a "violent attack."[113] In a war demanding youthful bodies and constitutions, older men encountered numerous aches and pains which reduced their fighting capability or precipitated discharges. Over 45 was considered "old" for both officers and enlisted. Private Frederick Dorn's (50) discharge for chronic rheumatism read: "His old age and camp life is fast wearing him out."[114] Private Henry Daniel (45) was transferred to the VRC in 1863. The man received mixed evaluations. Some comrades felt he "always had the cleanest gun and accoutrements of any man in the company (seemed to be his passion), because of his age was shielded from the more arduous duties, not by his request but by common consent." He was not strong, not fleshy, tall but skinny, and never shirked. Not as robust as others, he "looked like he had lumbago from the way he walked about the camp with a cane in stooped position." Other comrades differed. "Old Man" Daniel struggled. He would "lag behind or give out on marches." Some felt "the old man was a good deal of a shirk" who did little duty and was never in action.[115]

CHAPTER 11

Save My Arm, if You Can!: Medical Care

I was wounded by a 6-pound solid shot passing between my side and arm, the wind of the ball tearing the flesh from my side from the breast bone round to the backbone, 3 or 4" wide. The shot had first hit the sword and rolled it round nearly double, and in so doing the sword hit my elbow and shattered the arm terribly, breaking the elbow joint. The surgeon said, "The arm must come off!" I said, "No, save it if you can." They said, "No; it must come off." Doctor King said, "No, don't do it; he can't live three hours." But I did, though, and the next day I refused to have it taken off, and my poor arm is now able to answer very well the uses for which it was given me. — *Colonel Silas Colgrove* [1]

Colgrove's Peachtree Creek wound on June 22, 1864, frightened but stiffened the resolve of his men. Private Lawrence Over was of the same makeup. Five surgeons tried to amputate his right arm after he was shot while building earthworks before Atlanta. He refused: He would rather have a crippled arm than none at all. The surgeons relented, but hapless wounded soldiers gained few such victories.

Wounds were either mortal, severe or slight, the latter two called "other wounds." Mortal wounds might delay death for weeks, months or until after a member was discharged. Severe wounds required extensive hospitalization, often leading to a medical discharge. Slight wounds were treated either in a hospital or in camp. The patient was released to duty and often wore his dressing wrapped around head or limb. Wounds came from anywhere and the soldier had to beware of "straggling balls," or spent bullets, that deflected and killed. Some wounds were "lucky," bringing a trip to the rear, a furlough or rest. The father of Captain Josiah Clinton Williams, visiting him in a Georgetown, D.C., hospital, wrote of his "lucky" wound at Chancellorsville. "Josiah had a very narrow escape. He was pointing out to his men with his sword in what direction to shoot the rebels. In the meantime a rebel took his measure, the bullet hitting the guard of his sword, fluttered and glanced downward. We are indebted our relative is yet in the land of the living." [2]

Most wounded men of the 27th Indiana were hit but once, but nearly 20 percent of the killed and mortally wounded were hit in multiple actions (i.e., Buckton and Resaca). Multiple wounds in the same action (e.g., shell and bullet) were common. Wounded lying on the field could be injured by movements of horses, artillery, or falling trees, or forest fire. Gunshots, rifle or musket, pistol or buckshot, caused the most deaths and wounds (86.4 percent). Cannon fire, shell, solid, grape or canister caused 11.9 percent; and bayonet and saber cuts, 1.3 percent. Most hits (57.3 percent) were inflicted on the upper body and head. These figures approach Union statistics.

Only at Cedar Mountain and Resaca was there substantial hand-to-hand fighting. Abdominal gunshot wounds were the most difficult to repair and the most lethal. But Private Merrick S. Brown survived a Chancellorsville abdominal wound and captivity. The bullet "entered the anterior surface of the right thigh about 3" from and below hip and languished laterally and backward. Came or was taken out of left mater near the anus; wound at latter joint not quite healed. In its range the ball injured the urethra making difficult ever since occasionally to discharge the bladder."[3] Second in lethality were head and upper torso wounds, especially the heart and lungs. The least lethal were farthest from the heart on the extremities. Most amputations were legs and arms, although some feet and hands were amputated.

Some wounds were purely accidental, others self-inflicted. Private Ira Kyle was on picket duty on July 5, 1862. "Endeavoring to draw a load from his gun in order to dry it (the beak of which he had rested over a stone to facilitate its accomplishment)," he accidentally shot himself in the left hand.[4] Men who would wound themselves in the trigger finger or hand wanted quick disability discharges. Private Henry C. Austin never disproved the accusation he shot off his own toe to avoid duty. Teamster Stephen S. Harvey mysteriously lost a finger to a gunshot in his tent, then deserted, was captured, paroled, and disappeared. For years comrades sought the truth to questionable woundings. The most controversial was Sergeant James E. Smith, who sustained a hand wound at Chancellorsville. (See Appendix F)

Several men survived ordinarily fatal head wounds. Private Squire Samuel Fellows' right cranium was fractured, the necrosed bones removed, and he returned to duty. A gunshot smashed the top left side of Private Peter Ryne's skull. He was discharged in 1864 (the "only recorded case of recovery from that peculiar head wound"). Pieces of bone were extracted causing a 1" depression $5/8$" in the middle and $1/4$" deep. Examination in 1865 showed "loss of osseous tissue $1^1/2$" long and $3/4$" wide; suffers from vertigo and pain on stooping."[5] Yet he lived until 1914.

Private James M. Hall was shot in the shoulder at Antietam:

The ball had entered between the first and second ribs about 3" to the right of the sternum, passing obliquely backward and outward, and making its exit at the external edge of the scapula, about 1¹/₂" below the scronium, fracturing the head of the humerus. Shoulder very much swollen and extremely painful; constitutional disturbances considerable, loss of appetite, pulse at 100.[6]

Surgeons waited until October 4, hoping for a change. None came; so they resected the head and 1" of the shaft of the humerus [3" in all]. "Patient did not lose an ounce of blood. Had to saw the bone twice, having found it denuded below the line of the first cut." By October 28 he was doing well; the wound was "entirely filled with healthy granulations." Treatment included lint, water dressings, and granulations stimulated with basilicon ointment. The incision healed in six weeks with "tolerable use of arm and forearm." Hall was discharged in December 1862 but five months later could not move his arm. In 1873 "a number of bony material have since come out, impossible to use arm, at times very painful."[7] He lived until 1923.

Private Daniel Seibel lost an arm at New Hope Church, but which one is an example of records inconsistency. The ball struck the left arm and passed into the right as he was aiming to fire. One record indicates the left arm was amputated, but his pension record photo shows the right arm missing.[8] Bark splinters from shells striking trees struck Captain James Stephens in his left eye and right ear, and Private James T. Harden, hit by grapeshot in the left shoulder and side, broke his arm while falling.*

Colgrove also was wounded at Cedar Mountain (scalp), Gettysburg (hand) and Chancellorsville (near the hip joint, which passed through the saddle tree and lodged in the saddle blanket). At Peachtree "he was in much pain when I saw him but will recover by losing his arm permanently," predicted Captain Josiah Clinton Williams. Corporal John Michael Tomey agreed. The Hoosiers were concerned over their leader's "desperate wound." "Such was its terrific force that it lifted him up several feet and whirled him over and over. It was strange he was not killed." He recovered but never returned to his regiment. (He was in command for nearly three years.)[9] Colgrove remembered the field hospital. "The poor wounded men lay by scores upon hammocks dying with gangrene in the camp hospital. My side became black, and the flesh dropped off and new flesh formed. In 20 days I was brought home, and not long after was able for business."[10]

---

* New Hope Church wounds were distinctive. For numbers engaged, gunshot wounds to the hands, lower arms and shoulders, and wounds from artillery fire were higher than during any other engagement. Many gunshot wounds came while firing or shielding oneself on the ground, kneeling or standing behind trees.

Most wounds came from the conoidal leaden minie ball rifle bullet which ripped chunks of flesh, shattered fragile bones and severed arteries. No medics succored wounded on the field with first aid kits. Bandages were not supplied; so men used dirty cloths to cover wounds. Tourniquets were rarely applied in the field because of inexperience in using them. Wounded men lay for hours with unattended open wounds bleeding and rotting. In the carnage pits of Antietam and Gettysburg, bodies often covered each other. Pain was often lost in the anesthesia of shock that followed, which was mistakenly dosed with whiskey and opium.

Near Winchester in May 1862, a bullet ripped Private John Williams' right ankle, and he fell. "For God's sake boys, don't leave me for I am wounded!" he cried.[11] First Lieutenant James Stephens and Private Seth White rushed to comfort him and placed him on a passing wagon. He was off to the rear for questionable care from an army retreating fast. Hours later, a shell struck Captain Richmond M. Welman, a physician in private life, on the right kneecap and arm. Left behind, he dressed and bandaged his own wounds.

Most of the 27th Indiana's battles were extemporaneous or exigencies (e.g., Cedar Mountain and New Hope Church), and preparations to accommodate the wounded were late and inefficient. Even with planning for imminent combat, serious complications arose. Chancellorsville, where both armies were poised, left thousands of Union soldiers on the field. The sheer numbers at Gettysburg, where the 27th waited until the Third Day to fight, overwhelmed early attempts to establish facilities. Getting medical attention was difficult, even for officers. First Lieutenant John D. McKahin, hit in the right leg at Antietam, lay on the field all night and was taken by ambulance to Hagerstown, Maryland. "Because of my rank the Wisconsin surgeon-in-charge said there were too many wounded privates and the officers would have to shirk for themselves. I remember the bullet was cut from my leg by a civilian surgeon. Surgeons gave me occasional Dovers powder, about all the medical attention I got. Surgeons were not always from my own regiment. 'The conditions of the time were so exciting that we paid not the least attention to those things.'"[12]

A shell struck Private James Alexander at Chancellorsville. He headed for the rear and found a doctor who amputated his arm "and done it up the best he could." At Acquia Creek Landing he had little or no attention for about 10 days. Eventually he "left on his own accord," and reached a Washington hospital and Philadelphia where he was discharged.[13]

Assistant Surgeon Willis H. Twiford was unafraid to try something new on Chancellorsville wounded. A conscientious, ambitious physician, acting as chief operator of the division field hospital, he also sought recognition from the Indiana military agent: "I shall remember you for any effort

Typical Union Army Field Hospital

Leslie's Illustrated Weekly

that will give me the credit due in these cases."[14] In 1863, the army's surgeon general asked field surgeons to send specimens of amputated limbs and excised bone and tissue to Washington for study. Twiford was one who complied for some men wounded at Chancellorsville. Their specimens are preserved in the National Museum of Health and Medicine of the Armed Forces Institute of Pathology.*

Twiford was concerned with his five cases of "resection of a portion of the interior shaft of the femur" for 27th Privates William Mulkey, Joshua Chambers, and John S. McMains. McMains died but the others went to Washington. "There was not less than 2" of the entire shaft of the thigh bone removed in any of these cases, and Mulkey had 3¹/₂" removed," Twiford wrote to Indiana Military Agent Isaac W. Monfort. "Will you be so kind as to visit the hospital and give me some information? Remember me kindly to the boys. I think of them often and their suffering!"[15]

Until Chancellorsville, removal of battlefield wounded was unsystematic and uncontrolled. Some unharmed soldiers used it to absent themselves from combat on the pretense of helping a fallen friend. To rectify this, the (27th's) XII Corps directed the detailing of only one private from each company to transport wounded, identified by a green badge, and allowed no soldier to ride in an ambulance without medical permission. Wounded usually were taken to the rear in the bearer's arms or by blankets and stretchers of wood and canvas. Away from the field, wounded

---

* The author examined them. A number of specimens and their accompanying records are cited herein, particularly those of Corporal Joseph D. Trullinger (skull).

were placed on ambulances for transit or carried or led to their regimental or division/corps hospital outside artillery range.

The 27th detailed men to the ambulance corps for short periods. Private Barton Warren Mitchell, a co-finder of Lee's "Lost Order," was assigned to ambulance duty for the Atlanta Campaign to alleviate his suffering from an Antietam wound. The 27th usually employed two or three two-axle, four-wheel ambulances pulled by two horses. They could transport 2–4 men reasonably comfortably, provided the terrain accommodated, except those with serious fractures. Medical aid was unavailable until arrival at a field aid station or hospital. "Exhausted, ill-fed men who had endured the horrors of mismanaged ambulance transportation, fared much worse under surgery than the well-conditioned men."[16]

The army established ad hoc hospitals in the field near the battle as the primary stations for treating and performing surgery on wounds. Aid stations, when they existed, and field hospitals, however, were incapable of processing the humanity descended upon them and scenes were gruesome. Usually field hospital locations could be selected only at the time battle commenced, perhaps 1–2 miles behind the Union line. At Cedar Mountain, wounded came off the field under a flag of truce and were sent to Culpeper, where field hospitals were established in churches, the Depot, hotels and other edifices, and to Alexandria.

Assistant Surgeon Willis H. Twiford's actions at a Cedar Mountain field hospital drew this recognition.

> Early in the war the regiment's surgeons were near the field continuously during battle. During Cedar Mountain Twiford established the only field hospital giving temporary dressings before sending the wounded back to hospitals far away from the combat area. All wounded from the 1st Division of Banks' Corps came through his hospital. About 6:00 p.m., when ordered back, he refused and remained there, receiving supplies and conveyances, providing assistance until 3:00 p.m. August 10th, when all wounded had been dressed.[17]

Twiford hardly acted alone at Cedar Mountain. When action began, the 27th's division medical director selected the Brown house as a general depot for wounded, who next morning were sent to Culpeper hospitals. No time existed to organize other hospitals as troops moved rapidly through to the front, because medical supplies and subsistence remained eight miles away in Culpeper. At Antietam, Twiford had been on the field until 3:00 p.m. when ordered back to the field hospital. Later he was put in charge of the corps station at the Poffenberger farm and remained there until November 20. In early 1863, he was detailed to establish a corps hospital at Acquia Creek.

All kinds of requested or comandeered public and private structures were used as field hospitals depending on the circumstances. When none was available, outdoors under shade sufficed where light was better and flies no worse. Lacking tables, doors spread over barrels worked fine. One persistent problem was disposing of amputated and excised limbs, bones, and tissue. Piled on the ground or dining room floor, they were a distraction, hazard, and a vile portent for men waiting their turns.

Hospitals were put up all around Antietam's outskirts. Private Dawson Denney was with mortally wounded Captain Peter Kop at a private house in Boonsboro. Private William A. White was treated at a small house "just up" with bunks in it. White's bullet disappeared into his head until 1875 when it came out his mouth.[18] Private Lewis King recalled a Chancellorsville station. "The first sight which partook of the horrible was the regiment's first aid hospital. Here lay a number of our mortally wounded heroes. We had only time for a glance. I saw one of my company comrades lying there with an appeal for help in his eyes and a bullet hole in his breast. I could only pass him by."[19]

What King saw was ordinary. Once, after Second Bull Run, 27th non-wounded had to stay on the field to guard the hospital. It was only a shady place of several hundred badly wounded men lying on the ground "almost destitute of everything, including nursing and friendly sympathy," even a drink of water. Pitiable sufferers on acres of ground, nothing else over them and nothing under them except evergreen boughs. "In their soiled, bloodstained clothing," lying in an orchard and stubble field up to three days, many had no medical assistance. Surgeons had gone to find ambulances. After a while the men were loaded and left.[20]

The most repulsive field hospital scene was at Resaca where the enemy abandoned the field, leaving many items. "But the wildest and most inexcusable haste was shown in the heartless abandonment of their wounded," a Hoosier wrote. "An extreme case was a rebel major found upon the amputating table. The surgeons had doubtless abandoned him while in the very act of amputating his leg. The poor man was just coming out from the influence of anesthetics and begged piteously for someone to shoot him. He wanted to die rather than to suffer longer." The amputating table was a contrivance arranged under an old outshed near a poor loghouse. "All were entirely deserted! Not a surgeon or nurse about! Chivalry!"[21] Another concluded, "Our men took care of all as soon as possible."[22]

After Chancellorsville the division/corps field hospital was at Acquia Creek. Twiford, 3rd Brigade chief operator, "did his work skillfully."[23] Visiting commander Brigadier General Alpheus Starkey Williams said the 7–800 wounded were in large tents on the hills overlooking the Potomac as comfortable as possible:[24]

I saw and talked with every man of my division. But I had a terrible surfeit looking at amputated legs and arms, and all imaginable kinds of severe wounds. It is wonderful how men could survive some of them...shot through the lungs; one through both eyes and was stone blind....One poor fellow had had his leg amputated by the Rebs on the field and the flesh had sloughed off, leaving a long bone sticking out, and he was much reduced by secondary hemorrhage. One...had been wounded through the hips, and his feet had lain in the water until they were gangrened and more than half the flesh had fallen off, leaving the bones of the feet protruding fleshless, nothing but skeletons of toes and outer bones. The men appreciated the visit and said, "the general's medicine was better than the doctor's."

Some stayed forever and died at Acquia Creek. After a determined, persistent struggle for life, when there was no longer hope, they sent messages of love, comfort, and cheer to Indiana friends, while their parting words were as stirring as high bugle notes. More than one said it was hard to die; life had seemed so full of promise. But as the interest of the country required it, he could die cheerfully. With his last breath he exhorted us to loyalty and courage. —*ERB* [25]

With its thousands of wounded and dying, Gettysburg was the supreme test of medical personnel and facilities, and the ability of wounded men to cope. This scene at one of the field hospitals established immediately after the battle poignantly describes its awful conditions.

There stood the surgeons, their sleeves rolled up to their elbows, their bare arms as well as their linen aprons smeared with blood, their knives not seldom held between their teeth, while they were helping a patient on or off the table or had their hands otherwise occupied. As a wounded man was lifted on the table, often shrieking with pain as the attendants handled him, the surgeon quickly examined the wound and resolved upon cutting off the injured limb. Some ether was administered and the body put in position. The surgeon snatched the knife, wiped it rapidly once or twice across the bloodstained apron, and the cutting began. The operation accomplished, the surgeon would look around with a deep sigh, and then—"next!" — *About Field Hospitals at Gettysburg* [26]

"Never before have I seen the beauty of our system of relief as I now see it," Agent Monfort reported to Indiana Governor Oliver P. Morton regarding the field hospitals. "Every house in reach for 10 miles is a hospital. Upon our arrival we supplied linen and bandages. We gave to each wounded a little lint for the next dressing. The wounded who can walk are dressing wounds on our men."[27]

Monfort and his team worked against insurmountable odds as he approached Gettysburg on July 7, finding hundreds of wounded in church and school houses, barns, and shops. A few days after the battle, large field hospitals were established at Camp Letterman on the hills east of Gettysburg and remained in operation indefinitely as general hospitals. Many of the 27th's men came through Letterman, including Private Nathan D. F. Terhune, in all admitted to seven hospitals (most of any man) before his 1864 discharge. But Private Charles E. Wishmore's thigh wounds were so bad he could not be transferred to Letterman, and he died July 15 of tetanus in a field tent.

The army dispatched liberal supplies of alcohol, solution chloride of soda, tincture of iron, nitric acid, buckets, tin cups, bed sacks, and stationery for 10,000 men. Monfort's views on the lack of planning are hard to dispute, for no one in authority ever expected such a melee in one place at one time.

Early in the war regiments established their own hospitals to care primarily for the sick. The reaction of many men of the 27th Indiana is summarized in this statement of Private Joseph Dunn Laughlin: "I was too plucky and too ignorant to allow myself to be sent to a hospital. Was afraid my comrades would call me a 'playoff' as most were who went to hospitals."[28]

"Playoff" or not, going to the doctors for treatment—especially the regimental hospital—was not what always what sick or wounded had hoped. From fear of the unknown, complacency about foredoomed illness, rumors of poor service, or visible proof from a comrade, many men failed to report maladies or receive treatment. Fear drove Corporal Henry Lange to resist getting his Antietam shoulder shell wound dressed. Instead he washed it with soap bought from Thomas Holvey, a New York peddler, who was "selling to the boys."[29]

Early regimental hospitals were for all kinds of problems and long-term treatment. Success depended on the doctors' skills and interests and their working conditions. Outsiders inspecting the hospitals often found "inadequate supply and filthy conditions—'pigsties.'"[30] In some, like the 27th's, convalescing soldiers were the only nurses available, men without training and hardly able to move about. After Antietam, Private James Montgomery Foster, wounded in the right hand, was nursing in the Smoketown, Maryland, hospital. He contracted septic poisoning from dressing the wound of another soldier, which "well nigh cost him his life." The soldier wanted his leg dressed more often than the senior nurse would do it. Foster lost two joints of his index finger, paralyzed his right arm and hand, and was discharged a year later.[31]

The 27th's hospital, staffed by the regiment's own medical department, was a forerunner to the field hospital. Their first hospital was overcrowded tents. The first permanent hospital was a 20 x 24 feet loghouse with a stove. The sick filled the floors except one narrow aisle. As division and corps field hospitals began treating casualties, regimental hospitals became mostly sick call and first aid stations.

Doctors' lives usually were either short frantic periods of overwork or periods when their duties were less than an hour a day. The high point of the medical day was sick call, "when men who sought excuse from duty were paraded before the doctors by the 1st sergeants."[32] The diagnosis was whether to continue a man for duty, excuse him but allow him to remain in quarters, place him in the hospital, or assign him light duty. This gave doctors significant power, but no doctor could send a man to a general hospital or discharge him from the service.

During the Winter 1861–62, some sick were consigned to quarters. Friends would obtain rations for them and help them to the sinks, or latrines. Private James M. Johnson made sick call every day for six weeks while being treated in his hut for diarrhea. Commissary Sergeant Simpson Solomon Hamrick, suffering from rheumatism, moved into the private house of a Dr. Bell near Darnestown, Maryland. He had a "good room and all the attention that I could have at home. The doctor's wife is one of the kindest nurses in the world, besides two young ladies that give me every attention required. I am recovering almost as fast as I was taken." Regimental surgeons visited him anyway. Board was $5 a week, although $5–6 were "customary prices."[33]

> I was in our hospital in 1861 for 10 days. The first six nights seven men died. Every day a soldier mustered out. It was their fate to fall before seeing the foe, but they died for their country. —*ERB* [34]

Operating techniques, primitive by today's standards, nevertheless saved some lives, although many wounded men carried the deformities and scars of Civil War medicine for the rest of their lives. Private Joshua Chambers, wounded in the right thigh at Chancellorsville, was a prisoner of war for 10 days without medical attention. Once returned to Union hands, the following attempt was made to repair his limb.

> May 16, 1863. Patient under chloroform. Longitudinal incision 4" long made to the abscess giving exit to large quantities of pus. A conical bullet was discovered and extracted as it laid loose in the cavity. It was flattened. The finger introduced could detach many splinters which were removed through the opening. Some provisional callus had formed. Fragments represented 4" in length and $^1/_3$ of the middle $^1/_3$ of the femur. Limb placed in Smith's anterior splint.[35]

By June 2, he had "progressed very favorably, feels comfortable, good appetite, good spirits. The incised opening gives exit to a considerable discharge of 'healthy pus.'" His procedure, unorthodox today, at least extended his life for 19 months.[36]

Private Charles H. Bowen,
Company A

Photo shows healing stump with skin flaps and thigh bone specimen with bullet fracture hole.

Otis Historical Archives,
Professional Services,
Armed Forces Institute of Pathology

Surgeon General's Office.

ARMY MEDICAL MUSEUM.

PHOTOGRAPH No. 229. *Lower Half of the Left Femur Successfully Amputated.*

Private C. H. Bowen, Co. A, 27th Indiana Volunteers, had his left femur fractured by a musket ball, at the battle of Antietam, on September 17, 1862. He was admitted to Hospital No. 1, at Frederick, Maryland, where Buck's apparatus was applied. Nine months subsequently, he was removed to Baltimore. There were numerous abscesses, and the patient underwent two operations for the removal of necrosed bone. On September 7, 1863, he was discharged the service, with the limb greatly deformed. He received a pension, and was employed in the Interior Department. Owing to recurrence of abscesses he was admitted to Providence Hospital in the autumn of 1867, and on November 11th, the limb was amputated in the middle third by Dr. D. W. Bliss. The wound healed well, and a photograph was taken at the Army Medical Museum on January 9, 1868, at which time the stump was firm and healthy. The specimen, with the history, was contributed by the operator. The fragments are considerably overlapped, having undergone unusual disturbance, and the amount of callus exceeds what is necessary for complete union.

Photographed at the Army Medical Museum.
BY ORDER OF THE SURGEON GENERAL:

GEORGE A. OTIS,
Ass't Surg. U. S. A., Curator A. M. M.

Sergeant Joseph B. Sellers lay on the New Hope Church field 36 hours before the upper right tibia, 4" below the knee, could be amputated by a circular incision with chloroform. Private Nathan Richardson was shot in the breast and left shoulder joint at Chancellorsville. The head and 2¹/₃" of shaft of his humerus were excised and resectioned, the arm put upon a straight barrel stave splint extending from shoulder joint to tips of fingers. The arm eventually became useless and pieces of bone occasionally came out. He was treated in six hospitals before his discharge.

Not all surgery worked right the first time. Corporal Charles H. Bowen's left thigh was hit by gunshot at Antietam about 5" above his knee. It broke the femur and passed out directly opposite. Buck's apparatus was applied. On October 23 a deep but circumscribed abscess was opened and evacuated, and both entry and exit wounds were enlarged to evacuate pus more freely. By March 18, 1863, the wounds nearly healed and he could walk with crutches. On May 21, gangrene set in requiring strong nitric acid. When he was discharged in September the femur had only partially healed; the sciatic nerve was injured; his leg was partially and his foot entirely paralyzed. His condition worsened and in 1867 the limb was amputated.[37] He lived 10 years.

The case of Corporal Joseph D. Trullinger was indeed phenomenal, perhaps the most remarkable among 27th Indiana wounded.

> Corporal, Company F. Wounded at Chancellorsville, May 2, 1863. Compound fracture of cranium, right frontal and parietal bones, brain extensively torn into and crushed. Cerebellum inflamed and congested but no lesion otherwise. Ball entered right ventricle.[38]

Trullinger was leading his squad behind breastworks repelling the attack of Jackson's corps late on the second day. Suddenly he fell backward shot in the head, grasping his face and shrieking. Soon the regiment withdrew. Trullinger, his head bleeding and believed dead, was left on the field, captured, held for four days without medical treatment, and paroled.

On May 16, exhausted and sick, he was sufficiently strong enough to walk from an ambulance to a tent at the XII Corps field hospital at Acquia Creek. The rifle ball had struck the frontal bone, penetrated both tables and lodged in the right ventricle. On the seventeenth, 5th Connecticut Infantry Assistant Surgeon Andrew J. Gilson examined him. He became comatose, but exhibited no symptoms of cerebral lesion except his head, which felt "thick and heavy" and ached slightly. The pulse was normal, skin wet and moist, head warm, and tongue slightly furred and somewhat dry. His pupils were not dilated and he swallowed readily. He was easily aroused to answer questions and converse intelligently, seemed conscious of his condition, remembered and spoke about what had happened. His wound was suppurating.

Gilson found five loose fragments of bone and removed them, causing "free evacuation of pus" mixed with blood clots and pieces of membrane. The operation left an opening 1½ inches long by one inch wide. The edges of the opening were necrosed and in the process of separation. But the bullet could not be found. After the operation Trullinger expressed relief and was inclined to sleep. Cold water dressings were constantly applied. The wound was well cleaned twice a day and free suppuration allowed. For five days the patient showed no "natural change" but was "obstinately costive," probably produced by free administration of sulfate magnesium. He passed water easily and freely.

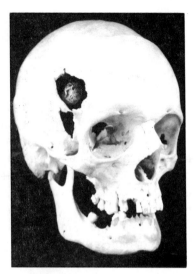

Skull of Corporal Joseph D. Trullinger

Died on May 20, 1863, after carrying a bullet in his brain for 18 days.

Anatomical Collection, National Museum of Health and Medicine, Armed Forces Institute of Pathology

He had no material change until May 21 when the ball appeared at the orifice of the wound, "expelled by action of the escaping pus," and was removed. Partial hemiplegia and complete coma supervened. He gradually weakened and died at 9 p.m.

Trullinger had carried the bullet in his brain for 18 days.

He endured for 14 more days before going to Acquia Creek to die. Autopsy revealed a compound fracture of right parietal and frontal bones. The brain substance was extensively lacerated, crushed and in a state of putridity. Over the right orbit the

Headstone of Corporal Joseph D. Trullinger

Fredericksburg National Cemetery.

Photo by author

track of ball was found leading to the right ventricle which was filled with pus, and the cerebellum was inflamed and congested.*

More unkind than kind things were said by the soldiers about army medicine, especially surgeons. The abilities of many were doubted, and some were outright feared. Commissary Sergeant Simpson Solomon Hamrick in May 1862 wrote home, "I hope the Governor will send the regiment an additional surgeon, for we have been sadly imposed by our present surgeons."[39] Six months later he wrote again. "We are the worst treated in the medical department than any other, miserably represented by doctors. What Governor Morton thinks of by appointing such men is more than we can account for. But this is a strangely managed war in many respects."[40]

Private John J. Smith "had such dislike for the regimental doctors that I would of dide rather than to of went to them for treatment of any kind."[41] Private Thomas Deputy blamed "very bad surgey" for maltreatment of the Potts fracture of his left ankle which caused anchylosis and contracting of the Achilles tendon.[42] Members of the 27th often whined and complained about surgeons and hospitals citing perfunctory treatment, inadequate pre-scriptions, or impersonal deafness to their ills.

The regiment usually had two doctors, or medical officers, with surgeon and assistant surgeon ranks. They performed all medical functions regardless of training or experience, assisted by a warrant officer hospital steward who dispensed medicines, performed minor surgery like bandaging and teeth extraction, and kept records. The small medical staff was augmented by untrained enlisted men as nurses, ambulance drivers, and stretcher bearers. Surgeon positions were political, highly sought, and like other senior field billets, appointed by the governor.

After the division/corps system was established in 1863, the surgeons were assigned in those hospitals during combat. Surgeon Twiford ran both 3rd Brigade and 1st Division hospitals at Acquia Creek. Surgeon Greenly

---

* Trullinger is buried in the Fredericksburg, Virginia, National Cemetery, one of three known members of the 27th buried there who died because of Chancellorsville. But the visitor will not find him without knowing that his sinking grave marker instead reads: "J. D. Fellinger." And, he is not all there. His head is missing. The skull was removed by the operators and is preserved in excellent condition—except for loose lower teeth—at the National Museum of Health and Medicine in three cleanly interlocking pieces. The twisted, leaden ball that smashed his skull still dangles in the 1½" wide round hole it made, attached by the same wire secured there by Gilson. The top was sliced off to allow autopsy, and snugly fits like a small yamulka. The lower jaw is unhinged but many teeth remain. The author assembled the pieces—a perfect fit—for the accompanying photograph of the skull.

Vinton Woollen sometimes sent sick men to Captain Jackson L. Moore, a physician and company commander. Woollen was captured at a hospital after Cedar Mountain and was imprisoned for over a month in Libby in Richmond, Virginia. Johnson, severely ruptured, was captured at Winchester and was retained two weeks by the Confederates to serve sick and wounded of both sides. His injury and Hospital Steward Aaron Allen's wound at New Hope Church were the only other staff casualties.

Much maligned—they had no "magic cures"—surgeons also endured the fatigue of long forced marches and shared dangers, poor food, and maladies, impacting their need for keen judgment. The penalties were fainting from exhaustion, paralysis of limbs, constant anxiety, and mental and physical strain. Civil War surgeons, at the end of a "dark age" of medical science, and untrained and unskilled in fundamentals commonly practiced a few years later, cannot be blamed totally for the failure of army medicine to save lives. They worked wonders on some men of the 27th Indiana and failed miserably on others. In the end, "the wounded man who wanted to recover stood the better chance."[43]

> What waste of life there was! Think of an active, spirited young fellow of 20, tingling with life and energy before now, doomed to lie in one position on his back for 11 long months, his thigh bone shattered, 4" of it removed, and his limb held in a swing suspended from above! This was a 27th Indiana soldier, never fully recovered from shock, who would die soon after the war. —ERB [44]

Army general hospitals, larger and more complete for handling sick and wounded cases of multiple causes, were located away from the war. Faced with indefinite convalescence in hard beds or wheel chairs, sick or wounded soldiers had abundant time to reflect on what might have been. Such was the situation for Private James W. Todd, who wrote in June 1863, "I am a cripple for life. It was done defending my country. My left hand shattered at battle of Chancellorsville. Had to be amputated."[45]

Eight months later in McClellan U.S. Army General Hospital (USAGH), in Philadelphia, Pennsylvania, Todd wrote after a furlough home: "My visit made me somewhat disatisfied with the hospital. I would like to be free from the army as I am of no benefit now. I expect to be home in the spring anyhow. I am to go to school and try to get a common education which I might have had if I had improved my time while I lived at your home. I fooled away my time which was so precious. But theres no time cry about misfortunes, will the best."[46] Todd altered his plans and in September 1863 transferred to the Veterans Reserve Corps (VRC), a non-combat unit for recovered men. In the spirit of his day he went west and, coincidentally, died near Greeley, Kansas, in 1881.

For wounded men of the 27th Indiana, the normal progression of care was field hospital to general hospital. Many were moved subsequently to other hospitals, sometimes in distant cities. For sick men the progression was the same, but sometimes they were sent direct to a general hospital and later returned to the regiment via a convalescent camp. A convalescent normally was detained longer than necessary whether recovered or not. Staff might release him without cure at his plea, even if unable to heal him. At home, perhaps a rural physician would treat him if he could afford one, or worse, he might die of service-connected problems. Private Orbagast R. Volmer was discharged from a Washington, D.C., USAGH on November 21, 1862, with chronic entera colitis. Before going home he died there in a civilian hospital on December 20 from chronic diarrhea abetted by colitis.

Until 1863, most general hospitals were located in churches, colleges, schools, mansions, or other such edifices. Beds, cots, and pads for the patients were usually crowded into parlors, bedrooms, studies, halls, or outdoors. The operating room was a large room equipped as adequately as possible. The government began constructing an array of custom-designed structures, such as the Indiana complexes at Jeffersonville, Madison, and New Albany, which in concept and functions resembled modern hospitals. The 27th's patients were treated in hospitals in at least 10 states and the District of Columbia, the site determined after each major battle or their camp location. In 1864, many men ended up in the new Indiana army hospitals, a move as politically inspired as humanitarian and often requested by the families.

Railroads were used extensively as ambulances on rails to transport sick and wounded to hospitals, particularly in the West. During the Atlanta Campaign a hospital train of 10–12 cars left daily from forward areas. During the Siege of Atlanta trains ran regularly from the front to base hospitals 472 miles away. The 27th's Army of the Cumberland had a travelling general hospital which followed them in Georgia down the Western and Atlantic line. Sick and wounded were kept together until they recovered or returned to duty. The railroad hospital consisted of 100 large tents equipped for 1,000 patients which were established at Ringgold, Resaca, Big Shanty, Marietta, Vinings Station, and Atlanta. Surgeons could attend patients only when the train stopped at a siding and many wounds went unattended for periods. An unsupervised nurse was in each car. In the East many 27th patients were moved on Central Virginia's Orange and Alexandria line to Washington, and the Baltimore and Ohio to Baltimore and other points eastward including Philadelphia.

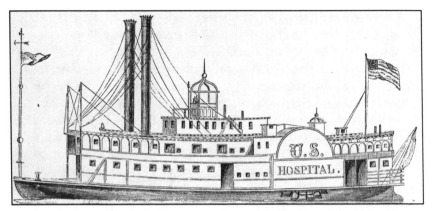

U.S. Army Hospital Steamer *D. A. January*

Wounded of the 27th Indiana were transported on this ship during Atlanta Campaign, 1864.
Medical and Surgical History of the War of the Rebellion, *Part 3, Vol 2.*

Water transportation was also used. Steamers like the workhorse *Mary Washington* shuttled patients to Washington from Acquia Creek after Chancellorsville, saving many Hoosier lives. Other steamers including the *Creole* and *Daniel Webster* hauled them to New York City. Perhaps the most perfect of the Western hospital boats was the *D. A. January,* which plied the Ohio River between Indiana, Ohio, Tennessee, and Kentucky hauling infirmed men of the 27th. Purchased for army use in 1862, *January* was a 450-ton sidewheeler, 230 feet long, with a 35-foot beam and 65-foot extreme width, and two high pressure steam engines. Her load was several hundred patients.

General hospital conditions varied greatly. Mr. Worthington B. Williams, father of Captain Williams, visited one of the best at the predominantly officers' Seminary USAGH in Georgetown, D.C., after Chancellorsville:

> It is a melancholy sight to see men stretched out this way, but those of sanguine temperament and who are disposed to put the best face on the matter will pass away the time if not too badly wounded in jokes at one another's expense—in recounting the battlefield—how things might have done better if all had been done right—of hair breadth escapes—of testimony as to bravery and cleverness of those who may have fallen never to rise again.[47]

His son's board in Seminary for 15 days was 75 cents per day, a total of $11.25. A Doctor Ducachet treated him and his wounded 27th comrade, Second Lieutenant Frazier Julian Hoffer. Williams recovered but Hoffer died June 22. Mr. Williams further observed:

On a little iron bedstead with neat white covering on his low couch I found my son reposing. An officer from the 14th Indiana good naturedly complained that Josiah and an Ohio officer shell him with their jokes, repartees, etc., until he is compelled to laugh, which frequently interferes with his wounds. Over each bed was a ticket or descriptive card giving the number of the bed, name, company and regiment, disease or injury, date of admission, date of discharge, where sent and by what authority. Physicians and nurses attended. Iced water in the hall was available for nurses to bathe the wounds. Much had been said about "red tape operations," but red tape means doing things decently and in order and the result of long experience. Josiah thought the bullet was preserved, but the person that stole his vest, watch, etc., also got the bullet, which as a relic of his narrow escape from death was of more value in his eyes than gold or silver. The [hospital] my son is now in is home in a far off land.[48]

Lack of proper cleanliness and sanitation were the worst deficiencies. "If cleanliness had been as highly esteemed as ventilation all would have been well. It was astonishing so much dirt was permitted. The majority were dirty in only one particular—their plumbing. Since intestinal diseases were more common no fault could have been worse."[49] Poor and unbalanced diets also prolonged recovery and increased susceptibility to other illnesses.

During the Winter 1863–64 in Tennessee, Assistant Surgeon Woollen was in charge of a Murfreesboro USAGH. He established a system of rigid inspections to cure some problems like filth and gangrene. Approaching one soldier's bed, he saw it clean and made up, arranged in "apple pie order." The occupant saluted and stood at attention. Woollen complimented him and moved on. The soldier said,"I see you don't know me, doctor." Woollen confessed he didn't. "Why, I belong to your regiment." Woollen expressed pleasure. The man said he had been detached duty when taken sick. "I have been engaged in the same occupation as yourself, doctor. I have been the brigade butcher."[50]

Because of its high death rate, "Camp Misery" was what thousands of Union soldiers called Alexandria's Convalescent Camp. Located at Fort Ellsworth on Shooter's Hill, it was both hospital and rehabilitation center for men en route their commands after leaving hospitals, and treated many Hoosiers. Opened in August 1862, it received some 75,000 convalescents, parolees, and stragglers in the first two months. Complaints were legion. Indiana Governor Oliver P. Morton sent someone to investigate. "I inspected it thoroughly," he wrote Morton in October 1862. "I think Colonel [camp commander J. S.] Belknap deserves great praise for his efforts to make the boys comfortable. The alleged neglect is incidental to the daily number changing. Some of the evils will be remedied speedily by added military and medical assistance. Vegetables, which they greatly need, will be supplied, I think. The hospitals in and around Washington you already know are well conducted and cleanly."[51] So much for oversight. Like many deficiencies in army administration, the "Camp Misery" plight seemed impervious to outside concern or pressure.

A more pleasant experience awaited 27th men convalescing in the Indianapolis Soldiers Home, representing Morton's "restless solicitude for the welfare of the State's troops." Indianapolis was the State's main depot, recruiting station, drill camp, and the chief resting place of transient troops. "Of course they always landed here hungry, dusty and tired, and a sound sleep and a good meal were sometimes worth a man's life," wrote an observer. The Soldiers Home, a sort of military hotel with free accommodations, was established on vacant ground south of depot with hospital tents and other conveniences. In 1862, a permanent home was established in a grove on the west side of Werst Street, just north of the Vandalia Railroad. Frame buildings were erected for 1,800 beds, and 8,000 daily meals were served. From August 1862 to June 1865, the home furnished 3,777,791 meals, in 1864 an average of 4,498 daily. A Ladies' Home to care for wives and children was opened near the Union depot in December 1863 and served an average 100 people daily during the war.[52]

Some wounded men lived.

> Face wound, partial anchylosis of lower maxilla. Ball entered left superior maxillary bone passing through the sinus into the mouth (the tongue escaping), and out the joint on the opposite side,"fracturing and considerably disorganizing the joint." Cold water dressing was applied. Removed [that which] had been thrown off by the ulceration process; several small fragments came out from time to time. January 1, 1863: "Patient may soon be well. Wounds are entirely healed, considerable anchylosis of lower jaw; can open his teeth about $1/2$." —*About Private Elisha Perkins* [53]

Can open his teeth about one-half inch! Perkins, a soldier for one month when wounded at Antietam, survived until 1899 with this handicap. Wounded Sergeant Joseph Vance Kenton recovered in Gettysburg's Letterman USAGH and was discharged December 3, 1863. His chart read:[54]

> 8-20-63 Was wounded July 3rd by minie ball entering to the left of anterior portion of upper third of left leg, passing between the bones obliquely backward & downward. Made exit at posterior portion of middle $1/3$. On July 5th both openings were enlarged in order to ascertain if either of the bones were injured, it was disclosed the fibula was slightly grazed. There was considerable hemorrhage & the tourniquet was applied over the femoral &

allowed to remain for 8–10 days. Admitted to this hospital in weak condition. Stimulants were administered every hour for a week & fortnight then showed signs of return to strength. Treatment: cold water & cerate dressings. Full diet.

8-21-63 The wounds are nearly healed & the patient suffers no inconvenience except a dull pain around the ankle joint & foot occasioned by one of the numerous branches of nerves that supply the parts which were struck by the ball. Treatment: cerate dressings.

"Cold water dressing, sugar and whiskey" was standard treatment for any wound. It helped save Privates Duncan E. Achor and Andrew White, both wounded at Resaca. Achor was hospitalized with a gunshot wound in the shoulder and breast and lived until 1923. White was shot in the left leg seven weeks after entering service and lived until 1915. Wounds and sickness healed more slowly than today, and hospitalization periods were decidedly longer, often requiring seriously wounded men to lie in one position for weeks. Lieutenant Joseph Balsley's Gettysburg thigh wound would not heal and was a running sore for several months as he resumed duty.

Harrison Lee was sick in Baltimore and Frederick for a year beginning in December 1862, and meanwhile was promoted several times from corporal to first sergeant during the absence. Contrarily, Private Alexander Andrews' amputation in a Gettysburg hospital healed quickly. A minie ball fractured the upper third of his right leg, severing main arteries. Admitted to a USAGH July 23, 1863, by August 20 he had "no bad symptoms. Stump healed with unusual rapidity owing, no doubt, to the great physical endurance and of hopeful mental constitution."[55]

Infirmed men caught other maladies. Fifer James T. McHolland, confined with diarrhea and measles, contracted typhoid during his two years of hospitalization before transferring to the VRC. Private Albert E. Ammons, wounded in the scalp at New Hope Church, went to a Chattanooga USAGH on June 1, 1864. There meningitis supervened, and he died June 10.

Most amputations were usually performed soon after the wounding, such as with Private John Forman. A ball smashed his right foot at Chancellorsville. Four days later he was admitted to Douglas USAGH in Washington, D.C.:[56]

5-18-63. Ball entered immediately posterior and below malleolus of right foot, remaining at front of entrance from which it was extracted by finger, small probe passed upward and forward 1¼" impinging against bone. Wounds has done well. Water dressing used.

5-21-63. Pulse 120 tongue moist slightly coated, skin inclined to heat and dry suppuration. Moderate appetite, no stool in 3 days. Swelling continues less pain from suppuration. Made thorough examination discovered joint to be involved. Amputation performed by Dr. Thomson, long anterior flap at joint of middle and lower $1/3$. Operation done well, lead sutures employed. Dry dressings. Milk punch freely.

5-24-63. Lower half in sloughing condition, no line of demarcation. Since 22nd has taken quinine and other medicines. Dressed the stump with bronium covered with oiled silk. No pain of consequence.

5-27-63. Nearly $3/4$ of flap has sloughed tolerably line of demarcation found. Pulse 120. Skin dry. Tongue moist, moderate appetite, no abnormal thirst. Continued quinate, continued yeast poultice.

6-1-63. Substitute eggnog for punch. Pulse 115, moderate appetite, fever normal. Painted leg with iodine. Cauterized.

6-6-63. Lower portion of leg again erysipelatous, and it was dressed with flaxseed poultice sprinkled with bromine in solution with bromide potassium and water. Bromine with glycerine in drop doses was given internally every 4 hours. In 48 hours the erysipelas had disappeared.

Forman had an "excellent stump, firm, well covered and with a narrow cicatrix, as in Teale's operation. The local and constitutional effects of bromine was undoubtedly beneficial. All the ankle joint wounds treated without early amputation have proved fatal."[57]

The government prescribed wood and metal prostheses in some instances. Private William N. W. Green lost his left forearm at Chancellorsville. A replacement leg was erroneously ordered, then corrected by B. Frank Palmer of Philadelphia, a manufacturer of artificial limbs. Private Jacob

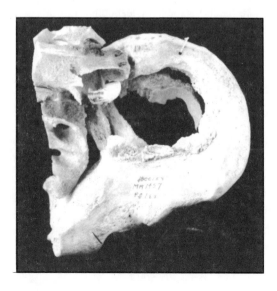

Left Hip Bone of Private Alfred Wilson, Company F

Wilson died on July 8, 1863, at Douglas Army Hospital, Washington, D.C.

Anatomical Collections, National Museum of Health and Medicine, Armed Forces Institute of Pathology

Mathias, shell wound at New Hope Church, applied to A. O. Forsberg, "Manufacturing of Trusses and Limbs of Every Description," Cincinnati, Ohio, for "part of a hand and four fingers for right arm will be constructed so as to enable him to write and do light handling of general life. The construction will be made according [to] his amputation. Price will range from $50–$75 (not sure exactly) as the work is more troublesome as a whole artificial arm."[58]

Some men died.

Chaplain, I wish to leave it as my dying testimony that I am glad that I entered the service of my country although it has cost me my life. My country! It is right! —*Private Alfred Wilson, July 1863* [59]

Wilson, wounded at Chancellorsville and struggling to live, was a victim of almost anything that could have gone wrong. Hit in the hip, he was unattended in captivity before being paroled and treated at the Acquia Creek field hospital. Doctor Carlos Carvello at Washington's Douglas USAGH prescribed an unusual regimen which did little to relieve or heal Wilson:[60]

6-15-63 Wounded gunshot left ilium. In hands of rebels. His wound was entirely neglected for 11 days, crackers & bread were his fare. This man never rallied after entrance into the hospital. Treatment: chicken broth for dinner, beef essence 3 times a day, styptic pills XXIV, take 2 pills every 3 hours;

W G eggnog twice a day.

6-16 Treatment: diarrhea pills continued. W G of beef essence every 3 hrs. One oz eggnog 3 times day. 6-19 Medicines: take tablespoonful 1 hr before each meal.

6-23 Diarrhea styptic pills renewed. Eggnog 3 times day. Egg for breakfast & dinner, brandy toddy twice a day.

6-27 Diarrhea pills continued.

6-28 Medicines: well shaken, take tablespoons 3 times a day.

6-30 Iced lemonade.

7-1 Same Rx as 6-28.

7-8 Died. Post mortem discovered extension fracture of the ilium ball passing through the center burying itself in the or sacrum within a line of the cerebral canal. Specimen preserved.

Wilson's autopsy read "death from exhaustion." A surgeon added, "The case was considered hopeless." Numerous bone fragments were removed; the bullet was found within half a line of the vertebral canal. Surgery was not advanced enough to remove it. Some men lived through similar wounds and carried the bullet for years. But Wilson was too weak, unaided by hospitalization.[61]

"Aunt" visited Private Eldridge Williams, recovering from an Antietam wound, in a Frederick hospital November 12, 1862:

I know that the news from Eldridge will grieve you very much. Kan does not think he can live thru today or at the utmost 1 or 2 days. His blood is absorbing the pus as he can take no nourishment he is going down very fast. Poor boy! He is constantly talking of what he is going to do when he gets well. He is very cheerful & patient & tries to laugh when I remind him of how much he & Jimmy used to get into the sugar jar. He is very much recued & looks very different from the Eldridge who came to see us before he went into the army. Today we moved Eldridge into a private room adjoining ours with a door opening between where he will be more comfortable.[62]

Williams died the same day. And more continued to die in general hospitals, as reported in the Indianapolis Journal: "The following of the 27th Infantry died in the hospital of wounds at Gettysburg: Company C. Daniel J. Colvin; D. Sgt. Elijah Tunney; I. Joseph Gilmore; K. Corp. Abednego Inman, Thomas Hall."[63]

"Hospital gangrene," which confronted hospital matron Elvira A. Powers while visiting the gangrene ward at Jeffersonville USAGH, was the most horrible surgical disease. Gangrene terrorized patients. First a dime-sized black spot appeared on a healing wound. Then the spot spread rapidly, engrossing the entire leg or arm, causing a rotten, evil-smelling mass of dead flesh. Necrosis (tissue death) was caused by blood circulation stoppage or bacterial infection and could be fatal. In extremis, amputation might halt the spread and its death agent. Otherwise, the best treatment was the tortuous bromine, lots of it and often. Powers recalled, "I never saw or scarcely imagined such suffering as the poor fellows undergo from the application of bromine, and do not wonder they have christened the place 'purgatory.'"[64]

Private Enoch Richardson, wounded in the left hand at Resaca, developed gangrene following hospitalization in the field, Chattanooga, Nashville and Louisville:[65]

7-3-64 No previous medical history, was received into gangrene ward on admission. Both thumb and finger amputated at the last joint on May 17th following wound at Resaca. He thinks gangrene set in one week before coming here. On admission the hand was very gangrenous covered with a greyish dirty slough omitting an intolerable odor. Patient suffering great pain, general health bad. Ordered tonics stimulants with generous diet. Removed small portions of slough by scissors & forceps. Treatment: Pure bromide applied by sponge followed with water dressings.

7-5-64 Removed some more sloughs. Wound looking better. Patient somewhat improved, appetite better.

8-25-64 Wound about healed, general health good. Ordered to Indianapolis to be mustered out.

Indiana Governor Morton, affectionately called the "Soldiers' Friend," built a model state military agency to receive and distribute all sanitary (medical, clothing, and related) supplies, supervising local agencies and other soldiers' relief. About him and his agents was written, "Through him their wants are made known. The 'Soldiers' friend' through his representatives or agents follows the soldier in his retreat...to their couches of sorrow, & illuminates the rooms with the light of their countenances & offers of humanitarian services, making the presence of relatives superfluous. An express agent, he brings a cane to one, a crutch to another, becoming almost the soldier's confidant & bosom friend."[66]

Morton did all within his power and authority to make the life of the Hoosier soldier, especially those at the front or hospitalized, as comfortable and meaningful as possible. His local agents in hospitals or the field reported to him on the condition of troops and hospitals in their charge and charter steamers to bring out wounded and bring in food, clothing, nurses, etc.

The agency allied with the State Sanitary Commission. Field agents attended to soldiers' health and comfort, wrote letters, handled burials, preserved relics, kept medical registers, and information for relatives and friends. Agents visited the "martial sons of Indiana" daily in hospitals. They turned offices into temporary soldiers' homes, assisted in transporting them home when they had no money or government passes, provided clothing,

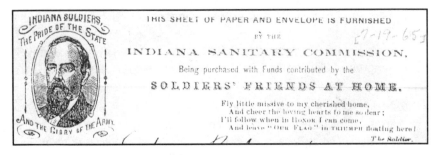

Oliver P. Morton
Indiana Governor and "The Soldiers' Friend."
Indiana Commission on Public Records, Archives Division

food and reading material, took charge of paroled prisoners, and were "careful watchful guardians." When possible the convalescents were sent home or to Northern hospitals.[67] Agent reverend Monfort published in an Indiana newspaper:

> Indiana Military Agency, No. 446 8th St.,
>
> 4 doors from Pennsylvania Avenue, Washington.
>
> The Governor of Indiana has established this agency for purposes of Relief and Information, in matters connected with Indiana Regiments serving in the Army of the East. The sick and disabled will be cared for and information furnished in regard to Sanitary Supplies, Furloughs, Discharges, Transportation, Pay, etc. N.B.—No charge made for services in any case.[68]

Agent T. Bullard visited the 27th Indiana in October 1862. "The boys greet anyone from home with pleasure. They cheerup and ask when Governor Morton is coming to visit them. They seem to expect that whenever there is a battle you or someone to represent you will soon be there to look after their wants. This adds to their courage and willingness to fight."[69] Monfort and Mr. William T. Dennis were close to the 27th's soldiers. Monfort in particular performed admirably and drew high marks.

From the Summer 1862 on, agents visited hospitals after battles reporting on casualties and the state of wounded and sick men: generally rosy, unalarming, and rarely critical. The agents, torch bearers of their politically ambitious governor, kept their avenues open and refrained from finding obvious faults, confining dissatisfaction to private messages. Agents worked closely with privately funded relief agencies which performed distinctive philanthropy, such as the Freedmen's and Christian Commissions. Indiana men organized the war's first Sanitary Commission. Citizens served without pay and followed the soldiers on the march, in camp, and in hospitals, with writing paper, toiletries, and other aids. Businessmen subscribed money, forwarded supplies, or accompanied materials to the front.

The Indianapolis *Journal*, circulated throughout Hoosier camps, was the favored clearinghouse for agent-supplied casualty and after-action information. The paper printed Chancellorsville deaths including Captain John Cassady and Private Joseph Beard as dead on the battlefield. However, Beard's was an example of frequent inaccuracy by both agents and newspapers. Actually Sergeant John P. Beard was mortally wounded and expired while a prisoner of war.

Some general hospital administrators were tougher than others on the patients, but usually every man eventually got his trip home for 15–30 days, depending on length of hospitalization. Whatever the reason, hospitalization was a drudgery at best and less than confinement at worst. Patients had some freedom to move around if able and were either on a rigid schedule or left alone, depending on the staff's training, motivation, and supervision. "The doctor in charge of the hospital will not give any furloughs," Private Andrew Jones wrote home in August 1863. "If there is any other way to get them we would like to know. Can you get that money that is coming to me for rations?"[70] Jones, wounded at Gettysburg and convalescing in the York, Pennsylvania, USAGH, sought help from Monfort.

Patient interests in reading, writing, and conversation were similar to today's. Men wrote letters for each other, or nurses did, and newspapers brought the war news. One of the most humane aspects of hospitals was the accessibility of families to visit and nurse their sons and brothers. However, few Hoosier families could afford the expense and time.

A weakness of the USAGH system, particularly early, was the lack of trained nurses, a major reason for the high mortality rate. Nursing was "no place for ladies"; so most nurses were men, including convalescents, contract alcoholics, or irresponsible idlers, with sometimes dire results for patients. Private William H. Chambers, dying of typhoid, was robbed of $26.25 in Fairfax Seminary Hospital, Alexandria, in 1862. The thief was John Rodana, an outsider acting as a nurse. The surgeon told the provost marshal to punish Rodana severely, "for the man he stole from has a family and will never get well." Chambers died October 17.[71]

In late 1862, nursing became stylish, popularized at Antietam by Clara Barton and her entourage, and more women entered nursing service. Comrades visited each other. Private Isaac Haddon saw Private John C. Haddon in the Fall 1862. Isaac, wounded in the right hand at Antietam, lost two fingers and had been discharged from service. John recalled Isaac's first two fingers were gone and the inside and back of his hand was sore, drawn out of shape, and a little cupped. John was recovering from a Cedar Mountain rupture, but would be discharged in December.

A medical historian wrote, "The wonder is not that so many patients died, but that so many survived. It was a tribute both to superb physicians and superb constitutions of patients."[72] Many a boy of the 27th Indiana warmed to the smile and aid of a female nurse in York, Washington, or Nashville, and could have shared his final words with her as well. One such nurse was author Louisa May Alcott, matron of an Alexandria hospital near "Camp Misery" which treated several members of the 27th.

There was much sickness and many fatalities at Camp Halleck in 1861–62, mostly from pneumonia and exposure, doubtless some of it unnecessary. There were well-equipped hospitals in Frederick. Some were taken there if they could be moved, but not enough. —ERB [73]

There was a finality about death in the Civil War.

Gillaspy, James R., Private, Company F. Gunshot wound at Antietam. Died, Mount Pleasant Hospital, Washington, DC, December 22, 1862.

I certify that the within named James R. Gillaspy, a Private of Captain David Van Buskirk's Company, of the 27th Regt. Indiana Vols., residence Monroe County, Indiana, 33 years of age, 5 feet 6 inches high; light complexion; hazel eyes; light hair and by profession a farmer, was enlisted by Peter Kop at Bloomington on the 18th day of April 1862, to serve during the war. The said James R. Gillaspy was last paid by Paymaster Maj. W. Sherman to include the 30th day of June 1862 and has pay due from that time to the day of his decease. He is indebted to the U.S. for clothing drawn in the amount of $30.09.

Station: Fairfax Station, Virginia

Date: January 13, 1863

/s/ David Van Buskirk, Capt., Cmdg.

Company F, 27th Indiana[74]

In the end, this routine, stiff, longhand note penned on a greasy lined sheet of tablet paper, officially closed the record on the service of a life the rebellion had already taken.

CHAPTER 12

The Men of the 27th Indiana: A Regimental Profile of Who They Were

World War II gave birth to a new slang term for the American soldier: "GI Joe." GI meant government issue, as everything in the Army was. Joe to match the soft repetitive "GiJ" sound, and, well, any popular first name might have done. But Joe is about as common and ambiguous a name as there is in English—all the better for these men. The term became synonymous with "characteristic," as of the military, or "ordinary," as in representing the norm. If you were a GI Joe, you were a common soldier. Combat cartoonist Bill Mauldin embellished the term with his portrayals of "Willie and Joe," two cigarette-smoking, unshaven, woebegone privates toughing out the war in Europe, usually from a wet foxhole.

As contemporary as the term remains, it could have applied 80 years earlier. For, during the Civil War, the United States Army had its own version of GI Joes. They were the men of the 27th Indiana Volunteer Infantry Regiment. Except for their unusually tall measure for that day (they were the tallest regiment in the Union Army), severe casualties, and huge manpower losses, the men of the 27th Indiana were normal, typical, or even average. They did things, thought things, said things the way one would expect of the Union common soldier.

Eleven hundred and eighty one men served in the regiment. Overwhelmingly they were farmers, reflecting midwestern society. Very few professional men enlisted. One-third were illiterate, and no more than half had the "common education" of the day. All men made coffee for each other, even in the rain. They were young like most of the Union Army. One-third were married, about the usual percentage. Their letters and diaries echo those of other Union soldiers. They wrote of furloughs, medical discharges, love for wife and children, sending money home, living through the last battle, whether slavery was "right" or "wrong," and what the "boys" were up to. All implored recipients to write more.

They would respond to a Confederate hollering "Yank!" at them across the Rappahannock River, but in no way called themselves Yankees. They were Hoosiers, Westerners, Indianians, and their state was Hoosierdom.

27th Indiana Regimental Flag

Carried in all Eastern engagements and stands about 6' high. Stored in Indiana War Memorial, Indianapolis.

Photo by author

They had a Medal of Honor recipient and men who ran from the enemy. They were controversial and criticized but also were acclaimed. Individual morale vacillated, more to suit the moment, but unit morale remained surprisingly high. Gallantry and performance often were rewarded with promotion, but some men deserted and others were court-martialed. Discipline was swift and just, some said excessive. Some officers were exceptional, some incompetent; most just did their jobs. They had generals who could lead and generals who could not.

Everyone complained, usually about health but also about not knowing what was to happen. After-action information often was late and muddled. Rumors were rampant. Administration was by trial-and-error and inconsistent, conditions which baffled historians. Paydays were few and far between. Many men who died almost always owed the government money for clothing and equipment.

There were moments for play, frivolity, and humor, not always just during long periods in camp. They tried baseball. The soldiers' penchants for gambling and alcohol were both prohibited and tolerated in cycles. They chewed tobacco, boiled lice from uniforms, and went barefooted when shoes fell apart. Stress and strain, though not properly diagnosed, were manifested curiously, perhaps the strangest being the phenomenon of "moonblindness"—inability to see at night due to vitamin deficiency—that confronted them during the Atlanta Campaign. They pined for and chased women. Venereal diseases, the scourge of armies, were visited on them. Religion was personal, not institutional. However, drudgery being relative, the Hoosier farm boy proved quite capable of coping with soldiering.

In some battles, such as Chancellorsville and Resaca, they gave a good accounting. In others, such as Winchester and Cedar Mountain, they were routed, though not entirely their fault. Their luck varied. At Antietam, they were thrust into total mayhem in the Cornfield. At bloody Peachtree Creek they were on the periphery, and at mismanaged Second Bull Run and Kennesaw Mountain, in reserve. They never grounded their arms or surrendered their colors, and won more battles than they lost. They were steady and resolute under fire and resilient afterwards. They were unusually composed for young volunteers even in untenable positions: the right flank against Jackson's flood at Winchester, the uphill charge to the Wheatfield in 98 degrees at Cedar Mountain, and the doomed assault at Gettysburg's Swale.

In an army fraught with disease and sickness, continually depleting the ranks through death, hospitalization, or discharges, surprisingly many men were present for every engagement, to face again survival's shrinking odds. These ordinarily independent and hard-willed men eventually responded to discipline and orders to attack, dig, countermarch, sleep on frozen ground, double-time on empty stomachs, or perhaps worse, just wait. When non-veterans mustered out, the numbers present had dwindled to one-fourth of the total who served. Not many were left.

Two-thirds of the members or their widows or families received a pension. Aging greatly aggravated amputations, crippling wounds and other disabilities, rendering many wasted men unable to work or care for themselves, and dependent upon families and the government. Service infirmities such as ruptures, camp diarrhea, soldier's rheumatism, prison scurvy, and heart disease cursed them until death, frequently abetting it. Even a cough from a common cold lasted forever. Most men died having improved their lot but little.

One-third of the survivors left Indiana after the war, most going West. Astonishingly, at least 424 lived into the Twentieth Century, but not many officers because they were older. They spawned no national figures. Their most prominent post-war member was both Indiana education superintendent and president of what became Oregon State University. Some achieved local notoriety in business or community work, or were elected to small posts.

War service was a catalyst to keep old comrades together through later years rather than as a slogan to be traded for personal gain. Through their regimental reunion group, they remained loyal to one another, their cause and their country. Their final survivor passed into eternity at 97 during the midst of the Depression and trans-oceanic airplanes, with Hitler's war and television a couple of years away.

Aside from the obvious, they were not so unlike us. Even though they are four generations removed, a number of their grandchildren live today. They wrote and spoke as we do, using many Hoosierisms which remain and four-letter words each new generation thinks it discovered. They used toothbrushes and canned goods, wore sized shirts, ate ice cream, put stamps on envelopes. Their logic and rationale was incredibly similar to ours. The values for which they consecrated themselves, preeminently the family, are the soul of the Midwest. The biggest difference is our world is just so much larger.

The Regimental Profile

National Tribune Editor John McElroy, reviewing the 27th Indiana regimental history in the late 1890s for the veteran-oriented periodical, said: "[They typify] the American people in 1861 and what kind of sons they reared in their schools, churches and homes...plain, everyday boys, who had ordinary appetites, passions and tempers, who dearly loved a full messpot and a good dinner, who made daily the most human mistakes and then had the manliness to laugh at them, but who were always instantly ready to rise to the loftiest planes of heroism, and self-sacrifice."[1]

To survey who were these typical American boys, this study examines both the Indiana common soldier and members of the 27th Indiana. Data includes heights, residences, education, ages, occupations, and names. About the Indiana soldier, actuary Dr. Benjamin Apthorp Gould wrote in 1869:

> The mean age at enlistment was 24.7 years, by far the lowest in the Union Army. Thirty percent of enlisted men were under 21; 60% were under 25. They had not become wedded to any particular occupation. His average weight was 141 pounds, and he generally had blue (42%) or gray (26%) eyes. Fifty eight out of 1000 had red hair.[2]

Gould said some characteristics of the "typical Hoosier soldier" were easier to quantify than others. For instance, 70 percent were natives of Indiana or Ohio, and 71 percent were farmers. Almost two-thirds had light complexions and either dark or sandy hair.[3] But most significantly he was: "Like a grand piece of mosaic in which all colors are united...,and enhancing the luster of each, the typical Hoosier is dependent on every element for completeness, yet as a whole is dissimilar to any part....Sensitive, excitable, bashful, and it may be boastful, enterprising, ardent, and industrious....No bully, yet is able to use his fist, and if he is accused of lying—the vice most repugnant to his nature—he loses not a moment in applying his fist in a free fight."[4]

A Hoosier soldier was always recognized among the crowd by this friendly custom: "If an Indiana boy catches your eye he says, 'How do you do, sir?' very politely, and this gives you a good opinion of the whole regiment."[5] One came to expect no less.

Mustered in on September 12, 1861, in Indianapolis, the regiment enrolled 1,181 men during its three years of service. Original members numbered 38 officers, 995 enlisted combatants, and 24 band members, a total of 1,057. Recruits numbered 124 and two transferred men returned for a total enrollment of 1,183. After non-veterans (those choosing not to reenlist) mustered out September 1, 1864, during the Siege of Atlanta, Georgia, the remnants consolidated with the 70th Indiana on November 4. The author did not count 139 veterans (reenlistees) as new enrollments, an artificial practice by some historians, which would have made the enrollment 1,322. Combatants—not counting band and field and staff—numbered 38 officers and 995 enlisted (1,033) original members, a total of 1,159.

The 1,183 disagrees with the frequently appearing 1,101 figure, origin unknown. The 27th's monuments at Chancellorsville and Gettysburg are inscribed with 1,101, the number used in writing the 1899 regimental history. William F. Fox used 1,101 in his 1898 authoritative work *Regimental Losses in the American Civil War*. Both writers may have accessed each other. Edmund Randolph Brown did not use War Department or Pension Office records and complained about the records of wartime Indiana Adjutant General William H. H. Terrell's office, although he probably used the latter. The 82-member difference is irreconcilable, although the author is close to some of Terrell's numbers.[6]

Citizens and other soldiers called them the "giants" or "tall boys." Wherever they went during their first two years, until their ranks were depleted, they drew comments and stares of awe, particularly when Captain David Campbell Van Buskirk of Company F was present. A comrade said of Van Buskirk in October 1861:

> The old Colonel took Big Lieutenant Buskirk out with him today as a kind of show, for he attracts attention and perfectly surprises them on the march. When we stop in a little town you will see a crowd gather about him. It tickles him to be noticed—looks to me like he tries to look as big as possible. [7]

Because of David Campbell Van Buskirk, the huge 6'10.5" soldier, and many others of less but yet imposing heights, the 27th Indiana was the tallest regiment in the Union Army. At an average height of five feet-nine inches per man, they rose at least one inch above the average height of the time for American white males of European stock.

Members of Van Buskirk Family of Monroe County, Indiana

Left to right: Second Lieutenant Isaac Van Buskirk ("Blue Ike"), Sergeant John ("Sandy");
David Campbell ("Big Dave") and Isaac ("Deaf Ike").

Provided by Patsy Powell

David Van Buskirk, one of five Company F member relatives from that family, was universally regarded as the army's tallest soldier, some said the world's. Weighing more than 300 pounds, he was a bonafide giant of his time, the possible equivalent of 7'2–4" today, and a headline show in Richmond, Virginia, after his 1862 capture at Winchester. The men were proud and sensitive of their fame and reacted vehemently to unfavorable remarks from brigade commander Brigadier General George Henry Gordon in 1862, such as his labeling them "disrespectfully" as "seven-foot Indiana volunteers." After the war the survivors wrote, "Now, to the eyes of Lilliputians [Gordon] we might have appeared to reach that sublime height, but generally we fell somewhere below. The 27th doubtless contained taller men than any other Indiana regiment, and the tallest man in it was only 6 feet 11 inches [*sic*]."[8]

Company F set high goals when filling its ranks. Recruited in Bloomington, it consisted of men from throughout Central and Southern Indiana, the "New Albany Railroad Company." Peter Kop, a French veteran of Napoleonic Wars well trained in infantry, watched David Van Buskirk walk up the south side of the square in Bloomington. The huge stature excited Kop with the idea of organizing a company of soldiers 5'10" or higher, and asked David to join him. The local newspaper of July 13, 1861, announced:

> RECRUITING: Peter Kop and several other gentlemen of this place are raising a company of grenadiers for United States Service. They admit no recruits under 5 feet 10 inches, and equally stout and able bodied. We pity the rebel upon whose neck the foot of "big Pete" shall come down with a vengeance.[9]

Kop, a 6'4.5" railroad conductor, almost succeeded. His men averaged 5'10.2". Sixty-five of their original 102 members were over 5'10", and 35 over 6'0".[10] When the company reached Indianapolis to be mustered into the 27th Regiment, the Indianapolis *Journal* reported:

> A few days ago a company of "six footers" arrived in this city from Monroe County and went into camp. The company is composed of the largest men we have seen from any section of the State. The Second Lieutenant [David Van Buskirk] is a "whale," but some others are whales too, but a trifle smaller. [11]

David's brother Corporal Isaac was 6'5". The five Van Buskirk relatives of Company F were all at least six feet tall and averaged nearly 6'3.5". History records no taller family in the army. Company F became "singularly renown," with men of "splendid physique whose intelligent faces bore out the impression conveyed by the strength of their form." This "strange company" was "perhaps the largest in the world, which would have delighted the heart of the eccentric Frederick of Prussia [a contemporary]."[12] Six members were from Washington County along the Louisville, New Albany and Chicago Railroad, headed by Sergeant John McKnight Bloss and Private Elijah McKnight, both 6'2". Their county was famous for its tall pioneers, the "Washington County Giants." When these men fit the company's mold their name was naturally assimilated by the company and then by the regiment, and the 27th Indiana became the "Giants" in perpetuity.[13]

Company B averaged 5'9.5", the Field and Staff and Company I 5'9.3". Company K at 5'7.6" was the only one falling short of the standard 5'8". Overall, 41.7 percent were 5'10" or better, and 16.9 percent reached at least six feet, remarkable numbers considering the preponderance of "short" men with undersized frames by today's standards for soldiers. Some soldiers, mainly drummer boys, were very short. Fearless Elisha H. Stephens,

15, was only 4'3". From loud drumming and cannonading at Chancellorsville and Gettysburg he suffered partial deafness, but completed his service. Another drummer, William Shaller Ottwell, 14, was 4'7.5". The shortest other enlisted men at 5' were Privates John Edward Hart and Elijah H. Tomy. Few were under 5'4". Because they had ceased growing, the older officers were taller. The shortest was Captain James Stephens at 5'5".

While researching the regiment, only the "Lost Order" melodrama captivated the author like the information on their heights. But few primary sources exist on heights of Civil War-era Americans. The government kept none. Disagreement exists among the few sources as to superlatives, forcing one to draw conclusions. A major inconsistency is failure to standardize measurement either with or without shoes (David Van Buskirk was measured in stocking feet). The minimum height established in August 1861 for the regular army was 63", but volunteers had no limit. The rule was that "the matter of stature should be considered only in general examination as to the physical fitness of the man for military service."[14] The average stature of original volunteers was greater than that of recruits subsequently enlisting. The most authoritative sources are journals and investigations of the Society of Actuaries in 1882, 1886, and 1912; Gould's 1869 work; and Terrell's 1869 Volume I.[15]

Gould, although frequently cited by period writers, was contradictory and scientifically suspect, using caveats and rambling inferences. Once he said Indiana soldiers were the army's tallest. Later he said he had examined measurements of taller Tennessee and Kentucky soldiers, but from a narrower data base.[16] He concluded that because people of the South were taller than those of the North, Southern Indianians ("27th Indiana country"), of mostly Southern stock, therefore were taller than other Indianians.[17]

Terrell calculated the average Indiana soldier's height at 5'8.1". Reports of Society of Actuaries (1881–82, 1886, 1912) indicate similar findings for American soldiers of the era.[18] Fox stated the average height of American soldiers from recruiting officer records was 5'8.25". Indiana men and others were slightly above this, including West Virginians at 5'9", but with such few West Virginia Union regiments the number was skewed.[19] The 1866 Provost Marshal General Report showed that for 346,744 Federal soldiers examined for service after March 6, 1863, U.S.-born men were taller (5'7.4") than European counterparts.[20]

Basically all sources agree that for the era, males reached maximum height at between 28–31 years. Union soldiers overwhelmingly were between 20–25, indicating a soldier reached peak growth after service. Spot checks of physical examination heights in hundreds of 27th Indiana pension records support that rationale. Comparing 5'8" with the Society's 1979 study showing the average male at 5'10.4" (20–24 years) and 5'10.5" (20–29), both with shoes with $^1/_2$-inch heel,[21] to the onlooker, 5'9" equated to at least 6 feet today.

Weights were not used to identify or classify soldiers. Scales sometimes were available and some men reported their weights, particularly to describe significant gains or losses. For example, two privates stated their weights dropped from 165 to 130 and 178 to 140 during their service, extreme cases, but few men gained. Musician Samuel P. McCormick was weighed (170 pounds) on September 12, 1861, but no other member reported a weight for that time. In early 1862 Sergeant William Parmemas Ellis gave the total weight of the 14 men in his mess as 2,245 pounds, an average of over 163. The heaviest was 184, the lightest 132. Another 27th Indiana soldier weighed 205. Gould tersely stated the average weight of men from Ohio and Indiana was 141.

The 27th had unusually wide cosmopolitan roots. Members came from 51 of the state's 90 counties (56.7 percent), 10 other states and three foreign countries. Nearly all members for whom a residence is known—1,110 (94.7 percent)—were Hoosiers by birth or choice, a remarkable statistic compared with the average Indiana soldier. The attraction of such geographically dispersed men was abnormal. An inland agricultural state like Indiana was less likely to draw transients than commercial or seaboard states. An expert on Hoosier life of that time said of the pioneer stock of the 27th Indiana:

> They were rural farmers, very reluctant and slow to change anything, particularly modernizing methods of farming. They were more backward than farmers in other states. Most settlers in Southern and South-Central Indiana were of Anglo stock, and the next most populous was German. Most were second generation, very few first generation. Most came from North Carolina, Tennessee, Kentucky, or Ohio.[22]

Also, in the early days of the war (original members enlisted in July–September 1861) whole infantry companies frequently were recruited from one county. Usually companies were filled at home from towns of men who were acquainted, and then were merged into a regiment. Likely unintentional, a plausible explanation centers around a principal railroad, the Louisville, New Albany and Chicago line, which sliced through Indiana from south to northwest. Many men joined the 27th from along this road, also called the Monon. Some were railroaders; most were neighboring farmers.

Despite the regiment's widespread nativity, 595 or 51.6 percent came from five principal counties. Seven of the 10 companies were assembled primarily from those counties. Daviess, with 193 (16.8 percent) in Companies B and E, and Putnam, with 141 (12.2) in Companies A and I, furnished

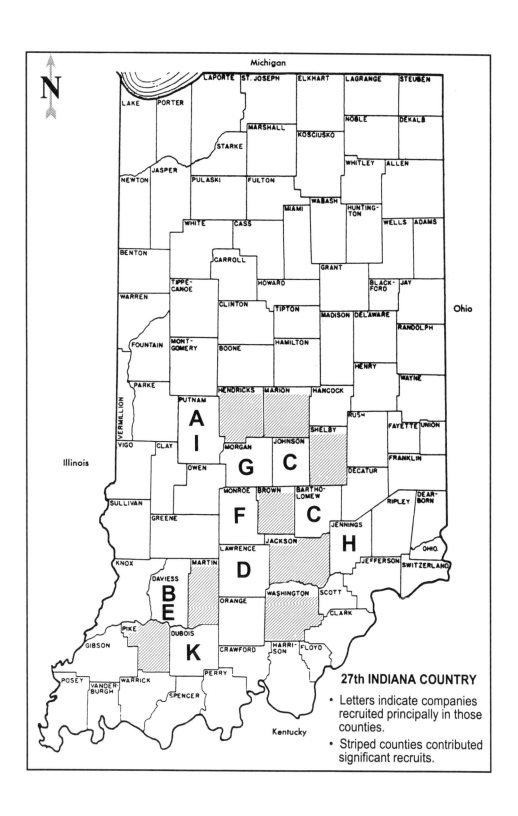

27th INDIANA COUNTRY

- Letters indicate companies recruited principally in those counties.
- Striped counties contributed significant recruits.

more than any other. Nineteen counties from every area of the state furnished one member each. Next door Ohio, Kentucky, and Illinois led outside states. Missing were foreign mercenaries frequently found in the Union infantry, and only three countries were represented. Germany was the original home of at least 25; Ireland was second with 12. The exclusive company—K, mostly of German descent, had only one original member from outside Dubois County, and two of three recruits were from Dubois, and many members were European immigrants or their sons.

Most members resided in the rural southern and southcentral parts of Indiana: "27th Indiana country." Bloomington was the epicenter. Many had Southern roots and combined with rural venue helped explain these notable features: the predominance of farming as an occupation; a resolute toughness of individual constitution; the lack of men with an advanced education; and the political and social dilemmas raised by the region's scattered but significant Confederate sympathy, the Copperhead movement. That became extremely contentious and affected the entire regiment especially during 1862–63 when Southern sentiment in Indiana peaked.

A small percentage of those who had moved from the South were intense haters of slavery, loyal to the Union, and saw the rebellion as a conspiracy of the slave oligarchy. However, most southern Indiana settlers had come north only to better their conditions and retained Southern loyalty—"They repeated,'*You never can conquer the South*.'"[23] With a "special aversion for the negro," they feared the "'niggers' might some time come up and live amongst us." However, they deceived Southern leaders regarding aid and material they might receive from them, and were contemptuously called "dough faces." They firmly believed the rebellion could not be suppressed. "Out of these conditions the 27th and most early [recruited] Indiana regiments sprung."[24]

> The men were largely from the farms and villages in the southern half of the state. Many of them were long when lying down and all of them were long in the Hoosier dialect and other colloquialisms and peculiarities of that period. But almost without exception they were sincere, manly young fellows, brave and courageous to a fault, and deeply interested in winning the war.
> —*ERB* [25]

Common educations, the equivalent of through the sixth grade, were the norm. When most men of the 27th were of school age in Indiana there were no grades, just one school attended by anyone. Some students starting school were seven, some older, but might be 18 if there was no school to attend previously, or his parents could not have afforded it. The teacher took them at whatever level and grouped them.

Since there was no public school system and no village or town laws requiring them to attend, parents decided whether a child should continue in school. (Private John Dearmin had been sent away to public schools in Bloomington.) Parents started a school and hired the teacher. Attendance was by subscription—$2.16 for a 3-month term in mid-winter when the children were not on the farms working fields until harvest's end. Curricula were not used. The students went six days a week, 7:00 a.m.to 4:00 p.m.or sun-up to sundown. Literate parents taught at home. Private Lewis King, who enlisted at 15, described his early education.

> I was a first class speller, a good reader, had studied geography success-fully, had gone pretty well through Ray's third part arithmetic, could write a fairly legible hand, etc. These things I had learned by firelight or chiplight on week days and by sunlight on Sundays, with very little instruction from any-body at the time. I learned nearly all before I was 10. After that time my service was more valuable in the house and out on the farm.[26]

No definition of literacy existed and no examination tested it, creating a gulf between literates and illiterates with no broad middle ground. The emphasis was on ability to write a fine, fair hand, because it enhanced chances of getting a job. If a student was not learning the parents would simply withdraw the child from school. The 1850 census showed Indiana had the highest illiteracy rate in the North, and the state slowly complied with the 1851 constitutional requirement for a "general and uniform system of common schools, wherein tuition shall be without charge, and equally open to all."[27] The backwoods Hoosier farmer was in a "condition of appall-ing ignorance and even sheer illiteracy."[28] An 1866 report on Indiana sol-diers stated, "No young State shows finer institutions of learning or of charity. Yet many a boy never sees the inside of a schoolhouse, and many a man drops into the ballot box a vote he cannot read, and makes the cross instead of his name to a deed of sale or purchase."[29] By 1860 the common school movement was under way and illiteracy among adults was declining.

Indications are approximately 33 percent of the 27th Indiana's mem-bers were illiterate, and 17 percent were borderline. Fifty percent appeared to have a common school education or higher and were considered liter-ate. Not all left written records, and some who did got others to read and write for them. Literacy was in ways we today might not expect: knowledge of Latin, Greek mythology, the Classics, the "paragon of education." We cannot judge by spelling and punctuation, which might be phonetic and poor, but perhaps had good structure and vocabulary.

Ability to pen ledgers, daybooks, and letters aided marketability; so there was further emphasis on writing fine script. Itinerant writing teachers taught the fancy Spencerian script of well-rounded, well-formed letters so popular during this period. Some people read haltingly, especially scripture (which was a real trial). Some had a knack for reading, and with little instruction could read well. Those without an aptitude for reading and writing just "went back to the fields and plowed ground."[30] A number of them later enrolled in the 27th Indiana, and their pension records are full of "X" marks instead of signatures.

Some Indiana and Ohio recruits were given education tests prior to entering the service. From the small sampling of 1,637 tested, 63 had no education, but the bulk—1,471 (89.8 percent)—had either limited or good "common school" educations—inferring some ability to read and write.[31]

In the "common education" experience, the fortunate student learned the "3 R's" and maybe some classics. Today that equates to less than an elementary school education. Private Silas Newton Whitted had a limited common school education because the nearest schoolhouse was some distance, fed by a pathway through dense woods. ERB recalled reading weekly and monthly papers "with avidity," and using school books with good selections of history and English literature. Before the war the only books he read were *Pilgrim's Progress* and the life of Benjamin Franklin. "Unknown to me were *Robinson Crusoe, Gulliver's Travels, Grimm's Fairy Tales,* American novelists, and Shakespeare."[32] Someone noted, "The teacher was usually master of the situation in everything except the subjects which he was required to teach."[33]

Only a few members attended college, and one, John McKnight Bloss, is known to have graduated. He obtained a bachelor's degree with honors from Hanover College in Indiana in 1860, and was principal of the Livonia public school before enlisting. Bloss gained the most post-war notoriety of any survivor by serving as Indiana State Superintendent of Public Instruction and president of what is now Oregon State University. Seven members were school teachers of a sort. Some of the eight doctors went to medical college. Captain Jackson L. Moore, a physician, graduated from Evansville (Indiana) Medical School. Physician Captain Richmond M. Welman attended school in "old time log schoolhouses," but he studied medicine as a boy under a Dr. Hazelwood and attended Cincinnati (Ohio) Medical College, graduating in 1859.[34] Assistant Surgeon Greenly Vinton Woollen received private instruction and studied medicine with Indianapolis doctors, and was attending Cincinnati College of Medicine when war broke out. Colonel Silas Colgrove, an attorney and post-war circuit court judge, studied law at an attorney's side, as was customary.

Only two men listed "student" as their occupation, Woollen and Drummer Ottwell. Putnam County's Company A had a "sprinkling" of men who attended college. The influence at Indiana Asbury (DePauw University) at

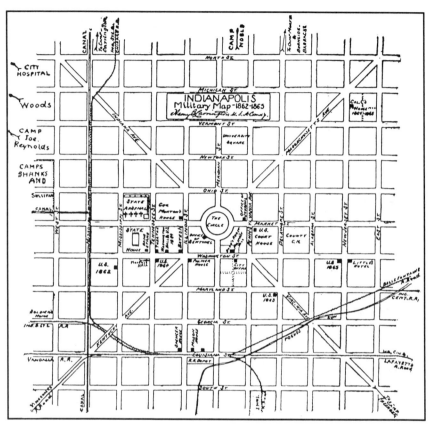

Military Map of Indianapolis, Indiana (1862–65)

Henry B. Carrington, "Indiana in the Civil War," in Oliver P. Morton correspondence, Indiana Commission on Public Records, Archives Division

Greencastle was "clearly noticeable in many other members." The company was known for having "more than the average wide-awake ambitious young men of some education and evident force and ability." [35] First Lieutenants George Tarvin Chapin and Jacob A. Lee probably attended. Company C had "more education than average, good manners, and personal neatness," attracting favorable comments on their soldierly appearance.

> The men had limited educations—but that's not saying they were unintelligent or not well informed. Throughout Indiana were to be found many men of large means and extensive and complicated business interests who were illiterate. Yet persons who tried to defraud them invariably would have his labor for his pains. The Union soldier knew what he was fighting for and what was expected of him. —*ERB* [36]

The average age of the 27th Indiana member, 23.6 years, was much lower than the Indiana average of 24.7, which itself was lower than the Union Army's. The regiment's officers averaged 28.7 and enlisted men 23.5, with a median age of 23.5. The vast spread of ages—13 to 61— spanned three generations of the nation's growth, from the untamed frontier of the new century's opening year to the industrial and railroad boom at mid-century.

The prescribed age limits of 18–45 in 1861 were flexible to allow for recruiting musicians or "sturdy or earnest" older men.[37] Many anxious, patriotic enlistees gave as their age either "18" or "45," and recruiters, eager to fill quotas, often acceded and fudged on ages. Presuming more very young men than very old joined, records are probably skewed higher than actual. The 27th's veterans commonly admitted in pension applications they had lied to reach the minimum age. Civil War soldiers weren't called "boys" as an expression alone. Probably many men in the 27th were underage. For example, in Company K twenty 18-year-olds and fourteen 19-year-olds enlisted, and none 17 or below. In Company B one 17-, twenty-eight 18-, and fourteen 19-year-olds enlisted. Only a handful of enlisted stated they were 46-plus.

The youngest member was Private Samuel Simpson, whose birthday was May 28, 1848 (13). The youngest officer was Major Theodore Frelinghausen Colgrove, at 17 the Adjutant. Both "youngest" remained for their full three years. Teamster William Suddeth, 61, was the oldest. After his discharge for health in January 1862, the oldest was Teamster Moses Fugate, 57, also later discharged for health. Two officers were 51, First Lieutenant Squire O. W. Garrett and First Lieutenant Francis Ottwell (No. 1). Both resigned by March 1863.

Farming, or agriculture, was the predominant occupation. More than three quarters, 870, or nearly 77 percent, listed farmer as their occupation when enlisting. That figure is higher than Gould's 71.5 percent for all Indiana soldiers and possibly in line with figures from other midwestern states. Farmers are tabulated in the *Manual Labor* category, which also included laborers, miners, and sawyers. This category represented 911 (80.4 percent) of the regiment. Adding laborers to farmers, the statistic reported in Gould for this category was 76.1 percent. Hogs, wheat, corn, and vegetables were the principal crops. Indiana was a major supplier of those products to the army.

Artisans constituted the next category with 166 (14.7 percent), including carpenters, the second leading occupation with 33 or 2.9 percent, blacksmiths (26), coopers, millers, shoemakers, wagon makers, and others skilled with their hands. There were five mechanics. Arbitrarily including Gould's mechanics and printers as the corresponding category, that figure was a close 17.7 percent. *Professionals* ranked third with 22 (1.9 percent), including seven each physicians/surgeons and school teachers, three each ministers and engineers, and two lawyers.

Transportation, including teamsters/wagoners and railroad and river men, provided 18 (1.6 percent). *White Collar* workers numbered 14 and included clerks, merchants and the like. This figure is close to Gould's 2.2 percent for its commercial category. The "*Other*" category were two students, the only members not employed at enlistment.

Apparently no one was engaged in manufacturing, except wagon, brick, and cabinet making. By significant numbers those not in farming supported it: the wagon makers, coopers, and millers, and those who toiled for the horse, the blacksmiths, teamsters, saddlers, and harness makers. If the regiment had been intact any time after muster-in (it was not) they could have utilized a wide but thin array of specialists, including a brewer, baker, artist, watch maker, fireman, gunsmith, and druggist.

Surnames and given names each numbered a couple of hundred. The multitude of surnames is noteworthy considering the tendency of mid-century rural families to intermarry, and probably resulted from the diverse births and lack of congregated residences as much as anything. Inaccuracy in recording names appeared to be symptomatic of Union Army administration, as the case of Private Joseph (James) S. Steele reported:

> When I enlisted at Greencastle in Captain Morrison's company, the company clerk Tarvin C. Stone enrolled me as James S. Steele. My name is Joseph S. Steele. I was young (18). They told me I would have to sign the

Union Volunteer Infantry Company
This is what the 27th Indiana probably looked like.

Brady Collection

muster rolls as James S. Steele, and I did. I signed all books, rolls, papers, etc., during my term of service as James. This has been a source of anoyance ever since I first was enrolled.[38]

Corporal Philburd S. Wright was discharged December 13, 1862, with a gunshot wound in the left leg received at Antietam. Private H. C. F. L. Pohlman was discharged two weeks later while "dragging out a miserable existence in camp with chronic hepititis and diarrhea, and dyspepsia in severe form." Corporal Abednego Innman was killed at Gettysburg by gunshot in the right side of his abdomen while carrying the colors in the charge. These three men had some of the regiment's most unusual names.

Close to matching modern Americans, Smith led the surnames with 17; Williams was second with 13; Jones was third (11), Davis fourth (10), and Brown/Baker/Kemp fifth (9). But these names represented only 9.1 percent. Other popular surnames were White, Wilson, Johnson, Allen, Edwards, and Evans. Smiths, merely 1.4 percent, included the Germanic "Schmidt." The leading given names fell into several categories, the first of which were traditional names: John (13.8), William (10.2), James, Thomas, George, Joseph, Robert, and Charles. These names accounted for nearly half: 45.3 percent.

No true Union regiment would be without its patriot names. Of the Georges, at least 29 were George Washington or George W. Benjamin Franklin (F.) and Andrew Jackson (J.) ranked high. There were sprinklings of Thomas J.'s, James M.'s, John Q. A.'s, and a Daniel Webster. Biblical names such as Abraham, Adam, Elisha/Elijah, Enoch, Isaac, and Joshua reflected a religious influence, and other names had biblical connotations: Daniel, David, Francis, Michael, Peter, and Samuel. Some names are out of vogue today: Abisha, Elihu, Erastus, Josephus, Marion, Silas, and Stark. Some had rhythmic flair: Bloomfield Beavers, Dory Kinneman, Ebenezer Quackenbush, Flavius Potter, Greensbury Hancock, Jabez Bradford, Jesse Jackson, McHewel Poindexter, Rezin Sumner, and Greenly Vinton Woollen.

Misspelled names are a major inconsistency in Civil War records, especially for enlisted men. A combination of sloppy signatures, illiteracy, recruiters' laziness, or incompetence completing enlistment papers, and poor administrative practices produced frequent multiple spellings. Consequently, many names were written phonetically and transcribed by hand erroneously, causing contemporary record-keeping problems and researchers' nightmares. For example, regimental records show Private George W. Gore as Gorer, Goar, and Goon. (The spelling used in this study is the one most frequently used in records.) Gore is easy compared to tracking Harv(r)ey M. (N.) Co(a)rrell (Coswell); Thomas Dossey (Dorsey) (Dorcet[t]) (Dawsey); Newton (Nathanial) H. (N.) Fitzgerald (Fitzgeare) (Fitzjiarl), Joseph Roelle (Re[a]ll[e]y) (Reilly); or Lawrence (Lorence) (Lorenz) Ov[b]er

(Offer). In the case of Smith (Schmidt), either the Dubois County Germans or the record keepers vascillated over whether to anglicize the name permanently. Therefore, as with Schumacher (Shoemaker) and Kemp(t) and others it appears both ways.

Many identifiable family combinations joined: father and sons, brothers, cousins, or mixes. The largest contingent were seven Deputy relatives from Jennings County in Company H, and their Jennings cousins Lewis King and James Milford Fowler. William Deputy was killed in action at Antietam and is buried in Antietam National Cemetery near brother Henry, who died of disease in Frederick, Maryland, in January 1863. Zachariah died of disease in Bellevue Hospital in New York City in August 1862. Joseph B. was discharged after typhoid fever in June 1862, and Thomas R. with lameness in August 1862. Within eight months three Deputys were dead and two were disabled.

Besides the Deputy group, the most exemplary patriotic family was Company C's 45-year-old father Charles Applegate and sons Joseph, 18, Americus, 16 and 5'0", a fifer, and Hiram, 14 and 4'8", a drummer boy. They were half the Wayne County contingent. Company K's six Dubois County Kemps, Benjamin, David, James, Silas, Wesley, and William, of Huntingburg, were the second largest family. The most famous was the Van Buskirks of Company F:

- Captain David Campbell of Gosport, "Big Dave," who resigned due to ill health on April 26, 1864;

- His brother Corporal Isaac (No. 2) of Gosport, "Deaf Ike," a POW at Winchester, who was discharged January 8, 1864, with deafness and tuberculosis;

- Their cousin Lieutenant Isaac (No. 1), of Gosport, "Blue Ike," also a POW at Winchester, wounded in right leg and POW at Chancellorsville, who died of wounds at Acquia Creek, Virginia, May 15, 1863;

- His brother First Sergeant John, of Gosport, "Sandy," wounded at Chancellorsville, mustered out December 27, 1864; and

- Everyone's cousin Corporal Michael Henry, of Bloomington, a prisoner of war at Winchester, wounded at New Hope Church, who mustered out September 1, 1864.

> Fortunately for me I was soon accorded a warm place among the men and later the survivors. Both men and officers have been my close personal friends through life. In fact, my acquaintance with them both during service and since has given me unbiding faith in the good sense and absolute trust of the plain, average people. —*ERB* [39]

EPILOGUE

As I studied the minutes of the 27th Indiana's Regimental Association and other material assembled on the 27th's survivors, I experienced unusual emotion and compassion for them. Those feelings had been commonplace as I had lived inside their uniforms for so long while writing their story, but this research struck me differently. They were no longer young men leaving plows, enlisting in the army, marching into battle, eating green corn, sleeping in mud-filled trenches or longing to be home. They were now at midlife or more, settled in some livelihood, many with grown children, and living with perpetual aches. But the absence of documents forced me to skip much of the time from the war to the reunion years of 1885 to 1928. Upon reaching the papers on Gettysburg's 50th anniversary in 1913, I was moved to rejoin them in reverie for all their reunions and track them until the last man died in 1936. I started rereading the minutes, and asked them to make more room for me. As at Gettysburg for the 125th commemoration, I became immersed in their lives.

Each year when they gathered, they saved me a place at their table and campfire, and passed me

Cedar Mountain Battlefield

Author stands on Slaughters Mountain surveying the Wheatfield where the 27th Indiana was routed on August 9, 1862.

Photo by author

224

a songsheet in case my own memory had slipped a bit, perhaps like their own. Each year the list of members got shorter, and I added my condolences to widows and children who, out of loyalty and devotion, steadfastly represented their men and helped keep the group going. Each year my comrades sat closer to the front, bending and turning their heads to hear a little better the adulations of a visiting GAR officer or a comrade from a sister regiment. "Without you Lee would have swept away Culp's Hill! Without you the Union would have been lost! Without you tyranny would have ruled!" And on. But, why not? I thought. They lived for these moments together to share, to renew their inner faith, to reinforce they had been in the right, even though they had forfeited their youth and mortgaged their health. The price had been steep, but I never met a man there who would not pay it again.

Each year I watched them grow old before my eyes. I saw them hobbling on canes through the meeting hall door, assisted by comrades with better legs, but only one arm. I saw them caressing their evening supper plates with long white beards, and raking their bony, leathery fingers through

Company K Veterans with Their Flag, Jasper, Indiana

Left to right: Corporal Conrad Eckert, Private Joseph Schrader, Private Mathias Smith (Schmidt), Sergeant Joseph P. Mehringer, First Sergeant Joseph Roelle, Private Anton Berger.

Provided by Doris Krelein and Ruth Buecher

thin, snowy hair. I heard their cracking, throaty renditions of "Marching Through Georgia," and "The Girl I Left behind Me," with the voice of a daughter at the piano coming through on the verses, but unnecessary on the still-familiar refrain. And I nearly lost myself when they finished each reunion with "God be with You Till We Meet Again."

As I had endured their pain in the briars at Cedar Mountain, and shared the sweltering heat of The Swale, and marveled at their clever ambush behind that knoll at Resaca where they captured the flag, I absorbed the revival of their glory days, their fighting spirit, their togetherness, true one-for-all and all-for-one, days when they were young. I dug into my own pocket for $5 to help Edmund Randolph Brown publish the long-awaited regimental history, a book of compassion for fellow man I would treasure as I wrote my own, and a dollar more so John Bresnahan could put up the regiment's monument at Chancellorsville. I watched men whose rugged and virile exteriors faced the cannon's mouth at New Hope Church be transformed into reciting humbling utterances from words of the Lord. Men whose Sunday mornings had been full of company inspections, boot black-ing and card games, now listened intently as their group chaplain led them in prayer in remembrance, and to boost their spirits.

Each year, how I grieved for them as their days moved on and their ranks withered. This year's reunion was over, and they would say, see you next year. One more year, then how many will be left? The saying of goodbyes was their hardest moment. Too quickly the meetings rolled by— 1897, 1910, and then 1928. Names I knew dropped from the rolls. By 1891, Prosser, Gaskins, Forlander were gone. By 1901, Gambold, Gentry, Landes. By 1905, Wallick, Ketchum, and John McKnight Bloss, my favor-ite soldier of all.

I was naturally drawn into their world and time. As the agent of their story, it had to be that way. I love the men of the 27th Indiana—who they were, what they accomplished, but mostly what they stood for, for their gifts to me as Hoosiers which allowed me to know and love their state. Their descendants are that way. I have never met a Hoosier who was not special.

As the survivors felt kindred spirit, so have I felt mine with them. It has been an escape by both drift and design, for it is so easy to abide while kneeling at a gravestone on a chilly, rainy day in Chattanooga, or strain-ing my eyes carefully unfolding their ancient muster rolls in poor light in the National Archives, or picking a ripe ear of corn—yes, picking it—from Miller's cornfield along Hagerstown Pike at Sharpsburg. Such musing and communication, misunderstood by any onlooker and sometimes by my own family who loyally and politely tolerated and supported my odyssey, frequently diverted me from my work, and watery eyes distracted me from returning to the task I had rewarded myself.

Thank you, Barton Warren Mitchell, and may you rest forever in peace in your home in Hartsville, Indiana.

27th Indiana Veterans at 50th Gettysburg Reunion, 1913
Captain Thomas J. Box, Company D, second from left.

Provided by Judi McMillen

APPENDIX A

Mitchell, Bloss, and Vance: The Lost Order

The letter First Sergeant John McKnight Bloss read was entitled "Confidential—Special Orders Number 191— Headquarters, Army of Northern Virginia—September 9, 1862." It was addressed to "Major General D. H. Hill, commanding division." Incredulous. The names of Generals Jackson, Longstreet, McLaws, Anderson, Walker, Hill, Stuart jumped off the paper. Bloss recognized them all whether the soldiers with him did or not. He read on: March tomorrow—part of the army to Hagerstown—Sharpsburg—part to cross Potomac—Martinsburg—Harpers Ferry—Boonsborough—Middletown—part to Maryland Heights—Loudoun Heights—rear guard—squadron of cavalry. Join the main body at Boonsborough or Hagerstown. And Colonel R. H. Chilton, assistant adjutant general, had signed it at the command of General R. E. Lee.[1]

Lee! At last, his whereabouts were known.

The copy of Confederate General Robert E. Lee's Special Orders No. 191 found near Frederick, Maryland, on September 13, 1862, was called the "Lost Order" in the North and the "Lost Dispatch" in the South. The discovery prompted Union commander Major General George Brinton McClellan to pursue Lee's divided army and force a decisive battle at Antietam four days later, a battle which redirected the Civil War and thwarted Confederate dreams of victory.

The story of the Lost Order also is the capstone story of the 27th Indiana.

Following their disaster at Second Bull Run in late August 1862, McClellan's stronger and reorganized Army of the Potomac inched northward from Washington through Maryland, following Lee's similar movements from Virginia. By September 4, all McClellan knew was Lee's army was crossing the Potomac River into Maryland. Not knowing Lee's intentions but fearing an attack on Washington or Baltimore, the cautious McClellan followed Lee at arm's length to protect the capital. The Union XII Corps, including the 27th Indiana, marched through Rockville to Ijamsville, a village on the Baltimore and Ohio Railroad, where they bivouacked on the twelfth.

Saturday, September 13, 1862.

Early a.m. Up before dawn, the XII Corps marched westward toward Frederick. The 27th went past the familiar William Clay and William Hoffman houses in Bartonsville and through the area of deserted cabins they had occupied the winter before. They learned that the bulk of Lee's army had been in Frederick until recently, and the Federals might encounter cavalry or outposts. One member recalled they always felt secure there, but "sudden and violent changes which the fortunes of war may bring" had changed that.[2]

The 27th formed the corps' skirmish line because of their knowledge of the area, and advanced between Urbanna and New Market. Reaching the narrow and knee-deep Monocacy River two miles east of town, the 27th waded across at Crums (Reich's) Ford, fanned out through woods down the river to the south, and turned back toward the city. Company F skirmishers, commanded by Bloss, were in the van. They rapidly reached the suburbs where the converging lines of other units caused them to halt.

9:00 a.m. Bloss ordered his line to rest in a clover field two miles south of Frederick which had been recently occupied by a large force, undoubtedly Confederates. They stopped several hundred yards above the river and 100 yards to the east of the Georgetown turnpike into Washington, near where the Baltimore and Ohio spur from Frederick intersects the main line. They discerned no movement ahead but saw artillery smoke rising west of town. The day was beautiful and warm, and the weary Hoosiers slumped to the ground in the shade on a relatively unspoiled grassy slope near a rail fence and bushes, speculated on the former occupants, and drank from canteens. In a group of four men, Bloss was on the right of three lying down, with Corporal Barton Warren Mitchell in the center, Private David Bur Vance on the left, and Private William H. Hostetter a few feet behind and to the right of Bloss.

Bloss and Mitchell conversed. Within a minute after halting, Bloss noticed a yellowish paper package lying in the grass between Vance and Mitchell. "What is it, Mitchell?" Bloss asked. "An envelope," was the reply. "Hand it to me," Bloss said. Vance picked up the unsealed package, and, as he passed it over Mitchell's body to Bloss, out fell three small cigars. Inside was a folded two-page letter.[3] Mitchell certainly knew what those were and fondled and playfully divided the cigars, then sought a match to smoke one. Bloss, glancing at the document, told Mitchell to wait until he had read the letter. Bloss then read it aloud to Mitchell, Vance, and others, including Hostetter and Privates Joseph Dunn Laughlin, John Campbell, George Washington Welsh, and Enoch G. Boicourt. As he read it "each line became more interesting," and he forgot the cigar.[4]

Clover Field South of Frederick, Maryland

Near Monocacy River where the 27th Indiana found General Lee's "Lost Order" on September 13, 1862.

Photo by author

Carefully emphasizing key names and words, Bloss was dumbfounded: Marching orders "giving plans for the next four days from that time" for all of Lee's army. If true, the information was extremely important. It had to be real. But why are they here? The bystanders were stunned and mumbled to each other. Mitchell again asked for a match, but Bloss told him to stuff the cigars back in the envelope and give them to him. "Boys," Bloss said, "this is of great importance, if genuine. I will take it to [Company F commander Peter] Captain Kop."[5] Then "the order created a general fusillade among the soldiers and excitement over the joy of the information."[6]

9:10 a.m. Bloss relinquished command of his unit temporarily and alone with the package headed for Kop, not a hundred yards away. Kop read the order quickly and agreed with Bloss: the colonel must see it immediately.

9:30 a.m. On foot, Kop and Bloss located Colonel Silas Colgrove, the regiment's commander, less than a half mile distant. Bloss handed the package to Colgrove who read the order and saw the three cigars. Up rode Brigadier General Nathan Kimball, and he also read it. Kimball suggested Colgrove bypass his brigade headquarters and go directly to Brigadier General Alpheus Starkey Williams, the acting XII Corps commander. Kop and Bloss returned to their men. The cigars disappeared, their fate unknown, but their role in history and lore secured.

9:45 a.m. Kimball and Colgrove rode to Williams' headquarters. He was not there, so they reported the find to Captain Samuel E. Pittman, his assistant adjutant general. "I immediately identified the signature of Colonel R. H. Chilton, Lee's Assistant Adjutant General," Pittman stated. Before the war, Pittman was a teller with the Michigan State Bank in Detroit, and Chilton was the paymaster for the army stationed there. As a signature expert, Pittman knew Chilton's, and with luck for the Federals, proved it was no "ruse de guerre." The signature and the orders thus were genuine.[7] But Pittman had to await Williams' return before forwarding the papers.

10:30 a.m. Pittman took Colgrove and reported to Williams with the order, Kimball accompanying. Williams directed Pittman to "lose no time in placing it in General McClellan's possession." Pittman "could not be spared" to deliver the papers, as a movement was expected. So he wrote a note for Williams to sign and sent a "trusty courier" to "ride fast" with the orders and note to McClellan's assistant adjutant general.[8] The Williams note, one of two contemporary records of the find, read: "I enclose a Special Order of General Lee, commanding rebel forces, which was found on the field where my corps is encamped. It is a document of interest and is also thought to be genuine."[9] Pittman was "about to copy the paper itself, recognizing that the finding of such an important document was likely to become an interesting fact of history, but General Williams would not permit a moment's delay."[10] Colgrove returned to his regiment and Kimball accompanied the courier.

12:00 noon. Major General Randolph B. Marcy, McClellan's chief of staff, took the papers to McClellan. Told they had been found by an Indiana soldier on grounds vacated by Lee's men, and with Chilton's signature verified, McClellan was satisfied that the orders were genuine and made no further inquiries. At the time meeting with a group of Frederick citizens, he excitedly opened the papers, read them silently, and hardly believed his eyes—and his luck. The orders corroborated his intelligence reports: Lee had divided his forces. He exclaimed, "Now I know what to do!"[11]

1:00 p.m. Within an hour after McClellan had the papers "the army was in motion, the lead troops in advance," orderlies and staff officers "flying off in all directions."[12] Progress thereafter was slow, but many troops began departing from the hastily assembled Frederick campsite, although the 27th Indiana would not leave until later. Armed with that extraordinary information, the Federals would now test the viability and execution of Lee's orders and attempt to destroy the Rebel forces.

With little dissent, history has anointed Corporal (not Private as some have written) Mitchell as the finder of the Lost Order, and Bloss as a bystander. Vance and Hostetter are not mentioned. But because Bloss,

Mitchell, and Vance each played a role in seeing, retrieving, and forwarding the Lost Order, each must be credited as a finder. Who first saw the package is forever arguable and of little consequence to either the outcome, Lee's defeat at Antietam, or one of the most intriguing mysteries of the war, who lost it. To slight any of them would levy an historic disservice, but if one is allowed to be the *most important finder,* it would have to be Bloss.

Constructing a case for any of them did not begin until 1884 at the earliest with the publication of a educational report apparently reflecting Bloss' version, which offered him as the finder and Mitchell as a bit player.[13] The foregoing scenario, taken from numerous sources, adjudicates the most logical sequence of events. The claims of Bloss and Vance on who found it first agree, then differ when Vance recanted and named himself. They are pitted against other declarations for Mitchell. (One of Bloss' two living [1990] grandsons and his

Captain John McKnight Bloss

Principal finder of General Lee's "Lost Order." Later served as Indiana superintendent of schools and president of what is now the Oregon State University.
Provided by Wilma and John M. Bloss (grandson)

namesake, believed the "Lost Dispatch" was really "The Stolen Dispatch." He believed a Union spy had infiltrated Lee's headquarters and instead of delivering it to Hill, took another route which put him in the path of Federal troops. For that he was captured and executed.[14] The other living grandson, John Bloss Lotz, said his aunt, Bloss' daughter-in-law, always called Mitchell a "country bumpkin."[15] Mitchell's descendants know only what has been published and aside from great-great-grandson Rudolph F. Rose, Jr., [1990] who represented the family at the 1963 Hartsville marker dedication, have shown scant interest in pursuing it.)[16]

When or if the 27th Indiana leadership learned of the Lost Order's consequences is unknown for it was not mentioned in any official report.

Private David Bur Vance,
Company F

Also a finder of General Lee's "Lost Order."

Provided by Harry M. Smith

After the war, Indianians were dis-inclined to read about it in South-ern publications. Eventually the matter surfaced from the 1880s on through memoirs of William Allan, John Esten Cooke, the Comte de Paris, Francis Winthrop Palfrey, and others; articles in *Century* Magazine, the *Southern Historical Society Papers*, and other journals; and veterans' speeches.

Corporal Edmund Randolph Brown, in writing the 27th's 1899 regimental history, named no one as finder, but cited the 1886 *Century* items by Colgrove and Mitchell's son as the stories in vogue in 1862. However, Brown said two other versions subse-quently had attracted interest years before the 27th's 1905 re-union group effort to get to the bot-tom of the story. But he went no further. Brown received no re-sponse in writing Mitchell's son after the *Century* item for evidence supporting his father's claim. Other-wise, the issue simply never energized the historian Brown.[17]

Let us examine more closely the principals involved in the discovery.

First Sergeant Bloss. Bloss was the best educated, most credible, and most apt to recognize their fortuitous coup. Seeing the envelope, the initial action, was pure chance. Picking it up and examining it, the next step, was logical, but really the inquisitiveness of bored soldiers. Reporting it up the chain of command, however, was the product of intelligence and initiative. Bloss was the regiment's only college graduate (Hanover) and eventually its most successful survivor. He rose from sergeant to captain and com-manded Company F in 1864. Wounded at Winchester, Antietam, Chancellorsville, and Resaca, he completed his term and was mustered out in October 1864. A career educator, he was a teacher, principal, Evans-ville superintendent of schools, Indiana State superintendent, and presi-dent of Oregon State University.

The Bloss version lacked corroboration for 43 years. Vance said he rarely saw Bloss after the war until 1904, and then at long intervals, and thus the subject had never surfaced between them. As Brown alluded, survivors undoubtedly fanned recollections after 1886. Bloss alone mentioned Kimball, Bloss' uncle by marriage. Colgrove, who could have added insight, lived in Washington, D.C. and Florida after 1886, did not mention it during the war, ignored reunion group activities, and left no known post-war manuscripts. Some speakers referred to the Lost Order before veterans groups, but Bloss was the one who spoke entirely on the subject, the 1892 paper presented to the Kansas Military Order of the Loyal Legion of the U.S.

After Bloss' death, his family sought not to "disparage or fail to give proper credit to any other comrade of the 27th Regiment who saw the document before it was read and its contents considered," but believed Bloss "fully comprehended the great importance of this document [and] took immediate steps to insure its prompt delivery at headquarters and bore it to his regimental commander with his own hands."[18] As he would have it, Bloss' gravestone in Muncie reads: "Finder of Lee's Lost Order No 191 at Frederick MD [sic] 1862." Two markers on the Lost Order, each claiming comrade soldiers—Bloss and Mitchell, men as different as night and day—as finder, grace Indiana's byways. Yet Vance's grave in Brownstown ignores any such reference.

Corporal Mitchell. Mitchell might well have seen the envelope first but if so, like Vance, left it alone. A smoker, had Mitchell picked up and opened it, to his delight he would have seen "three fragrant Confederate cigars" plummet to the ground, a miracle for a front line soldier.[19] Both Mitchell and Vance were 5'10" and ruddy and even with the disparate ages (Mitchell, 46, Vance, 20) could have been mistaken by those who said they saw Mitchell retrieve it. Mitchell could scribble his name but otherwise was illiterate. He could not have read the order and he left no manuscripts. His military and pension records ignore the issue, except for Campbell's affidavit on behalf of wife Jemima's pension application. Had Colgrove not written *Century* in 1886, the world might never have associated Mitchell with the Lost Order, or perhaps anyone else.

Mitchell began service in September 1861 as a private, was promoted to corporal in 1862, and over 13 months advanced five steps within that grade. Disability from an Antietam leg wound forced him to request a detail assignment to the ambulance corps from September 1863 to July 1864 when he rejoined the regiment before Atlanta. On October 31, 1863, overgraded for ambulance duty, he voluntarily became a private until mustering out on September 1, 1864. Unable to work because of his wound, Mitchell, 51, died a wrecked man on January 29, 1868, in Hartsville, his family's wartime residence. In 1886, *Century* also reported unsuccessful attempts of Mitchell's

WIDOW'S PENSION.

Claimant _Jemima A Mitchell_ Soldier _Barton W Mitchell_

P.O. _Jacyque_ Rank _Private_ Co. _F_

County _Fenn_, State _Kansas_ Regiment _27 Indiana Vol Inf_

Rate, $ _8_ per month, commencing _January 29_, 18 _68_, and _$12 from March 19 86_

and two dollars a month additional for each child, as follows:

By former marriage	Born, ____, 18	Sixteen, ____, 18	Commencing ____; 18
	Born, ____, 18	Sixteen, ____, 18	" ____, 18
	Born, ____, 18	Sixteen, ____, 18	" ____, 18
By last marriage _William Ansel_	Born, January 22, 1860	Sixteen, " 21, 1876	" January 29 1868
Eldredge Hopkins	Born, September 10, 1865	Sixteen, " 9, 1881	" " 29 1868
	Born, ____, 18	Sixteen, ____, 18	" ____, 18
	Born, ____, 18	Sixteen, ____, 18	" ____, 18
	Born, ____, 18	Sixteen, ____, 18	" ____, 18

Payments on all former certificates covering any portion of same time to be deducted.

All pension to terminate ____, 18 , date of ____

RECOGNIZED ATTORNEY:

Name _Stoddart & Co._ Fee $ _20_ Agent ____ to pay.

P.O. _Washington DC_ Articles filed _May 12_, 18 _86_

APPROVALS:

Submitted for _Admission_, May 2, 188 _9_, _H P MacNeal_ Examiner.

Approved for _admission_, origin of _Wdg of both legs and Chr Rheumatism_ accepted,

M S Roberts

May 6, 188 _9_, Legal Reviewer.

Approved for _admission_; death resulted from _Disease of heart_ due to _Rheumatism_ which has been legally accepted,

W H Coe May 10, 188 _9_, Medical Reviewer.

____, Re-Reviewer. ____, Medical Referee.

IMPORTANT DATES:

Enlisted _Sept 1_, 186 _1_.

Mustered " _1_, 186 _1_.

Discharged _Jan 1_, 186 _4_.

Died _Jany 29_, 18 _68_.

Declaration filed _Jany 7_, 186 _7_.

Invalid application filed _None_, 18

Invalid last paid to " ____, 18

Former marriage ____ " ____, 18

Death of former wife " ____, 18

Claimant's marriage to soldier, ____

Mark _M.C._

Widow's Pension Form

For Barton Warren Mitchell.

Pension Records of the 27th Indiana, National Archives

"destitute" family to obtain a pension for Jemima. Colgrove, then a Pension Office employee, said no such applications had been filed. However, about then she did receive a pension which lasted until her death in 1900.[20]

Private Vance. Vance said nothing until 1904 and then supported the story that Bloss found the order and told Vance, not Mitchell, to give it to him. Vance soon changed his mind—claiming himself as the finder—but always credited Bloss, not Mitchell, with taking it to his superiors. Vance left no known manuscripts except for the 1905 references, but he was a student of Bloss before the war in Washington County. The two shared another loose thread, Dr. Moses Elrod, of Columbus, Indiana, who was postmaster in Orleans while Bloss was the academy principal there in 1866–70. Elrod later practiced medicine in Hartsville from 1877–97 and, as a member of the U.S. Board of Medical Examining Surgeons for 13 years, may have been contacted by William Ansel Mitchell regarding Jemima's pension. In 1904–05, Elrod wrote both Bloss and Vance about the Lost Order.[21] Elrod did nothing with the information and Vance let the issue drop, as did the rest of the survivors.

Vance was discharged in December 1862 because of his Antietam wounds. Recovered, he reentered the army in September 1863 with the 117th Indiana Infantry, becoming a captain. In 1885 he moved to Brownstown where he was postmaster, the electric and water company manager, town clerk, civic leader, and businessman. He died in 1917.

The Special Orders

The original copy of Special Orders No. 191 follows (Lee later modified Longstreet's order and sent him to Hagerstown):

Confidential Special Orders No. 191

Hdqrs., Army of Northern Virginia   September 9, 1862

I. The citizens of Fredericktown being unwilling, while overrun by members of this army, to open their stores, in order to give them confidence, and to secure to officers and men purchasing supplies for benefit of this command, all officers and men of this army are strictly prohibited from visiting Fredericktown except on business, in which case they will bear evidence of this in writing from division commanders. The provost marshal in Fredericktown will see that his guard rigidly enforces this order.

II. Major Taylor will proceed to Leesburg, Virginia, and arrange for transportation of the sick and those unable to walk to Winchester, securing the transportation of the country for this purpose. The route between this and Culpeper Court House east of the mountains being unsafe will no longer be traveled. Those on the way to this army already across the river will move up promptly; all others will proceed to Winchester collectively and under command of officers, at which point, being the general depot of this army, its movement will be known and instructions given by commanding officers regulating further movements.

III. The army will resume its march to-morrow, taking the Hagerstown road. General Jackson's command will form the advance, and, after passing Middletown, with such portion as he may select, take the route toward Sharpsburg, cross the Potomac as the most convenient point, and by Friday morning take possession of the Baltimore and Ohio Railroad, capture such of them as may be at Martinsburg, and intercept such as may attempt to escape from Harper's Ferry.

IV. General Longstreet's command will pursue the main road as far as Boonsborough, where it will halt, with reserve, supply, and baggage trains of the army.

V. General McLaws, with his own division and that of General R H Anderson, will follow General Longstreet. On reaching Middletown will take the route to Harper's Ferry, and by Friday morning possess himself of the Maryland Heights and endeavor to capture the enemy at Harper's Ferry and vicinity.

VI. General Walker, with his division, after accomplishing the object in which he is now engaged, will cross the Potomac at Cheek's Ford, ascend its right bank to Lovettsville, take possession of Loudon Heights, if practicable, by Friday morning, Keys' Ford on his left, and the road between the end of the mountain and the Potomac on his right. He will, as far as practicable, co-operate with Generals McLaws and Jackson, and intercept retreat of the enemy.

VII. General D. H. Hill's division will form the rear guard of the army, pursuing the roads taken by the main body. The reserve artillery, ordnance, and supply trains, etc., will precede General Hill.

VIII. General Stuart will detach a squadron of cavalry to accompany the commands of Generals Longstreet, Jackson, and McLaws, and, with the main body of the cavalry, will cover the route of the army, bringing up all stragglers that may have been left behind.

IX. The commands of Generals Jackson, McLaws, and Walker, after accomplishing the objects for which they have been detached, will join the main body of the army at Boonsborough or Hagerstown.

X. Each regiment on the march will habitually carry its axes in the regimental ordnance wagons, for use of the men at their encampments, to procure woods, etc.

By command of General R. E. Lee:

R. H. CHILTON
Assistant Adjutant-General[22]

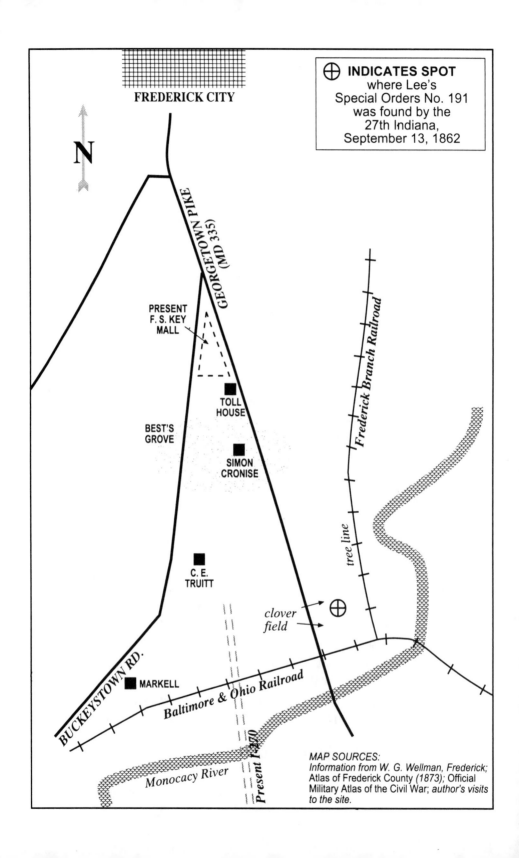

Colonel Robert Hall Chilton made seven copies of the original for: Major Generals Stonewall Jackson and James Longstreet, Lee's wing commanders; Major General J. E. B. Stuart, his cavalry commander; Major General John G. Walker, Major General Lafayette McLaws, and Major Walter H. Taylor, independent commanders under the orders; and a copy for Chilton's files (apparently the basis for the foregoing copy in the *Official Records*).

Two copies were made for Hill both eliminating the irrelevant first two paragraphs: the copy Jackson himself wrote for Hill which he received, and Chilton's copy addressed to him, which became the Lost Order. There was a total of nine copies. Later, Chilton sent a partial copy to the war department in Richmond, received there on the sixteenth. No copy was made for Major General Richard H. Anderson.[23]

Jackson memorized his copy and burned it.[24] Longstreet memorized his, temporarily gave it to his aide, Major G. Moxley Sorrel, shredded it, and "then used as some persons use a little cut of tobacco"—chewed it up.[25] (Sorrel, the officer responsible for Longstreet's correspondence, stated, "It [the order] was so full that when a copy came into my possession I wondered what could be done with it in event of my falling into enemy hands.")[26] Walker got his copy from Lee's courier on the afternoon of the ninth and pinned it securely in an inside pocket.[27] Stuart, McLaws, and Taylor never said whether they received a copy. What happened to any of these copies is unknown. Hill's copy from Jackson is in the North Carolina State Archives.

Where the Lost Order Rests

McClellan kept the Lost Order. It rests with his papers in the Library of Congress, a matter ignored by researchers. Thus, two copies exist. The front of a plain white 3x5" envelope with it has undated handwritten notations: "Gen. Lee's Gen. order"; "This is the original order found and on which McC. was able to plan his movements to South Mt. & Antietam"; and the initials "WIP" [Major William I. Paine of McClellan's staff].[28]

The orders are two sheets of white lined paper, approximately 8x12", of texture and style similar to today's lined tablet used in schools and offices. The order was written hurriedly but legibly in pencil. Judging from Chilton's correspondence in other collections, it appears to be his handwriting. The top of the first sheet contains the word "Confidential." The bottom of the second sheet contains the phrase: "For Maj. Gen. D. H. Hill Comdg. Division." Chilton signed his abbreviated title: "A. A. General."[29] The envelope is not the one in which the orders were found (it was discarded) although the order's folds correspond to the original's size.

The Copy of the "Lost Order"

Addressed to D. H. Hill and presented to Major General George B. McClellan.

McClellan Papers, Library of Congress

Chronological Versions of How the Lost Order was Found

McClellan—1862. He wired the army General-in-Chief, Lee's order addressed to D. H. Hill "has come accidentally into my hands this evening," [*sic*] which gave disposition of Lee's forces. [Sent at 11:00 p.m. on September 13, it was the first official disclosure.[30]

McClellan—1869. He received the order from his staff; it was found by some of the troops on Lee's campground. Believed genuine, he made no further inquiries. It probably got to him through his adjutant general.[31]

McClellan—1879. He could not recall name of finder, but believed it was a private of an Indiana regiment. A member of his staff handed him paper.[32] [He was replying to a letter from Mitchell's son, William Ansel.]

John W. Holcombe, historian—1884. Bloss saw it, asked Mitchell to hand it over. Mitchell picked it up, found 2 cigars, and a folded letter. Mitchell divided cigars and gave letter to "the officer."[33]

William Ansel Mitchell, Mitchell's son—1886. Attempting to secure a pension for his mother, he said his father found it.[34]

Colonel Silas Colgrove, 27th Indiana—June 2, 1886. A few minutes after halting Mitchell and Bloss took it to Colgrove. Both said Mitchell found it. It was wrapped around 3 cigars, the condition Mitchell said it was in when found.[35]

First Lieutenant Josiah Clinton Williams, 27th Indiana—June 14, 1886. While standing in line, Mitchell found it wrapped around 3 cigars. Mitchell and Bloss took it to Colgrove via the adjutant.[36] [Coincidentally Williams wrote *Century* 12 days after Colgrove. The inference is he wrote from his diary. If so, it and the General Williams' note are the only contemporary records.]

Private John Campbell, 27th Indiana—March 4, 1889. He was with Mitchell when he picked up the order. He looked over Mitchell's shoulder and read it with him.[37]

Bloss—January 6, 1892. He saw a large envelope beyond Mitchell, asked him to give it to him. It was unsealed; 2 cigars and a paper fell out. Bloss read it, took it to Kop; both took it to Colgrove who was with Kimball.[38]

Colonel Ezra Ayers Carmen, 13th New Jersey—ca. 1890s. Bloss saw a long envelope near Mitchell, asked Mitchell to hand it to him.[39]

Private Joseph Dunn Laughlin, 27th Indiana—ca. 1900. He saw Mitchell pick it up, and Mitchell and Bloss took it to Colgrove.[40]

Bloss and Vance discussed the Lost Order during the regiment's 1904 reunion, set out to straighten the record, and together credited Bloss. Some survivors gave affidavits supporting Bloss (marked as follows with [A]).

Bloss—March 18, 1905. Bloss saw over Mitchell's shoulder a long yellow envelope and asked him to hand it to him, but Vance picked it up and passed it. Two cigars dropped. Mitchell smoked one and Bloss read papers. Bloss went to Kop; he read it, then went to Colgrove.[41] [Bloss died April 26.]

Vance—May 2, 1905. Mitchell neither found nor held the order. He was lying in the center with Vance on his left and Bloss on his right. Bloss saw a large yellow envelope and asked Vance to pass it to him; Vance picked it up and passed it; 2–3 cigars fell out. Mitchell grabbed two. Bloss read the papers aloud, and took them to Kop [42] [He was aware of Bloss' death and continued trying to obtain affidavits.]

Private George Washington Welsh, 27th Indiana—July 24, 1905 (A). Bloss read it and took it to Colgrove and thence to headquarters.[43]

Mrs. Bloss—September 13, 1905. At the reunion she echoed Bloss.[44]

Vance—September 15, 1905 (A). A large envelope lay to Vance's left; he reached for it and read the address. Bloss asked him to hand it to him and Vance passed it over Mitchell's body. Mitchell picked up one fallen cigar.[45] [Four months later, Bloss dead, Vance changed the finder to himself.]

Private William H. Hostetter, 27th Indiana—December 18, 1905 (A). Someone picked up the envelope near him. Bloss took papers from an envelope and read them. He went to rear alone and gave them to Colgrove. Bloss alone handled the papers.[46]

Private Enoch Boicourt, 27th Indiana—July 30, 1906 (A). Someone gave Bloss an envelope. He took out an order read it aloud and took it to Kop and Colgrove.[47]

G. W. H. Kemper, historian—1908. Bloss noticed papers near a comrade who handed them to him. The man divided the 2 cigars inside but handed him the papers. Bloss immediately sent them to McClellan.[48] [Kemper's Delaware County, Indiana, history would favor the late Bloss, a prominent local citizen.]

Second Lieutenant Joseph Balsley, 27th Indiana—1908. Mitchell, Bloss, and Vance were lying down. Bloss asked Mitchell to pass him an envelope. Mitchell passed it to Vance who gave it to Bloss. Vance was "one of the star performers in this eventful episode."[49]

Indiana Magazine of History—1939. Mitchell saw a scrap of paper with cigars wrapped with string. He untied it, unwrapped the paper, and understood the contents. He took it to Bloss, who took Mitchell to Colgrove. All 3 went to Williams' headquarters.[50]

James V. Murfin, author—1962, 1965. Mitchell "noticed an interesting piece of paper on the ground." Bloss read it; both took it to Colgrove.[51]

John W. Schildt, author—1980. Both men found it and took it to Colgrove.[52]

Stephen W. Sears, author—1983. Mitchell saw and picked up a bulky envelope. He and Bloss scanned the papers and took them to Kop who hurried them to Colgrove. General Williams wrote McClellan that a 27th Indiana corporal found them.[53]

Fred L. Frechette, author—1990. Mitchell found the papers near the regiment's old winter quarters on the way into Frederick.[54]

APPENDIX B

Living with Carnage:
Casualties and Losses

Somehow our great loss at Antietam did not hit us fully until September 19th. The whole regiment was formed temporarily into four small companies. Gaps in our ranks were desperate. Companies A, C, D, F, and H had no commissioned officers present for duty. In several companies only 2–3 non-commissioned officers were present. For many days we were almost inconsolable. —*The aftermath* [1]

Battlefield carnage wrought extensive manpower losses and suffering on the 27th Indiana. The regiment fought in six major campaigns consisting of 11 battles and other engagements, including three of the war's most fearsome conflicts: Antietam, Chancellorsville, and Gettysburg, and withstood the arduous four-month Atlanta Campaign and its vicious firefights at Resaca, New Hope Church, and Peachtree Creek.

When the 27th's service to country ended on September 1, 1864, hundreds of Hoosier farm families had sacrificed for the loyalty, fleeting glory, and eternal pain of their sons. Consequently, its heavy casualties and other losses were one significant reason the 27th Indiana was set apart from the average Union infantry regiment.*

The author counted a casualty when a combatant was killed in action, mortally wounded, otherwise wounded, injured or missing in action, or captured as a prisoner of war (POW). Manpower losses were men who never returned to the regiment after being a casualty death, non-casualty death or included in "other attrition," which included discharges, resignations, transfers, and desertions.

At Antietam, the 27th carried 443 effectives to the foe. Few of the POWs from the Shenandoah Valley Campaign were exchanged in time to join them, and many others were previous casualties or absent with

---

* Casualties and other losses are compiled and reconciled from numerous sources, including regimental, War Department, Pension Office, and Indiana government records.

sickness. Gunshots caused all but a few wounds. Antietam casualty numbers point to the inconsistency of Civil War records. An expert of casualty numbers, William F. Fox, whose 1898 work honored the 27th as a Union "Fighting Regiment," found 209 casualties, calling it tenth worst among Union regiments there, but third among number of wounded.[2] However, the author reconstructed larger numbers:

Killed in action	18	(1-17) (officers-enlisted)
Mortally wounded	18	(3-15)
	36	(4-32)
Other wounded	235	(5-230)
Injured	1	(0-1)
Prisoners of war	2	(0-2, counted as wounded)
	238	(236)
Total net casualties	272	(9-263)
Deserted	1	(0-1)
Killed/mortally wounded:	36	(4-32)
Others who did not eventually return to regiment:		
	78	(0-78)
Total permanent losses:	114	(4-110)

The regiment's total casualties represented 61.4 percent of the effectives—almost two out every three men. Historians normally attribute the 14th Indiana Infantry with its 56 percent casualties as the highest percentage among the Indiana units at Antietam. Removing the other 27th casualty who was not killed or wounded, the 27th's percentage is still 61.2 percent.

Total wartime regimental casualties included:

- 158 men, 10 officers and 148 enlisted, lost their lives directly from combat, representing 13.6 percent of the regiment's combatants.

- 706 men, 37 officers and 669 enlisted, 61 percent of the regiment's combatants, were a casualty at least once. Most were knocked out of action, and many never returned to the regiment for duty.

- 172 men, 6 officers and 166 enlisted, became POWs, two-thirds of them captured at Buckton Station and Winchester.

Every action meant fewer men were available next time, for replacement recruits never came close to making up the difference in numbers. The author frequently disagrees with Fox regarding casualties. For example, Fox listed them as 169 killed and mortally wounded, 15.3 percent of the number enrolled. The rationale for 169 is unclear; he may have included the few who died of wounds after discharge. The author stopped when a man was out of service, or when the non-veterans mustered out, because it is impossible to determine in most cases the causes of post-service deaths. Fox records 21 killed and mortally wounded at Cedar Mountain, vice the author's 19; 41 at Antietam vice 36; 32 at Chancellorsville vice 35. The biggest difference is deaths from disease and sickness: Fox 133 to 95.[3] However, the author shows one "other killed" and 13 deaths from "other or unknown causes," whereas Fox treats only directly attributable deaths. The author's advantage included access to more complete records, including the 1899 regimental history.

Statistics were calculated from the original 38 officer and 995 enlisted combatants (1,033), plus the 124 combatant recruits added during service, and two transferred men who returned (38-1,121). Regimental band non-combatants (24) are excluded. The relative effect of total casualties on strength at any time is revealing. For instance, excluding the killed in action and mortally wounded, there were 665 "other wounded." In the regiment's three major battles, Antietam inflicted 235 "other wounded" (35.3 percent of the 665), Chancellorsville 145 (21.8 percent), and Gettysburg 103 (15.5 percent). Percentages are larger when calculated against numbers actually present or available for duty (effectives): Antietam (53 percent of 443 men), Chancellorsville (32.2 percent of 450), and Gettysburg (31 percent of 331).

The author adds "injured" to the traditional Civil War casualty categories, more accurately portraying the regiment's body count. A man disabled with a torn ankle or knee, unable to continue fighting or requiring attention in the rear, was as costly as a loss to a bullet. Historians have ignored the impact of injuries on unit readiness or fighting efficiency. Combatants bruised, burned, cut, and sprained themselves; were hit by splintering trees or rocks; discharged a rifle near a comrade's ear; or otherwise suffered and caused debilitating accidents which distracted or immobilized someone. Included as casualties are individuals wounded by "friendly fire," when known, another neglected observation. Not included are sunstroke cases or injuries unrelated to combat.

The first casualty was Private Henry McCaslin, mistakenly killed by a comrade on Harrison's Island in the Potomac River on October 24, 1861. Neither he nor his uniform were recognized, and he made motions as if shooting. His comrade, a crack shot, aimed at 400 yards. One bullet killed him instantly. The picket "went out of reason when told."[4] The first casualty in an outright fight was Private Alonzo C. Buher, wounded during a skirmish at New Market, Virginia, on April 15.

The first man killed by enemy action was Private John H. Cheatham, while on picket duty near Smithfield, Virginia, March 13, 1862. He and Private William M. Devet went to a farmhouse near the picket line to buy something for breakfast. Confederate cavalry rode up and shot Cheatham through the head. Devet was captured, the first of the regiment's 122 prisoners of war during the Valley Campaign.

The last member killed or mortally wounded before the three years were completed was Private George W. Stout, mortally wounded in the Atlanta trenches on August 10, 1864. The last man shot was Private William Alexander Callehan on August 29, 1864.

Nearly 6 of every 10 members were lost to combat, disease, disability, or desertion. There were:

-    108 non-casualty deaths (9.2 percent of the 1,159 members), which includes POWs who died in captivity;

-    266 total deaths (22.6 percent);

-    426 members (36.1 percent) who did not return to the regiment after being a casualty; and

-    420 members (35.6 percent) who did not return to the regiment because of other attrition (includes some numbers by transfer and discharge, etc., from the above 426 number); for a total of

-    686 members (266 + 420) who were permanently lost to the regiment during the war, an exceptionally high 58 percent.

Several companies were mauled. Company E, primarily from Daviess County, had the most members as casualties: three officers and 83 men (68.8 percent of enrollment); 27 suffered wounds in multiple actions. Perhaps because of their high losses they received the most recruits, 24. Company C, mostly Johnson and Bartholomew Counties, had the highest casualty percentage: 77 for 72.6 percent of their enrollment; 27 also were wounded in multiple actions. Contrarily, Company G, mostly Morgan County, was conspicuous with the fewest casualties: 11 deaths and 36 wounded among their 49.1 percent. Company F's (Monroe County) numbers steadily dwindled. At Cedar Mountain, 11 months after mustering in, 2 officers and 72 enlisted out of 92 were present. At Antietam one month later it was 1 officer, 62 enlisted; on April 11, 1863, 48 men of 64 were present; and on December 31, 1863, 31 of 48.

As the companies shrunk, so did the regiment. The day before mustering out, Company K (Dubois County) was down to 2 officers and 46 enlisted, but only 29 were present for duty, and Company I (Putnam County) had only 18 on duty out of 1 officer and 37 men. Company D (Lawrence County) carried 2 officers and less than 30 men at Resaca on May 15,

1864, and 9 were wounded. Notably, the following 1862–63 figures reflect losses and gains such as Winter 1861–62 disease and sickness; Spring recruiting; Winchester, Cedar Mountain, and Antietam; band discharges, wounded and sick; and return of Winchester POWs, etc.:[5]

February 1, 1862. Camp Halleck, Maryland

> 35 officers/940 enlisted assigned (975 in regiment).

> However, 32/888 present for duty (920—94.4 percent)

April 8, 1862. Edinburg, Virginia

> 32/910 assigned (942)

> 32/791 present (823—87.4 percent)

June 2, 1862. Williamsport, Maryland

> 33/819 (852)

> 31/705 (736—86.4 percent)

October 1, 1862. Maryland Heights, Maryland

> 31/875 (906)

> 21/487 (608—67.1 percent)

January 2, 1863. Fairfax Station, Virginia

> 34/741 (775)

> 31/477 (508—65.5 percent).

Mid-April 1863. Stafford Court House, Virginia

> 525—44.5 percent

October 1863. Tullahoma, Tennessee

> 320—27 percent

On January 2, 1863—after only 16 months of service— the number present was 52 percent of those assigned 11 months previously, and only 48.1 percent of the original 1,057 assigned, including the band. Those enrolled and present for duty during service with the Army of the Cumberland in 1863–64 are difficult to reconstruct. However, after New Hope Church there were 247, and the day after Kolbs Farm they reported only 101 men were present for duty; more than half of the remainder were permanently disabled.

When the non-veterans mustered out September 1, 1864, the regiment stood at 497 men, 42 percent of the total of 1,183 enrolled. Allowing for absences for hospitalizations, convalescence, furloughs, and detached service, around 300 were present on the Chattahoochee River near Atlanta for the final farewell:

- 237 were non-veterans mustered out on September 1 or within several weeks from the Chattahoochee, Atlanta, Indianapolis, and other locations, who headed for home;
- 22 more mustered were out over succeeding months;
- 139 were veterans who had reenlisted January 24, 1864, for three more years and, wherever they were, awaited transfer to the 70th Indiana on November 4;
- 49 were recruits, wherever they were, who awaited the same transfer;
- The remainder were 23 officers, also wherever they were, most of whom resigned in November, or those unaccountable.

TOTAL CASUALTIES

CASUALTIES:

K = Killed in Action; D WDS = Mortally Wounded; W = Other Wounded;

M = Missing; INJ = Injured; POW = Prisoner of War

ALSO SHOWN (NON-CASUALTIES):

Died of Other Causes (While POW); Deserters; Casualties which Did Not Return to Regiment (Permanent Losses)

Officers—Enlisted

[Total counts as casualty only once those who were

(1) W/INJ and also POWDeserter, and (2) POW & also Died Other]

NET TOTAL NUMBER OF CASUALTIES:

GROSS

Add	K	=	85	(5-80)
	D WDS	=	73	(5-68)
	W	=	665	(34-631)
	INJ	=	44	(2-42)
	POW	=	173	(6-167)
	M	=	3	(0-3)
			1043	(52-991)
Subtract	POW also W/INJ	=	54	(3-51)
	(counted as W/INJ)			
	NET		989	(49-940)

The 989 does not mean different members, rather 989 times death, wounds, capture, injury, or missing were suffered. Many were a casualty in multiple actions. For example, one was wounded in five different battles; several were wounded in four; many were wounded in one action and died in a later one. The intent is analyzing the number taken out of or limited in action by being a casualty. Thus, a member who was W and also a POW, or POW and D as a POW, during the same action is counted only once—one loss. The 989 does not include members who died of disease, sickness, or other causes.

TOTAL MEN WHO WERE CASUALTIES

                                            37-669   = 706 (59.9 percent)

TOTAL NON-DEATH NET CASUALTIES

                                            39-148   = 387 (32.8 percent)

DID NOT RETURN TO REGIMENT

As the result of being a casualty, permanent losses were

                                            18-408   = 426 (36.1 percent)

NON-CASUALTY DEATHS

Killed Other   0-1   = 1

Died Disease & Sickness   1-94   = 95

Died Other/Unknown Causes   0-13   = 13

TOTAL NON-CASUALTY DEATHS

                                            2-106   = 108 (9.2 percent)

TOTAL DEATHS

                                            12-254   = 266 (22.6 percent)

OTHER ATTRITION

Discharged   7-260 (0-1 returned)   266

Resigned   27-0   = 27

Transferred USA   0-42   = 42

Transferred VRC   0-50 (0-2 returned)   = 48

Deserted   0-47 for 50 times (13 returned)   = 37

MEMBERS LOST THROUGH OTHER ATTRITION

                                            34-386   =   420 (35.6 percent)

TOTAL MEMBERS LOST DURING SERVICE

(CASUALTIES, NON-CASUALTY DEATHS AND OTHER ATTRITION)

                                            46-640   =   686 (58.2 percent)

APPENDIX C

The Biggest Yankee in the World

Second Lieutenant David Campbell Van Buskirk, 6'10.5" tall, was captured outside Winchester during Banks' retreat. He was taken to Lynchburg, Virginia, Salisbury, North Carolina, and finally to Libby Prison in Richmond, where he was a star attraction.

One local newspaper said Confederate President Jefferson Davis visited him in prison and inquired about his home and family. Van Buskirk answered, "Back home at Bloomington, Indiana, I have six sisters. When they told me goodbye, as I was standing with my company, they all walked up, leaned down, and kissed me on top of the head."[1]

Captain David Campbell Van Buskirk

The tallest soldier in the Union Army at 6'10.5". He was a POW at Libby Prison, Richmond, Virginia in 1862.

Provided by Patsy Powell

He was billed as "The Biggest Yankee in the World," and became the talk of the town as word spread. Young girls and matrons teased their military friends for passes to Libby. The enterprising Confederates removed Van Buskirk to a downtown Richmond room where for one month he became the chief exhibit in a freak show. Van Buskirk agreed on one condition—provided he had "all he could eat." Consequently he was probably one of the few POWs gaining weight during captivity.[2] Southerners flocked to the show, paying to see the Yankee who "was so big nobody could believe it" reportedly weighing over 400 pounds during imprisonment.[3]

He was paroled at Aikens Landing, Virginia, on September 13, 1862, landed at Camp Parole, Maryland, on September 17, and eventually returned to the regiment October 6.

While in Washington, D.C., on parole, the parolees, including Van Buskirk, were being paid from one of the windows of the U.S. Treasury. He sensed himself the object of pity and curiosity:

> I was dirty, ragged and lousy. My clothing was in tatters. I was broke, and it seemed to me that everyone in Washington was gazing at me, and oh, how humiliating.! My plight was dreadful. I was an officer, and it was up to me to make out my own pay account, so I was informed that I would find blanks for that purpose at a nearby office, to which I repaired. Upon entering, to my horror, there sat several ladies, who were clad in fine silk, and they were conversing with an officer who ranked as a Colonel, and who seemed to want to heap coals on me to keep the fire of humiliation burning. He inquired what I wanted, speaking to me like a ruffian. I informed him that I wished blanks on which to make out my pay account. He thrust them through the window. I made them out and passed them to him, and then he said to me, "If you made as poor out at fighting as you do filling out a blank, you made a very poor fight."[4]

Humiliated, Van Buskirk lost his temper but restrained himself because of the officer's rank, and presented the paycheck. It was numbered 276 but filled out for $976, the reverse of what was correct. The paymaster gave him the money, then saw he had drawn more than entitled, and asked if the check called for that amount. He was informed that it did. The paymaster said, "Is it wrong?" "Yes." "Then go back and have the check corrected."[5] He wrote:

> I thought my chance had come to show my fighting qualities, and for the first and only time in my life I had murder in my mind, for I intended to kill that officer if I could get my hands on him. So I entered the office and in his gruff and insulting manner he demanded to know what I wanted now. I said that I had come back to tell him that is he made as poor effort at fighting as he did filling out a blank check, he would make a poor fight. I came back here to show you that there is fight in me, and if you will step out from behind the screen so that I can get in lick at you, I will kill you. The officer very promptly declined the invitation.[6]

The following morning a Washington paper reported on the big Hoosier. President Lincoln ordered him taken to Fortress Monroe, Virginia, and given all the privileges.

APPENDIX D

Silas Colgrove, 1816–1907

Silas Colgrove was born in Steuben County, New York, May 24, 1816, one of 18 children. He received a common education. In 1837 he married Rebecca P. Stone in New York and soon went westward to Winchester, Indiana. He completed law study and began practicing there in 1839. In 1852 he was elected district prosecuting attorney, and in 1856 was elected to the Indiana House of Representatives, switching from the Whig to the new Republican Party. When war broke out he enlisted as a private for three months' service. He was quickly elected a company captain in the 8th Indiana Infantry Regiment, and later promoted to lieutenant colonel. The 8th served in Western Virginia and fought at Rich Mountain. After his service expired he was assigned to the 27th just forming in Indianapolis in September.

Following his resignation as brigadier general in late 1864, he was appointed to a judgeship in Winchester and elected president of the Cincinnati, Fort Wayne & Grand Rapids Railroad. In 1865 he was elected circuit judge for Randolph and Delaware Counties for six years, and elected again in 1873 for six more. He retired as a judge and practiced law in Winchester. Colgrove's wife died August 9, 1887, and is buried in Winchester's Fountain Park Cemetery. In 1888 he moved to Washington, D.C., to work for the Pension Office until health forced him to resign in 1893. He had 11 children; one was killed performing as an aeronaut. Colgrove died January 13, 1907, at the home of his granddaughter, Mrs. Lula R. Steap, Lake Wales, Florida, at 90. His ashes are believed scattered.

On his death he was remembered as "a lawyer of the Old School, a hard but fair fighter, always unswervingly devoted to the interests of his client, making his client's case his own. His forte was his knowledge of men and his natural powers to command." As a judge was "clear headed and pure hearted," fair and impartial. He possessed "excellent judgement, such strong common sense, such comprehensive knowledge of the affairs of life, that he seldom made mistakes" on the bench, with a "keen sense of natural justice."[1] The Randolph County bar resolved:

> That in the death of Judge Colgrove the country has lost a brave, patriotic citizen, whose record as a military chieftain is made brilliant with heroic deeds performed on many battlefields, for the preservation and perpetuation of our Government our bar has lost as honored member, and the Bench, an upright, just Judge.[2]

APPENDIX E

Captain Thomas J. Box
and the Medal of Honor

The Medal of Honor was awarded to Captain Thomas J. Box for the regiment's most conspicuous display of valor, capturing the battle flag and colonel of the 38th Alabama Infantry Regiment at Resaca. The Civil War medal was not called "Congressional," but was the forerunner to the present citation. It was the only decoration awarded by the Union for valor during the war, and thus does not have the same significance as the modern medal.

Box's medal was issued April 7, 1865, five months after he mustered out. Presumably it was mailed to him and received without ceremony. No record exists that he ever wore or exhibited the medal publicly.

Box, of Bedford, helped form and maintain the Regimental Association and Lawrence County reunions. However, he must have been well aware of the sentiment against his being awarded the medal, a topic of the veterans' concern. The feeling was less against Box than for Private Elijah White, whom some believed regimental commander Colonel Silas Colgrove had treated unfairly, and against Colgrove's superiors and the War Department. Some felt Box was not precisely there when White seized the flag and thus White deserved a medal. The feeling simmered for years and prompted the veterans to

Captain Thomas J. Box,
Company D

Medal of Honor recipient at Resaca for capturing flag ot 38th Alabama Infantry.
Provided by Judi McMillan

New Headstone for Captain Thomas J. Box

Ceremony at Greenhill Cemetery, Bedford, Indiana. *Right* Frances Asbell, great-granddaughter of Thomas Box, and *left,* Judi McMillen, great-great-granddaughter.

Photo by author

plead for a similar medal for White as late as 1898, to no avail. The regimental historian raised the issue to new heights and ignored Box's participation and demeaned him by innuendo: "Though the label upon this [Alabama] flag in the State House divides the honor between White and another, the prevalent sentiment of the men who were present is certainly decidedly against it."[1] Box never opposed any effort to obtain White's medal.

Box is not known to have written on the matter. The medal's whereabouts are unknown, in spite of efforts through descendants. Rumors were Box in the immediate post-war years was a drug addict, not uncommon among veterans because of the widespread use of opiates in medical treatment. If true, as he grew older he regretted the embarrassment, which, regardless of his reunion efforts, then compelled him to keep the medal issue out of sight.

The State displayed the flag in Indianapolis before sending it to the War Department, where it was stored as late as 1898. Years later the government returned all captured items to the states. The Alabama Department of Archives and History holds it.

APPENDIX F

The Anti-Hero[1]

Smith seemed to be sort of a coward & was always cussing the government about not getting enough to eat. We got tired of it. —*Private Noah J. Palmer about Sergeant James E. Smith*

Was it a combat wound, or self-inflicted? In Smith's controversial Chancellorsville case, nothing was ever proven. Opinions were he had shot himself intentionally to avoid the upcoming battle. Because of his reputation, "some of the boys was running on him at the time about it." In line of battle a gunshot rang out in the rear rank. Smith was seen stooping with his right hand raised over his smoking gun which he grasped in his left hand, his right index finger bloody. He arose and ran to the rear, "going a little over double quick."

Private Elijah Wilkinson saw Smith's "right hand at muzzle & right forefinger was off close to the joint." Major Theodore Freelinghausen Colgrove called out, "Halt! You goddam coward!" When he failed to stop the Major shouted, "Shoot the son of a bitch! Shoot the damned coward!" and fired at him. A 2nd Massachusetts officer hollered, "God damn fool!" Smith ran to the rear holding his hand in the air and shaking the top of his finger.

The regiment was not operating under an order to fire when the shot went off. Private William H. Hostetter believed "it was lack of courage." Palmer said, "We knew the Major would not have hollered the way he did if everything had been all right." Strangely, Smith was never disciplined. First Sergeant John Robert Rankin felt the reason Smith was not reduced in rank was, "His captain was from same neighborhood & I think shielded him all he could." Smith defended himself, claiming the wound was accidental. "I have heard of reports it was self-inflicted but I was never charged." The reports were "political" and circulated by his enemies. "If they had any proof they would have court martialed me & reduced me to the ranks but they did not. My company captain was an enemy before I went into service (he was not captain when I enlisted). It was an old grudge. I knew I had enemies in the company because of my politics—I was a Democrat, but I always tried to do my duty as a soldier."

Thereafter Smith definitely became a marked man. His reputation caught up with him before Kennesaw Mountain near Atlanta. Sick with a headache, and not expecting action, he neglected to get an excuse when ordered out on advance and refused to go. A court-martial reduced him to private for "hanging back."

APPENDIX G

Love, Liberty, and Pursuing a Discharge

> I hope it wont be long before I can home with an honorable discharge. Am homesick fighting for liberty for wife and children. But as long as I am here I am here to fight for my country. Come life come death or my liberty and liberty for you and children. That was all that ever induced me to come. —
> *Private George Edwards, September 22, 1861* [1]

However motivated for joining, by the time many soldiers tasted army life they wanted out. Requests for discharges and furloughs under myriad pretenses glutted the system. Most were legitimate, based on improvised or real needs, but others were outright shams. Some succeeded and quickly the number of members began dwindling. Convincing medical officers was easier if a request was tied to a disability. The religious Edwards, husband and father, loyal and lonely, homesick and frustrated, was typically torn. On October 11, 1861, in Darnestown, Maryland, Edwards wrote his wife:

> There is a good that has now my love for I am trying to live as near right as I can. Now I want you to be religious and pray for me that I may prove faithful and serve God so that when I come to die that I may look back on a well spent life and I hope and pray that we may live so that when we leave this world we can meet in heaven. If we never fore meet on this earth I want you take good care of yourself and the children as you can and as I cannot be there to help you and I got the hair around my wrist as you wanted me to. [2]

In April 1862, he wrote:

> It is nearly eight months since I left home and it seems to be three times that long. I would rather suffer a little than for the south to rule. There is a good many of the boys is wishing they had not volunteered at all. I do not wish any such wishes as that. [3]

In December 1862, Edwards, a paroled prisoner of war recovering in an army hospital from Winchester wounds, still pursued his discharge:

It appears I cannot get an examination for a discharge. [The doctor] would not give it to me. So I went before the board with a fellow from Pennsylvania and they examined the other fellow. I am satisfied that I will get my discharge and be home in one month from today. And I can pay Dugger for that property in full so he may rest contented and the other little drips that I owe.[4]

From a hospital at Frederick, Maryland, he wrote in January 1863:

I have not been examined for discharge yet and it appears I aint. The small-pox is here in camp and they have almost quit discharging hear. At least I have been vacinated.[5]

Edwards, both good family man and good soldier, stayed in uniform. He died at Resaca in May 1864.

APPENDIX H

Looking for Uncle Whit

I made a search but could find nothing of Uncle Whit's body. [Private] Dan Beck saw him into the ambulance & sent [away] with his sword on, although money, pistol & watch were gone. All officers were sent to Washington to be embalmed. I could not find the officer that superintended the removal but will search further. —*About First Lieutenant George Whitfield Reed* [1]

Reed, 33, was "Uncle Whit" to Second Lieutenant Josiah Clinton Williams, 22. From Putnamville, they were close, single, and together had joined the forerunner of Company I in May 1861. Reed's sister was Williams' mother, Mrs. Worthington B. Williams. His father was Reverend Isaac Reed, well known as a pioneer of early Indiana Christianity. The officers were in the van of the futile charge to Cedar Mountain's wheatfield when Reed was shot in the face and died almost immediately. The grieving Williams soon wrote home:

> Here while the bullets flew like hail I am sorry to inform you uncle Whitfield was killed by being shot. He was only about 10 feet from me when he threw up his hand and fell forward upon his face. When uncle Whit was shot a full 20 men fell around me. I had not time to get him from the field or see to his things, we being between 2 fires. [2]

Williams remembered how earlier Reed "had tired of the tedium of inactive military life and longed for more stirring scenes" and later wrote:

> Thus died a soldier as brave a man as the best. When the war commenced he was following the peaceful pursuit of agriculture. No one would have taken him for a military man. Probably he was a quiet unobstrusive say nothing type of person except upon subjects when his feelings were enlisted and then he was fluent. He was a hard worker. As a military man he was a disciplinarian. He was ardent thoroughly devoted to his country and an honest and completely unselfish man that drew the sword in battle. [3]

The day after the battle Williams "made a diligent and fruitless search" for the body. It was hard to accept him dead—had the enemy recovered him and treated his wounds? When there was no word of capture he accepted

259

reality. Weeks later Williams received three letters from his parents containing sympathies and "those dear remembrances of old friends. The tribute to Uncle Whit's memory is quite good as do many others that have read it. I miss him very much at times."[4] Confirmation came early in 1863:

> I must sadly state there is no possibility of Uncle Whit being alive. Yesterday Lt. Thomas Box arrived back in camp from being home says Reed was shot twice, once through the cheek or jaw (thus passing along sideways), instead of through his head as I formerly supposed. Box was by him when that shot struck him, when he whirled around and said he was shot, started to the rear, then run a few steps and fell. Box said he was shot again somewhere through his body he thinks.[5]

Before Cedar Mountain, Reed had written, "If my life must be taken in this war let it be on the battlefield amid the flashing of sabres the waving of colors amid the roll of drums and the roar of artillery and let me hear the glad shout of victory."[6] In the briars and brush, craving water so his voice failed to issue commands, at once he had all except victory.*

---

* Reed's body, believed buried on the battlefield, was never found, a fact not lost on the author as he walked the fields and woods of the 27th Indiana's positions. He has for certain visited Williams in Greencastle.

APPENDIX I

Soldiers and Descendants

Sergeant Andrew Streigel,
Company K
Provided by Urban Streigel

Grandchildren of Sergeant Andrew Streigel
Left to right: Tony Streigel, Lucille Streigel, Veronica Streigel, Urban Streigel, of Jasper.
Photo by author

Private James M. Fowler,
Company H
Provided by Betty Clemmens

Granddaughter of Private
James M. Fowler
Betty Clemmens, Atlanta, Georgia.
Photo by author

Corporal Conrad Eckert, Company K

Typical early uniform worn by diverse companies before they formed the 27th Indiana.

Provided by Ruth Buecher

Granddaughter of Corporal Conrad Eckert

Ruth Buecher in front of Soldiers' and Sailors' Monument in Dubois County, holds furled flag carried by Company K during the war.

Photo by author

264

First Lieutenant Thomas W. Casey, Company B

Severely wounded at Gettysburg, died in 1899, and buried at Raglesville, Indiana.
Provided by Virginia May

Granddaughter of First Lieutenant Thomas W. Casey

Virginia May, Indianapolis.
Photo by author

NOTES

Chapter 1—Giants in the Cornfield:
Bloodletting at Antietam

1. Ezra Ayers Carmen. Undated draft memoirs, Box 1. Ezra A. Carmen Papers, Library of Congress. [Carmen was colonel of the 13th New Jersey.]
2. Diary of Josiah Clinton Williams. Josiah Clinton Williams Papers, Vigo County Public Library, Terre Haute, Ind.; Edmund Randolph Brown, *The Twenty-Seventh Indiana Volunteer Infantry in the War of the Rebellion,* 1899. Reprint: Gaithersburg, Md., Butternut Press, 233–34. Hereafter cited as ERB.
3. ERB, 235.
4. Josiah Clinton Williams diary.
5. Edwin E. Bryant, *History of the Third Regiment of Wisconsin Veteran Volunteer Infantry, 1861–65* (Madison: 1891), 123.
6. ERB, 236.
7. Ronald H. Bailey, *The Bloodiest Day: The Battle of Antietam* (Alexandria, Va.: Time-Life Books, 1984), 65.
8. Ibid., 67.
9. Edwin E. Bryant, 123.
10. ERB, 237–38.
11. Ibid., 238–39.
12. Ibid., 239.
13. Ibid., 237.
14. Lewis King, "Scraps from My Army Life." Unpublished monograph, Lewis King Collection, Box L-83, Indiana State Library, Indiana Division.
15. ERB, 241; Josiah Clinton Williams diary.
16. Lewis King.
17. Simpson Solomon Hamrick to his Father, September 30, 1862. The Civil War Letters of Simpson Solomon Hamrick, Roy O. West Library, Depauw University.
18. ERB, 242–43.
19. Lewis King.
20. Josiah Clinton Williams to his Parents, September 28, 1862. Josiah Clinton Williams Papers.
21. Josiah Clinton Williams to *Century* Magazine, June 14, 1886. Josiah Clinton Williams Papers.
22. ERB, 243.
23. *Official Records of the Union and Confederate Armies in the War of the Rebellion* 19, ser. 1, pt. 1. Hereafter cited as *OR.* Report of Colonel Silas Colgrove, 498.
24. ERB, 246.
25. *OR* Report of Colonel William Tatum Wofford, 928.
26. ERB, 247.
27. *OR* Report of Lieutenant Colonel Philip A. Work, 932.
28. ERB, 263.
29. *OR* Wofford's report, 928.
30. *OR* Report of Brigadier General John Bell Hood, 923.
31. *The Soldier of Indiana in the War for the Union* 2 (Indianapolis: 1866), 33–34.

32. Eldridge Williams to Uncle Jack, September 20, 1862. Provided by Jay Wilson, Oolitic, Ind.
33. *OR* Gordon's report.
34. ERB, 247, 249.
35. Ibid.
36. Lewis King.
37. Pension Record of James Burk. National Archives. Hereafter cited as PR.
38. PR of Daniel Burk.
39. Josiah Clinton Williams to Brother [believed Ed], September 17, 1862. Josiah Clinton Williams Papers.
40. ERB, 249–50.
41. Ibid., 249.
42. PR of William C. Riley.
43. *OR* Gordon's report, 494–95.
44. ERB, 250.
45. Stephen W. Sears, *Landscape Turned Red: The Battle of Antietam* (New York: Ticknor & Fields, 1983), 208.
46. ERB, 250.
47. *OR* Colgrove's report, 498.
48. ERB, 251.
49. PR of Theodore M. Nance.
50. John L. Files in the Fairbanks MSS, Lilly Library, Indiana University.
51. *OR* Colgrove's report, 499.
52. Brigadier General Alpheus Starkey Williams quoted in Stephen W. Sears, 215.
53. Edwin E. Bryant, 123.
54. *OR* Colgrove's report.
55. Julian Wisner Hinkley, *Service with the Third Wisconsin Infantry* (Madison: Historical Commission, 1912), 57.
56. Josiah Clinton Williams diary; Josiah Clinton Williams to *Century.*
57. PR of Philip A. Lane.
58. PR of George P. Mehringer.
59. PR of John L. Files; PR of William Thomson.
60. PR of John D. McKahin.
61. PR of Josiah W. Tobias.
62. ERB, 252.
63. *The Soldier of Indiana*, 34.
64. Milo M. Quaife, ed. *From the Cannon's Mouth: The Civil War Letters of Alpheus Starkey Williams* (Detroit, Mich.: Detroit Historical Society and Wayne State University Press, 1959), 126–27, 130.
65. Simpson Solomon Hamrick to his Father, September 22, 1862. Hamrick Letters.
66. Ibid.
67. Simpson Solomon Hamrick to his Father, November 16, 1862. Hamrick Letters.
68. Ibid., September 22, 1862.
69. *OR* Colgrove's report, 499.
70. *OR* Gordon's report, 494–95.
71. Francis Winthrop Palfrey, *Campaigns of the Civil War: The Antietam and Fredericksburg* (New York: 1882), 79.
72. G. F. R. Henderson, *Stonewall Jackson and the American Civil War* 2 (London: Longmans, Green & Co., 1898), 305.
73. Hamrick to his Father, September 30, 1862.
74. Ibid., September 22, 1862.
75. Milo M. Quaife, 130; ERB, 254.
76. Marker at The Cornfield, Antietam National Battlefield; Major General Joseph Hooker quoted in Ronald H. Bailey, 70.

77. Milo M. Quaife, 130.
78. *OR* Gordon's report, 497.
79. Rufus Williams to Jack, September 20, 1862. Provided by Jay Wilson, Oolitic, Ind.
80. Ibid.
81. Josiah Clinton Williams to his Parents, September 28, 1862. Josiah Clinton Williams Papers.
82. George Tarvin Chapin to his Brother, September 18, 1862. The Chapin Family Papers, Roy. O. West Library, Depauw University.
83. Josiah Clinton Williams diary.
84. Lewis King.
85. ERB, 266.
86. Ibid., 260.
87. Indianapolis, Ind. *Journal*, October 22, 1862.
88. New York, N.Y. *Times*, September 21, 1862.

Chapter 2—For Union, Flag, and Lincoln: Cause, Morale, and External Interactions

1. John McElroy, ed. *National Tribune* (ca. 1899–1900), noted in Edmund Randolph Brown Manuscripts File and Private Book. Edmund Randolph Brown Papers. Indiana Historical Society. Hereafter cited as ERB Papers.
2. Edmund Randolph Brown, "Brief Autobiography." Edmund Randolph Brown Private Book, ERB Papers.
3. Welman to Doane, June 18, 1862.
4. "Dubois Volunteer," September 9, 1861, in the Jasper, Ind., *Weekly Courier*, September 18, 1861.
5. Welman to Doane, June 18, 1862.
6. Josiah Clinton Williams to his Grandfather, October 30, 1861. Papers of Josiah Clinton Williams, Vigo County Public Library, Terre Haute, Ind.
7. Harden Edwards to George Edwards, December 28, 1861. Letters of George Edwards, Indiana Historical Society.
8. Silas Colgrove to Adjutant General Noble, February 5, 1862. Records of the 27th Indiana, Box 61. Indiana Commission on Public Records, Archives Division.
9. Simpson Solomon Hamrick to his Father, January 14, 1863. The Civil War Letters of Simpson Solomon Hamrick, Roy O. West Library, Depauw University.
10. John L. Gilmore, April 4, 1863, in the Putnam County, Ind., *Republican Banner,* April 16, 1863.
11. Ibid.
12. Ferdinand Grass to Editor, October 14, 1861.
13. Silas Colgrove to Oliver P. Morton, October 26, 1861. Oliver P. Morton Correspondence, Box 1. Indiana Commission on Public Records, Archives Division.
14. Simpson Solomon Hamrick to his Sister Lou, October 12, 1861. Hamrick Letters.
15. Simpson Solomon Hamrick to his Father, September 10, 1862. Hamrick Letters.
16. Richmond M. Welman in the Jasper, Ind. *Weekly Courier*, February 26, 1862.
17. Edmund Randolph Brown, *The Twenty-Seventh Indiana Volunteer Infantry in the War of the Rebellion* (1899), 224. Reprint: Gaithersburg, Md.: Butternut Press. Hereafter cited as ERB.
18. Ibid., 258.
19. Ibid., 260.
20. Simpson Solomon Hamrick to his Father, February 12, 1862. Hamrick Letters.
21. ERB, 124.
22. Milo M. Quaife, ed. *From the Cannons Mouth: The Civil War Letters of Alpheus Starkey Williams* (Detroit, Mich.: Detroit Historical Society and Wayne State University Press, 1959), 91.

23. Josiah Clinton Williams to his Parents, September 8, 1862. Williams Papers.
24. Welman to Doane, June 18, 1862.
25. ERB, 260.
26. Simpson Solomon Hamrick to his Father, January 8, 1863, and January 14, 1863. Hamrick Letters.
27. Ibid., January 14, 1863.
28. John A. Crose [nom de plume "40"] in the Putnam County, Ind. *Republican Banner*, April 23, 1863.
29. Ibid.
30. Ibid.
31. T. Bullard to Oliver P. Morton, October 15, 1862, in the Indianapolis, Ind. *Journal*, October 22, 1862.
32. Simpson Solomon Hamrick to his Father, October 13, 1862. Hamrick Letters.
33. ERB, 271.
34. Simpson Solomon Hamrick to his Brother Charley, January 16, 1863. Hamrick Letters.
35. Josiah Clinton Williams to his Brother, February 5, 1863. Williams Papers.
36. Thomas W. Casey to his Brother and Sister, March 13, 1863. Provided by Virginia May, Indianapolis, Ind.
37. Simpson Solomon Hamrick to his Father, December 17, 1862. Hamrick Letters.
38. Ibid., December 30, 1862.
39. Ibid., January 8, 1863.
40. Ibid., February 12, 1863.
41. Ibid., June 25, 1862.
42. ERB, 513; Diary of Josiah Clinton Williams. Williams Papers; Diary of John Michael Tomey. Morgan County Public Library, Martinsville, Ind.
43. ERB, 93.
44. ERB, 82.
45. Ibid., 283.
46. Ibid., 349–50.
47. Ibid., 351.
48. George Edwards, May 13, 1863. Edwards Letters.
49. George Whitfield Reed to Miss J. E. Williams, October 5, 1861. Williams Papers.
50. The Comte de Paris, *The Civil War in America* 2, Henry Coppee, ed. (Philadelphia, Pa.: 1907), 723–25; "A Journey Among the Contrabands: The Diary of Walter Totten Carpenter." *Indiana Magazine of History* 73 (1977), 203.
51. Simpson Solomon Hamrick to his Sister Lou, October 12, 1861. Hamrick Letters.
52. Simpson Solomon Hamrick to his Father, July 28, 1862. Hamrick Letters.
53. Theodore H. Nance to A. D. Hamrick, July 27, 1862. Hamrick Letters.
54. Simpson Solomon Hamrick to his Father, January 7, 1862; ERB, 91.
55. Simpson Solomon Hamrick to his Father, November 18, 1861. Hamrick Letters.
56. Ibid., January 20, 1862.
57. Ibid., January 23, 1862.
58. Josiah Clinton Williams to his Father, April 21, 1862. Williams Papers.
59. ERB, 186.
60. Josiah Clinton Williams to his Sister, December 1, 1862. Williams Papers.
61. ERB, 446–47.
62. Van Buskirk diary.
63. ERB, 512–13.
64. George Tarvin Chapin to his Brother, January 12, 1864. Letters of George T. Chapin in Chapin Family Papers, Indiana Historical Society.
65. ERB, 130–31.
66. Richmond M. Welman to Friend Doane [editor], June 18, 1862, in the Jasper, Ind., *Weekly Courier,* July 2, 1862.

67. Simpson Solomon Hamrick to his Father, March 9, 1862. Hamrick Letters.
68. Edward G. Fugate, ca. 1863. Letters of Edward G. Fewgate in the Neely MSS, Lilly Library, Indiana University.
69. John Parham to his Sister Henrity, April 22, 1863. Hiram Reid Letters, Box F83, Indiana Historical Society.
70. George Tarvin Chapin to his Brother, January 12, 1864. Chapin Papers.
71. Silas Colgrove to A. D. Hamrick, July 24, 1862. Civil War Miscellany, Drawer 106, Indiana Commission on Public Records, Archives Division.
72. Simpson Solomon Hamrick to his Father, June 5, 1862. Hamrick Letters.
73. Ibid., June 14, 1862.
74. Ibid., May 26, 1862.
75. Welman to Doane, June 18, 1862.
76. Ibid.
77. Colgrove to A. D. Hamrick.
78. ERB, 161, 168.
79. Ibid., 162.
80. Ibid., 191.
81. Ibid., 156.
82. *Slocum and His Men; A History of the 12th and 20th Army Corps* (AKA) *In Memoriam: Henry Warner Slocum* (Albany, N.Y.: 1904), 47.
83. Ibid., 437–38.
84. John A. Crose ["40"] in the Indianapolis, Ind. *Journal*, February 16, 1864.
85. Alpheus Starkey Williams quoted in *Slocum and His Men*, 224.
86. Simpson Solomon Hamrick to his Brother Charley, March 14, 1863. Hamrick Letters.
87. "Perkins" in the Indianapolis, Ind. *Journal*, June 4, 1863.
88. John A. Crose ["40"], June 12, 1862, in the Indianapolis, Ind. *Journal*, July 2, 1862; ERB, 402–03.
89. ERB, 438.
90. Linzey C. Lamb to Wife Mary, May 20, 1864. Lindsay Lamb Letters, Lilly Library, Indiana University.
91. Robert Lewis Dabney, *Life and Times of Lt. General Thomas J. Jackson*, 504. Reprint: Harrisonburg, Va.: Sprinkle Press, 1976.
92. Simpson Solomon Hamrick to his Father, March 9, 1862.
93. Josiah Clinton Williams diary.
94. Milo M. Quaife, 328.
95. ERB, 510–11.
96. Ibid., 515–16, 533.
97. Edwin E. Bryant, *History of the Third Regiment of Wisconsin Veteran Volunteer Infantry, 1861–65* (Madison: 1891), 263.
98. Josiah Clinton Williams Diary.
99. John McKnight Bloss, May 18, 1864. Provided by John McKnight Bloss (grandson), Paris, Ill.
100. ERB, 498.
101. Ibid., 497.
102. John Michael Tomey diary.
103. ERB, 481, 501.
104. Ibid., 521–22; Lewis King, "Scraps From My Army Life." Unpublished, undated monograph. Lewis King Collection, Box L-83, Indiana State Library, Indiana Division.
105. ERB, 506, 512–13.
106. *bid.*, 501.
107. Diary of Michael Henry Van Buskirk. Provided by Patricia Peruch, Carmichael, Calif.; Diary of Roger Sherman Loughry. Provided by Dick Loughery, McLean, Va.; John Michael Tomey diary.
108. ERB, 540.

109. Abraham Lincoln to William Tecumseh Sherman, September 3, 1864. Quoted in Thomas B. VanHorne, *History of the Army of the Cumberland* 2 (Cincinnati, Ohio: 1875), 153.
110. *Official Records of the Union and Confederate Armies in the War of the Rebellion* 38, ser. 1, pt. 2. Report of Brigadier General Alpheus Starkey Williams, 36.

Chapter 3—Colonel Colgrove, His Officers, and Other Enemies: Insurrection, Leadership, and Politics

1. 27th Indiana Officers to Oliver P. Morton, November 28, 1861. Adjutant General Muster Rolls of the 27th Indiana, Box 61. Indiana Commission on Public Records, Archives Division.
2. Ibid.
3. Adjutant General Muster Rolls, Box 61.
4. Simpson Solomon Hamrick to his Father, December 1, 1861. Civil War Letters of Simpson Solomon Hamrick, Roy O. West Library, Depauw University.
5. Ibid., December 1, 1861.
6. Ibid., November 18, 1861.
7. Simpson Solomon Hamrick, December 9, 1861. Hamrick Letters.
8. William F. Fox, *Regimental Losses in the Civil War* (Albany, N.Y.: 1894), 346.
9. Edmund Randolph Brown, *The Twenty-Seventh Indiana Volunteer Infantry in the War of the Rebellion* (1899), 37–38. Reprint: Gaithersburg, Md.: Butternut Press. Hereafter cited as ERB.
10. Simpson Solomon Hamrick to his Father, January 20, 1862. Hamrick Letters.
11. Compiled Military Service Record of John Forlander. Records of the 27th Indiana, National Archives. Hereafter cited as CMSR.
12. ERB, 37.
13. Simpson Solomon Hamrick to his Father, June 28, 1862. Hamrick Letters.
14. Ibid., March 20, 1862.
15. Ibid., April 10, 1862.
16. Ibid.
17. Ibid., April 30, 1862.
18. Ibid., June 28, 1862.
19. Ibid., June 5, 1862.
20. George Tarvin Chapin, February 17, 1863. Letters of George T. Chapin in the Chapin Family Papers, Indiana Historical Society.
21. Simpson Solomon Hamrick to his Father, March 19, 1863. Hamrick Letters.
22. Ibid., April 30, 1862.
23. G. C. Colbert to Oliver P. Morton, May 20, 1862. Muster Rolls, Box 61.
24. Abisha S. Morrison to General [George Henry] Gordon, July 27, 1862, in CMSR of Silas Colgrove.
25. Simpson Solomon Hamrick to his Father, undated [circa July 1862]. Hamrick Letters.
26. Ibid.
27. Ibid., July 16, 1862.
28. ERB, 213.
29. Simpson Solomon Hamrick to his Father, June 5, 1862. Hamrick Letters.
30. Silas Colgrove to the Indiana Adjutant General, February 5, 1862. Muster Rolls, Box 60.
31. Ibid, September 27, 1862.
32. H. B. Hill to Oliver P. Morton, December 11, 1863. Oliver P. Morton Correspondence, Box 7. Indiana Commission on Public Records, Archives Division.
33. Jasper, Ind. *Weekly Courier*, March 26, 1862.
34. Josiah Clinton Williams to [his Brother] Ed, January 13, 1863. Papers of Josiah Clinton Williams, Vigo County Public Library, Terre Haute, Ind.

35. Putnam [County, Ind.] *Republican Banner*, April 23, 1963.
36. Letter from "The 27th Indiana," February 9, 1864, in Indianapolis, Ind. *Journal*, February 16, 1864.
37. James A. Hardie to Oliver P. Morton, August 9, 1864. Morton Correspondence, Box 7. Colgrove earned the appointment with steadfast hard work and achievement, overcoming personality differences, clashes of wills, and controversial activities.
38. Joseph Balsley in Pension Record of Elihu M. Wells. National Archives. Hereafter cited as PR.
39. Josiah Clinton Williams to his Parents, July 27, 1862. Williams Papers.
40. Diary of Josiah Clinton Williams. Williams Papers.
41. Simpson Solomon Hamrick to his Father and Family, February 12, 1862. Hamrick Letters.
42. Simpson Solomon Hamrick to his Father, October 13, 1862. Hamrick Letters.
43. Calvin Arthur in PR of John D. McKahin.
44. Williams Parmemas Ellis to his Father, April 3, 1864. Provided by Eleanor Purdue, Washington, Ind.
45. George Tarvin Chapin, November 8, 1861. Chapin Letters.
46. Simpson Solomon Hamrick to his Father and Family, October 13, 1861. Hamrick Letters.
47. Simpson Solomon Hamrick to Father, January 20, 1862. Hamrick Letters.
48. CMSR of Archibald Irvin Harrison; Simpson Solomon Hamrick to his Father and Friends, October 31, 1861. Hamrick Letters.
49. Simpson Solomon Hamrick to his Father, November 18, 1861. Hamrick Letters.
50. Ibid., June 28, 1862.
51. ERB, 162–63.
52. George Tarvin Chapin, February 17, 1863. Chapin Letters; Simpson Solomon Hamrick to his Father, December 30, 1862. Hamrick Letters.
53. Jarvis J. Johnson, May 2, 1862. Papers of Jarvis J. Johnson, Indiana Historical Society.
54. Simpson Solomon Hamrick to his Father, November 18, 1861. Hamrick Letters.
55. Ibid., December 30, 1862.
56. CMSR of John Mehringer.
57. Simpson Solomon Hamrick to his Father, June 26, 1862. Hamrick Letters.
58. CMSR of William S. Johnson.
59. Simpson Solomon Hamrick to his Father, July 10, 1862. Hamrick Letters.

Chapter 4—Likely I May Then Fall:
Bravery and Bravado

1. James C. Thomas to his Brother, May 10, 1863, in Jasper, Ind. *Weekly Courier*, May 16, 1863.
2. Thomas W. Casey to his Brother and Sister, September 25, 1862. Provided by Virginia May, Indianapolis, Ind.
3. George Edwards, May 13, 1863. Letters of George Edwards, Indiana Historical Society.
4. Ibid., May 8, 1863.
5. Josiah Clinton Williams to his Sister, October 28, 1861. Papers of Josiah Clinton Williams, Vigo County Public Library, Terre Haute, Ind.
6. Simpson Solomon Hamrick to his Father and Family, October 13, 1861. Civil War Letters of Simpson Solomon Hamrick, Roy O. West Library, Depauw University.
7. Edmund Randolph Brown, *The Twenty-Seventh Indiana Volunteer Infantry in the War of the Rebellion* (1899), 57, 59–61. Reprint: Gaithersburg, Md.: Butternut Press. Hereafter cited as ERB.
8. George Edwards, March 12, 1862. Edwards Letters.
9. ERB, 124.
10. Ibid., 137.
11. Ibid., 128–29.

12. Ibid., 135–36.
13. Ibid., 136.
14. Diary of Michael Henry Van Buskirk. Provided by Patricia Peruch, Carmichael, Calif.
15. *Official Records of the Union and Confederate Armies in the War of the Rebellion*, 12, ser. 1, pt. 1, 619. Hereafter cited as *OR*. Report of Colonel Silas Colgrove.
16. ERB, 145.
17. Ibid.
18. Ibid., 145–46.
19. George Edwards, June 5, 1862. Edwards Letters.
20. Clemens Johnson to his Father, May 30, 1862, in Pension Record of Clemens Johnson. National Archives. Hereafter cited as PR.
21. ERB, 148.
22. Ibid., 202. The 27th charged into the face of galling fire three times during its service: Cedar Mountain, Gettysburg, and New Hope Church. Nowhere were physical conditions as constraining as here.
23. Ibid., 201.
24. Ibid., 202.
25. Ibid., 203.
26. Ibid.
27. Ibid., 206.
28. *OR* 12, ser. 1, pt. 1, 156. Colgrove report; Diary of Josiah Clinton Williams. Williams Papers.
29. Josiah Clinton Williams to his Parents, August 9, 1862. Williams Papers.
30. Edmund Randolph Brown Brief Autobiography. Edmund Randolph Brown Private Book, Edmund Randolph Brown Papers, Indiana Historical Society.
31. ERB, 209, 212.
32. Indianapolis, Ind. *Journal*, May, 11, 1863.
33. George Edwards, May 13, 1863. Edwards Letters.
34. James C. Thomas to his Brother, May 10, 1863.
35. Milo M. Quaife, ed. *From the Cannons Mouth: The Civil War Letters of Alpheus Starkey Williams* (Detroit, Mich.: Detroit Historical Society and Wayne State University Press, 1959), 187.
36. *OR* 25, ser. 1, pt. 1, 710–12. Report of Colonel Silas Colgrove; ERB, 323.
37. Milo M. Quaife, 187.
38. *OR* 25, ser. 1, pt. 1, 710–12. Colgrove report.
39. ERB, 320–22.
40. Michael Henry Van Buskirk diary.
41. *OR* 25, ser. 1, pt. 1, 710–12. Colgrove Report.
42. Edwin E. Bryant, *History of the Third Regiment of Wisconsin Veteran Volunteer Infantry, 1861–65* (Madison: 1891), 156.
43. Ibid., 157.
44. John L. Files. Letters from the Civil War Papers of John L. Files, Fairbanks MSS, Lilly Library, Indiana University.
45. ERB, 336.
46. *OR* 25, ser. 1, pt. 1, 710–12. Colgrove report.
47. Ibid., 707–10. Report of Brigadier General Thomas Howard Ruger.
48. Ibid., 415–16. Report of Brigadier General Charles K. Graham.
49. Family Records of Joseph Dunn Laughlin. Provided by Kerry V. Armstrong, Indianapolis, Ind.
50. [Probably Father of Josiah Clinton Williams to his Wife], May 11, 1863. Williams Papers.
51. PR of Alfred Keck.
52. Jim Sharp to Jerome T. Armstrong, May 12, 1863. Roger Sherman Loughry Letters. Provided by Dick Loughery, McLean, Va.

53. ERB, 341.
54. Ibid., 379.
55. Ibid., 382–83, 393.
56. Silas Colgrove to Oliver P. Morton, May 22, 1864. Adjutant General Muster Rolls of the 27th Indiana, Box 61. Indiana Commission on Public Records, Archives Division.
57. ERB, 470.
58. OR 38, ser. 1, pt. 2, 64. Report of Lieutenant Colonel John Roush Fesler; ERB, 472.
59. "Indiana at Antietam." *Report of the Indiana Antietam Monument Commission* (Indianapolis: 1911), Atlanta Campaign section, 136–37; ERB, 472.
60. ERB, 472.
61. Edwin E. Bryant, 233–34.
62. ERB, 475–76; Muster Rolls, Box 60; "Indiana at Antietam," 136–37.
63. Biographical sketch of Thomas J. Box. Provided by Jay Wilson, Oolitic, Ind.; "Indiana at Antietam," 136–37.
64. ERB, 475.
65. Diary of Roger Sherman Loughry. Provided by Dick Loughery, McLean, Va.
66. Josiah Clinton Williams diary.
67. Lewis King, "Scraps from My Army Life." Undated, unpublished monograph. Lewis King Collection, Box L-83, Indiana State Library, Indiana Division.
68. Michael Henry Van Buskirk diary.
69. ERB, 486.
70. OR 38, ser. 1, pt. 2, 30. Report of Brigadier General Alpheus Starkey Williams. He felt he never got credit from seniors or the press on his command's exploits, and wrote that his XX Corps commander, Major General Joseph Hooker, said of the 1st Division's charge at New Hope Church: "It was the most magnificent sight of the war." Williams continued: "I lost 800 men killed and wounded. My horse got a ball in his hind leg." After three years at the front he was numb to carnage. (Milo M. Quaife, 313.)
71. ERB, 487–88.
72. Diary of John Michael Tomey. Morgan County Public Library, Martinsville, Ind.
73. Roger Sherman Loughry diary.
74. Josiah Clinton Williams diary.
75. ERB, 488.
76. Ibid.
77. Josiah Clinton Williams to his Parents, May 29, 1864. Williams Papers.
78. John Michael Tomey diary.
79. K. Jack Bauer, ed. *Soldiering; The Civil War Diary of Rice Bull* (San Rafael, Cal.: Presidio Press, 1977), 148–49.
80. Richmond M. Welman to Friend Doane, *Weekly Courier*, August 20, 1864.
81. George Edwards, October 6, 1863. Edwards Letters.

Chapter 5—Boredom in Polecat Den:
Picket Duty

1. Diary of Michael Henry Van Buskirk. Provided by Patricia Peruch, Carmichael, Calif.
2. Edmund Randolph Brown, *The Twenty-Seventh Indiana Infantry in the War of the Rebellion* (1899), 293–94. Reprint: Gaithersburg, Md., Butternut Press. Hereafter cited as ERB.
3. Ibid.
4. Lewis King, "Scraps from My Army Life." Unpublished, undated monograph. Lewis King Collection, Box L-83. Indiana State Library, Indiana Division.
5. Joseph B. Sellers in Pension Record of Thomas Faith. National Archives. Hereafter cited as PR.
6. PR of Michael Leikauff.
7. Lewis King.

8. Josiah Clinton Williams to his Parents, October 21, 1862. Papers of Josiah Clinton Williams, Vigo County Public Library, Terre Haute, Ind.

9. ERB, 69.

10. Ibid., 413–14.

11. Josiah Clinton Williams to his Parents, December 15, 1861. Williams Papers.

12. Ibid., May 18, 1862.

13. Ibid., November 2 and 8, 1862.

14. Ibid., May 18, 1862.

15. Ibid.

16. Milo M. Quaife, ed. *Into the Cannons Mouth: The Civil War Letters of Alpheus Starkey Williams* (Detroit, Mich.: Detroit Historical Society and Wayne State University Press, 1959), 330.

17. Lewis King.

18. Michael Henry Van Buskirk diary.

19. PR of Dawson Denney.

20. PR of Joseph R. Jones.

21. Josiah Clinton Williams to his Parents, August 2, 1863. Williams Papers.

22. Lewis King.

23. Diary of John Michael Tomey. Morgan County Public Library, Martinsville, Ind.

24. ERB, 455–57.

25. Joshua Deputy to his Brother and Sister, March 5, 1864. Lewis King Collection.

26. George Tarvin Chapin to his Brother, January 12, 1864. Letters of George T. Chapin in Chapin Family Papers, Indiana Historical Society.

27. PR of Bricen Carter.

28. ERB, 451.

29. PR of Roger Sherman Loughry.

30. Michael Henry Van Buskirk diary.

31. John Michael Tomey diary.

32. Ibid.

33. Ibid.

34. ERB, 67.

Chapter 6—Letters, Loved Ones, and Likenesses: Families and Friends

1. Josiah Clinton Williams to his Sister, December 1, 1862. Papers of Josiah Clinton Williams, Vigo County Public Library, Terre Haute, Ind.

2. Josiah Clinton Williams to [his Sister] Edistina, April 2, 1863. Williams papers.

3. Josiah Clinton Williams to his Parents, September 14, 1861, and November 1, 1862. Williams Papers.

4. Wesley Slider to [his Sister] Mary F., August 2, 1862, in Pension Record of Wesley Slider. National Archives. Hereafter cited as PR.

5. Josiah Clinton Williams to his Parents, July 30, 1862. Williams Papers.

6. Enoch Anderson to his Father, January 29, 1862, in PR of Enoch Anderson.

7. Simpson Solomon Hamrick to his Father, January 14, 1863. Civil War Letters of Simpson Solomon Hamrick, Roy O. West Library, Depauw University.

8. William Parmemas Ellis to his Father, April 3, 1864. Provided by Eleanor Purdue, Washington, Ind.

9. Andy [believed Hart] to Jerome T. Armstrong, March 27, 1863. Roger Sherman Loughry Letters. Provided by Dick Loughery, McLean, Va.

10. Josiah Clinton Williams to his Parents, October 25, 1862. Williams Papers.

11. Clemens Johnson to his Parents, July 27, 1862, in PR of Clemens Johnson.

12. PR of Stephen J. Rayburn.

13. Simpson Solomon Hamrick to his Father, December 30, 1862. Hamrick Letters.

14. Simpson Solomon Hamrick to his Brother Charlie, January 16, 1863. Hamrick Letters.

15. Josiah Clinton Williams to his Grandfather, October 30, 1861. Williams Papers.

16. Linzey Lamb to [his Wife] Mary, May 2, 1864. Letters of Lindsay Lamb, Lilly Library, Indiana University.

17. George Whitfield Reed, February 9, 1862. Collection of Letters from George Whitfield Reed, Indiana Historical Society.

18. John McKnight Bloss to Emma McPheeters, August 9, 1861. Provided by John McKnight Bloss (grandson), Paris, Ill.

19. John D. Billings, *Hardtack and Coffee; Or, the Unwritten Story of Army Life* (1887), 62. Reprint: Williamstown, Mass.: Corner House Publishers, 1984.

20. George Edwards, September 21, 1861. Letters of George Edwards, Indiana Historical Society.

21. Ibid., April 5, 1862.

22. Josiah Clinton Williams to his Parents, October 21, 1862. Williams Papers.

23. Clemens Johnson to his Parents, March 16, 1862, in Johnson PR.

24. William Thomson to his Wife, December 5, 1862. Provided by John D. Steele, Odon, Ind.

25. Albert Dodd to George Edwards, November 28, 1862. Edwards Letters.

26. Josiah Clinton Williams to his Parents, July 9, 1862. Williams Papers; Simpson Solomon Hamrick to his Father, July 14, 1862. Hamrick Letters.

27. Hamrick to his Father, January 8, 1863. Hamrick Letters.

28. PR of George Donica.

29. Ellis to his Father, February 19, 1863. Eleanor Purdue.

30. Edmund Randolph Brown, *The Twenty-Seventh Indiana Volunteer Infantry in the War of the Rebellion* (1899), 287. Reprint: Gaithersburg, Md.: Butternut Press. Hereafter cited as ERB.

31. William Parmemas Ellis to his Parents, January 2, 1862. Eleanor Purdue.

32. Vinson Williams to his Parents, March 7, 1863, in PR of Vinson Williams.

33. Linzey Lamb to [his Wife] Mary, April 23, 1864. Lamb Letters.

34. Simpson Solomon Hamrick to his Father, October 27, 1862. Hamrick Letters.

35. Simpson Solomon Hamrick to his Brother Charlie, April 17, 1863. Hamrick Letters.

36. His Sister to Thomas W. Casey, June 4, 1862. Provided by Virginia May, Indianapolis, Ind.

37. Linzey Lamb to [his Wife] Mary, May 20, 1864. Lamb Letters.

38. PR of Henry Albright. Many of the financial interests in pensions emanated from the deceased son being the family's only support.

39. PR of Elijah McKnight.

40. PR of Samuel Lemming.

41. PR of Joseph Fiddler.

42. Simpson Solomon Hamrick to his Father, March 10, 1862. Hamrick Letters.

43. Nancy R. McClanahan to Isaac W. Monfort, July 6, 1863. Adjutant General Muster Rolls of the 27th Indiana, Box 61. Indiana Commission on Public Records, Archives Division.

44. Compiled Military Service Record of John W. Wilcoxsen. Records of the 27th Indiana, National Archives. Hereafter cited as CMSR.

45. PR of Joseph B. Stimson.

46. Mary A. Livermore, *A Woman's Narrative of Four Years Personal Experience* (Hartford, Conn.: 1888), 587.

47. PR of Sylvester Layton.

48. George Tarvin Chapin to his Brother, November 25, 1863. Letters of George T. Chapin in Chapin Family Papers, Indiana Historical Society.

49. Josiah Clinton Williams to his Parents, September 4, 1862. Williams Papers.
50. Ibid., November 1, 1862.
51. Josiah Clinton Williams to his Father, June 21, 1862. Williams Papers.
52. Simpson Solomon Hamrick, December 9, 1861. Hamrick Letters.
53. Simpson Solomon Hamrick to his Father, June 5, 1862. Hamrick Letters.
54. T. A. Goodwin, December 7, 1863, and January 15, 1864, in "Report of the Allotment Commissioner on the Transmission of Money for Soldiers, to the Governor" (Indianapolis: 1865), 3, 5.
55. Simpson Solomon Hamrick to his Father, December 30, 1862. Hamrick Letters.
56. PR of Earl Moore.
57. Vinson Williams to his Parents, August 5, 1862, in Vinson Williams PR.
58. Ibid., September 8, 1862.
59. Josiah Clinton Williams to his Father, [believed October], 1861. Williams Papers.
60. Josiah Clinton Williams to his Parents, October 25, 1862. Williams Papers.
61. Ibid., February 6, 1863.
62. Ibid., November 29, 1863.
63. John S. Hackler to his Parents, September 5, 1861, in PR of John S. Hackler.
64. John S. Hackler to his Parents and Family, November 29, 1861, in Hackler PR.
65. William Parmemas Ellis to his Parents, January 2, 1862. Eleanor Purdue.
66. Simpson Solomon Hamrick, December 9, 1861. Hamrick Letters.
67. Josiah Clinton Williams to Sister, December 1, 1862. Williams Papers.
68. His Mother to Thomas W. Casey, January 26, 1864. Virginia May.
69. Josiah Clinton Williams to his Father, December 28, 1861. Williams Papers.
70. Diary of Michael Henry Van Buskirk. Provided by Patricia Peruch, Carmichael, Calif.
71. George Edwards, December 6, 1863. Edwards Letters.
72. George Whitfield Reed in the Putnam [County, Ind.] *Republican Banner*, December 8, 1861.
73. Josiah Clinton Williams to his Parents, February 6, 1863. Williams Papers.
74. His Sister to Thomas W. Casey, June 4, 1862. Virginia May.
75. His Parents to Thomas W. Casey, August 31, 1862. Virginia May.
76. His Mother to Thomas W. Casey, January 26, 1864. Virginia May.
77. Ibid., May 20, 1864.
78. Josiah Clinton Williams to his Parents, October 25, 1862. Williams Papers.
79. "The Haversack" newspaper of the 27th Indiana, March 26, 1862. Adjutant General Muster Rolls, Box 61. "Haversack," the Regiment's only newspaper, was printed three times that month in Berryville, Va. One issue survives.
80. William Dinsian to Cousin Mary [believed October] 28, 1862. Lucius C. Embree Papers, Indiana State Library, Indiana Division.
81. G. H. Voss to Oliver P. Morton, October 3, 1862. Muster Rolls, Box 61.
82. Oliver P. Morton Correspondence, Box 9.
83. Letter petition from Citizens of Edinburgh, Ind., to Oliver P. Morton, January 24, 1863. Muster Rolls, Box 60.
84. William J. Wells to Isaac W. Monfort, undated [ca. 1863]. Muster Rolls, Box 61.
85. George East to Isaac W. Monfort, undated [ca. August 1863]. Muster Rolls, Box 60.
86. CMSR of James O. Laughlin.
87. John A. Cassady to Isaih Slider, April 10, 1863, in PR of Wesley Slider.
88. Jackson L. Moore to S. P. Hackler, December 12, 1861, in John S. Hackler PR.
89. PR of James Cooper.
90. Indianapolis, Ind. *Journal*, May 4, 1863.
91. Earl Moore PR.
92. Abraham Landes to Isaac W. Monfort, June 5, 1863. Muster Rolls, Box 61; Putnam [County, Ind.] *Republican Banner*, May 21, 1863.

93. Worthington B. Williams, May 13, 1863, in Putnam [County, Ind.] *Republican Banner*, May 21, 1863.
94. Ibid.
95. Philip Jones to Isaac W. Monfort, July 26, 1863. Muster Rolls, Box 61.
96. His Sister to Thomas W. Casey, April 19, 1863. Virginia May.
97. His Wife Katy to Jarvis J. Johnson, June 12, 1862. Jarvis J. Johnson Papers, Indiana Historical Society.
98. John Parham to his Friend, February 4, 1863, in PR of John Parham.
99. John Parham to his Sister Henrity, April 22, 1863. Hiram Reid Letters, Box F83, Indiana Historical Society.
100. PR of Thomas Bacon.
101. Michael Henry Van Buskirk diary.
102. William Parmemas Ellis to his Father, February 19, 1863. Eleanor Purdue.
103. Daniel B. Williams to his Cousin Mahala, January 15, 1862. Provided by Jay Wilson, Oolitic, Ind.
104. Thomas W. David to John G. Cain, December 26, 1861, in PR of George W. Kane.
105. Benjamin Arthur to Sarah Edwards, May 21, 1864. Edwards Letters.
106. George Edwards, undated [circa Spring 1864]. Edwards Letters.

Chapter 7—God and Good Boys: Religion and Morals

1. New Albany, Ind., U.S. Army General Hospital, *The Reveille: For the Soldier in the Field and Hospital*, February 24, 1864.
2. *Report on the Unveiling and Dedication of the Indiana Monument at Andersonville, Georgia* (Indianapolis: Wm. B. Burford, 1909), 47.
3. Edmund Randolph Brown, *The Twenty-Seventh Indiana Volunteer Infantry in the War of the Rebellion* (1899), 502. Reprint: Gaithersburg, Md.: Butternut Press. Hereafter cited as ERB.
4. Diary of Josiah Clinton Williams. Papers of Josiah Clinton Williams, Vigo County Public Library, Terre Haute, Ind.
5. G. S. Bradley, *The Star Corps* (Milwaukee, Wisc.: 1865), 294.
6. ERB, 71–72.
7. *The Soldier of Indiana in the War for the Union 2* (Indianapolis: 1866), 708.
8. Simpson Solomon Hamrick to his Father, December 1, 1861. Civil War Letters of Simpson Solomon Hamrick, Roy O. West Library, Depauw University.
9. Ibid., November 2, 1862.
10. George Tarvin Chapin to his Brother, November 8, 1861. The Chapin Family Papers, Roy O. West Library, Depauw University.
11. Diary of Michael Henry Van Buskirk. Provided by Patricia Peruch, Carmichael, Calif.
12. Joshua Deputy to his Sister, March 5, 1864. Lewis King Collection, Box L-83, Indiana State Library, Indiana Division.
13. Michael Henry Van Buskirk diary.
14. ERB, 48.
15. "Letter from the 27th Indiana," August 4, 1862, in Indianapolis, Ind. *Journal*, August 12, 1862.
16. Simpson Solomon Hamrick to his Father, November 29, 1862. Hamrick Letters.
17. Milo M. Quaife, ed. *From the Cannons Mouth: The Civil War Letters of Alpheus Starkey Williams* (Detroit, Mich.: Detroit Historical Society and Wayne State University Press, 1959), 252.
18. Michael Henry Van Buskirk diary.
19. Richmond M. Welman to Margaret Cooper, January 23, 1862, in Pension Record of James Cooper. Hereafter cited as PR.

20. ERB, 152.
21. Daniel B. Williams to Cousin Mahala, [January] 23, 1863. Provided by Jay Wilson, Oolitic, Ind.
22. Lewis King Collection, Box L-83.
23. PR of Meredith Leach.
24. *History of Lawrence County, Ind.* (1884), 197. Reprint: Paoli, Ind.: Stout's Print Shop, 1965.
25. George Edwards, March 23, 1863. Letters of George Edwards, Indiana Historical Society.
26. John Parham to Friends, May 24, 1864, in PR of John Parham.
27. PR of Clemens Johnson.
28. PR of Vinson Williams.
29. Daniel B. Williams to Cousin Mahala, January 15, 1862. Jay Wilson.
30. John McKnight Bloss, ca. October 1862. Provided by John McKnight Bloss (grandson), Paris, Ill.
31. Michael Henry Van Buskirk diary; ERB, 502–03.
32. John H. Holliday, *Indianapolis and the Civil War* 4, no. 9 (Indianapolis: Edward J. Hecker, 1911), 568.
33. ERB, 412.
34. Indianapolis, Ind. *Journal*, May 25, 1863.
35. Ibid.

Chapter 8—Scalawags, Courts, and Guardhouses: Order and Discipline

1. Headquarters 1st Division, 12th Army Corps, General Court Martial February 26, 1863. Records of the 27th Indiana, Regimental Journal and Letter Book. National Archives.
2. Compiled Military Service Record of John Meek. Records of the 27th Indiana, National Archives. Hereafter cited as CMSR; Pension Record of John D. McKahin. National Archives. Hereafter cited as PR.
3. Calvin Arthur about John D. McKahin in McKahin PR.
4. CMSR of John D. McKahin.
5. Simpson Solomon Hamrick to [his Brother] Charlie, March 14, 1863. Civil War Letters of Simpson Solomon Hamrick, Roy O. West Library, Depauw University.
6. Ibid.
7. Josiah Clinton Williams to his Parents, September 14, 1861. Papers of Josiah Clinton Williams, Vigo County Public Library, Terre Haute, Ind.; Edmund Randolph Brown, *The Twenty-Seventh Indiana Volunteer Infantry in the War of the Rebellion* (1899), 29–30. Reprint: Gaithersburg, Md.: Butternut Press. Hereafter cited as ERB.
8. ERB, 89; Simpson Solomon Hamrick to his Father, February 3, 1862. Hamrick Letters.
9. Diary of Michael Henry Van Buskirk. Provided by Patricia Peruch, Carmichael, Calif.
10. ERB, 424.
11. PR of George W. Morgan.
12. ERB, 429.
13. George Whitfield Reed, June 25, 1862. Collection of Letters from George Whitfield Reed, Indiana Historical Society.
14. Josiah Clinton Williams to his Father, June 21, 1862. Williams Papers.
15. Diary of Josiah Clinton Williams. Williams Papers.
16. ERB, 296–97.
17. CMSR of Anderson Dichert.
18. ERB, 178–79.
19. PR of Shelly Martin.
20. PR of Smith Turner.

21. Records of the 27th Indiana, Box 909. National Archives.
22. Milo M. Quaife, ed. *From the Cannon's Mouth: The Civil War Letters of Alpheus Starkey Williams* (Detroit, Mich.: Detroit Historical Society and Wayne State University Press, 1959), 257.
23. ERB, 432–33.
24. Lewis King, "Scraps from My Army Life." Undated, unpublished monograph. Lewis King Collection, Box L-83, Indiana State Library, Indiana Division.
25. CMSR of Henry K. Hendricks.
26. Headquarters 1st Division, 12th Corps, General Order No. 28, November 24, 1862, in CMSR of George W. Wright; ERB, 296–97.
27. CMSR of John T. Boyle.
28. Ibid.
29. CMSR of Silas Colgrove.
30. Michael Henry Van Buskirk diary.
31. Headquarters Army of the Potomac General Orders No. 178, October 20, 1862, in CMSR of Nehemiah Walton.
32. Nehemiah Walton CMSR.
33. CMSR of Peter Fesler.
34. ERB, 124.

Chapter 9—Skeletons and Scurvy:
Prisoners of War

1. Mary A. Livermore, *A Woman's Narrative of Four Years Personal Experience* (Hartford, Conn.: 1888), 687.
2. Edmund Randolph Brown, *The Twenty-Seventh Indiana Volunteer Infantry in the War of the Rebellion* (1899), 152. Reprint: Gaithersburg, Md.: Butternut Press. Hereafter cited as ERB.
3. Simpson Solomon Hamrick to his Father, November 16, 1862. The Civil War Letters of Simpson Solomon Hamrick, Roy O. West Library, Depauw University.
4. Pension Record of James C. Thomas. National Archives. Hereafter cited as PR.
5. PR of John Russell.
6. Simpson Solomon Hamrick to his father, June 17, 1862. Hamrick Letters.
7. Compiled Military Service Record of Henry K. Hendricks. Records of the 27th Indiana. National Archives. Hereafter cited as CMSR.
8. Jonas Davis in PR of Andrew J. Vest.
9. PRs of Robert L. S. Foster, James Sharp, Andrew Jones, and John McConnell.
10. PR of Michael Corcoran.
11. PR of Michael Wallick.
12. Andrew J. Arnold to Samuel S. and Charles Weaver, September 26, 1891. Collection of Letters of Samuel S. Weaver. Lilly Library, Indiana University.
13. Joseph W. Morton, Jr., ed. *Sparks from the Campfire* (Philadelphia: Keystone Publishing, 1890), 194–95.
14. CMSR of James N. McKowen.
15. George L. Fesler to Mrs. J. J. Johnson, May 30, 1862. Papers of Jarvis J. Johnson. Indiana Historical Society.
16. Jarvis J. Johnson to his wife Katy, June 2, 1862. Johnson Papers.
17. Ibid, June 6, 1862. Johnson Papers.
18. Green V. Woollen, "A Recollection, "*War Papers Read Before the Indiana Commandery, Military Order of the Loyal Legion of the United States* (Indianapolis: 1898), 428–32.
19. Diary of Michael Henry Van Buskirk. Provided by Patricia Peruch, Carmichael, Calif.
20. Ibid.
21. George Sangster to W. T. Dennis, December 27, 1862. Oliver P. Morton Correspondence, Box 11. Indiana Commission on Public Records, Archives Division.

22. Mary A. Livermore, 688; Robert B. Roberts, *Encyclopedia of Historic Forts* (New York: Macmillan, 1988), 387–88; Author's interview with Major Pete Whitenack, USMC, November 21, 1988.
23. Indianapolis, Ind. *Journal*, October 6, 1862.
24. Mary A. Livermore, 688.
25. Adjutant General Muster Rolls of the 27th Indiana, Box 60. Indiana Commission on Public Records, Archives Division.
26. Indianapolis, Ind. *Journal*, June 20, 1863.
27. ERB, 490–91.
28. ERB, 491.

Chapter 10—Typhoid, Catarrh, and Soldier's Rheumatism: Health and Fitness

1. George Edwards, May 17, 1862. Letters of George Edwards, Indiana Historical Society.
2. Simpson Solomon Hamrick to his Father, March 10, 1862. Civil War Letters of Simpson Solomon Hamrick, Roy O. West Library, Depauw University.
3. Pension Record of Samuel Waln. National Archives. Hereafter cited as PR.
4. Michael Henry Van Buskirk to [his Grandmother] Catherine Gabbert, October 6, 1861. Provided by Patricia Peruch, Carmichael, Calif.
5. John R. Rankin in PR of Linzey C. Lamb.
6. Paul E. Steiner, *Disease in the Civil War* (Springfield, Ill.: Charles C. Thomas, 1968), 37–38.
7. Simpson Solomon Hamrick to his Father, November 25, 1861. Hamrick Letters.
8. Ira Broshears in Booneville, Ind. *Democrat*, February 3, 1862, extracted in Jasper, Ind. *Weekly Courier*, February 26, 1862.
9. PR of Charles Lutz.
10. George Edwards, December 23, 1861. Edwards Letters.
11. PR of John Conklin.
12. Edmund Randolph Brown, *The Twenty-Seventh Indiana Volunteer Infantry Regiment in the War of the Rebellion* (1899), 74–75. Reprint: Gaithersburg, Md.: Butternut Press. Hereafter cited as ERB.
13. Simpson Solomon Hamrick to his Father, January 20, 1862. Hamrick Letters.
14. PR of William Shaller Ottwell.
15. John D. Billings, *Hardtack and Coffee; Or, the Unwritten Story of Army Life* (1887), 83–84. Reprint: Williamstown, Mass.: Corner House Publishers, 1984.
16. Regimental General Order No. 6, October 1861. Records of the 27th Indiana, Regimental Journal and Letter Book. National Archives.
17. "Report of the Operations of the Sanitary Commission," U.S. Sanitary Commission #40 (Washington, D.C.: December 1861), 25.
18. Regimental Order No. 12, November 9, 1861. Records of the 27th Indiana, Box 910, Letter Book. Regimental Order hereafter cited as R. O.
19. Ibid. R. O. No. 72, March 20, 1862.
20. Diary of Michael Henry Van Buskirk. Patricia Peruch.
21. George Worthington Adams, *Doctors in Blue: The Medical History of the Union Army in the Civil War* (New York: Henry Schuman, 1952), 198.
22. R. O. No. 119, April 11, 1863. Records of the 27th Indiana, Regimental Journal and Letter Book.
23. Robert I. Alotta, *Stop the Evil: A Civil War History of Desertion and Murder* (San Rafael, Calif.: Presidio Press, 1978), 31.
24. Simpson Solomon Hamrick to his Father, July 31, 1862. Hamrick Letters.
25. Josiah Clinton Williams to his Parents, July 9, 1862. Papers of Josiah Clinton Williams. Vigo County Public Library, Terre Haute, Ind. Hereafter cited as Williams Papers.

26. ERB, 515; Diary of John Michael Tomey. Morgan County Public Library, Martinsville, Ind.; Michael Henry Van Buskirk diary.
27. PR of Thomas H. Chiles.
28. Compiled Military Service Record of Archibald Irvin Harrison. Records of the 27th Indiana, National Archives. Hereafter cited as CMSR.
29. PR of Edgar E. Barnes.
30. PR of Theodore E. Buehler.
31. Michael Henry Van Buskirk diary.
32. PR of Enoch M. Bruner.
33. PR of Elijah S. Crawford.
34. PR of William Shaller Ottwell.
35. PR of William D. Burch.
36. Paul E. Steiner, 13–14.
37. PR of Conrad Beck.
38. PR of Joshua L. Foster.
39. Paul E. Steiner, 16.
40. PR of Joseph Schrader.
41. PR of John Roush Fesler.
42. PR of Michael Leikauff.
43. PR of Mathias Smith.
44. PR of Peter Jacobs.
45. PR of Jonathan Baker.
46. James F. Herendon in PR of John Hayes.
47. PR of Peter Fesler.
48. PR of John D. McKahin.
49. PR of Samuel A. Duzan.
50. PR of Thomas H. Chiles.
51. PR of James Burke.
52. PR of John Parham.
53. John Parham to his Friends, May 24, 1864, in Parham PR.
54. PR of Daniel Monahan.
55. Robert J. Hicks, "Night-Blindness in the Confederate Army." *Richmond Medical Journal* 3 (Richmond, Va.: 1867), 34–38.
56. PR of James Sharp.
57. Compiled Military Service Record of John McKaskay. Records of the 27th Indiana, National Archives. Hereafter cited as CMSR.
58. CMSR of Jesse Younger.
59. *The Medical and Surgical History of the War of the Rebellion* 1, pt. 3, Medical (Washington: Government Printing Office, 1880), 893.
60. Ibid.
61. Ibid., 894.
62. PR of Asbury Allen.
63. CMSR of William Dodson.
64. PR of William H. Holloway.
65. Samuel A. Duzan PR.
66. Pension Record of Isaac Adams. Department of Veterans Affairs.
67. PR of William H. O'Neal.
68. PR of Arthur B. Douglas.
69. Josiah Clinton Williams to his Parents, July 9, 1862. Williams Papers.
70. *Medical and Surgical History*, 854–55.
71. PR of Flavius Potter.
72. ERB, 194–95.
73. Ibid., 195.

74. Ibid.
75. PR of William C. Riley.
76. PR of James Edwards.
77. Pension Record of Robert W. Coffee. Department of Veterans Affairs.
78. PR of Zachariah J. Rood.
79. PR of George W. Earhart.
80. CMSR of John W. Hutchison.
81. James Street, Jr., "Under the Influence." *Civil War Times Illustrated* (May, 1988).
82. David T. Courtwright, *Dark Paradise: Opiate Addiction in America Before 1940* (Cambridge, Mass.: Harvard University Press, 1982), quoted in Ibid.
83. PR of Peter D. Jacobs.
84. Ibid.
85. PR of George W. Frazier.
86. Michael Henry Van Buskirk diary.
87. Ibid.
88. Josiah Clinton Williams to his Parents, December 15, 1862. Williams Papers.
89. ERB, 190.
90. Diary of Roger Sherman Loughry. Provided by Dick Loughery, McLean, Va.
91. Michael Henry Van Buskirk diary.
92. Ibid.
93. Ibid.
94. John Michael Tomey diary.
95. PR of Robert Kutzich.
96. William H. Holloway PR.
97. Indianapolis, Ind. *Journal*, May 23, 1863.
98. PR of Henry Daniel.
99. PR of Peter Jacobs.
100. Diary of Josiah Clinton Williams. Williams Papers.
101. CMSR of Jehu Davis.
102. Simpson Solomon Hamrick to his Father, March 10, 1862. Hamrick Letters.
103. PR of Joseph Rice.
104. PR and CMSR of James Edwards.
105. CMSR of Edward A. Hoskins.
106. "Report of the Operations of the Sanitary Commission," 27.
107. PRs of Arthur Pratt and Dawson Denney.
108. George Edwards, November 7, 1861. Edwards Letters.
109. CMSR of Jacob R. Gilmore.
110. PR of Enoch M. Bruner.
111. PR of Tighlman Howard Nance.
112. PR of Robert L. S. Foster.
113. PR of William H. O'Neal.
114. CMSR of Frederick Dorn.
115. PR of Henry Daniel.

Chapter 11—Save My Arm, if You Can!:
Medical Care

1. E. Tucker, *History of Randolph County, Indiana* (A. L. Kingman: Chicago,1882), 290.
2. Worthington B. Williams [probably] to Gertrude [probably Josiah's mother], May 11, 1863. Papers of Josiah Clinton Williams. Vigo County Public Library, Terre Haute, Indiana. Hereafter cited as Williams Papers.
3. Pension Record of Merrick C. Brown. National Archives. Hereafter cited as PR.
4. Compiled Military Service Record of Ira Kyle. Records of the 27th Indiana. National Archives. Hereafter cited as CMSR.

5. *Medical and Surgical History of the War of the Rebellion, 1861–65* (Washington: Government Printing Office), pt. 1, surgery, 250.
6. Ibid., 582.
7. Ibid.
8. PR of Daniel Siebel.
9. Diary of John Michael Tomey. Morgan County Public Library, Martinsville, Ind.; Diary of Josiah Clinton Williams. Williams Papers; Edmund Randolph Brown, *The Twenty-Seventh Indiana Volunteer Infantry Regiment in the War of the Rebellion* (1899), 520. Reprint: Gaithersburg, Md.: Butternut Press. Hereafter cited as ERB.
10. E. Tucker, 290.
11. PR of John Williams.
12. PR of John D. McKahin.
13. PR of James Alexander.
14. Willis H. Twiford to Isaac W. Monfort, August 13, 1863. Records of the 27th Indiana, Box 61. Indiana Commission on Public Records, Archives Division.
15. Ibid.
16. George Worthington Adams, *Doctors in Blue: The Medical History of the Union Army in the Civil War* (New York: Henry Schuman, 1952), 128, 132.
17. PR of Willis H. Twiford.
18. PR of William A. White.
19. Lewis King, "Scraps from My Army Life," unpublished monograph. Lewis King Collection, Box L-83. Indiana State Library, Indiana Division.
20. ERB, 221–22; Josiah Clinton Williams to Parents, September 4, 1862. Williams Papers.
21. ERB, 478–79.
22. Lewis King.
23. Alonzo H. Quint, *The Record of the Second Massachusetts Infantry 1861–65* (Boston, 1867), 170.
24. Milo M. Quaife, ed., *From the Cannons Mouth: The Civil War Letters of Alpheus Starkey Williams* (Detroit, Mich.: Detroit Historical Society and Wayne State University Press, 1959), 219.
25. ERB, 354.
26. Carl Schurz quoted in George Worthington Adams, 118.
27. Isaac W. Monfort to Oliver P. Morton, undated [shortly after Gettysburg]. Oliver P. Morton Correspondence, Box 9. Indiana Commission on Public Records, Archives Division.
28. PR of Joseph Dunn Laughlin.
29. PR of Henry Lange.
30. George Worthington Adams, 64.
31. PR of James Montgomery Foster.
32. George Washington Adams, 65–66.
33. Simpson Solomon Hamrick to his Father and Friends, October 31, 1861. Civil War Letters of Simpson Solomon Hamrick. Roy O. West Library, DePauw University.
34. ERB, 94.
35. Anatomical Collections of the National Museum of Health and Medicine, Armed Forces Institute of Pathology. Hereafter cited as Anatomical Collections. Specimen MN 1442 —Joshua Chambers.
36. Ibid.
37. *Medical and Surgical History,* 2, pt. 3, 311; CMSR of Charles M. Bowen.
38. CMSR of Joseph D. Trullinger; *Medical and Surgical History* pt. 1, surgery, 250; Anatomical Collections. Specimen 1267 Section I, AMM. AFIP #1001066 – Joseph D. Trullinger.
39. Simpson Solomon Hamrick to his Father, May 14, 1862. Hamrick Letters.
40. Ibid., November 2, 1862.

41. PR of John J. Smith.
42. CMSR of Thomas Deputy.
43. George Worthington Adams, 128.
44. ERB, 354.
45. James W. Todd to the Shilladay Family, June 6, 1863. Civil War Letters of Isaac Holman Rowland and the Shilladay Family, Indiana Historical Society.
46. James W. Todd to Cynthia [Shilladay], February 15, 1864. Rowland-Shilladay Letters.
47. "W" [Worthington B. Williams], May 13, 1863, in Putnam [County, Ind.] *Republican Banner*, May 21, 1863.
48. Ibid.
49. George Worthington Adams, 168–69.
50. ERB, 462–63.
51. T. Bullard to Oliver P. Morton, October 15, 1862, in Indianapolis, Ind. *Journal*, October 22, 1862.
52. B. R. Sulgrove, *History of Indianapolis and Marion County, Ind.* (Philadelphia, Pa.: L. H. Everts, 1884), 316.
53. Carded Medical Record of Elisha Perkins. Records of the 27th Indiana. National Archives.
54. Ibid.
55. Compiled Military Service Record of Alexander Andrews. Records of the 27th Indiana, National Archives. Hereafter cited as CMSR.
56. Case of John Forman. AMM Specimen No. 1851, AFIP #1000275. National Museum of Medicine and Health, Armed Forces Institute of Pathology.
57. Ibid.
58. CMSR of Jacob Mathias.
59. CMSR of Alfred Wilson.
60. Case of Alfred Wilson. AMM No. 1641, Specimen #MM 1457, AFIP #1000159. National Museum of Medicine and Health.
61. Ibid.
62. "Aunt" to Abram [Williams], November 12, 1862. Provided by Jay Wilson, Oolitic, Ind.
63. Washington, D.C., *Chronicle* quoted in Indianapolis, Ind. *Journal*, July 18, 1863.
64. Elvira J. Powers, *Hospital Pencillings: Being a Diary* (Boston, Mass.: 1866), 123–24.
65. CMSR of Enoch Richardson.
66. "W" [believed Worthington B. Williams], May 13, 1863, in Putnam [County, Ind.] *Republican Banner*, May 21, 1863.
67. John H. Holliday, *Indianapolis and the Civil War* (Indianapolis: Indiana Historical Society Publications 4, no. 9, 1911), 566–67; William H. H. Terrell, *Report of the Adjutant General of the State of Indiana* 1 (Indianapolis: 1869), 402–03.
68. Putnam *Republican Banner*, May 21, 1863.
69. T. Bullard to Oliver P. Morton, October 15, 1862, in Indianapolis *Journal*, October 22, 1862.
70. Andrew Jones to Isaac W. Monfort, August 9, 1863. Adjutant General Muster Rolls of the 27th Indiana, Box 61. Indiana Commission on Public Records, Archives Division.
71. CMSR of William H. Chambers.
72. Sylvia G. L. Dannett, *Noble Women of the North* (New York: Sagamore Press, 1959), 61.
73. ERB, 93–94.
74. CMSR of James R. Gillaspy.

Chapter 12—The Men of the 27th Indiana:
A Regimental Profile of Who They Were

1. John McElroy, ed. *National Tribune* (ca. 1899–1900), noted in Edmund Randolph Brown Manuscripts File and Private Book. Edmund Randolph Brown Papers. Indiana Historical Society. Hereafter cited as ERB Manuscripts.

2. Benjamin Apthorp Gould, *Investigations in the Military and Anthropological Statistics of American Soldiers* (U.S. Sanitary Commission)(Cambridge, Mass.: Hurd and Houghton; New York: Riverside Press, 1869), 53, 58, 200, 206, 210–12, 403.

3. Carl A. Zenor, "Indiana Goes to War" (Indianapolis: Indiana Civil War Commission, 1961).

4. *The Soldier of Indiana in the War for the Union* 1 (Indianapolis: 1866), 2. Hereafter cited as *Soldier of Indiana*.

5. Ibid., 163.

6. National Archives records of the 27th Indiana indicate approximately 30 other names appeared one or more times as assigned to the Regiment. The author exhaustively cross-checked these names and determined they were in error. Without duplicating processes, records were copied by longhand. Regimental, War Department, and Pension Office clerks were liable for errors as shown by inconsistencies, incompleteness, and inaccuracies. These 30 names probably belonged to other units such as the "37th Indiana" or "27th Illinois."

7. Simpson Solomon Hamrick to his father and family, October 31, 1861. Civil War Letters of Simpson Solomon Hamrick, Roy O. West Library, DePauw University.

8. 27th Indiana Regimental Association, "Report on Exchange of Compliments with General George H. Gordon" (Indianapolis, 1886). 27th Indiana Regimental Association Collection. Indiana State Library, Indiana Division.

9. Bloomington, Ind. *Republican*, July 13, 1861.

10. A number of historians, beginning with Gould, have misinterpreted these numbers regarding Company F and regimental height. They have erroneously claimed the company recruited 65 of its original members over 6 feet tall. Instead that should read 5'10", which was their height goal, certainly the equivalent of 6 feet today. How these observers found such information is unknown unless they quoted Gould. Gould probably did not measure the men himself or have it done.

11. Indianapolis, Ind. *Journal*, August 16, 1861.

12. John W. Holcombe, *Thirty Second Report of the Superintendent of Public Instruction of the State of Indiana; Years Ending August 1883 and 1884* to the General Assembly (Indianapolis, 1884), 68.

13. Harvey Morris, *Washington County Giants* (Greenfield, Ind.: 1921), 373– 74; Jacob Piatt Dunn, *Indiana and Indianians* 2 (Chicago and New York, 1919), 1199.

14. Benjamin Apthorp Gould, 90 [for white troops only].

15. William H. H. Terrell, *Reports of the Adjutant General of the State of Indiana* 1 (Indianapolis, 1869).

16. Morris, 367.

17. Benjamin Apthorp Gould, 129.

18. *Medico-Actuarial Mortality Investigations* 1 (New York, 1912), 11–22; *Journal of the Institute of Actuaries* 25, (London, 1886), 250–57; *Institute of Actuaries and Assurance Magazine* 23 (London, 1882), 62–65.

19. William F. Fox, *Regimental Losses in the American Civil War* (Albany, New York, 1898), 62. Reprint: Morningside Bookshop, Dayton, Ohio, 1974.

20. *Report of the Provost Marshal General* (Washington, 1866), 698; sometimes called "The Dr. J. H. Baxter Statistics." Only a handful of recruits entered the 27th Indiana after March 3, 1863.

21. Society of Actuaries, "Build and Blood Pressure Study" (1979); Author's interview with Donna Richardson, Society of Actuaries, April 14, 1989.

22. Author's interview with Dr. David Vanderstel, senior historian, Conner Prairie Settlement, Noblesville, Ind., August 26, 1988.

23. Edmund Randolph Brown, *The Twenty-Seventh Indiana Volunteer Infantry in the War of the Rebellion* (1899), 16. Reprint: Gaithersburg, Md.: Butternut Press. Hereafter cited as ERB.

24. Ibid., 17.

25. Edmund Randolph Brown, Brief Autobiography. Edmund Randolph Brown Private Book, Edmund Randolph Brown Papers. Indiana Historical Society. Hereafter cited as ERB Autobiography.
26. Lewis King, "Scraps from My Army Life." Unpublished, undated monograph, Lewis King Collection, Box L-83. Indiana State Library, Indiana Division.
27. *Encyclopedia of the United States: Indiana* (St. Clair Shores, Mich.: Somerset Publishers, 1976), 142.
28. Federal Writers' Project, *Indiana: A Guide to the Hoosier State*. Reprint: New York: Oxford University Press (1973), 100.
29. *Soldier of Indiana*, 2.
30. Author's interviews with period interpreters, Conner Prairie Settlement, Noblesville, Ind. August 26, 1988.
31. Benjamin Apthorp Gould, 570.
32. ERB Autobiography.
33. *History of Hendricks County [Indiana]* (Chicago: Interstate Publishing Co., 1885), 441.
34. Pension Record of Richmond M. Welman. National Archives. Hereafter cited as PR.
35. ERB, 564.
36. Ibid., 85.
37. *Encyclopedia of the United States*, 56.
38. PR of Joseph (James) S. Steele.
39. ERB Autobiography.

Appendix A—Mitchell, Bloss, and Vance: The Lost Order

1. *Official Records of the Union and Confederate Armies in the War of the Rebellion*, 19, ser. 1, pt. 2. Hereafter cited as *OR* Army of Northern Virginia Special Orders No. 191, September 9, 1862, 603–04; Modified copy of Special Orders No. 191 (the Lost Order) is in the George B. McClellan Papers, Library of Congress, Manuscripts Division.
2. Edmund Randolph Brown, *The Twenty-Seventh Indiana Volunteer Infantry Regiment in the War of the Rebellion* (1899), 227–28. Reprint: Gaithersburg, Md.: Butternut Press. Hereafter cited as ERB.
3. Minute Book, 27th Indiana Regimental Association Collection. Indiana State Library, Indiana Division; G. W. H. Kemper, *A Twentieth Century History of Delaware County, Indiana* 1 (Chicago: Lewis Publishing Co., 1908), 900; John W. Holcombe, Superintendent, *Thirty-Second Report of the Superintendent of Public Instruction of the State of Indiana, Years Ending August 1883 and 1884* (Indianapolis, 1884), 70–71; Affidavit of David Bur Vance in the "Report of the Committee Appointed by the 27th Indiana Regimental Association to Investigate the John M. Bloss Claim regarding the Lost Order," September 15, 1905. Provided by John Bloss Lotz, Royerton, Ind.
4. John McKnight Bloss, "Antietam and the Lost Dispatch." Paper presented to the Kansas Commandery of the Military Order of the Loyal Legion of the U.S., January 6, 1892.
5. Ibid.
6. Affidavit of William H. Hostetter in "Report of the Committee." December 18, 1905.
7. David Bur Vance, September 15, 1905; Affidavit of George Washington Welsh in "Report of the Committee," July 24, 1905.
8. Samuel E. Pittman in the *National Tribune*, June 25, 1925.
9. Ibid.
10. George B. McClellan Papers, Reel 31. Library of Congress, Manuscripts Division.
11. Ezra A. Carmen undated draft memoirs. Ezra Ayers Carmen Papers, Library of Congress, Manuscripts Division.

12. Douglas Southall Freeman, *Lee's Lieutenants* 2 (New York: Charles Scribner's Sons, 1943), 718.
13. John W. Holcombe.
14. John McKnight Bloss (grandson) to the author, October 1, 1988.
15. John Bloss Lotz to the author, February 1988.
16. The author's interview with Rudolph F. Rose, Jr., February 15, 1988.
17. ERB, 231.
18. John McKnight Bloss Family Papers. Provided by John Bloss Lotz.
19. James Longstreet, *From Manassas to Appomattox*, James I. Robertson, Jr., ed. (Bloomington: Indiana University Press, 1960), 213–14.
20. *Battle and Leaders of the Civil War* 2 (New York: Century, 1887), 603.
21. Moses N. Elrod to John McKnight Bloss, ca. late 1904 or January 1905. Elrod to Vance, May 1, 1905. References provided by Richard C. Datzman, New Orleans, La. Datzman's 1970s unpublished monograph on how it was found was very helpful.
22. *OR,* 603–04.
23. Copies were made for Taylor and each general mentioned except Anderson. The war department copy is cited in Army of Northern Virginia Orders and Circulars, 1861–65. Record Group 109, Entry 68, National Archives; Anderson is cited in D. H. Hill to R. H. Chilton, December 11, 1867. Papers of Robert Hall Chilton, Museum of the Confederacy.
24. John W. Schildt, *September Echoes* (Shippensburg, Pa.: Beidel Printing House, 1980), 19.
25. James Longstreet, 213; *Battles and Leaders* 2, 607.
26. G. Moxley Sorrel, *Recollections of a Confederate Staff Officer*, Bell I. Wiley, ed. (Jackson, Tenn.: McGowan-Mercer Press, 1958), 99.
27. *Battles and Leaders* 2, 606–07.
28. The Lost Order in McClellan Papers.
29. Ibid.
30. *OR* Report of McClellan, 281.
31. McClellan to Hill, July 1, 1869. Hill Papers, Virginia State Library.
32. *Battles and Leaders* 2, 603.
33. John W. Holcombe, 70–71.
34. *Battles and Leaders* 2, 603.
35. Ibid.
36. Josiah Clinton Williams to *Century*, June 14, 1886. Josiah Clinton Williams Papers, Vigo County Public Library, Terre Haute, Ind..
37. Affidavit of John Campbell in Pension Record of Barton Warren Mitchell. National Archives.
38. John McKnight Bloss, January 6, 1892.
39. Ezra A. Carmen.
40. Family Records of Joseph Dunn Laughlin. Provided by Kerry V. Armstrong, Indianapolis, Ind..
41. John McKnight Bloss to Moses Elrod, March 18, 1905. Richard C. Datzman.
42. David Bur Vance to Moses Elrod, May 2, 1905. Bartholomew County, Ind. Historical Society.
43. George Washington Welsh.
44. Minute Book, 27th Indiana.
45. Affidavit of Vance in "Report of the Committee," September 15, 1905.
46. William H. Hostetter.
47. Affidavit of Enoch G. Boicourt in "Report of the Committee," July 30, 1906.
48. G. W. H. Kemper, 900.
49. Joseph Balsley in the *National Tribune,* March 26, 1908.
50. "Commemoration of Antietam and Gettysburg," *Indiana Magazine of History* 35, 3, September 1939, 237.

51. James V. Murfin, "The Lost Orders," *Civil War Times Illustrated*, August 1962; and Murfin, *Gleam of Bayonets* (New York: Thomas Yoseloff, 1965), 332.
52. John W. Schildt, 19.
53. Stephen W. Sears, *A Landscape Turned Red* (New Haven, Conn.: Ticknor and Fields, 1983), 112–13.
54. Fred L. Frechette, "The Lost Hero of the Lost Dispatch," *Civil War* 8, 3, May-June 1990, 24–31.

Appendix B—Living with Carnage: Casualties and Losses

1. Edmund Randolph Brown, *The Twenty-Seventh Indiana Volunteer Infantry in the War of the Rebellion* (1899), 267–68. Reprint: Butternut Press, Gaithersburg, Md. Hereafter cited as ERB.
2. William F. Fox, *Regimental Losses in the American Civil War* (Albany, N.Y.: Brandow Printing Co., 1898), 8, 10, 122, 346, 501.
3. Ibid., 346.
4. ERB, 61.
5. Records of the 27th Indiana, Box 909. National Archives.

Appendix C—The Biggest Yankee in the World

1. *Indiana History Bulletin* 51, no. 3 (March 1974), 32–36; Bloomington, Ind. *Herald-Telephone*, April 14, 1943; Roger S. Durham, "The Biggest Yankee in the World," *Civil War Times Illustrated* (May 1974); Roger S. Durham, "The Biggest Yankee in the World," *Blue & Gray* Magazine (November 1985).
2. Ibid.
3. Roger S. Durham, both *Civil War Times Illustrated* and *Blue & Gray.*
4. *Indiana Battle Flags* (Indianapolis: Indiana Battle Flags Commission, 1929), 202–03.
5. Ibid.
6. Ibid.

Appendix D—Silas Colgrove, 1816–1907

1. Winchester, Ind., *Journal*, January 16, 1907.
2. Ibid.

Appendix E—Captain Thomas J. Box and the Medal of Honor

1. ERB, 476.

Appendix F—The Anti-Hero

1. Pension Record of James E. Smith, National Archives.

Appendix G—Love, Liberty, and Pursuing a Discharge

1. George Edwards, September 22, 1861. Letters of George Edwards. Indiana Historical Society.
2. Edwards to his Wife and Children, October 11, 1861.
3. Edwards, April 5, 1862.
4. Ibid., December 21, 1862.
5. Ibid., January 20, 1863.

Appendix H—Looking for Uncle Whit

1. Josiah Clinton Williams to his Parents, August 31, 1862. Papers of Josiah Clinton William, Vigo County Public Library, Terre Haute, Ind.
2. Unknown relative [believed Williams] to Friends and Relatives about the death of George Whitfield Reed, ca. August 1862. Collection of Letters from George Whitfield Reed, Indiana Historical Society.
3. Ibid.
4. Williams to his Parents, September 4, 1862, and diary of Williams. Williams Papers.
5. Williams to his Parents, January 2, 1863. Williams Papers.
6. Reed quoted by unknown relative [believed Williams] writing about his death to Friends and Relatives, ca. August 1862. Reed Collection.

BIBLIOGRAPHY

This Select Bibliography excludes standard Civil War references including:

Atlas to Accompany the Official Records; Battles and Leaders of the Civil War; A Compendium of the War of the Rebellion; Encyclopedia of Historic Forts; The Medical and Surgical History of the War of the Rebellion; Numbers and Losses in the Civil War in America; The Photographic History of the Civil War; Regimental Losses in the Civil War; The Sanitary Commission Bulletin; The Union Army—History of Military Affairs and Records of Regiments, and Cyclopedia of Battles; The War of the Rebellion: Official Records of the Union and Confederate Armies.

Books on Indiana

American Biographical History of Emminent and Self-Made Men of the State of Indiana. Vol. 1. Cincinnati: 1880.

Barnhardt, John D. *The Impact of the Civil War on Indiana.* Indianapolis: Indiana Civil War Centennial Commission, 1962.

Barnhart, John D., and Donald F. Carmony. *Indiana: From Frontier to Industrial Commonwealth.* New York: Lerwis Historical Publishing, 1954.

Beckurch's History of Montgomery County, Indiana. Crawfordsville, Ind.: 1887.

Bergan, John V. *Johnson County* [Indiana] *Atlas.* 1983-84.

Biographical and Historical Record of Putnam County, Indiana. Chicago: Lewis Publishing, 1887.

Blanchard, Charles, ed. *Counties of Morgan, Monroe and Brown, Indiana.* Chicago: F. A. Battey, 1884.

Blanchard, Charles, ed. *History of Owen County* [Indiana] (1884). Reprint. Spencer, Ind.: Owen County Historical Society, 1977.

Bowen's History of Montgomery County, Indiana. Crawfordsville, Ind.: 1913.

Bowman, Heath. *Hoosier.* Indianapolis: Bobbs-Merrill, 1941.

Branigan, Elba L. *History of Johnson County, Indiana.* Indianapolis: B. F. Bowen, 1913.

Brown, Edmund Randolph. *The Twenty-Seventh Indiana Volunteer Infantry in the War of the Rebellion, 1861 to 1865* (1899). Reprint. Gaithersburg, Md.: Butternut Press.

A Chronology of Indiana in the Civil War, 1861-1865. Civil War Centennial Series. Bloomington: Indiana University Press, 1958.

A Chronology of Indiana in the Civil War, 1861-1865. Indianapolis: Indiana Civil War Centennial Commission, 1964.

Coffman, Helen. *Soldiers from Bartholomew County* [Indiana] *in the Civil War.* Columbus: Bartholomew County Historical Society, 1983.

Counties of White and Pulaski, Indiana. Monticello, Ind.: White County Historical Society, 1883.

Dunn, Jacob Piatt. *Greater Indianapolis.* Vol. 2. Chicago: 1910.

Esarey, Logan. *History of Indiana.* Indianapolis: Hoosier Heritage Press, 1970.

Fulkerson, A. O., ed. *History of Daviess County, Indiana.* Indianapolis: B. F. Bowen, 1915.

Funk, Orville L. *Hoosiers in the Civil War.* Chicago: Adams Press, 1967.

Harden, Samuel. *Those I Have Met, or the Boys in Blue.* Anderson, Ind.: 1888.

Historic Jasper, Inc. *Jasper Area History.* Paducah, Ky.: Turner Publishing, 1989.

History of Bartholomew County, Indiana, through 1888. Columbus: Bartholomew County Historical Society, 1976.

History of Hendricks County, Indiana. Chicago: Inter-State Publishing, 1885.

History of Jackson County, Indiana. Chicago: Brant & Fuller, 1886.

History of Johnson County, Indiana. Chicago: Brant & Fuller, 1888.

History of Knox and Daviess Counties, Indiana. Chicago: Goodspeed Publishing, 1866.

History of La Porte County, Indiana. Chicago: Chas. C. Chapman, 1880.

History of Lawrence County, Indiana. Reprint: Paoli, Ind.: Stout's Print Shop, 1965.

History of Lawrence and Monroe Counties, Indiana. Indianapolis: B. F. Bowen, 1914.

History of Pike & Dubois Counties, Indiana. Chicago: Goodspeed Bros., 1885.

History of Randolph County [Indiana]. Historical & Genealogical Society of Randolph County, 1882.

Holliday, John H. *Indianapolis and the Civil War.* Indiana Historical Society Publications, Vol. 5, no. 9. Indianapolis: Edward J. Hecker, 1911.

Indiana: A Guide to the Hoosier State. Federal Writers' Project. Reprint. New York: Oxford University Press, 1973.

Indiana Battle Flags: A Record of Indiana Organizations in the Mexican, Civil and Spanish-American Wars. Indianapolis: Indiana Battle Flag Commission, 1929.

Kemper, G. W. H. *A Twentieth Century History of Delaware County, Indiana.* Chicago: Lewis Publishing, 1908.

Kreitzer, John Alves. *A History of Northeast Dubois County in Indiana.* Oxford, Ind.: Richard B. Cross, 1970.

Levering, Julia Henderson. *Historic Indiana.* New York: G. P. Putnam's Sons, 1909.

Madison, James H. *The Indiana Way: A State History.* Bloomington: Indiana University Press, 1986.

Madison, James H. *The Indiana Way: The Politics of the Civil War Era, 1850-1873.* Indianapolis: Indiana Historical Society and Indiana University Press, 1986.

Majors, Noah J. *The Pioneers of Morgan County* [Indiana]. Indianapolis: Edward J. Hecker, Printer, 1915.

Merrill, Samuel. *The Seventieth Indiana Volunteer Infantry in the War of the Rebellion.* Indianapolis: The Bowen-Merrill Co., 1900.

McBride, John R. *History of the Thirty-Third Indiana Veteran Volunteer Infantry.* Indianapolis: William B. Burford, 1900.

Moore, Edward E. *A Century of Indiana.* New York: American Book, 1910.

Morris, Harvey. *Washington County Giants.* Greenfield, Ind.: William Mitchell Publishing, 1921.

Packard, Jasper. *History of La Porte County, Indiana.* La Porte, Ind.: S. E. Taylor, 1876.

Pitman, Benn, ed. *The Trials for Treason at Indianapolis.* Cincinnati: Moore, Wilstach & Baldwin, 1865.

A Portrait and Biographical Record of Boone and Clinton Counties, Indiana. Chicago: A. W. Bowen, 1895.

Pumroy, Eric, and Brockman, Paul. *A Guide to Manuscript Collection of the Indiana Historical Society and Indiana State Library.* Indianapolis: Indiana Historical Society, 1986.

Putnam County History. Putnam County Sesquecentennial Committee, 1966.

Riker, Dorothy, and Gayle Thornburgh, eds. *Indiana Historical Collection.* Vol. 36. Indianapolis: Indiana Historical Bureau, 1956.

Roll, Charles. *Indiana: One Hundred and Fifty Years of American Development.* Vol 2. Chicago: Lewis Publishing, 1931.

Shelby County Civil War Centennial Committee. *Shelby County in the Civil War.* Shelbyville, Ind.: Tippecanoe Press.

Simmerman, Jack and Linda. *History of Clay and Owen Counties* [Indiana]. Spencer, Ind.

The Soldier of Indiana in the War for the Union. Vols. 1-2. Indianapolis: Merrill, 1866, 1869.

Stampp, Kenneth M. *Indiana Politics During the Civil War.* Indianapolis: Indiana Historical Bureau, 1949.

Stevens, Warder W. *Centennial History of Washington County, Indiana.* Indianapolis: B. F. Bowen, 1916.

Stevenson, David. *Indiana's Roll of Honor.* Vol. 1. Indianapolis: A. D. Streight, 1864.

Sulgrove, B. R. *History of Indianapolis and Marion County, Indiana.* Philadelphia: L. H. Everts, 1884.

Sweeney, Margaret. *Fact, Fiction and Folklore of Southern Indiana.* New York: Vantage Press, 1967.

Thornburgh, Emma Lou. *Indiana in the Civil War Era, 1850-1880.* Indianapolis: Indiana Historical Bureau and Indiana Historical Society, 1965.

Tucker, E. *History of Randolph County, Indiana.* Chicago: A. L. Kingman, 1882.

Turner, Ann. *Guide to Indiana Civil War Manuscripts.* Indianapolis: Indiana Civil War Centennial Commission, 1965.

Vexler, Robert I., ed. *Chronology and Documentary Handbook of the State of Indiana.* Dobbs Ferry, N.Y.: Oceana Publications, 1978.

Weik, Jessee W. *History of Putnam County, Indiana.* Indianapolis: B. F. Bowen, 1910.

Wilson, George R. *History and Art Souvenir of Dubois County* [Indiana]. 1896.

Wilson, George R. *History of Dubois County* [Indiana] *from its Primitive Days to 1910.* Jasper, Ind.: 1910.

Winslow, Hattie Lou, and Joseph R. H. Moore. *Camp Morton, 1861-1865: Indianapolis Prison Camp.* Indianapolis: Indiana Historical Society, 1940.

Civil War Books

Adams, George Worthington. *Doctors in Blue: The Medical History of the Union Army in the Civil War.* New York: Henry Schuman, 1952.

Allan, William. *The Army of Northern Virginia in 1862.* Boston: Houghton-Mifflin, 1892.

Allan, William. *History of the Campaign of Gen. T. J. (Stonewall) Jackson in the Shenandoah Valley of Virginia.* Reprint. Dayton, Ohio: Morningside, 1974.

Alotta, Robert I. *Stop the Evil: A Civil War History of Desertion and Murder.* San Rafael, Calif.: Presidio Press, 1978.

Army Register of the Volunteer Force. Vol. 6. Reprint. Gaithersburg, Md.: Olde Soldier Books, 1987.

Bailey, Donald H., and Editors. *Battles for Atlanta: Sherman Moves East.* Alexandria, Va.: Time-Life, 1985.

Barton, Michael. *Goodmen: The Character of Civil War Soldiers.* State College: Pennsylvania State University Press, 1981.

Bauer, Jack, ed. *Soldiering: The Civil War Diary of Rice C. Bull.* San Rafael, Calif.: Presidio Press, 1977.

Beck, Brandon H., and Charles S. Grunder. *Three Battles of Winchester: A History and Guided Tour.* Berryville, Va.: Country Publishers, 1988.

Billings, John D. *Hardtack and Coffee: Or, The Unwritten Story of Army Life* (1887). Reprint. Williamstown, Mass.: Corner House Publishers, 1984.

Borcke, Heros Von. *Memoirs of the Confederate War for Independence.* New York: Peter Smith, 1938.

Bowman, S. M., and Irwin, R. B. *Sherman and His Campaigns.* New York: Charles B. Richardson, 1865.

Brewer, W. *Alabama: Her History, Resources, War Record and Public Men.* Reprint. Tuscaloosa, Ala.: Willo Publishing, 1964.

Bryant, Edwin E. *History of the Third Regiment of Wisconsin Veteran Volunteer Infantry, 1861-1865*. Madison: Veterans Association of the Regiment, 1891.

Cavada, F. F. *Libby Life: Experiences of a Prisoner of War* (1865). Reprint. Lanham, Md.: University Press of America, 1985.

Cist, Henry M. *Campaigns of the Civil War: The Army of the Cumberland*. New York: Charles Scribner's Sons, 1882.

Clark, Champ, and the Editors. *Gettysburg: The Confederate High Tide*. Alexandria, Va.: Time-Life, 1985.

Clark, Walter, ed. *Histories of the Several Regiments and Battalions from North Carolina in the Great War, 1861-65*. Vols. 1 and 4. Raleigh, 1901.

Commager, Henry Steele, ed. *The Blue and The Gray: Two Volumes in One*. New York: Fairfax Press, 1982.

The Comte de Paris. *The History of the Civil War in America*. Philadelphia: Porters & Coates, 1886.

The Comte de Paris. *The History of the Civil War in America*. Vol. 2. Edited by Henry Coppee. Philadelphia: John C. Winston, 1907.

Cooke, John Esten. *Wearing of the Grey*. Reprint. New York: Kraus Reprint, 1969.

Crute, Joseph H., Jr. *Confederate Staff Officers, 1861-1865*. Powhatan, Va.: Derwent Books, 1982.

Dannett, Sylvia G. L. *Noble Women of the North*. New York: Sagamore Press, 1959.

Doubleday, Abner. *Campaigns of the Civil War: Chancellorsville and Gettysburg*. New York: Charles Scribner's Sons, 1882.

Douglas, Henry Kyd. *I Rode with Stonewall*. Chapel Hill: University of North Carolina Press, 1940.

Dowdey, Clifford. *The Land They Fought For*. Garden City, N.J.: Doubleday, 1955.

Dowdey, Clifford, ed. *The Wartime Papers of Robert E. Lee*. Boston: Little, Brown, 1961.

Driver, Robert J., Jr. *52nd Virginia Infantry*. 1st ed. Lynchburg, Va.: H. E. Howard, 1984.

Dwight, Theodore F. *The Virginia Campaign of 1862 Under General Pope*. Boston: Houghton, Mifflin and Co.; Cambridge, Mass.: Cambridge Press, 1895.

Early, Jubal Anderson. *War Memories*. Edited by Frank Vandiver. Bloomington: Indiana University Press, 1960.

The Editors. *Lee Takes Command: From Seven Days to Bull Run*. Alexandria, Va.: Time-Life, 1984.

Evans, Clement A. *Confederate Military History*. Vols. 4 and 7. Atlanta: Confederate Publishing Co., 1899.

Fiebeger, G. J. *Campaigns of the American Civil War*. West Point, N.Y.: U.S. Military Academy, 1914.

Foote, Shelby. *The Civil War: A Narrative; Fort Sumter to Perryville.* New York: Vantage Books, 1986.

Freeman, Douglas Southall. *Lee's Lieutenants: A Study in Command.* Vols. 1 and 2. New York: Charles Scribner's Sons, 1943.

Freeman, Douglas Southall. *R. E. Lee: A Biography.* Vol. 2. New York: Charles Scribner's Sons, 1934.

Fry, James B. *New York and the Conscription of 1863.* New York: G. P. Putnam's Sons, 1885.

Frye, Dennis E. *2nd Virginia Infantry.* 2nd ed. Lynchburg, Va.: H. E. Howard, 1984.

Goolrick, William K., and the Editors. *Rebels Resurgent: Fredericksburg to Chancellorsville.* Alexandria, Va.: Time-Life, 1985.

Gordon, George H. *Brook Farm to Cedar Mountain in the War of the Rebellion, 1861-62.* Boston: James R. Osgood, 1883.

Gordon, George H. *History of the Campaign of the Army of Virginia.* Cambridge, Mass.: Riverside Press, 1880.

Gordon, George H. *A War Diary of Events in the Great War of the Rebellion, 1863-65.* Boston: James R. Osgood, 1882.

Gould, Benjamin Apthorp. *Investigations in the Military and Anthropological Statistics of American Soldiers.* Cambridge, Mass.: Hurd and Houghton; New York: Riverside Press, 1869.

Hale, Laura Virginia, and Stanley S. Phillips.*History of the Forty-Ninth Virginia Infantry, CSA.* 1981.

Headley, P. C. *Massachusetts in the Rebellion.* Boston: Walker, Fuller, 1866.

Henderson, G. F. R. *Stonewall Jackson and the American Civil War.* Vol. 2. London: Longmans, Green, 1898.

Henderson, Lillian. *Roster of the Confederate Soldiers of Georgia, 1861-65.* Vol. 2. Hopeville, Ga.: 1956.

Henry, Robert Selph. *The Story of the Confederacy.* Indianapolis: Bobbs-Merrill, 1931.

Hess, Geo. *The Maryland Campaign and History of the Antietam National Cemetery.* Hagerstown, Md.: 1890.

Historical Register and Dictionary of the United States Army, September 29, 1789–March 2, 1903. Vol. 1. Washington: Government Printing Office, 1903.

In Memorium: Henry Warner Slocum, 1826-1894. Contains *History of the Twelfth and Twentieth Army Corps.* New York Monuments Commission. Albany, N.Y.: J. B. Lyon, 1904.

Johnston, Joseph E. *Narrative of Military Operations.* New York: D. Appleton, 1874.

Jones, Chas. Edgeworth. *Georgia in the War, 1861-1865.* Augusta, Ga.: 1909.

Jones, J. William. *Army of Northern Virginia: Memorial Volume; Virginia Division of the Army of Northern Virginia.* Richmond: J. W. Randolph & English, 1880.

Jones, Terry L. *Lee's Tigers: The Louisiana Infantry in the Army of North-ern Virginia.* Baton Rouge: Louisiana State University Press, 1987.

Klement, Frank L. *Dark Lanterns: Secret Societies, Conspiracies, and Trea-son Trials in the Civil War.* Baton Rouge: Louisiana State University Press, 1984.

Klement, Frank L. *The Copperheads in the Middle West.* Chicago: Univer-sity of Chicago Press, 1960.

Lindsley, John Berrien, ed. *The Military Annals of Tennessee.* Reprint. Spartanburg, S.C., 1974.

List of Staff Officers of the Confederate States Army, 1861-1865. Wash-ington: Government Printing Office, 1891.

Livermore, Mary A. *My Story of the War: A Woman's Narrative of Four Years Personal Experience.* Hartford, Conn.: A. D. Worthington, 1888.

Longstreet, James. *From Manassas to Appomattox: Memoirs of the Civil War in America.* Edited by James I. Robertson, Jr. Bloomington: Indi-ana University Press, 1960.

Lonn, Ella. *Desertion During the Civil War.* (1928). Reprint: Gloucester, Mass.: Appleton-Century Crofts, 1966.

Lord, Francis A. *Civil War Sutlers and Their Wares.* Cranbury, N.J.: Tho-mas Yoseloff, 1969.

Lossing, Benson J. *A History of the Civil War Illustrated with Reproduc-tions of the Brady War Photographs.* New York: War Memorial Associa-tion, 1912.

Loudoun County (Virginia) Civil War Centennial Commission and the Loudoun County Board of Supervisors. *Loudoun County and the Civil War.* Leesburg: Potomac Press, 1961.

Luvaas, Jay, and Harold W. Nelson, eds. *The U.S. Army War College Guide to the Battle of Antietam.* Carlisle, Pa.: South Mountain Press, 1987.

McClellan, George B. *McClellan's Own Story: The War for the Union.* New York: Charles L. Webster, 1887.

McClellan, George B. *Report on the Organization and Campaigns of the Army of the Potomac.* New York: Sheldon, 1864.

McDonough, James Lee, and James Pickett Jones. *War So Terrible: Sherman and Atlanta.* New York: W. W. Norton, 1987.

McGuire, Hunter, and George L. Christian. *The Confederate Cause and Conduct in the War Between the States.* Richmond: L. H. Jenkins, 1907.

McMurry, Richard M. *John Bell Hood and the War for Southern Indepen-dence.* Lexington: University of Kentucky Press, 1982.

Meade, George Gordon. *The Life and Letters of George Gordon Meade.* Vol. 2. New York: Charles Scribner's Sons, 1913.

Moore, John W. *Roster of the North Carolina Troops in the War Between the States.* Vol. 1. Raleigh: 1882.

Morton, Joseph W., Jr., ed. *Sparks from the Campfire.* Philadelphia: Key-stone Publishing, 1890.

Munden, Kenneth W., and Henry Putney Beers. *Guide to Federal Archives Relating to the Civil War.* Washington: National Archives, 1962.

Murfin, James V. *The Gleam of Bayonets: The Battle of Antietam and the Maryland Campaign of 1862.* New York: Thomas Yoseloff, 1965.

Murphy, Terrence V. *10th Virginia Infantry.* Lynchburg, Va.: H. E. Howard, 1989.

Naisawald, L. Van Loan. *Grape and Canister: The Story of Field Artillery of the Army of the Potomac, 1861-1865.* New York: Oxford University Press, 1960.

North Carolina Troops, 1861-1865: A Roster; Infantry. Vols. 1, 3, 4, 6, 8. Raleigh: Office of Archives & History, 1971, 1973, 1977, 1981.

Palfrey, Francis Winthrop. *Campaigns of the Civil War: The Antietam and Fredericksburg.* New York: 1882.

Palumbo, Frank A. *George Henry Thomas, Major General, USA: The Dependable General.* Dayton, Ohio: Morningside, 1983.

Papers of the Military Historical Society of Massachusetts. Campaigns in Virginia, Maryland, and Pennsylvania, 1862-1863. Vol. 3. Boston: Griffith—Stallings Press, 1903.

Papers of the Military Historical Society of Massachusetts. Petersburg, Chancellorsville, Gettysburg. Vol. 5. Boston: The Military Historical Society of Massachusetts, 1906.

Phisterer, Frederick. *Statistical Record of the Armies of the United States.* New York: Charles Scribner's Sons, 1884.

Pollard, Edward A. *The Lost Cause: A New Southern History of the War of the Confederates.* New York: E. B. Treat, 1866.

Pollard, Edward A. *The Second Year of the War: A Southern History of the War.* New York: Charles B. Richardson, 1864.

Polley, J. B. *Hood's Texas Brigade; Its Marches; Its Battles; Its Achievements.* Reprint. Dayton, Ohio: Morningside, 1976.

Powell, William S. *Dictionary of North Carolina Biography.* Vol. 3, H-K. Chapel Hill: University of North Carolina Press, 1988.

Powers, Elvira J. *Hospital Pencillings: A Diary.* Boston: Edward L. Mitchell, 1866.

Quaife, Milo, ed. *From the Cannon's Mouth: Civil War Letters of General Alpheus Starkey Williams.* Detroit: Detroit Historical Society and Wayne State University Press, 1959.

Quint, Alonzo H. *The Record of the Second Massachusetts Infantry, 1861-65.* Boston: 1867.

Rankin, Thomas M. *23rd Virginia Infantry.* Lynchburg, Va.: H. E. Howard, 1985.

Rankin, Thomas M. *37th Virginia Infantry.* Lynchburg, Va.: H. E. Howard, 1987.

Roberts, Robert B. *Encyclopedia of Historic Forts.* New York: Macmillan Publishing, 1988.

Robertson, James I., Jr. *General A. P. Hill: The Story of a Confederate Warrior.* New York: Random House, 1987.

Rodenbaugh, Theo. F., ed. *Uncle Sam's Medal of Honor, 1861-1886.* New York: G. P. Putnam's Sons, 1886.

Salley, A. S., Jr. *South Carolina Troops in Confederate Service.* Vol. 1. Columbia, S.C.: R. L. Bryan, 1913.

Scaife, William R. *The Campaign for Atlanta.* Atlanta: William R. Scaife, 1985.

Scharf, J. Thomas. *History of Western Maryland.* 2 vols. Philadelphia: 1882.

Schildt, John W. *Antietam Hospitals.* Chewsville, Md.: Antietam Publications, 1987.

Schildt, John W. *September Echoes: A Study of the Maryland Campaign of 1862.* Shippensburg, Pa.: Beidel Printing House, 1980.

Sears, Stephen W. *A Landscape Turned Red: The Battle of Antietam.* New Haven, Conn.: Ticknor and Fields, 1983.

Shannon, Fred Albert. *The Organization and Administration of the Union Army, 1861-1865.* 2 vols. Cleveland: The Arthur H. Clark Co., 1928.

Simpson, Harold B. *Hood's Texas Brigade: A Compendium.* Hillsboro, Tex.: Hill Jr. College Press, 1977.

Slocum, Charles Elihu. *The Life and Services of Major General H. W. Slocum.* Toledo, Ohio: Slocum Publishing, 1913.

Sobel, Donald J. *The Lost Dispatch.* New York: Franklin Watts, 1958.

Stackpole, Edward J. *Chancellorsville: Lee's Greatest Battle.* Harrisburg, Pa.: Stackpole, 1958.

Steiner, Paul E. *Disease in the Civil War.* Springfield, Ill.: Charles C. Thomas, 1968.

Stine, J. H. *History of the Army of the Potomac.* Philadelphia: Jas. B. Rodgers, 1892.

Swinton, William. *Campaigns of the Army of the Potomac.* New York: Charles Scribner's Sons, 1882.

Tanner, Robert G. *Stonewall in the Valley.* Garden City, N.Y.: Doubleday, 1976.

Thomason, John W., Jr. *Jeb Stuart.* New York: Charles Scribner's Sons, 1934.

Toombs, Samuel. *New Jersey Troops in the Gettysburg Campaign.* Orange, N.J.: 1888.

Turner, George Edgar. *Victory Rode the Rails: The Strategic Place of the Railroads in the Civil War.* Indianapolis: Bobbs-Merrill, 1953.

The United States Sanitary Commission. *The Sanitary Commission of the United States Army.* New York: 1864.

Vandiver, Frank E. *Mighty Stonewall.* New York: McGraw-Hill, New York, 1957.

Van Horne, Thomas B. *History of the Army of the Cumberland.* Vol. 2 and Atlas. Cincinnati: Robert Clarke, 1875.

Wallace, Lee A., Jr. *A Guide to Virginia Military Organizations, 1861-1865.* Richmond: Virginia Civil War Commission, 1964.

Warner, Ezra J. *Generals in Blue: Lives of the Union Commanders.* Baton Rouge: Louisiana State University Press, 1964.

Weber, Gustavus A. *The Bureau of Pensions: Its History, Activities and Organization.* Baltimore, Md.: Johns Hopkins Press, 1923.

Weber, Thomas. *The Northern Railroads in the Civil War, 1861-1865.* New York: King's Crown Press, Columbia University, 1952.

Wiley, Bell Irvin. *The Life of Billy Yank: The Common Soldier of the Union.* Baton Rouge: Louisiana State University Press, 1971.

Wiley, Bell Irwin. *They Who Fought Here.* New York: The Macmillan, 1959.

Williams, Kenneth P. *Lincoln Finds a General: A Military Study of the Civil War, Vol.* 1. Bloomington: Indiana University Press, 1949.

Williams, T. Harry. *Lincoln and His Generals.* New York: Alfred A. Knopf, 1952.

Manuscript Collections

Bachelder, Jonathan B. Papers. New Hampshire Historical Society. Copies in Gettysburg National Military Park. Gettysburg, Pa.

Bloss, John McKnight. Family Papers. Provided by John Bloss Lutz, Royerton, Ind.

Bloss, John McKnight. Letters. Provided by John M. Bloss, Paris, Ill.

Brown, Edmund Randolph. Collection. Indiana Historical Society. Indianapolis.

Carmen, Ezra Ayers. Papers. Library of Congress.

Carrington, Henry B. Papers. In Morton, Oliver P., Correspondence. Indiana Commission on Public Records, Archives Division. Indianapolis.

Chapin Family. Papers. Roy O. West Library, DePauw University, Greencastle, Ind.

Chapin, George T. Letters. Civil War Letters of the Chapin Family Papers. Indiana Historical Society, Indianapolis.

Chilton, Robert Hall. Papers. Museum of the Confederacy, Richmond, Va.

Edwards, George. Letters. Indiana Historical Society, Indianapolis.

Ellis, William P. Letters. Provided by Eleanor Purdue, Washington, Ind.

Embree, Lucius C. Collection. Indiana State Library. Indianapolis.

Files, John L. Letters. Lilly Library, Indiana University, Bloomington.

Freeman, Douglas Southall. Papers. Library of Congress.

Fugate, Edward G. Letters. Neely MSS. Lilly Library, Indiana University, Bloomington.

Hamrick, Simpson Solomon. Letters. Roy O. West Library, DePauw University, Greencastle, Ind.

Johnson, Jarvis J. Papers. Indiana Historical Society, Indianapolis.

King, Lewis. Collection. Indiana State Library. Indianapolis.

Lamb, Lindsay. Letters. Lilly Library, Indiana University, Bloomington.

Loughry, Roger S. Letters. Provided by Richard Loughery, McLean, Va.

McClellan, George B. Papers. Library of Congress, Washington.

Morton, Oliver P. Correspondence. Indiana Commission on Public Records, Archives Division. Indianapolis.

Parsley, Eliza Hall. Papers. Southern Historical Collection, University of North Carolina Library, Chapel Hill.

Pendleton, William Nelson. Papers. Southern Historical Collection, University of North Carolina Library, Chapel Hill.

Reid, George Whitfield. Letters. Indiana Historical Society, Indianapolis.

Reid, Hiram, and Relatives. Letters. Indiana Historical Society. Indianapolis.

Rowland, Isaac Holman, Todd, James M. and the Shilladay Family. Letters. Indiana Historical Society, Indianapolis.

Starbuck, Julietta. MSS. Indiana Historical Society. Indianapolis.

Tomey, John Michael. Diary. Morgan County [Indiana] Public Library, Martinsville, Ind.

Van Buskirk, Michael Henry. Diary. Provided by Patricia A. Peruch, Carmichael, Calif.

Weaver, Samuel S. Papers. Lilly Library, Indiana University, Bloomington.

Williams, Eldridge, Letters. Provided by Jay Wilson, Oolitic, Ind.

Williams, Josiah. Diaries. Worthington B. Williams Collection. Indiana Historical Society, Indianapolis.

Williams, Rufus. Letters. Provided by Jay Wilson, Oolitic, Ind.

Family Histories

Ackerman, Dr. C. W. Family Records. Dubois County Public Library, Jasper, Ind.

Deputy and Fowler Families of Jennings County, Indiana. Genealogies. Provided by Betty Clemmens, Atlanta, Ga.

Dinn and Allied Families Genealogies. Wright Hageman Public Library, Edinburgh, Ind.

Fesler-Roush Family of Morgan County [Indiana]. Genealogies. Franklin, Ind.: 1940.

Fleener Family of Indiana. Genealogies. Provided by Larry Fleenor, Rushville, Ind.

Melchior, J. T. Melchior Family. History. Dubois County Public Library, Jasper, Ind.

Roelle Family. Papers. Dubois County Public Library, Jasper, Ind.

Wilson, John and Lydia Owens Family. Historical paper. Putnam County Historical Society, Greencastle, Ind.

Periodicals

Excludes most references to *Indiana Magazine of History.*

"The Biggest Yankee in the World." *Civil War Times Illustrated.* Vol. 13 (May 1974).

Bridges, Hal., ed. "Lee's Letter on the Lost Dispatch." *The Virginia Magazine of History and Biography* 66 (1968).

Canup, Charles E. "Conscription and Draft in Indiana during The Civil War." *Indiana Magazine of History.* Vol. 10.

"The Commemoration of Antietam and Gettysburg." *Indiana Magazine of History.* Vol. 35, no. 3 (1939).

Feuer, A. B. "John McGrady and the Confederate Prisoners at Camp Morton." *Civil War Quarterly.* Vol. 10.

Harrison, Kathy Georg. "Gettysburg The Third Day." *Blue and Gray* Magazine (July 1988).

Harstad, Peter T. "Billy Yank Through the Eyes of the Medical Examiner." *Rendezvous: Journal of Arts and Letters.* Vol. 1, no. 1 (Spring 1966).

Indiana History Bulletin. Vol. 33, no. 1 (January 1956).

Indiana Teacher Magazine (November 1954).

Journal of the Institute of Actuaries and Assurance. Vols. 23 (1882), and 25 (1886).

"List of Civil War Regiments by Indiana Counties." *Indiana History Bulletin.* Vol. 38, nos. 10 and 12 (October and December 1961).

Murfin, James V. "The Lost Orders." *Civil War Times Illustrated* (August 1862).

McMurry, Richard M. "Atlanta Campaign: The Battles of May 1864." *Blue and Gray* Magazine. 6, no. 4 (April 1989).

Morris, Roy, Jr., and Phil Noblitt. "History of a Failure." *Civil War Times Illustrated* (September 1988).

"Pioneer Folk of Early Southern Indiana." Indiana University *Alumni Quarterly.* Vol. 23, no. 4 (Fall 1936).

Sears, Stephen. "The Grand Campaign." *Civil War Times Illustrated* (September 1988).

"Special Edition: Antietam." *Civil War Quarterly.* Vol. 9.

Wabash [College] *Magazine* (March 1868 and June 1868).

Wert, Jeffry. "Gettysburg: The Special Issue." *Civil War Times Illustrated* (Summer 1988).

Newspapers

All Indiana except where noted.

Bedford *Daily Mail.* 1900, 1905, 1912.

Crawfordsville *Daily Journal.* 1893.

Daviess *County Democrat.* 1901, 1911-12.

Edinburgh *Courier.* 1863, 1878.

[Columbus] *Evening Republican.* 1963.

Franklin *Democrat.* 1884, 1912-13.

Gettysburg [Pa.] *Star and Sentinel.* 1885.

Hamilton County *Ledger.* 1908.

Indianapolis *Daily Journal.* 1861-1864.

Indianapolis *News.* 1914.

Indianapolis *Sentinel.* 1861-64.

Jasper *Courier,* 1861-64, 1866, 1871, 1880, 1894.

Jasper *Herald,* 1900, 1932.

Jennings County *Plain Dealer.* 1917.

Martinsville *Republican.* 1888.

Michigan City *Evening News.* 1898.

Muncie *Morning Star.* 1905.

Odon *Journal.* 1899, 1909, 1911, 1924-27.

Pike County *Democrat*. 1913, 1919.

Pulaski County *Democrat*. 1922, 1930.

Republican [Columbus], November 15, 1984.

The Reveille Newspaper: "For the Soldier in the Field and Hospital." U.S. Army General Hospital No. 6, New Albany, Ind. 1864-65.

Salem *Democrat*. 1905.

Shelby *Democrat*. 1909, 1913, 1922.

[Bloomington] *Telephone*. 1886.

Union City *Times*. 1907.

Vincennes *Capital*, 1892, 1903.

Washington *Democrat*. 1899, 1905, 1909, 1911-12, 1916, 1918, 1923, 1925, 1935.

Washington [D.C.] *Star*. 1913.

Winchester *Journal*. 1907.

Winimac *Republican*. 1938.

Records, Reports, and Other Indiana Documents

Excludes cemetery, census, and church records.

Bloss, John McKnight. "Antietam and the Lost Dispatch." Paper presented before the Kansas Commandery, Military Order of the Loyal Legion of the United States. January 6, 1892.

Book on the Soldiers and Sailors Monument. Dubois County Court House, Jasper, Ind.

Brownstown Area Sesquicentennial, 1816-1966. Brownstown, Ind.: Brownstown Sesquicentennial, Inc., 1966.

Celestine Centennial Book. Dubois County, Ind.

Cloverdale Then and Now, 1839-1939. Cloverdale, Ind.: Cloverdale Centennial Celebration, 1938.

Doane, Lillian, ed. Excerpts from the Jasper *Weekly Courier* During the Civil War, Jasper, Ind., undated.

"Fiftieth Anniversary of the Battle of Gettysburg: Report of the Pennsylvania Commission on the Battle of Gettysburg." Harrisburg, 1913.

Gordon, George H. "The Second Massachusetts and Stonewall Jackson." Paper presented at the annual meeting of the Second Massachusetts Infantry Association. May 11, 1875.

"Hoosier Tall Stories." American Guide Series, Federal Writers' Project. Indianapolis: Works Progress Administration, 1939.

Hannaman, William. "Report of Indiana Military Agencies, to the Governor." Indianapolis: W. R. Holloway, State Printer, 1865.

"Indiana at the Fiftieth Anniversary of the Battle of Gettysburg." Report of the Fiftieth Anniversary Commission of the Battle of Gettysburg, of Indiana. Indianapolis: 1913.

"Indiana at Antietam: Report on the Indiana Monument Commission and Ceremonies at the Dedication of the Monument." Indianapolis: 1911.

"Journal of the Fifty First Annual Encampment of the Department of Indiana, Grand Army of the Republic. Held at Wabash, June 9-12, 1930." Vol. 2. Fort Wayne, Ind.: Fort Wayne Printing Co., 1930.

Morse, Charles F. "History of the Second Massachusetts Regiment of Infantry; Gettysburg." Paper presented at the officers' reunion in Boston. May 10, 1878.

Pension Records (approximately 20) of Survivors of the 27th Indiana. U.S. Department of Veterans Affairs. Washington.

Records of the 27th Indiana Regimental Association. Indiana State Library, Indianapolis.

Records of the John A. Martin Post 153, Grand Army of the Republic. Soldiers Home, Los Angeles County, Cal.

Records of R. M. Kelly Post 217, Grand Army of the Republic. Edinburgh, Ind.

"Report on the Unveiling and Dedication of Indiana Monument at Andersonville, Georgia (National Cemetery), Thursday, November 26, 1908." Commission on Indiana Monuments. Indianapolis: Wm. B. Burford, 1909.

"Report of the Allotment Commissioner on the Transmission of Money for Soldiers, to the Governor." Indianapolis: W. R. Holloway, State Printer, 1865.

"Report of the Committee on Exchange of Compliments, of the 27th Indiana Regimental Association, with General George H. Gordon." Indianapolis: 1886.

Records of the Anatomical Collections. National Museum of Health and Medicine of the Armed Forces Institute of Pathology. Washington.

"Report of Committee appointed by the Association of the 27th Regiment of Indiana Volunteer Infantry. Re: Claim of John M. Bloss and finding of Lost Dispatch." September 13, 1905.

"A Report to the Secretary of War on the Operations of the Sanitary Commission." Washington: McGill and Witherow Printers, 1861.

"Stars and Stripes Songster." Personal song book of John Auten, first Indiana soldier killed in Civil War. Published by Robert M. DeWitt, N.Y., for Union soldiers. Lilly Library, Indiana University, Bloomington.

"State of Indiana, Department of Public Instruction, 23rd Biannual Report of the Indiana State Superintendent of Public Instruction." Indianapolis: 1906.

"Thirty Second Report of the Superintendent of Public Instruction of the State of Indiana." Indianapolis: 1884.

The Underground Railroad in Indiana File. Indiana State Library. Indianapolis.

War Papers Read before the Indiana Commandery, Military Order of the Loyal Legion of the United States. Indianapolis: The Commandery, 1898.

Official Records. National Archives

Bound Regimental Record Books. Volunteer Organizations of the Civil War. Indiana—27th Infantry. 3 vols.

Carded Medical Records. Volunteers—Civil War. 27th Indiana. Boxes 617-19.

Compiled Military Service Records. Civil War (Union)—27th Indiana Infantry. Boxes 6436-6456.

Monthly Returns of Regiment. Records of the 27th Indiana.

Muster Rolls. Volunteer Organizations of the Civil War. Indiana—27th Infantry. Boxes 908-11.

Pension Records (approximately 800) of Survivors of the 27th Indiana.

Quarterly Returns of Deceased Soldiers. Records of the 27th Indiana. Box 909.

Records of Deaths and Discharges. 27th Indiana Volunteer Infantry Regiment.

Official Records. Indiana Commission on Public Records, Archives Division

The Adjutant General's Muster Rolls of the 27th Regiment.

Casualty List. Indiana Adjutant General's Office. File A3852.

Clothing Book. Companies F, G, I and K, 27th Infantry. Indiana Adjutant General's Office. File A6370.

Paroled and Exchanged Prisoners of War. Indiana Adjutant General's Office. File L727.

Register of Men Unaccounted For, including 27th Infantry. Indiana Adjutant General's Office. File A6429.

Terrell, W. H. H. *Indiana in the War of the Rebellion. Report of the Adjutant General of Indiana, 1861-1865.* Vols. 1-4, 8. Indianapolis: Vols. 1-2, 1865; Vol. 3, 1868; Vol. 4, 1866; Vol. 5, 1868.

Unpublished Manuscripts

Carmen, Ezra A. Memoirs. Ezra A. Carmen Papers. Library of Congress, Manuscripts Division.

Doane, Lillian. "Governor Oliver P. Morton—Civil War Years." Lillian Doane, Jasper Ind.

King, Lewis. "Scraps from My Army Life." Lewis King Collection. Indiana State Library, Indianapolis.

Rankin, John R. [presumed]. "What I Thought at Antietam." Oliver S. Rankin Papers. Indiana Historical Society, Indianapolis.

Wilson, George R. "The Pioneers of Their Earth" (1930). Dubois County Public Library, Jasper, Ind.

Miscellaneous Documents

Bachelder, Jonathan B. Gettysburg Battlefield Maps (Bachelder Maps). New Hampshire Historical Society. Copies in Gettysburg National Battlefield Park.

Bridgewater, Betty Anderson, ed. "Tullahoma: Episodes from the Past." Vol. 6, nos. 3-4. Coffee County [Tennessee] *Historical Society Quarterly.*

Coffee County Conservation Board. *Coffee County* [Tennessee]: *From Arrowheads to Rockets; A· History of Coffee County.* Tullahoma, Tenn.: 1969.

"Libby Prison, Richmond, Virginia." Richmond, Va.: Richmond Civil War Centennial Committee, 1961.

McMahan, Basil R. *Coffee County* [Tennessee], *Then and Now.* 1983.

Medico-Actuarial Mortality Investigation. Vol. 1. New York: The Association of Life Insurance Medical Directors & The Actuarial Society of America, 1912.

Mitchell, William Ansell. *Linn County, Kansas: A History.* Kansas City, Kans.: Campbell-Gates and Charno Bindery, 1928.

Newstead, Robert. "Rules for Holy Living; with Questions for Self-Examination." New York: G. Lane & L. Scott, 1849.

Ourand, Charles H. "Carman-Copes" Maps of the Antietam Battlefield. Antietam Battlefield Board, 1899. Antietam National Military Battlefield.

Rose, Eleanor Mitchell, La Cygne, Kans., to author, February 5, 1988.

Selzer, Jack. Baseball in the Nineteenth Century: An Overview. Cooperstown, N.Y.: National Baseball Hall of Fame and Museum, Inc., 1986.

Vance, David B. Letter to Moses Elrod, May 2, 1865. Discusses B. W. Mitchell's role in finding Lost Order. Bartholomew County (Indiana) Historical Society, Columbus.

Vizzard, William Raymond, Jr. "Prisoner of War Policy in Relation to Changing Concepts of War." Ph.D. diss., University of California, 1961.

Willmann, Wm. G., Historical Society of Frederick County, Inc. to author, December 29, 1987.

INDEX

27TH INDIANA

GENERAL INDEX

A